St. Teresa of Avila

100 THEMES ON HER LIFE AND WORK

By
Tomás Alvarez

TRANSLATED BY
Kieran Kavanaugh, O.C.D.

ICS Publications
Institute of Carmelite Studies
Washington, DC

2011

ICS Publications
2131 Lincoln Road. NE
Washington, D.C. 20002-1199
www. icspublications.org

The Original Spanish Edition was published in
2007 under the title
100 Fichas Sobre Teresa de Jesús
Para Aprender y Enseñar
by Monte Carmelo

Alvarez, Tomas
[100 Fichas Sobre Teresa de Jesus, English]
St. Teresa of Avila : 100 Themes on her Life and Work /
By Tomas Alvarez :
translated by Kieran Kavanaugh, O.C.D.
 pages cm
"The Original Spanish Edition was published in 2007 under
the title 100 Fichas Sobre
Teresa de Jesus, Para Aprender y Ensenar, by Monte Carmelo."
ISBN 978-0-935216-83-7
1. Teresa of Avila, Saint, 1515-1582. I. Title.
BX4700.T4A5713 2011
282.092-dc22
                    2010043565

I owe a debt of gratitude to
Mother Ana of Port Tobacco Carmel
for checking my translation and
for her valued suggestions.

Table of Contents

Themes Abbreviations

BMC ' Biblioteca Mistica Carmelitana

C ' *The Constitutions*

F ' *The Book of Her Foundations*

IC ' *The Interior Castle*

L ' *The Book of Her Life*

Ltr ' *The Letters*

M ' *Meditations on the Song of Songs*

MHCT ' Monumenta Historica Carmeli Teresiani

ST ' *The Spiritual Testimonies*

Sol ' T*he Soliloquies*

Themes Presentation

The goal of my writing on these One Hundred Themes is to offer the reader a number of other facets of St. Teresa's image: the cultural and family context in which she lived, her biographical profile, her leadership qualities as a founder, and her work as a writer.

Given the density and amplitude of the teresian horizon, we have opted to maintain the maximum thematic balance:

30 themes on the context of her image

30 on her work as founder and writer

30 on her written production

10 on her doctorate

This last section remains open to a further study confronting Teresa's teaching with the actual religious thinking.

As the first woman to be given the title of doctor of the church, she continues to exercise her teaching authority in the world today both within and outside the boundaries of the church.

By the present group of themes we would only wish to create a favorable approach to her person and a comprehensive reading of her writings.

I
Historical Content

We are interested in situating St. Teresa in her cultural and social context. We will explore this from a strictly teresian perspective: only those periods and social aspects that are related to Teresa or that in some way may have conditioned her existence. First of all, we will give an elemental presentation of the person of Teresa and in an appendix we will present her portrait.

1. Saint Teresa: General Data

Her family name was Teresa Sanchez de Cepeda y Ahumada, although she signed her name simply Teresa de Ahumada. From the time of her foundation of the new Carmel, she signed her name Teresa of Jesus, or rather Teresa of Jesus Carmelite. She had no academic titles. Some of her well known posthumous titles are: Mother Founder, "the Saint," Mother of Spiritual Seekers, Mystical Doctor, Doctor of the Church, and Patroness, in many different respects [Patroness of Spain is one that is highly contested], Teresa of Avila to distinguish her from Thérèse of Lisieux, and so on.

DATES THAT MARK THE COURSE OF HER LIFE:

1515: She was born in Avila - died in Alba de Tormes,
      1582 at age 67

1529: Her mother died when she was fourteen years old.

1535: She entered the Carmelite monastery of the Incarnation;
      made profession in 1537.

1539: She became sick and went to Becedas for a cure;
      a paralysis followed.

1543: Her father died when she was 28 years old.

1554: She underwent a profound conversion; a new life began,
      one of maturity and plenitude.

1554: Her mystical life began: an experience of the Christian
      mystery.

1560. She began her work as a writer: her first writing to reach us
      is *Spiritual Testimony*1.

1562: She began her task as founder: the foundation of her first
      Carmel, in Avila

1567: Her first exit as founder: the journey to Medina del Campo.

1575: Her brother Lorenzo and his family returned to Spain from the Indies.

1581: Her last journey: Avila-Burgos-Alba de Tormes.

1582: Her death in Alba de Tormes (4-15 October 1582).

THE MOST NOTABLE PERIODS IN HER LIFE:

20 years in her paternal home (1515-1535)

27 years in the Carmelite monastery of the Incarnation (1535-1562)

28 Years of profound mystical experience (1554-1582)

22 Years as writer and founder (1560-1582)

THE GEOGRAPHICAL BOUNDARIES OF
TERESA THE "GADABOUT"

Her real geography: Teresa traveled about a thousand miles in a covered wagon or riding a mule or on foot. She founded Carmels in Avila, Medina, Valladolid, Toledo, Malagón, Salamanca, Alba, Pastrana (Guadalajara), Segovia, Beas (Jaén), Sevilla, Villanueva de la Jara (Cuenca), Palencia, Soria, Burgos. She collaborated in foundations of the friars in Duruelo and Pastrana. Other travels took her to Gotarrendura, Guadalupe, Madrid, Torrijos, Becedas,.

The *geography of her mental world* was much more spacious than the former. In Spain: Caravaca, (Murcia), Granada, Cantabria, the Basque Country, Valencia, Pamplona, and Barcelona. In Europe: France, Italy, Portugal, and Poland; Africa, Turkey, Abyssinia, and Japan; Above all, South America, where she sent numerous letters, with much tension and stress because of her brothers and in favor of the Indians, and as a prolongation of her mystical life (cases of bilocation?).

Writer: Teresa is a writer, but not one who sought to publish. About 2,000 autograph pages have reached us, but she wrote much more than this, the greater part in Avila:

Four major works: Her *Life, The Way of Perfection, The Interior Castle,* and *The Foundations*.

Various minor works: *Meditations on The Song of Songs, Spiritual Testimonies, Constitutions, On Making a Visitation, Soliloquies,* and *Poems*.

Letters: almost five hundred have come down to us, but she must have written a couple thousand. (Over a hundred to Padre Gracián).

Lost writings: In addition to the lost letters (all of her correspondence with St. John of the Cross), various Spiritual Testimonies, the first redaction of her *Life,* a part of her *Meditations on the Song of Songs,* and an unknown writing when she was fourteen years of age in the style of a novel of chivalry.

Among all of her writings, her *Life* is the most introspective, the best evaluation of her own life. *The Interior Castle* is her best doctrinal synthesis. *The Way of Perfection* is her best pedagogical work, the only work she decided to publish during her lifetime, although it wasn't actually published until after her death, in 1583 in Evora.

Characteristics: Teresa is a woman from Avila, a Carmelite nun, a mystic and a humanist, contemplative and active, a self-taught writer, a founder and a leader, an enterprising, business woman, a saint, a teacher, and a spiritual mother.

Fragile Health. Chronically ill, but psychically strong, her spirit never succumbed to her bodily illnesses; open to transcendental values: to God, Christ, the church, the soul . . .; ready to undertake daily tasks [a good cook]. Among the traits of greater contrast: her sense of transcendence (the mystical), and her gifts for business and social life (realism and humanism)..

On *social life:* open to friendship and to community with other persons; among her personal relationships *we* can separate out some of the most notable ones: St. Francis Borgia, St. Peter of Alcántara,

Don Alvaro de Mendoza, St. John of the Cross, Padre Giovanni Bautista Rossi (the General of the Order), St. John of Avila, (only through correspondence), and Padre Jerónimo Gracián. Occasionally St. Juan de Ribera and St. Luis Beltrán.

Her largest share of relationships came from her own Carmelite nuns. Most notable among these were Ven. Anne of Jesus and Bl. Anne of St. Bartholomew, María de San José, María de Jesús, the founder of Carmel of the Infant Jesus in Acalá, three children who entered the Carmels in their childhood,. and a number of sick nuns.

The meaning of her life: with pen in hand, Teresa thought a great deal about the meaning of her life. She did this through ill-fated days, struggles and times of crisis, yet without breaking down, moving forward in one direction. She identified with her religious vocation (to be a nun was the *greatest favor)*. Not without a certain feminine inferiority complex: *someone like myself, weak and wretched, a little woman like myself without learning or having lived a good life*. Only in the phase of maturity did she grasp fully the meaning of her existence. She identified it with her mystical experience and her prophetic mission: a mystical dynamism and a mission both transcendent and earthly. To be a witness of Christ and a promoter of the religious undertaking. A woman capable of giving testimony to God's presence in the world and in history.

For this reason her personality surpassed the travels of her earthly life and lives on even today.

2. Avila And Its Surroundings

1. Avila, Teresa's birthplace, was an important city in Old Castile during the golden age. A short distance from Madrid, Valladolid, and Salamanca, it was located on a height of the Castilian Meseta 3, 710 feet above sea level. It is surrounded by a medieval warriors' wall, which at its highest point incorporates the bastion of the cathedral. The climate is severe. In appearance and structure Avila is a soldiers' fortress, with a sober and chivalric population, faithful to its secular history, adorned with palaces and genealogical heraldry. The palace of the Velas lies next to Teresa's family home. The city has been justly called or defined as "Avila of the Knights. "

2. Around 1561, during Teresa's lifetime, Avila counted in its midst 3,156 families, that is to say approximately 10,000 inhabitants. It was one of the most populated cities in Old Castile, surpassed only by Valladolid, Segovia, and Salamanca. Avila had a higher number even than Burgos and León. The population of Avila was divided into six sections (San Juan, Santisteban, San Pedro, San Andrés, La Trinidad, and San Nicolás). The most numerous section was San Juan, to which the family of Teresa belonged.

3. Avila was governed by the lords of the city council, presided over by the governor (or governors), and in the name of the king, ruled by the chief magistrate. At least on two occasions Teresa experienced serious friction with the city council: in 1562 when St. Joseph's was founded, because of the channel of water that flowed nearby; and in 1577, when Fray John of the Cross was taken prisoner. In both cases the matter passed on to the city council and then, in the second case, went on to Madrid. Teresa even wrote to the king to plead in favor of Fray John of the Cross.

4. Avila, like Castile in the fifteenth century, continued Spanish medieval society in that three religions lived together in relative harmony: Christian, Muslim (Moors), and Jewish. Now in Teresa's century strong tensions arose among the three groups, between Christians and Muslims (Moors) after the fall of Granada. Teresa from the time she was a child alludes to the hostile land of the Moors and to a possible martyrdom in it; then later on returning from Seville she referred to the war of the Alpujarras (Ltr 347. 14). Yet much more tense and dramatic was the Judeo-Christian tension from the time of the expulsion of the Jews at the end of the previous century. This was so especially in Avila. Here there was orchestrated the process of the "*Niño de la Guardia*" (1491), followed by the terrible auto de fe in the field where the burnings took place near the bridge of the Holy Spirit (1491), which immediately resulted in the expulsion of 1492. A number of Jewish merchant families abandoned their homes in the Caldeandrín, precisely where, a little while later, Teresa's father set up his merchant's shop. Likewise the Carmelite community of the Incarnation was set up in a large building on the Calle de Lomo that had been in use as a Jewish synagogue and then built the definitive monastery on a site that had served as a Jewish ossuary. But once the Jews were exiled, the tension was transferred and intensified toward the *conversos* and their descendants, who couldn't prove *limpieza de sangre* (purity of blood) or occupy relevant social positions. Teresa came from this group (see Theme 11), although she never shows any symptoms of such tension, neither in her person, nor in her family. But unavoidably she breathed in such an atmosphere.

5. The active life in the city was intense and complex. From a detailed census taken in 1561, we can point out the most numerous offices and services. That year in the city there were: twenty millers, twenty-five notaries, twenty-five gardeners, twenty-eight

carriers, thirty-one farm laborers, thirty-two hosiers, forty-seven stonemasons, sixty-four weavers, eighty-one carpenters, ninety-five tailors, one hundred shoemakers, one hundred two wool combers and so on. The strong industry of the city was that of wool exported, although with difficulty, to northern nations. Teresa's family were cloth merchants, which called for sixteen skilled workers. These high numbers contrast with the scarce number of children's teachers; only five; eleven lawyers, one mayor of the fortress, one member of the court, and four alderman. There were only a few kinds of work assigned to women seven seamstresses, thirteen laundresses, twelve spinners (and seven more at the spinning wheel), one maker of leather straps, and twenty-one bakers. It is not easy to assign one of these work places to Teresa. Her parents and family belonged to the group of merchants. Yet they had possessions and country work in Gotarrrendura.

6. The city had a high number of poor. But for them there were the hospitals that were not always dedicated to the care of the sick, but to providing for temporary lodging or nightly hospitality to beggars, the sick, or vagabonds. In the city and its surroundings there existed at least nine little hospitals: Ssnta Escolástica, the Poor Souls, San Vicente, San Segundo, San Martín, the Trinity, Our Lady of Sonsoles, San Julián, God the Father, and Santa Escolástica which was found right next to the house of the Cepeda-Ahumada family. It would have been normal for Teresa to come in contact more than once with the numerous poor and sick that roamed about there. One of her friends, Gaspar Daza, had promoted the foundation of the Confraternity of Mercy to help the poor and the destitute.

7. Avila, for its social climate, usages, customs, and urban structure, still reflected the key roll the city recovered after the reconquest of the peninsula. Among the people of Avila was told (and relived) the legendary heroic deed of the heroine Doña Jimena,

who in the absence of soldiers in the city, called together the women and disguised them as soldiers so as to defend successfully the walls of the city against the advancing enemy. In the city, the story nourished the warrior spirit. Captains continued to go forth from Avila to the wars in Africa, Navarra (in which Teresa's father took part) and Italy. In Italy, Teresa's oldest brother, Juan, died. All Teresa's other brothers yielded to the warlike lure of the Indies. To the enthusiasm of the conquistador, Teresa instinctively lends a missionary interpretation: *the millions of souls that are being lost there.* Later on she clarified her ideas. When the war between Castile and Portugal was announced about how the different bands of Teresa's friends ought to intervene, she was horrified and to one of them she wrote that she would prefer to die than to see another war break out among Christians. From the time she was a child she had to be present from close at hand to the war of the *'comuneros'* who had established their headquarters in Avila.

8. The life, the customs, and the image itself of Avila, in granite, and raised high in a fortress-like warrior's bastion, had its influence on Teresa's personality, on her manner of being and thinking, on the imagery used in her writings, including the most distinguished of her symbols, the *interior castle*. This image influenced her not only because Teresa spent the first third of her life inside the walls of the city and the following thirty years having engraved before her eyes those walls or the bastion of the cathedral, but also because this was the atmosphere that she breathed and that the majority of those dear to her shared.

9. In the social environment of that time, the cult of honor was depressing, to the point of influencing the mentality and laws in favor of purity of blood. Teresa will insist in her protest against *the accursed honor,* and she will not yield to the social demands of purity of blood (she does not admit them into her Constitutions, nor

in her lexicon does she find room for this idea of old Christians. She mocks, as we shall see in what follows, the jargon used in titles and the treatment of the nobility: *God deliver me from these lords who can do everything*, but she does share along with the popular masses veneration at all costs of the king, of whom she gives the title "defender of Christianity."

3. Saint Teresa in 16th Century Spain

1. The Spain that Teresa knew was of recent coinage. It was unified territorially after the conquest of Granada (1492) and the later attachment of Navarra (1512), in which Teresa's father, Don Alonso, and other future friends of Teresa's, had intervened. The unification of the peninsula culminated toward the end of Teresa's life with the aggregation of Portugal (1579). This aggregation did not last long, however, but it it did have a special repercussion on Teresa, as much for the tragic episode of the death of king Don Sebastián in Marruecos (Ltr. 258.2) as for the subsequent war of annexation (Ltr. 305). As the Iberian nation, the peninsula, had found its unity under the Catholic Monarchs, Isabel and Ferdinand. (In her writings Teresa never alludes to Queen Isabel, who for contemporary writers was an outstanding model as a woman.)

2. In this century Teresa's life extended the length of two great reigns: the imperial period of Charles V (1516-1556), with its triumphal extension of horizons and frontiers to almost half the world; and next the reign of Philip II (1556-1598), who was harassed and nervous, tense, watchful, and controlling. Teresa was born and educated in the first period, and her activity and personality developed in the second. Yet she acted with a mentality that was shaped during the imperial period. She saw the emperor Charles in his pompous passing through Avila, where he assisted in the Mercado Chico at a great bull run, actually when she was 19 years old and about to enter the cloister (1534). On the other hand it doesn't seem she had seen Philip II. (The letter in which Teresa gives an account of her personal meeting with the king is apocryphal.) Yet she does manifest the reverent gesture in the introduction of her letter to him as king:

to His Sacred, Catholic Imperial royal Majesty, the Lord King. (Ltr. 52). Afterward she will write to him with an openness, almost with familiarity. She is thankful to him for the favors he grants to her work as founder. Ultimately, she owes to the royal favor the overcoming of the most serious crisis and hostility in which her work was ensnared. The king, in 1581, for his part gave decisive support (a royal action at the chapter of Alcalá) to the Teresian Carmel as a separate province. Teresa maintains equally good relations with the court, yet she doesn't dissimulate her displeasure with the slow pace of the bureaucracy. Because of this, ironically, the plenipotentiary, Mauricio Pazos, the president of the council of Castile, was nicknamed El Pausado (the Slowpoke) (Ltr. 272). He was successor to the diligent Covarrubias.

3. The provincial regions still showed their own personality, although very much diminished because of the courts tendency to centralize. Avila also revolves around this center in Madrid. The regions most represented in Teresa's writings are the two most populated: Castile and Andalusia. To give a detailed sign of what was most present in Teresa's mind, some simple data and statistics can be of help: she mentions Spain in her writings hardly 12 times; Castile 18 times and Andalusia 23 times. Still the world to which Teresa related was overpopulated by Castilians. Teresa was and felt like a Castilian. Castile had no approach to the sea. She never contemplated the sea, although she referred to it a number of times.

4. In Teresa's time Castile ceased being a region recollected and closed in on itself, but opened to larger spaces: to European horizons, to Italy, France, and Flanders (Teresa will be especially sensitive to happenings in France (WP 1.2); and to Lutherans; and so also to the African world (although she never mentions Africa explicitly, she carried in the depth of her soul a worry about Africa and about the Turks). But most of all, she turns her gaze away from Castile,

the peninsula, (and Europe) and directs it to the Mediterranean and the West, and now with her gaze directed much more toward the Ocean and the Indies recently discovered in the West. Teresa not only suffered because of the breakdown of Christianity, but she was especially sensitive to the vast panorama of America and its problems. From her youth she watched the flow of young migrants from Avila, and almost all of her brothers, to American lands. She then kept up intense relations with them. From one of them she received money for the foundation of her first Carmel. And when the missionary Padre Maldonado arrived in Avila and revealed the problem of the *conquistadores* in America, she adopted a mental attitude clearly defined in a human, Christian, and missionary key. A window had been opened for her that was clarifying, and Teresa was converted into an Avilan with a realistic gaze toward the American world recently discovered. In small details, her correspondence echoes the news about things coming from America, like potatoes, resin, balsam poplar, and coconut. On a higher plane, she formulates her personal involvement in that historical fact: "I am very anxious about those Indians (Ltr 24.13).

5. In that monarchical Spain of the sixteenth century, Avila did not have a good reputation, from the episode of the symbolic dethronement of Henry IV and from its close connection with the war of the *comuneros,* with the seat of the *Santa Junta* in Avila, after Toledo (1521). Castile (and all of Spain) continued to be poor. Exposed to cycles of famine and epidemics—remember the universal influenza which struck down Teresa herself (1580). It experienced great difficulties for interior commerce on account of its battered and improvised chain of roads: Teresa will have to walk and travel them so much! The middle class had already arisen, made up of contractors and bankers with easy international relations (Genoa, France, Germany, America), but with little benefit to the interior of

the nation. Great were the difficulties in the intersection of lives and relationships between the rich and the poor. (It should be enough to recall the case of the parents of Fray John of the Cross.) The proliferation of outlaws and unsavory characters, with great pockets of bandits in specific regions there was a strong repressive system: hanging or the galleys. There persisted in Spain as well as in other parts of Europe the marginal social phenomenon of slavery, not present in the family of Don Alonso, but in his milieu. (Let us remember the episode of the slaves brought by Christopher Columbus in one of his voyages, and later "freed" by Queen Isabel at her own expense.)

6. In the *Book of her Life*, Teresa criticizes the three great false values of that society: the cult of honor; the urge for money; and what she labels as a search after delights (*L* 20). *It [the soul] would want to cry out in order to make known how deceived they are– sometimes it even does so, and a thousand persecutions rain down on its head (L 20.25).* The cult of honor – *the accursed honor* she writes – derives from the laws of purity of blood. Teresa will protest against these and she will not yield to the social demands of purity of blood; she males no room for them in her *Constitutions*. Nor in her lexicon does she have any place for the idea of "old and new Christians." She mocked, as we shall see, the jargon surrounding titles and treatment in society, but she will share along with the masses veneration to the extreme of the person of the king. And she herself will inevitably become involved in the system of social classes that made up the framework of the nation, as we shall see in the following theme.

[It would be interesting to designate the historical personages of every kind that penetrated the little world of Teresa. Or better, what were the greatest happenings that had their repercussions in her writings and which ones, on the other hand, left no trace.]

4. Teresa And The Social Classes Of Her Time

We are not interested here in class as a social problem in Spain's golden century. Our interest lies in Teresa's attitude before the tangle of social classes, titles, treatment, abuses, complications and so on. What tribute did she pay to these, what were her reactions to them?

1. *"Avila of the Knights"* reflects quite well the texture of the Spanish society derived from the re-conquest and from medieval feudalism. Clearly, the city itself could be labeled as "Avila *of the merchants"* or even *"Avila of the commoners."* Yet the city of Avila as much in the material proliferation of palaces and heraldry, as for the number of lordly lineages, was characterized by the first title. According to the testimony of its contemporaries, the city gave shelter to some 330 lineages of noble people: Aguilas, Acuñas, Arellanos, Ayalas, Adras, Arévalos and so on. Teresa will find them represented in the Incarnation; among the nuns is a large group of Doñas who observed in the monastery the class structures of the street. This was something that evidently affected the young Teresa – she also was called and signed her name Doña Teresa — yet when she organized on her own the new Carmel of St. Joseph she did not allow the use of titles: "Never should the prioress or any of the Sisters use the title Doña." And a little before: "The Mother prioress should be the first on the list for sweeping so that she might give a good example to all." (C 30, 22)

2. Notwithstanding this, Teresa entered on the wrong footing that mechanism of social classes and ladders. In her blood family, her father like her uncles struggled (as we shall see in Theme 16) to acquire a degree of nobility which they in fact did not have and that cost Don Alonso as it did many other Castilians much trouble and

money. From this mistaken social situation of Don Alonso, Teresa's journey along the grid of social classes began when she was a child. She was enrolled in the group of merchants to which her father belonged, in whose service were a number of young men and girls. (Teresa will recall the servants, L 1, 1, and the maids L 2. 6.) In Gotarrendura, on the other hand, shepherds, laborers, and commoners worked for her father. Later, in her task as founder, Teresa comes to know and deal in depth with the other extreme of the social ladder, Dukes, Counts, Ladies, and Courtiers.

3. The ladder of social classes was made up, mostly, of three levels: the high nobility, the new bourgeoisie, and the marginalized. Among the nobility figured the privileged members of society, "the Grandees of the Kingdom," all those who showed the titles and escutcheons of nobility, including an inferior level the "hidalgos" or "hijosdalgo." At the peak of this social pyramid stood the dignitaries of the Court. Teresa will enter into relations above all with the ladies of the nobility. She will live a half year in the Toledan palace of Doña Luisa de la Cerda; she will become an intimate friend of Doña Guiomar de Ulloa; in Alba, she is friendly with the Duke and Duchess; she will live in much tension with the Princess of Eboli; and she has an incredible admiration for Doña Catalina de Cardona, and so on. In the *Book of Her Foundations she* gives an extensive account of the episode surrounding Casilda de Padilla and her family of Greater Governors of Castile for whom the whole family problem consisted in a transmission of title and name. The episode was brought to a conclusion years later, when Casilda left Teresa's monastery for another monastery where she would receive the honorific title Abbess, with the brief comment by Teresa: *"May God deliver me from these all-powerful lords with their strange reversals"*(Ltr. 408.3).

4. With the intermediate classes — merchants, men of the ancient nobility, bankers, and so on – Teresa will come to know

countless representatives of various social backgrounds. She traveled to Duruelo accompanied by merchants, "my friends", she founded the Carmel of Medina with the backing of the most celebrated banker of her time, Simón Ruiz, with whom she will soon feel obliged to break. She was a friend of the royal postmen and of the forest guardians of His Majesty, such as Roque de Huerta and Casademonte. In Burgos she established a good friendship with Doctor Aguiar. For her correspondence she had constant recourse to the services of the muleteers (she spoke with them – Gracián assures us – as if she had been a muleteer all her life), in travels as founder she became a good friend with Antonio Ruiz, a cattle dealer, and so on .

5. But the most numerous and humble class was made up of the marginalized, those without any special office. The census in Avila, 1561, which was mentioned, numbered about 250 poor people without work or a known office. The most relevant case in the history of the Teresian foundations is the recourse of Teresa to the services of the very poor Andrada in the noble city of Toledo. From her childhood she knew about the presence of slaves in the service of noble ladies. She shares with her father, Don Alonso, the rejection of this social abuse . And when in 1577 she heard that a slave wanted to become a Carmelite in the community of Seville she wrote a terrific letter to the prioress of the Carmel in Seville, María de San José: "As to whether the little slave girl should enter, by no means oppose it *"* (Ltr 198. 5).

6. In Teresa's biography there is a moment in which there emerges in a very special way her position about the poor. It occurred at the beginning of her mystical life and she left a record of this in her first writings: "It seems to me I have much more compassion for the poor than I used to. I feel such great pity and desire to find relief for them that if it were up to me I would give them the clothes off my back. I feel no repugnance whatsoever toward them, toward speaking to or touching them. This I now see is a gift given

by God. For even though I used to give alms for love of him, I didn't have the natural compassion. I feel a very noticeable improvement in this matter" *((ST 2.4)*.

7. At least twice Teresa gives in writing her value judgment with respect to the high social class that was then dominant. Once in her *Life* when she took stock of her experience in the Toledan palace of Doña Luisa de la Cerda (*L* 34.4): "I derived a very beneficial insight, and I told her about it. . . . how little should be our esteem for the status of nobility . . . As a result, I totally abhorred a desire to become a lady of nobility – God deliver me from faulty composure – this is a kind of subservience that makes calling such persons lords and ladies one of the world's lies, for it doesn't seem to me they are anything but slaves to a thousand things". All of this came as a result of a meticulous analysis of the conventional practices of this social group ("this farce in this life. . ."). She will return to this theme some pages further on in contrasting the lordship of God with the lordships of society: "those we have as lords here on earth, all of whose lordship consists in artificial display . . . Here on earth if a king were all by himself, he would fail to be recognized as king, he wouldn't be believed; he would have no more to show than anyone else. . . It is necessary that one see the reason for believing he is a king, and that is the purpose of these artificial displays. If he didn't have them, no one would esteem him at all; the appearance of power doesn't come from him"*(L* 37.5-6). Still in later pages in the *Way of Perfection* (27. 5) she turns again to trace in a brief flash an outbreak of class structures in the heart of the families of her time, and also in the university environment.

5. Environment And Cultural Levels

1. In past centuries the education of every child or young nobleman centered on the acquisition of good manners, on learning how to hunt and go on cavalcades, to use every kind of arms, and to play every kind of game. So at least it was understood by the songwriters for King Alfonso and their successors. Now in the height of the renaissance, the culture is measured by different parameters. The basic one was to learn how to read and write. Learning that, nevertheless, continued to be the achievement of a minority in that society. According to M. Fernández-Alvarez, "the overwhelming mass of illiterates [in the middle of the sixteenth century] could have reached 80 to 85 per cent of the population. And I believe that I might be too small in my estimate."

2. To this change in the culture, printing is what contributed above all. Coming from the central Europe, it quickly (in the fifteenth century) got set up in Spanish cities: Segovia, Valencia, Barcelona, Zaragosa, Seville, Burgos; and still before the century of the incunabula came to an end, in Salamanca, Valladolid, Zamora, Toledo, Coria, León, and so on. It took longer for it to arrive in Avila (Avila produced no incunabula nor post incunabula). Printers sent out to the public merchants large collections of books, including the classics (the Bible, Cicero, Virgil, Seneca, for example) and more recent ones, whether European (from Flanders, Italy, Germany and so on) or already in the Spanish romance language, as will be the whole series of post-incunabula (1500-1520) of the period of Cisneros. Many books were printed and read that reached Teresa. It is important above all the share of spiritual books (Franciscan spirituality) that got into the hands of the humble people, especially women who now

devoted themselves to reading. The books most widely disseminated among these humble readers were the Flos Sanctorum, the *Life of Christ*, books of prayer (the daily hours of the liturgy, meditations), and books on the practice of recollection, which included precious works by Osuna, Laredo, Palma, and Granada. A flood of lower literature with books of chivalry, which in the end were turned "*a lo divino*" (given a religious meaning). In the higher spheres there began to form household libraries of Latin classics and Spanish poets of the 14th -15th centuries. Likewise there were the small libraries of humble people, Teresa herself for example.

3. Nonetheless, the printed books did not eliminate the use of manuscripts. In the Avilan census of 1561 there still figured the service of copyists and the office for book copying: eight scribes, one writer; two copywriters of books. . . Teresa herself will read in manuscript form the most important books for her Carmelite formation at the Incarnation: the *Rule*, the *Constitutions,* and some other books of great importance (cf.Theme 25).

4. In the customs of the century, the child, at least in families that were well off, learned to read soon. Perhaps between the ages of 3 and 5 years! For herself, Teresa insinuates between 6 and 7 years. For this the well off families made use of primers, so numerous at the time. There existed as well the books of doctrine, in which together with the task of learning the alphabet and spelling the child learned the rudiments of the Christian faith (the prayers, the sacraments, the commandments, the seven deadly sins, and so on). In the recent facsimile publication of the primer and book of doctrines (34 bibliographical entries) made by Victor Infantes, there is one primer that is contemporary with Teresa, entitled: *A Primer to show young people how to read with Christian doctrine that is sung (Toledo 1526)*. It contains a musical poem to memorize. The synthesis of the Christian doctrine: "*Beloved brothers/ since we are Christians/* the

arms of Jesus/ *that we take up is the cross/. . . .And then we pray/ what we know/ what the Roman Church/ teaches us/. . .*" And while the poetic string continues announcing themes to the child are suggested the movements that ought to accompany them: "*Here the child should humble himself /Here the child should make the sign of the cross /Here he must raise his arms . . .*" It is easy to imagine that Teresa with this or a similar primer was introduced to Christian doctrine at home, perhaps by her mother or perhaps with the help of a young teacher.

5. The cultural level of that time was not something exact but rather in a movement of ascent. It was much more profound in the final third of the century than in the first. As a point of reference it should be enough to mention what occurred in the publication of the works of Teresa. In a little more than twelve months, the edition prepared by Fray Luis de Leon (the complete works) was published three times: in Salamanca 1588 / in Barcelona 1588 / in Salamanca 1589. It was a text in Spanish. We don't know the number of copies in each printing. But the receptivity on the part of readers is clear (they were then humble readers), they were capable of absorbing quickly the three editions. We know that from this lower plane, Teresa's works penetrated the University of Salamanca, the Andalusian and Catalonian environments, and a writer from Segovia [John of the Cross].

6. Also at the cultural level occurred something similar to the social structures of the social classes. At the summit of the cultural world were the learned men, the university professors, the writers. At the middle level were situated the group of readers and beginners more or less eager to learn. At a lower level, the illiterate and the underprivileged. In the first group a tremendous boom in universities occurred throughout the century (socially close to Teresa: Salamanca, Alcalá, Palencia, Guadalajara) and the typical oral

teaching of the university professors, very numerous in the Teresian environment. In the second group, there is a growing popular interest in a large collection of books in Spanish (from the *Life of Christ* by the Carthusian, books by the Spiritual Franciscans and at the end of the century by Fray Luis de León). A sign of this could be that Teresa herself did not conceive the structure of a Carmel without the presence of a little library of select books, in Spanish, for the "spiritual nourishment" of the nuns. The third group made use above all of the insistent oral teaching of preachers and catechists. Some were very powerful, such as Maestro Avila. Or thanks also to the Jesuit schools rapidly increasing. Recall the case of the little poor boy Juan de Yepes [John of the Cross] in the School for Doctrine in Medina or the attendance of Teresa's nephews at the College of San Gil in Avila. What is important anyway is that on all three levels the cultural ferment was on the increase.

7. Avila included a copious service of sermons in the cathedral and in the parishes. The sermons at that time made up for the mass media of our times. Inside the city, besides the College of San Gil, Daza and Honcala had organized a College of Mercy. And the diocese conserved the embers of two illustrious prelates: Tostado and Hernando de Talavera (at the end of the fifteenth century). The first had written – among other pages –a manual for confession, highly instructive and practical for the sacramental formation of simple people and for the instruction of the confessors. The second, on the other hand, wrote "*A brief and very beneficial summary of doctrine that every Christian should know* (Granada 1496). Among other things this summary proposed an entire plan of daily life for the family, very similar to that – in the middle of the century – proposed by Diego Gracián for the education of his future wife. All of this was very close to the environment in which Teresa was educated.

6. The Contemporary Woman In Teresa's Time, Culture, And Social Level

1. Although the sixteenth century began under the presidency of an exceptional woman, Queen Isabel (d. 1504), Spanish society of that time was pervaded with antifeminism: a contempt for women: keeping them on the margin in public life, in a permanent state of being a minor. Women met with difficulty in accessing the sources of culture; they were not admitted into the universities, nor were other centers of study or promotion open to them. They were threatened "with the sword of fire" that they not drink from the Bible, and also the official prohibitions of books that went along with it. Teresa will protest in *The Way of Perfection* against this situation: "Since the world's judges are sons of Adam and all of them men, there is no virtue in women that they do not hold suspect Yes, indeed, the day will come, my King when all will be known" (3,7). It is certain that there existed here and there private schools for the education of young girls from wealthy families. So, for example, that of *Our Lady of Grace* in Avila or the *College for Noble Young Ladies* in Toledo (founded by Cardinal Siliceo). But the education of young girls was mainly directed toward household tasks and good customs without any special opening to other cultural horizons.

2. In the census of 1561 for Avila, few are the women who exercised a public service. Only humble services. It merits the pain of numbering them one by one. In more or less public services, they acted as women laborers: makers of shoe laces, button makers, cap makers, jacket makers, woolen clothiers, weavers, dyers, jewelry shopkeeper, silversmith, makers of methaglin, pastry maker, candle makers, wax chandlers, cheap restaurant owners, fruit sellers, bakers, kneaders of bread, fish sellers, tavern keepers, shopkeepers, and mar-

ket women. In other domestic jobs: house keeper, seamstress, maid, embroiderer, laundress. They were not assigned any employment in construction, transportation, health, Church-culture- teaching, the arts, administration of justice. Symptomatic and overwhelming was the high number of "poor widows" or "women alone and poor," or widows in the hospitals: In the little square of San Juan alone, the census numbered 66 in this situation.

3. It is certain that during the time of Queen Isabel there emerged in the Court (Madrid and Lisbon) a group of select women, educated and learned in classic literature, called "the learned girls" (Nebrija, Medrano, .Galindo). Among them were some who were extraordinary, like the one from Burgos (or Toledo), Luisa Sigea, who managed to reach a cultural eminence in her knowledge of Biblical languages, as well as of Greek and Latin philosophers. She writes in Latin her *Duarum virginum colloquium de vita aulica et privata* (*Colloquy between two young ladies on life at the court and in private*), in which one of the dialoguers pleads for life (feminine) at the court and the other for life in the town, with a profusion of quotations in Greek and in Hebrew. The only difficulty is that Sigea never published her book, and when in 1582, Saint Teresa comes to make her foundation in Burgos, the author had already died and Teresa established excellent relations with Francisco de Cuevas, the author's husband ("He has always helped us when there was need" *F* 31. 28). Yet these groups of *"learned girls,"* some of whom attained momentarily to teaching positions at Alcalá and Salamanca, were elite, due to exceptional circumstances. They were without effect in the rise to any cultural level among the masses of Spanish women..

4. To gain an idea of the cultural possibilities for women in that society, we can make use of two extreme books, one at the beginning and the other at the end of the century. The first is entitled *De Institutione feminae christianae,* by the great humanist Luis Vives;

the other at the end of the century is *The Perfect Wife,* by Luis de León. The first was written in Latin, difficult to read by the great masses of readers. The second was written in a brilliant Castilian, and was much more accessible to them. Both authors were exponents of the current humanist culture, and at the same time witnesses of the dominant popular mentality, which at bottom was misogynist. For the marriageable woman, or one already married and a mother of a family, they propose the ideal of housework: sewing, spinning, and housekeeping. Insofar as an introduction to the cultivation of the woman, they are both absolutely sparse and more negative. It is certain that Vives, among the tasks that he assigns to the woman, is that of being a mother and in her role of mother, he proposes that of teaching her children personally the primary courses: "If the mother has the knowledge, she should herself teach the children." but still the thesis remains in its depth: "since the woman is in her being weak and in her judgment insecure and very much exposed to deception (as Eve demonstrated), she is not suited for teaching, once she has been persuaded of a false opinion" (This attitude coincides with the persistent complex of Teresa, "a weak woman / without learning or a good life"*).* Likewise Fray Luis, on the topic of feminine culture, is not very far from Vives. For him, "since women are by nature weak and fragile more than any other animal. Nature did not make them suitable for the study of the sciences or for negotiations in difficulties, but only for one office alone simple and domestic, so their intelligence is limited, and as a consequence they are sparing with words." It is certain that a little after, when Fray Luis was given the task of publishing the works of St. Teresa he discovered wonders in them " I doubt that in our language there is a writer who can equal her." Yet in the end St. Teresa, according to him, is a pure exception. And definitely the exception confirms the rule.

     5. In this cultural antifeminist context, the posture of Teresa

is clear and well defined. In founding her new Carmel, she places herself at the head of a group of young women. In principle she does not admit the illiterate: she demands that "the nuns have the ability to recite the office [in Latin] and help in the choir" [*Const 6, 1*]. Yet a little after she wrote this norm, an illiterate shepherdess from Almendral, Ana García (Anne of St. Bartholomew). knocked at the door of her Carmel. Teresa broke with her criterion and accepted her. She taught her how to read and write. More than once she dictated her own letters to her. And after Teresa's death, Anne becomes prioress of the Teresian Carmel in Paris and Flanders, and she will write enough letters and small works to fill two large volumes in the recent edition of her writings edited by Julián Urkiza. In the new Teresian Carmel, Teresa will be a friend of books, of learning and learned men, of verses, and the canticles of St. John of the Cross. And after her, there will follow at the end of the century and beginning of the seventeenth century a whole entourage of learned Carmeltie nuns, among whom without doubt are the three greatest ones: María de San José (*Ramillete de mirra, Libro de recreaciones, poemas*); Cecilia del Nacimiento, a poet and writer, and Ana de la Trinidad (the Calagurritana). They wrote spiritual literature strictly feminine. A good indication of this literary movement is the book of *Romances* y *coplas del Carmelo de Valladolid,* edited by Victor García de la Concha..

     6. To sum up: Teresa. a self taught reader, does not pertain to the select group of "*puellae doctae,*" but to the popular mass of women avid to learn. She does not write in Latin or in learned Spanish. She connects with the spiritual literature in Spanish of the Cisnerian and Postcisnerian period . She herself writes in a popular Avilan, Spanish style. And she promotes within her Carmels a movement of feminine culture that includes excellent representatives.

7. The Milieu Of Popular Religion

1. Spanish society during the golden age was ostentatiously religious in its structures, customs, and feelings. It was normal in this society for popular religion to be converted into an agent of an all-inclusive formation. Perhaps in Castile something more sober existed than in other regions of the nation. But by and large, popular religion was present at all levels with a tendency to overflow and distort. As a child Teresa breathed it within her family. Later, she lived with different forms of it throughout her religious life, in counterpoint with the convent liturgy. And in the end, she incorporated it, now very purified, into her mystical life. From this whole ambient we will gather only the aspects that more directly affected the life of Teresa. We will note at once some of its negative, superstitious aspects.

2. In the city of Avila the manifestations of popular religion were strictly tied to the structure of the life itself of the people: numerous chapels dedicated to the saints, a ring of hermitages outside the walls of the city, a little chapel at each of the gates of the walls so as to pray on going forth and to give thanks on returning from each trip (the "Cuatro Postes" still stands), processions, and pilgrimages, lighted candles, crosses, votive offerings, pleas, recourse to holy water, and so on. The possible – and frequent – popular excesses were held in check by two regulatory forces: the council and the decrees of the Inquisition. The council of Trent in one of its last decrees "on the invocation, veneration, and relics of the saints and of holy images" (session 23, 1563), at bottom supports popular religion. And the index of forbidden books of 1559, in which the Inquisition gives a whole series cutting back and calling attention to "truculent images" (omnes picturae), pictures of death, practical books about magic ("books about magic or about how to invoke the

devil"), false Diurnals and Books of the Hours, and countless prayers in the vernacular (*"a prayer for the confined,"* *"a prayer of the testament of Christ,"* *"a prayer for the count"* *"a prayer for a just judge,"* *"a prayer to Saint Marina,"* and so on. (*Indice* p. 46).

3. Teresa from the time she was a child was introduced to the practice of a healthy piety which her mother inculcated in her ("my devotions, the rosary, being devoted to Our Lady . . . "). Recall how when her mother died Teresa went before a statue of our Lady and took our Lady for her mother. In the Incarnation she followed the life and customs of the community, in which they practiced fervently processions, like that of *Corpus Christi*, and where there flourished from 1560 on the confraternity of the Transpiercing of Our Lady (which became a great Marian devotion of Teresa's). On receiving word about the death or the wounds suffered by her brothers in the battle of Iñaquitos (Perú 1546), Teresa made a pilgrimage to the shrine of Guadalupe in Spain. The most powerful episode of all occurred in the years 1560-1562 when King Philip II sent a petition to the monastery – as he did to many others – containing a plea for urgent prayers and processions for unity among Christians and for religious peace in France. The plea was promptly seconded in the monastery of the Incarnation. It has a special resonance in the first chapters of the *Way of Perfection* and in the Carmel of St. Joseph. Yet, unfortunately, a little before (1531) the popular religious misunderstanding had a bad effect on the pious practices of the monastery. As a harsh example: iIn Avila, as in all of Castile, it was in vogue to be preoccupied about one's own life after death. One of the well-off Lords of the city (Señor Robles) obsessed with thoughts about security of his soul after death, left to the monastery his wealth, on the condition that his remains be buried in the presbytery of the church and that "there, before his tomb the nuns of the monastery take their turn day and night watching in prayer with a lighted candle in hand

praying for his eternal rest, "in such a way that always there will be a nun praying and begging God for him." All of this was as absurd as it was unbearable for the nuns. Only Teresa when she was elected prioress obtained a permutation.

4. The biographical period most important is without doubt the third. Teresa lived in depth the mystical experience and in it the mystery of God, the Humanity of Christ, the Eucharist and so on. Yet at the same time she followed faithfully the practices of popular religion: she sowed hermitages in the new Carmel of St. Joseph, she holds processions with the "Santo Cristo del Amor"; or even includes humorous ones, she cultivates in depth devotion to St Joseph; when she returns to the Incarnation as prioress, she enthrones a statue of the Virgin Mary in the prioress's seat, she trains the nuns in the practice of converting the profane into the divine, that is popular songs and dances were given a religious meaning at Christmas time and for other feasts. In the caravan for her foundations she always brought a statue of Christ (or of St. Joseph, or the Virgin Mary), who presided over the expedition. She visited the *Santo Cristo* in Burgos. She carried a long series of blessings in her personal breviary (blessing of St. Albert's water, for travelers, for Agnusdeis, for the house, for grapes, for figs, cheese, for fire, for a boat, for children, and so on). Yet the most striking fact in her mystical experience was her devotion to holy water (L 31.4) and her enthusiasm for religious images (portraits of Christ or of the saints).

5. There is in all this a discordant note: it is called "demonism." Popular religion of the whole century, as well as in previous times, grew out of a constant temptation to demonism. It was an attachment to the marvelous or miraculous, but in the inverse. One lived in the firm belief that the Christian life (of every man and woman) suffered a constant harassment and being spied on by the devil. From this arose the implacable persecutions of witches. And the use and abuse

of superstitious practices came about. (Already from the time she was young Teresa assures us that she did not fall into such customs: "I never cared for other devotions that some people practice, especially women, with those ceremonies, intolerable to me" *(L. 6. 6);* "may God deliver us from foolish devotions" *(L 13, 16)*. But she too became a victim of this popular superstition. It was aggravated by the learned men (theologians) precisely in the period of her mystical experience. They inculcated in her the thought that her experience was from a bad spirit. They insisted on this and it was very painful for Teresa. They did so even to the extreme of advising her to make the fig at her visions of Christ – although she couldn't manage to believe that they were right – which would serve to frighten the devil away. In fact for years, Teresa had to battle against two extremes: the fear of being a victim of the devil, as they say, and the other the absolute conviction of the nullity and powerlessness of the malignant spirits: "I pay no more attention to them than to flies . . .there was no doubt in my opinion, that they were afraid of me. I think they're such cowards . . . .and a fig for all the devils" (L 25. 20-22). But the fact is that Teresa continued to experience his occasional presence at determined moments in her life.

6. What was most relevant of all was the union of popular religion with mystical experience: Teresa experienced day by day the astounding beauty of the face of Christ, she lived in a Trinitarian experience, and so on. Nevertheless in the daily practices of the community, images, holy water, processions, singing songs were almost indispensable. Symptomatic was her exclamation: "Unfortunate are those heretics who through their own fault have lost this consolation of images. It is then a wonderful comfort to see an image of One whom we have so much reason to love. Wherever I turn my eyes, I would want to see his image" (WP 34. 11). Teresa had made mystical experience and popular religion compatible.

8. The Contemporary Clergy

1. The clergy is the social class nearest Teresa. Also it was the most influential for a religious like herself. Of the two branches in which it was divided – secular and religious – we are going to consider here only the first. In the Spain of that time the secular clergy were organized as a pyramid: at the base was the lower clergy (country curates, city parish priests, chaplains): then the higher clergy of bishops, archbishops, exempt abbots; and finally representatives of the ecclesiastical center of Rome: nuncios, officials from the Roman curia, and the Supreme Pontiff. Teresa counts in her family one priest, Don Alonso's brother, to whom she never alludes. On the other hand, she had the fortune of maintaining personal relations with members from the different strata on the ecclesiastical ladder. She knew not only individual persons but unavoidably the official bureaucracy. But, above all, she depended on this knowledge in her activity as founder. Therefore, this came about at the beginning of the third period of her life (1560).

2. She established relationships with the summit of the high clergy. Hardly does she decide to found a Carmel than she realizes that it all depends on Rome. The pope at the time was Pius IV (the pope who closed the Council of Trent). And from Rome there arrived successively three permissions for a foundation. The first was useless. She had to solicit and pay for a second (which came addressed not to her but to her friends Aldonza and Guiomar). And still she needed to seek a third (L 39. 14). This was her first experience with Roman bureaucracy. In the future she will have to come to an understanding with the papal nuncios in Madrid. First with the nuncio Crivelli. Afterward with the good Nicolás Ormaneto (of the school of St.

Charles Borromeo). And finally with an adversary, Felipe Sega, who evidently judged women without much benevolence ("*Of me they say that I am a restless vagabond"* Ltr. 269, no. 3). In reality, Sega never deigned to take account of the work or person of this "woman."

3. The Spanish church at that time was divided into ecclesiastical provinces. The two most important were considered metropolises, one in Toledo, the other in Santiago de Compostela. Toledo was the most powerful (it extended from Valladolid to the Mediterranean). But Avila belonged to the province of Santiago, even though Teresa had strong relations with the Archbishop of Toledo, Cardinal Quiroga. (She also had them with the future Archbishop of Santiago, Dr. Alonso Velázquez, her confessor.) Avila included a copious and powerful city chapter, not always friendly toward Teresa. Surely she knew about the tremendous trauma suffered by the Toledan church: the sequestration and imprisonment of Archbishop Carranza out of pure envy on the part of his fellow soldiers, followed by the vile politics of Philip II. When Teresa makes her foundation in Toledo, the diocese – she says – lacks a prelate and she had to energetically confront a substitute governor, Gómez Tello Girón, so as to gain the permission. Toledo was at the time a good peephole for observing the gloomy Spanish horizon.

4. Teresa deals personally with at least ten Spanish bishops and one Portuguese. The one who collaborated with her the most unselfishly was the Bishop of Avila, Don Alvaro de Mendoza (from 1562 until 1582 after the death of Teresa). Other great friends of Teresa's and collaborators were the Bishop of Osma, Alonso Velázquez, the Bishop of Evora, and Don Teutonio de Braganza (the first editor of a teresian work). A great admirer of her work was the Patriarch of Valencia, St Juan de Ribera. A wholehearted supporter of hers was the Bishop of Salamanca, Don Jerónimo Manrique, who a little after Teresa's death had the university professors investigate the miracle

of her incorrupt body and immediately began on his own the process for her canonization (1591). From being an adversary to becoming an admirer and friend was the Cardinal Archbishop of Seville, Cristóbal de Rojas. The only one who continued for a long time being hostile toward her was the Archbishop of Burgos, Cristóbal Vela (who came from Avila). The entire list of prelates more or less involved in Teresa's activities can be found in the *Diccionario de Santa Teresa* under the term *"Obispos."* The number comes to 23 prelates. A good indicator of how Teresa came to affect this ecclesiastical sector.

5. The strata of the lower clergy helped Teresa to get a glimpse of the ecclesiastical state of mind, not only in Spain but in Europe. In the teresian biography the episode most known and ventilated was her encounter with the curate in Becedas, when she was only 24 year old, gravely ill, and in need of spiritual assistance. In her travels as founder there accompanied her another humble chaplain, who was called "her squire," Julián de Avila. She will experience in Seville the false friendship with Garciálvarez whom she had to remove from her Spanish Carmel. Another failed friendship was that of the famous Padilla (Ardapilla her code name for him), an ex-missionary, a fiery reformer, who will end up in the prison of the Inquisition. Up until the end of her life, Teresa will count priests of quality, sharing jointly in her work, unconditionally, such as the two from Palencia, Salinas and Reinoso, who assisted her in the foundation in Burgos.

6. Another thing is the attitude or value judgments stated by Teresa. She had a high esteem for numerous persons in the episcopate whom she knew. She had an equal veneration for the Nuncio Ormaneto. The only exception was the Nuncio Felipe Sega in the measure that he made use of his powers. Sega had begun on the wrong foot, maximizing his powers as lord of the gallows and the knife (cf. MHCT 3, 610). On the part of Teresa, it is enough to note the salient moments. She is astonished by the kind of curial language

used in the condemnation of Gracián without hearing anything in his favor ("God forgive me, for I am still unable to believe . . . in that style" Ltr. 254. 8)). She has a serious fear that Gracián will fall into the hands of the nuncio ("Watch carefully that if he is placed under the authority of the nuncio his safety will be guaranteed" (Ltr. 255. 1); "It would be folly to submit to the nuncio" (Ltr 261. 2). She has recourse to the nuncio's confessor so as "to oblige him [the nuncio] in conscience" (Ltr. 269. 9). She labels the conduct of the nuncio with an unusual word from her pen: "For since the nuncio is so touchy . . ." (Ltr 296. 7). All of this is out of the ordinary yet a revealing occurrence on the pen of Teresa: the marginalized woman, who is Teresa, faces up to someone who represents the summit of ecclesiastical powers.

7. Her assessment of the lower clergy is more univocal. The priest, for her, is not an official employee. At the crucial moment in which the church is living, the priest is a standard bearer, a kind of commander-in-chief for Christians. He is a defender of the cause of Christ. So as to exercise his high duty there is demanded of him quality: perfection. "This is not the time for seeing imperfections in those who must teach . . . One who is perfect will do much more than many who are not . . . They are the persons who must strengthen people who are weak, and encourage the little ones. A fine state things would be in – soldiers without captains! These persons must live among men, deal with men, live in palaces, and even sometimes outwardly behave as such men do. "Do you think, my daughters, that little is required for them to deal with the world, live in the world, engage in its business, and, as I said, resemble it in its conversations, while interiorly remaining its strangers, its enemies, in sum, not being men but angels? For if they do not live in this way, they do not deserve to be called captains, nor may the Lord allow them to leave their cells" (WP 3. 5, 3). What would become of the Church without them?

9. Teresa In The Sight Of The Spanish Inquisition

1. In the church, as in the Spanish society of that century, the inquisition was one of the most determinant, and also pernicious, institutions of that time. It was so also in Teresa's life. The inquisitors questioned both her person and her first and main work, *The Book of Her Life*. She, for her part, replied in different forms to the famous *Index of Forbidden Books* of 1559. It is common to present Teresa among the persons not only repressed intellectually but harassed by the inquisitors, above all by the impact of that social force on freedom of thought, of life, and of action in that society.

2. From the social point of view, the inquisition exercised a disastrous influence. Its expressed or hidden presence was everywhere. Also its almost unlimited power and gloomy autos-da-fe – necessarily known by Teresa – gave rise to a wave of fear especially in the religious sectors. Clearly this wave of fear also grazed the climate and soul of Teresa. When the uncontrollable mystical graces burst forth in the years 1554-60, her novice assessors who recalled the cases of recent pseudo-visionaries about whom the inquisition intervened, "came to me with great fear to tell me we were in trouble and that it could happen that others might accuse me of something and report me to the inquisition." Despite the profound disturbance that Teresa was undergoing at this time, she gives an account of her reaction before this great fear:

"This amused me and made me laugh, for I never had any fear of such a possibility . . . I told them they shouldn't be afraid about these possible accusations . . .that I thought that if I did have something to fear I'd go myself to seek out the inquisitors" (L 33, 5).

We do not know whether her response seemed boastful to these assessors. Yet certainly with respect to fearing or not fearing, Teresa distanced herself from the common denominator. Let us underline her affirmation that she never had any fear of the inquisition. Nonetheless in the successive events of her life there occurred a series of incidents, in regard to her writings and person, that reveal to what degree she fell into the inquisitorial orbit. It is enough to list them.

3. Above all, in her first writing that she redacted for the instruction of her nuns at St. Joseph's, *The Way of Perfection*, she adopts a frank position: in her famous apology for women: *"since the world's judges are sons of Adam and all of them men, there is no virtue in women that they do not hold suspect."* With the subsequent tacit appeal to the tribunal of the supreme judge she just as directly alludes to the inquisitorial abuses, which her friend the censor – Padre García de Toledo – hastened to erase, an entire paragraph, which doesn't pass into the second redaction of the book. What does remain in the second redaction are the categorical allusions to the fact that the inquisition took away from spiritual readers books on prayer (mentioned repeatedly, and also noted by the censor, but not erased).

4. Much more serious is the incident surrounding *The Book of Her Life*. It occurred in 1575 and the following years until after the death of the author. Denounced at the same time in Andalusia and Castile, the inquisition sequestered it that year. Don Alvaro de Mendoza handed it over in February. In July, Padre Báñez signed his favorable vote to the work, but it remained sequestered. In 1577, being now the grand inquisitor and archbishop of Toledo, García de Quiroga, along with Teresa and Gracián, asked the inquisition to restore it but in vain. The book continued "in prison" until Teresa's death in Alba (1582). And it was only allowed out in 1587 for the preparation of its edition.. Then it passed into the hands of Anne of Jesus and from hers to those of Fray Luis de León, who published it

in 1588. Fortunately the autograph did not suffer from deletions or annotations (only a few by a benevolent hand), nor bad handling. Yet its diffusion was impeded. And Teresa had suffered as if her soul had been taken prisoner.

5. The same dates that her *Life* had been implicated before the inquisition, the "person" of Teresa was too. She was in the Carmel of Seville. Under suspicion and denounced by diverse Andalusian channels, finally a *beata* who had tried the Carmelite life in the Seville Carmel informed against Teresa. And the inquisition presented itself with all its pomp to investigate the case and the spirit of Saint Teresa, who came out of the misfortune ostentatiously unharmed. Two of those consulted by the inquisition (P. Rodrigo and P. Enríquez) were friendly admirers of Teresa. For them she wrote *Spiritual Testimonies* 58 & 59. The first was to give an account of the learned and spiritual men who had been her directors; the other was for the purpose of giving an account of the stages of mystical prayer as she had expounded them in the little treatise on prayer in her *Life* (chaps. 11-22).

6. In speaking of the inquisitorial pressure, it is usually told how Teresa threw the autograph of her meditations on the biblical book the *Song of Songs* into the fire, an episode that took place very probably during the five years in which Fray Luis de León was held in the prison of the inquisition for translating into Spanish this biblical work. It is possible that the inquisitorial climate of the moment had its influence on this incident in Teresa's life. But the fact happened, according to a witness in this way: "Padre Yanguas told this witness that the said Madre Teresa had written a book on the Song of Songs, and it seemed to him that this wasn't right that a woman should be writing a book on Scripture, and he told her so, and she was so prompt in obedience and following the advice of her confessor that she burned it at once . . ." María Gracián gave this testimony

(BMC 18, 320). According to her it was not the inquisition that was the cause of its being thrown into the fire but the antifeminist prejudice of the theologian from Segovia, Diego de Yanguas.

7. The attitude of Teresa before the decisions of the inquisition remains clear in the primitive text of the Teresian *Constitutions*. In specifying the books preferred for the little library of a Carmel, she does not hesitate to include on the list the books of Fray Luis de Granada, when he was recently still included on the *Index of Forbidden Books*, although he may have already been rehabilitated by Rome. The most harsh and persistent denunciations of Teresa to the inquisition occurred after her death. At the root of this was the publication of her books by Fray Luis de León, after they had already initiated in Salamanca the process for her canonization (cf. E. Llamas. *Santa Teresa y la Inquisición*. Madrid 1972).

8. To sum up: it is likely that, from the time she was a child, Teresa knew about the sambenito (a penitential garment) imposed by the inquisition on her grandfather and family in Toledo. Nevertheless, no trace remains in her writings of this event. What remains firmly established is that she did not succumb to the ambient of anti-inquisitorial fear that spread through Castile. Also, she was a victim of the inquisitorial prohibition of spiritual books in the vernacular. Personally she was investigated by the inquisitors in Seville. During the last years of her life, her autobiography was sequestered by the inquisition. In 1577-78, as soon as she had finished *The Interior Castle*, she sent the autograph to Seville so that it would be in the safe hands of Madre María de San José, but she finds no problem in the fact that one of the inquisitorial councilors, Padre Rodrigo, knows about it. In short, neither the person of Teresa nor the sequestered *Book of Her Life*, suffered ill-treatment or bad handling from the inquisition.

10. In The Wake Of The Counter-Reform Of Trent

1. In the history of the church, Teresa, like St. Ignatius of Loyola or St. John of the Cross, was enrolled in the movement of the counter-reform that started up in the middle of the XVI century and was led in a special way by the Council of Trent. By counter-reform we mean the vital mood that arose in the church in its becoming aware of the of the great break in unity produced in the west. This came not only in reaction to the reform initiated by Luther, but as a new spirit, that nourished the Christian life, the arts, theology, and the seminaries. It had its highest examples in the saints, or in the church itself, as much in the manner of actualizing the Christian mystery as in the reaction to the splintering that separated from Rome. We are interested in situating Teresa in this great current. What was her relation to the Council of Trent. What place did she occupy in the life of the church of the counter-reformation. What attitude did she adopt before the dissident church in Europe.

2. In general terms, her mystical life as well as her activity as founder coincides with the celebration and execution of the Council of Trent, which she frequently refers to as the *holy Council.* It should be enough to give some simple dates:

Council	Teresa
1545: Opening: first period	1544: Death of Teresa's father. Time of struggle.
1547: Second period (Bologna)	1554: The beginning of Teresa's mystical life
1560-63: Third period (Trent)	1560: First writings and foundations

1565-1582: The Spanish   1582 - 1588: Death and spread
councils of implementation   of her work

Other contextual dates:4 December 1563 the Council of Trent is closed; 26 January 1564, the Bull of Pius IV approving the council's decrees; with the proclamation of 12 July 1564, Philip II accepts the implementation of the council; and there follows in Spain a series of provincial councils for the implementation of the decrees; the last of these known by Teresa was celebrated in Toledo (1582) with the assistance of two bishop friends of hers: Gaspar de Quiroga (who presided) and Alvaro de Mendoza (Bishop of Palencia) who met her in Valladolid on his way to Toledo, and she gave him some errands (2 September 1582), about a month before her death (see Ltrs 463 and 466). During this period (1564-1582) there existed in Spain great tension, ecclesiastical and political, in regard to the reception of the council.

3. It is normal that these tensions would have repercussions on Teresa and her work. Yet even before, during the final sessions of the council, there arrived in Avila the reports of Dominican and Jesuit theologians, that referred to the internal events of the assembly, the things debated in it, the arrival of Cardinal Lorena who gave a pathetic account of the terrible situation in France, and so on; this information finds a strong echo in the first chapters of *Way of Perfection* (1566), "At that time news reached me of the harm being done in France and of the havoc the Lutherans had caused and how much this miserable sect was growing" (WP *1.2).*

4. Among the doctrinal decisions of the decrees of the council, those that had the greatest repercussion on Teresa were the canons of session VI (1547) on justification and the security or insecurity of being in the state of grace. A problem arose throughout her writings, from her *Life* to the *Interior Castle*, and passing through the *Spiritual Testimonies* (no. 24). More concretely the practical decrees

of reform affect her: in reference to monastic poverty, it made her change her opinion and decide to modify what was established in her *Constitutions* (Ltr 376.7; F 9.3; 20. 1); and in reference to the necessary recourse to the respective ordinary for each new foundation (F 24. 15); or in reference to the situation of the first two discalced Carmelites in Pastrana (F 17. 8), and other small details (Ltr 89.3). Yet, affecting her above all were the norms about the enclosure of nuns (session 25. 5). She had already before the decision at Trent opted for "much enclosure" for her Carmels, but not with the material rigor dictated by the council and the successive decrees implementing it. Teresa had to adjust to these criteria, with a certain delay, the enclosure of her monasteries (Ltr 412.15; 451.14).

5. This same decree occasioned strong interferences with her task as founder: the persistent opposition to her leaving the enclosure to make foundations; first the rumors (ST 15) widespread among the theologians (including the insults of a professor at the University of Salamanca); later the objections of the papal nuncios, Ormaneto and Sega ("I must choose a house and remain there permanently and make no more foundations, for I can no longer go out, because of the council" (Ltr 98.3); "about me they say that I am a restless vagabond and that the monasteries I have founded were established without permission from the pope or general"(Ltr 269.3); and under the strong opposition of her provincial, Angel de Salazar ("Melchizedek says that according to the council I cannot make foundations and that our Most Reverend Father [Rossi] has expressly declared this" Ltr 134. 3*)*. For this reason Teresa had to suspend the foundations for more than four years, from 1576 until 1580.

6. Nevertheless, these were not just episodes that characterize Teresa's contribution to the movement of reform initiated by the council of Trent. She is not one reformer more of the religious life. In that moment of crisis to church unity, her position is clear. Above

all, she maintains a combative position with the dissidents – she calls them Lutherans – for breaking church unity, for their desecration of images and of the Eucharist, and for the wars they stirred up . . . (even if she opposes the military reaction of Philip II: not "with force of arms" (WP 3.1); a passage crossed out by the censor. In the epilogue of the *Interior Castle*, she prays for the "increase of his church and for light for the Lutherans."

7. Likewise she maintains her strong option for the church – the holy Roman Catholic Church, she writes two times, in the prologue and the epilogue of *The Interior Castle*, not only in reference to the church mystery but expressly to its structure and earthly existence ."If anyone were to see that I went against the slightest ceremony of the church in a matter of faith, I myself knew well that I would also die a thousand deaths for the faith or for any truth of Sacred Scripture" (L 33.5). "For one fraction of an increase in faith and for having given some light to the heretics such a king would be willing to lose a thousand kingdoms" (L 21.1).

8. It is characteristic of her Christian humanism, that she write for people essentially open to transcendental values. All her symbols (the *castle*, the *garden* of the soul, the *worm-butterfly*, the two *founts*) present human persons as destined for transcendence and open from the depths of their being to a relationship with God. Equally her mysticism is prophetic: she speaks of God, of Christ, of the soul, not from theoretical outlines but from experience. Teresa is definitively a witness of God, present in the world and in the history of humankind. Christian humanism and mysticism are the strongest contributions of Teresa to the counter-reform movement led by the council.

II
Teresa in Her Family

The family is the space in which Teresa opened up to life and took her first steps. We are interested in specifying what we know about her: the environment, the duties, the persons, the cultural level .

Also the family decline: Teresa will assist at the dispersion and splitting up of the family home, at leaving behind her house of birth. And afterward at the partial restoration of the family, but no longer in the old homestead.

11. Teresa's Home

1. In Teresa's time the hearth was *the place where light and fire were enkindled for the common service of a household* (Covarrubias). And around the material fire so necessary in a place as cold as Avila, there was at the same time the human and affectionate warmth that unites and reunites the members of the family, a little cell of life that is born and grows and creates the space and the humus adequate for intimacy. In this theme we will be occupied only with the material aspects of the hearth, the house or houses where Teresa was born and grew, at least during the first 20 years of her life. This home was situated in the built-up area of Avila, not far from the south wall, and there was a kind of occasional extension into the town of Gotarrendura. That is we are speaking of an urban home inside the walls of the city with a supplementary rural home in the open country.

2. The Cepeda-Ahumada family had paternal roots in Toledo, where the father, Don Alonso, and the grandfather, Don Juan Sánchez, had resided. On the maternal side the family was rooted in Olmedo, where the maternal grandparents, Juan de Ahumada and Teresa de las Cuevas had resided. Teresa de las Cuevas was the only ancestor known by Teresa. But having roots in Toledo was the most determining factor. There her grandfather and his family lived a Judaizing life – also Teresa's father. For this they were later penalized by the inquisition as *conversos*, at the end of the previous century. There family business as merchants had flourished. In the last decade of the fifteenth century the business expanded into Avila, where little by little the sons of Juan Sánchez emigrated, and were known as "the Toledans." Don Alonso settled in the Caldeandrín. There he married Catalina del Peso, with whom he established his first home in 1505. With her he moved

to the neighborhood of Santo Domingo, to the House of the Currency which became his definitive residence and where Teresa was born.

3. In 1507 Doña Catalina died. A shadow of solitude and cold fell upon the home. Don Alonso then had to do an inventory of" the estate that existed at the time that my wife, Catalina del Peso, may she have holy glory, died, that is without the debts and other things that are in another notebook." And a few years after (1509) he entered into a second marriage with Doña Beatriz de Ahumada, who would become Teresa's mother. They both established a second home in the same House of the Currency. At the beginning this was a large old and abandoned house that no longer served as a mint.

4. After this, that habitat of Don Alonso's with his new family became ample and comfortable with the acquisition of some large houses somewhat grouped together with their respective yards and large gardens watered by a water wheel, which in time would be known and perhaps used by the adolescent Teresa. Fortunately the inventory of 1507 that was mentioned has reached us and through it we know something of the life and hustle and bustle of the house. Above all, Don Alonso has in his service a group of young men servants and another group of young girl maids, and also some little girl maids. They were not considered to be occasionally employed .but permanent servants, so they resided in the house day and night. To protect his possessions he used a battery of small and large chests (no less than ten) that contained the merchandise for sale: in the large jewelry chest the gold was kept:" two gold chains, that have four turns, six small gold rings, six gold bracelets, a large broken gold flask, two gold necklaces worth 400; other necklaces, a cross for its workmanship worth 80. Linens of every kind: cloth from France, Holland, Rouen, London, Milan, Toledo, Valencia, Segovia, gold damask., and a harness with little bells of gold thread, and cords from Arabia, with a scarlet ball. " There are also various foodstuffs: "sixteen kinds of cheese that exist

in Avila; another sixteen kinds of cheese from Parral, what is more another six kinds of cheese brought form Guadanil; preserves , honey and other little things. A little bit of musk and sweet gum and a large flask of oak oil, and in another flask a little bit, and some small, empty glass bottles for oil." Noted in the inventory are " pledged objects," such as money owed to the queen: "I owe our lady the queen 10,154 maravedis, " and so on. These are samples of the huge inventory. In all, there are more than 330 articles that filled the chests of the merchant, carefully numbered, fixed with their respective price and mixed with clothing and objects for the private use of Don Alonso (for example, "my arms, my black sword, belt, and black dagger"), all in great disorder, provoked probably by the recent absence of his dead first wife.

5. It was the world of commerce in which the little family enterprise moved, wide open to the clientele of the city and that extended normally into the following decade, when Teresa enters the scene as a little girl. It is very possible that this little world of buying and selling had influenced her, that years later she nicknamed herself the "bargainer" and "negotiator," very wise in the use of money and in business matters.

6. Beyond this inventory of 1507, there occurred the important second marriage of Don Alonso with the newly arrived Doña Beatriz to the Avilan home. This new lady of the house had brought with her a dowry of new riches and goods: the houses and a dovecote in Gotarrendura, with property and lands, plus "two pieces of land and three vines " in the spacious fields of the surrounding area and a large flock of wool-bearing sheep which in time numbered 2,000 heads (the number given precisely by the townspeople). This means that at least a small number of country people, farmers and shepherds in charge of this estate were bound to the family of Don Alonso. It disposed of some litters for ladies, fully adorned with girdles covered in fine woven, new cloth that cost a thousand maravedis, plus a horse and

a young mule for the move of Doña Beatriz and perhaps Teresa to Gatarrendura. The most likely thing is that for Teresa when a child or young girl from the city, the encounter with doves and herds and shepherds and tenant farmers had a special charm, at least it opened more spacious horizons than the restricted area enclosed by the walls of the city of Avila. Gotarrendura was the place where the wedding between Don Alonso and Doña Beatriz was celebrated. And that is where Doña Beatriz came to give up her last breath, when Teresa was still very young, only fourteen years old. It is important that the childhood dwelling places of Teresa had this double horizon: urban and country.

We shall see in what follows the formation of the family and of each of its constituent parts.

12. Teresa's Father, Don Alonso Sanchez De Cepeda

1. Almost all that we know about Don Alonso we owe to his daughter, Teresa. She begins *The Book of Her Life*: "My father was fond of reading good books and thus he also had books in Spanish for his children to read." (Despite this, Don Alonso did not belong to the association of cultured humanists, but to the modest popular group, who were desirous to learn, like Teresa herself). She continues on to speak of her father's affection and predilection for her: "I was the most loved of my father." And still she goes on in this first page of her *Life* to present a sketch of Don Alonso: "My father was a man very charitable with the poor and compassionate toward the sick" [next door was the hospital of Santa Escolástica] "and even toward servants; so great was his compassion that nobody was ever able to convince him to accept slaves . . . He was very honest No one ever saw him swear or engage in fault-finding. He was an upright man" (L 1.1).

2. He was born in Toledo about 1480. At the end of the century he moved to Avila. In 1505 he married Catalina del Peso and with her had his two first children., María and Juan. Widowed in 1507, he celebrated his second marriage with DoZa Beatriz de Ahumada in 1509 and with her became the father of many children, he had ten with his second wife ("we were," Teresa writes, "in all three sisters and nine brothers"). He was a merchant and had a number of employees. Teresa recalls that he was against the reading of long novels of chivalry, which, hidden from him, her mother and she read. Despite his judeo-converso origin there is not a trace of it, which he denounced, in his conduct. But yes, an uncontrollable hunger for the title of nobility. To obtain it, he associated with his brothers residing in Avila and bordering regions and undertook a large lawsuit before the chancery of Valladolid, 1519-

51

1521. (We will analyze this in Theme 16.). Previously Don Alonso had taken part in the war of Navarre, with the show of being a knight well armored (1512). In 1515 his preferred daughter, Teresa, was born, "at five in the morning . . .almost at dawn."

3. In 1528/29 DoZa Beatriz died and for the second time Don Alonso was widowed. He was 48 years old and responsible for the eleven children that lived at home. (Juan his first born had departed for Italy, where he died a little afterward.) It was at this time that he decided to send Teresa for her education as a boarder to the Avilan school of Our Lady of Grace (1531). Yet a short time afterward, he roundly opposed her Carmelite vocation. In the meantime she served as housekeeper. But Teresa's vocation to be a nun was irrevocable and Don Alsonso surrendered to his daughter's wish (1535). She recalls that "when I left my father's house I felt that separation so keenly that the feeling will not be greater, I think, when I die, for it seemed that every bone in my body was being sundered" (L.4. 1). When she made her profession two years later Don Alonso granted her a lavish dowry ("40 bushels of bread as rent, one half wheat and one half barley, that the property yields in the place and boundaries of Gotarrendura . . . and in its defect 200 gold ducats": *BMC 1. 93)*. This was such that Teresa figured among the DoZas in the monastery for being the "daughter of noble parents."

4. Two years later poor Don Alonso took charge of his recently professed daughter in her grave illness. He took her out of the convent and brought her to his brother Pedro's house in Hortigosa; then he accompanied her to Becedas to leave her in the hands of a well known quack, and already in 1539, when she returned to Avila he received her into his own large house. But she entered into a deep coma, and despite her apparent death, he opposed her burial. He thus saved Teresa's life. His last days arrived, which generally modern authors present in a somber way with a failed and bitter Don Alonso. On the contrary,

Teresa – the only historical source for this final days – recalls how she had previously coached her father in prayer, she gave him books on how to practice it and he made most notable progress becoming a spiritual person in the style of his brother Don Pedro. Don Alonso went down frequently from his large family home to the speak room at the Incarnation. He and Teresa conversed about prayer. And they practiced it in depth. He above all. In December of 1543, at the age of 63, he became sick and died. He accepted the loving care and the counsels of Teresa who had left her monastery to assist him and she recalls his last breath: "when I saw him coming to the end of his life, it seemed my soul was being wrenched form me, for I loved him dearly." And she comments: "He looked like an angel. This it seems to me he was, so to speak, in soul and character, for he preserved his soul very well" (L 7.14 -16).

5.. Avoiding the thicket of modern biographies of Teresa with a propensity to cast a shadow over these last days in the life of Don Alonso, we can sketch the figure of the old merchant with a simple balance sheet. It is certain that in these last years Don Alonso neglected the home, the estate, and the merchandise. The inventory of his goods made at the time close to his death is much more modest than that done in 1507 at the death of his first wife. Also it is possible and absolutely normal that a shadow of sadness should come upon his countenance and in the depths of his soul after having lost DoZa Beatriz in the flower of her age, and then to see his sons leave home at the call to the Americas: from 1532, at least five of his sons embarked for this destination. Remaining at home were the youngest, Antonio, Agustín, and Pedro. And perhaps the last daughter Juana, if she had not yet taken refuge at the side of Teresa in the Incarnation. Yet we lack documents that inform us about the degree of sadness and dejection that had fallen on the home. The only source that we have are Teresa's writings .In these, the figure of the old merchant is purified, grows, and is spiritualized. Don Alonso passes beyond financial problems. He finds strength in the faith and the Christian life. He grows in one direction in his appreciation and love for Teresa. And she with a normal dose of filial partiality, yet with a lucid and objective gaze, forms a high concept of him. Of the kind that in her soul, the death of her father was a shock. And it brought about a profound change in her life. She instinctively turned to the Dominican friar that was her father's confessor that he might encourage and guide her.

6. From this moment begins for her the period of struggle to overcome the preceding mistaken life and prepare in depth for the immanent bursting forth of her mystical life. She herself sums up this period of struggle: "I wanted to live (for I well understood that I was not living but was struggling with a shadow of death), but I had no one to give me life" (L 8.12).

1. Teresa's mother was Doña Beatriz de Ahumada. She married

13. Teresa's Mother

Don Alonso in 1509 when she was 14 years old. Born in Olmedo in the year 1495, she was the daughter of Juan de Ahumada and Teresa de las Cuevas. Her father died when she was young girl, with only one brother alive, Juan de Ahumada. she had had four other brothers, all now deceased. The marriage was celebrated in Gotarrendura. She was richly endowed by her mother. Don Alonso, her spouse offered a magnificent donation as a "pledge of her virginity: I oblige myself to pay a generous gift to Beatriz de Ahumada . . .my bride and wife who will be pleasing to God in honor of her virginity and for the increase of her dowry, one thousand gold florins, good ones, of a just weight and value according to the law and stamp of Aragón "(Serrano y Sanz 2,488).

2. Almost the only source of information we have about the person and life of Doña Beatriz we owe to her daughter Teresa in the account given of her mother in her *Life*. It is precisely the approach that interests us here: how did Doña Beatriz appear to her daughter, and to what degree was she for her a model of femininity? In fact Teresa's autobiography begins intentionally with two biographical sketches, one of her father and the other of her mother. She presents her mother as young, beautiful, virtuous, intelligent, hard-working, and dedicated to her children and, like Don Alonso, fond of reading. That is to say, Doña Beatriz did not belong to the great mass of illiterate women of that time. (Her own mother, Teresa de las Cuevas., did not know how to sign her name). Perhaps for that reason it was due to her that none of Beatriz's many children were ignorant of the art of reading and writing.

3. The portrait Teresa drew of her mother is unsurpassable: "My mother also had many virtues. And she suffered much sickness during

her life. She was extremely modest. Although very beautiful, she never gave occasion to anyone to think she paid any attention to her beauty. For at the time of her death at the age of thirty-three, her clothes were already those of a much older person. She was gentle and very intelligent. Great were the trials she suffered during her life. Her death was a truly Christian one" (*L* 1.2).

4. Among the physical and moral traits of her mother, Teresa underlines three times the precarious state of her mother's health. One time she states expressly:"And she suffered much sickness during her life." Then, somewhat more confused: "Great were the trials they suffered during her life" (trials that both spouses suffered?). And for a third time: "Perhaps she did this reading to escape thinking of the great trials she had to bear" (L 2. 1). In fact, Doña Beatriz had her first child, Hernando, at the age of 15. And in the eighteen following years, eight or nine other children. Teresa is the fourth in the series, born when her mother was 20 years old. The last recollections she had of her mother date from when Teresa was 13 or 14 years old. She recalls them in the account of her *Life* when she approaches 50 and is a nun in the Carmel of St. Joseph, submerged now in the high sea of mystical experience.

5. In the account of her *Life* there appear the remembrances of her childhood and adolescence. Of her childhood she recalls the pious practices instilled in her by her mother: "my devotions, and they were many, especially the rosary, to which my mother was very devoted: and she made me devoted to it too. " And perhaps her diligence in giving alms to the poor prompted Teresa to do so as well, "although I could only give a little." In this sheaf of memories, that of the death of Doña Beatriz stands out. It marked at the same time the trauma of being deprived of her mother that Teresa suffered in her adolescence and that drove her to turn to the Mother of heaven: "I remember that when my mother died I was twelve years old or a little less" [a couple of years more]."When I began to understand what I had lost, I went

afflicted before an image of our Lady and besought her with many tears to be my mother. It seems to me that although I did this in simplicity it helped me, for I have found favor with this sovereign Virgin in everything I have asked of her . . ." (L 1.7). The event influenced Teresa not only in her adolescence but in the depth of her soul for her whole life. Perhaps this moment of "many tears" marked the passage from conventional devotions to a first act of profound religiosity, clearly Marian.

6. An apparently negative note was the attachment of Doña Beatriz to reading books of chivalry. She did so in opposition to the will of Don Alonso, who at another time was himself attached to them, but now he disapproved of this addiction. Teresa confesses that she was an accomplice in this practice, and that both she and her mother did so, hiding it from Don Alonso. With the special note in which she recalls it in her *Life*, she also shares its negative standard, although adding kindheartedly two mitigating circumstances in favor of Doña Beatriz: "she didn't fail to do her duties. Perhaps she did this reading to escape thinking of the great trails she had to bear and to busy her children with something so that they would not turn to other things dangerous to them" (L 2.1). This seems to insinuate that it was not only Teresa but her brothers as well who shared this forbidden reading.

7. We don't know any of the titles of the novels that at that time got into the home. We only know, with enough probability, that among the books read by Teresa was found Las Sergas de Esplancián [The Adventures of Esplancián] (one of the Amadises). Yet in that third part of the century there were very many that the Castilian presses released on the public market. This explains the avidity of the young reader, Teresa: "I was so completely taken up with this reading that I didn't think I could be happy if I didn't have a new book" (L 2.1). It is normal for the modern historian to disagree on this point with the negative judgment of Don Alonso and of his daughter. In that context of illiter-

ate women, Doña Beatriz was capable of becoming impassioned over reading, and this precisely for books of fantasy so as to escape from the stress of family worries, capable also of gaining independence from her husband in this matter and in not seeing any problem in passing on this same passion to her adolescent daughter Teresa. A connivance that reveals a special confidence and intimacy between mother and daughter. We shall see further on the importance that these readings had on Teresa's literary formation. For the moment, let us underline only the convergence of mother and daughter on this cultural fringe. If, as it seems, it was the mother who coached Teresa the child in the art of reading, Teresa's present passion for books would be a normal prolongation of this training.

8. Like her mother, Teresa also had fragile health all her life. She was more robust in spirit, but possessed a large supply of traits inherited from her mother. In a summary evaluation we could condense them into three or four traits. Above all, an introduction to the practices of popular religiosity that Teresa will cultivate as she grows throughout her whole life. A love for learning and reading. Politeness and gentleness of manners, together with love of the family group. We have previously noted that Teresa traced this maternal profile when she was already immersed in the mystical experience. From the depths of this experience Doña Beatriz emerges once more at her husband's side: ". . . a spiritual rapture came upon me so forcefully that I had no power to resist it. It seemed to me I was brought into heaven, and the first persons I saw there were my father and mother. . . . I indeed remained outside myself" (L 38.1). This took place about the year 1565.

14. Teresa's Brothers And Sisters

"We were in all three sisters and nine brothers. All resembled their parents in being virtuous "(L. 1.3) .

"My brothers and sisters did not in any way hold me back from the service of God" (L 1. 4)

1. These were the two brush strokes with which Teresa introduced her brothers and sisters in the account of her *Life*. They were twelve, like the biblical patriarchs. We do not have a biographical portrait of any of them. The first of all, María de Cepeda, is nine years older than Teresa. The youngest, Juana, was born when Teresa was 13 years old. Teresa was the second of the three sisters. She also occupied the central place when counting all the children together: sixth place among the twelve. They formed two different groups, but they got on well: the two oldest, María and Juan came from the first marriage of Don Alonso. The ten remaining were children of Doña Beatriz. The disagreements between the two groups arose only when their father died (1543), when the time came for the inheritance and the distribution of money (cf. Theme 17)..

2. Little by little the twelve went their own way. The oldest, Juan, enlisted in the Italian regiment, where he died. María established her own home in Castellanos de la Cañada (1531), a little after the death of Doña Beatriz. And then began rapidly the diaspora of the eight men en route to the Americas. Four (or five) of them left during the lifetime of Don Alonso, the last three after his death. Those who enlisted in the armed retinue of the Avilan Blasco Nuñez Vela entered combat under his orders in the battle of Iñaquitos, in which Antonio died (the one who aspired to become a Dominican friar at the time Teresa was aspiring to become a Carmelite nun). A little after that, word arrived

of the death of Rodrigo – the one who tried as a child with Teresa to go to the land of the moors – in the land of the American Southern Cone. One of the youngest, Agustín, had traveled under the orders of the Viceroy, Francisco de Toledo, a protégé of Teresa's adviser, the Dominican García de Toledo. A peculiar note of all of them is their cultural initiation. It seems that all of them knew how to read and write. Juana the youngest of all corresponded with Teresa regularly. If as seems certain the number of illiterates in that society were about eighty or ninety percent of the population, Teresa's brothers and sisters found themselves situated at a privileged level

3. Throughout her life Teresa kept up special relations with some of them; the more loved ones? There is no trace of her friendship with her preferred Rodrigo, once he embarked for America, although before leaving Avila he renounced his maternal inheritance in favor of Teresa. The one she was most fond of was Juana, her younger sister, for whom she acted as a mother. On an unknown date, perhaps at the time of Don Alonso's illness, Teresa brought her to live with her at the Incarnation, where she was prepared not for the life of a nun but for marriage. And when Juana married Juan de Ovalle and took up residence in Alba de Tormes, Teresa continued to serve as her regular counselor and share in her thorny family problems. They corresponded with each other frequently: "For goodness' sake don't neglect to write to me," Teresa asks her (Ltr 367.5). The last letter, written in August 1581 during a most painful trip in return from Soria to Avila, is a moving one. She asks her brother-in-law to give permission to Juana and her daughter to meet her in Avila: "even though there may be some obstacles to this and he would have to stay and watch the house . . . Since I am coming from such a great distance. Beg him to let you come" (Ltr. 404.2). Juana has left us no less than 15 letters from her sister.

4. More intense and troubled was the relationship with Lorenzo. Seventeen of Teresa's letters to him are conserved. In the first she is

highly interested in his family life in Quito, and grateful to him for the economic help he gave to her and her two sisters. She insists on his return to Spain ("that we both join together to procure more honor and glory for God"). And when in the end he returned to the peninsula, she taught him about prayer and the spiritual life, helped him to establish himself in Avila and to organize a retired life in La Serna. She put him in contact with Fray John of the Cross and enrolled him in the little group that shared the Satirical Critique of the mysterious words "Búscate in mi" (seek yourself in me). (Lorenzo took part with a composition in verse). The time came when Lorenzo growing in fervor, wanted to give up the estate and the material tasks, but Teresa corrects his plan: "What you spend on La Serna will be well spent" (Ltr. 172.11).

5. In Avila Lorenzo lived with a painful fraternal problem. He received into his house his brother Pedro – the black sheep of the family – sick and neurasthenic – always unsuccessful who one day left home and took up the life of a vagabond. Hungry and half crazy he arrived at the Carmel in Toledo and sought refuge from his sister Teresa. Teresa took on the role of mediator and wrote a touching letter to her brother Lorenzo pleading for her poor, unruly brother and suggesting an exceptional solution: that Lorenzo give economic help "to this poor man," but that he allow him to go his own way."And so I beg you for the love of our Lord, to do me the favor of not bringing him back into your house no matter how much he begs and great his need . . .Indeed in this matter of wanting to stay with you, he is crazy, although he may not be so in other things . . . And truly I have this fear that some disaster will befall him" (Ltr. 337. 1). And then after proposing a costly solution, she reminds him: "Believe me that God wants anyone to whom he grants the favors he gives you to make such sacrifice" (337.4).

6. In the end, when Lorenzo died on his property in La Serna (Avila), Teresa gave spontaneously his funeral eulogy: "He died

entrusting himself to God, like a saint . . .He was so in the end in such a way [God's servant] that he wanted nothing to do with anything earthly. . . II I were able to write some of the details about his soul . . . It has made me, more than anyone else, feel very sad" (Ltr. 363. 3.4). He arranged to have his mortal remains rest in a chapel of St. Joseph in Avila, thinking that there he would lie next to his sister.

7. The relations with her other brothers were more sporadic and painful. It is dramatic her relation with the stubborn and neurotic Pedro, who after the death of Lorenzo started a lawsuit against Lorenzo's son . . . for his money. Likewise painful was her relation with her two younger brothers, Agustín and Jerónimo, lost far away in the pampas and mountains of South America. Teresa knew that years before her brother Lorenzo had to support two daughters that each one of her brothers had begotten outside marriage. Also with these brothers Teresa insisted that they return to Spain.

8. In summary: Teresa lived her fraternal relations in a first home-loving and idyllic period. Next she lived through the breakup of the home and the distant journeys of her brothers. Precisely in the period of her life as founder two of the family members became associates with her in her work, Lorenzo and the couple in Alba. Equally, in the intense years of her mystical life, she shared it with her brother Lorenzo, and with him and with him she lives the most intense of her fraternal relations.She also shared at the same time the dark drama of her brother Pedro. (We believe that even though this complex aspect of Teresa's biography has not been studied in depth, it in great part coincides with the stage of her mystical life.).

15. Teresa's Family In America
Teresa's Thought About America

1. Teresa was about seventeen years old when the exodus of her brothers for America (the Indies as Teresa called it) began. From this moment she never stopped turning her gaze to the American continent. The stress over it went on increasing until the eve of her death. For us the intersection of this stress with the wave of her mystical life is interesting. During the last two decades of her life the Americas form a part of her interior landscape. Let us begin by establishing chronologically the most important milestones:

1532: Her cousin Hernando de Cepeda and her brother Hernando de Ahumada depart for America

1535: Departure of her brother Rodrigo de Cepeda with the governor Pedro de Mendoza toward Rio de la Plata. Rodrigo renounces his maternal inheritance in favor of Teresa.

1540: Departure of her brothers Lorenzo and Jerónimo under the orders of Vaca de Castro.

1544: Departure of her brother Antonio de Ahumada.

1546: The battle of Iñaquito, in which various brothers of Teresa participated. Among the wounded, Antonio died. Hernandoand Lorenzo suffered serious wounds.

1546: Arrival in Peru of Teresa's youngest brother, Agustín de Ahumada, under the orders of La Gasca.

1547: Teresa goes on pilgrimage to the Extremaduran shrine of Guadalupe so as to pray for her brothers in the battle of Iñaquito.

1549: Three of Teresa's brothers, Lorenzo, Jerónimo, and Agustín take part in the victorious battle of Jaquihuana (8 April).

155?: Her brother Rodrigo dies in Chile fighting against the Araucanos.

1561:   In Avila, while preparing the foundation of St. Joseph's, Teresa receives through various channels the money sent from Quito by her brother Lorenzo. One of the messengers, Captain Antonio Morån, is exceptional (L 33. 12).

1561:   A long letter by Teresa to her brother Lorenzo (Ltr. 2), acknowledging receipt of his letter, the first of a series. (Only one other letter from her to Lorenzo in Quito, Ltr 24, is conserved). The remaining letters to him are written after his return to Spain.

1565:   Her brother Hernando dies in Pasto (Columbia).

1566:   A missionary from the Americas, the Franciscan Alonso Maldonado, preaches to the nuns in St. Joseph on the state of the American Indians (F 1.7).

1569:   Padre García de Toledo, O.P., Teresa's friend and counselor, for whom she wrote *The Book of her Life*, now the religious assistant to the viceroy Francisco de Toledo,. departs for Perú.

1575:   Lorenzo and two brothers undertake a voyage back to Spain. One of the brothers, Jerónimo, died in Panama, then called "Nombre de Dios."

1576:   Lorenzo with his three children and brother Pedro arrive back in Spain.

1580:   Lorenzo's son Lorenzo sets sail for Perú. His oldest son, Francisco, will also return to the Americas in 1591.

1581:   Padre García de Toledo returns from the Americas. Teresa learns of this in January of this year (Ltr. 366.8).. She comments in a letter to Lorenzo (the son) in Quito: "the viceroy has already arrived, and Padre García is well, although I have not seen him. It is a hard thing to undertake so dangerous a journey at such an advanced age for the sake of a fortune," [she is alluding to the voyage that her brother Agustín de Ahumada is planning] "when we shouldn't be attending to anything else than preparing for heaven" (Ltr. 427. 10).

2. Regarding Teresa's attitude toward the Americas, the topic often repeated is that of money that arrives from there and the new kinds of little things that came from across the ocean, such as potatoes, resin, a medicinal gum, the coconut, and so on. All of that was just a diversion. In reality Teresa lived the problem of America at a deeper level, and she underwent a radical evolution in this regard. We do not know what her first impressions were. Perhaps they arose in her childhood years. It seems impossible that in the Avilan environment and in Don Alonso's house there was no echo of the lavish reception given in Toledo around 1527 and 1528 to the famous *conquistadores* Hernán Cortês and Pizarro, who came from the two great empires, Mexico and Perú. Teresa at that time was 12 or 13 years old and in the immediate campaign the two Hernandos, her cousin and her older brother, enlisted, Neither do we know the kind of reactions that were hers as she said good-bye to each brother – some very close to her – who set sail for the Americas.

3. Probably the first serious information, although slanted, was given to her at the end of 1561 by Antonio Morán and his companions Varrrona and Alonso Rodríguez carriers of the gold pesos sent by Lorenzo. Morán was an old soldier, full of American adventures and landscapes. He brought with him one of his brothers, who had gone insane, to entrust him to his elderly mother. Teresa had received Morán in the speak room of the monastery of the Incarnation a couple of days before her departure for Toledo to the palace of Doña Luisa de la Cerda. Certainly, she took advantage in depth of the knowledge and loquacity of good old Morán, from which she was left with an excellent impression, but she tells us little or nothing of the American news about his task as *conquistador* and her own brothers, *conquistadores*. At this time it is probable that she considered them little less than "defenders of the faith," as she will say of Rodrigo, who died a martyr in Araucania. Among Teresa's informers about America is one of her closest friends, the Dominican, Padre García de Toledo, who

had passed his young years in Mexico and then in 1569 he said goodby
to her and set sail again as a religious assessor for the new viceroy
of Perú, his cousin Francisco de Toledo. Given the total confidence
that existed between her and the one for whom she wrote her *Life*, it
would be unlikely that he did not speak to her more than once about
the American venture.

4. Despite all this, the event and the decisive information came
about when in 1565 there passed through the Carmel of St. Joseph
the fiery and talkative Franciscan missionary Alonso Maldonado. A
disciple and follower of Padre Las Casas, Maldonado was en route to
the Court in Madrid to speak for the cause of the American Indians.
He was really opposed to the undertaking of the conquistadores, and
in favor of the missionaries. In listening to him Teresa was profoundly
moved and she could not help but withdraw to a hermitage alone in
the garden and plead to God "for the many millions of souls being lost
there. " At once an immense horizon opened before her of a totally new
outline.There fell a shadow on the plan of the *conquista*, and the world
of souls was lit up for her (F ch. 1).

5. From this time her correspondence with her brothers residing
in America will be an insistent and unvaried cry: "that you return and
that we join here to attend to the business of the soul." In one of these
passages there springs from her pen one of the hardest expressions in
her whole correspondence: "I don't know what to say except that we
are worse than animals; we do not understand the great dignity of our
souls" (Ltr. 24.13). A little before, strangely involved in the problem
of the Indians, she had assured herself : "and I am very anxious about
those Indians"(Ltr. 24.13). It is at this time that Teresa discovered
the Americas, the immensity of its regions and above all the sense
of a double problem: the *"conquista"* and the missions. In any case,
America vastly expanded Teresa's existential space.

16. The Lawsuit For Nobility Of Don Alonso And His Brothers

1. The lawsuit for nobility transfers us from Teresa's home to the great family of the Sánchez-Cepeda. There are four brothers who are interested personally in the lawsuit: Pedro, Alonso (Teresa's father), Ruy, and Francisco. Yet in it the other brothers were implicated, also Teresa's grandfather Juan Sánchez de Cepeda, now dead, and her great-grandfather Alonso Sánchez. The lawsuit began in 1519, when Teresa was four years old, and concluded in 1523, when she was eight. Don Alonso was thirty-nine at the start and forty-three at the end. The lawsuit was brought up with a fiction of rights infringed on by the commoners of Ortigosa and Majalbálago (Avilan towns) and was formalized before the Royal Chancery of Valladolid. At one moment the tribunal was transferred to Avila to hear the witnesses, right near Don Alonso's family home. A similar investigation was made in Toledo. From all of this, what interests us mainly is the possible impact this turbulent family episode had on the person of Teresa.

2. If we consider the reason for the lawsuit, it wasn't brought against the brothers Sánchez-Cepeda, but on the contrary was initiated by them. They had a double motive: above all to obtain a patent letter of nobility to erase or cover over the presumed stain of judeo-converso origin of the four and settle the question of their pure blood; and secondly, a motive more vulgar, to be exempt on their being declared noble,. from paying taxes and tributes.

3. The proceedings of the lawsuit quickly became complicated and the verdict returned was against the four: first the prosecutor discovered that the witnesses were bought; and then he discovered the allegation of the Jewish origin of the Cepedas, upon learning about the episode in Toledo (1485) when the father, Don Juan, with some of

his sons, had to be reconciled and wear the corresponding penitential garb *(sambenito)* in the parish of Santa Leocadia, for having judaized. Repeated to the point of satiety, this second denunciation turned against the four brothers in an especially disturbing form when the tribunal had to institute proceedings in Avila, in the most compromising social environment. Perhaps it was at this moment that the family's greatest secret about the lawsuit on their origins got to the watchful eyes of Teresa, a child of about seven or eight years old..

4. The tribunal's verdicts. The judges dictated a sentence with two successive verdicts. First in favor of the nobility of the four brothers (1520); this was appealed on the part of their adversaries and after a new revision, was modified by the tribunal (1522) with the addition that the nobility of the four was reduced to and recognized Aonly@ in the city of Avila and the towns of Ortigosa and Majálbalago. In the proceedings it reads: "the said Alonso Sánchez de Cepeda and his four brothers will keep possession of their nobility . . . only in the city of Avila and in the council of Majalbálago and Ortigosa."

5. Appealed and then ratified, this sentence in reality undermined the pretensions of the four brothers, since obviously they as well as their children needed the title to cover a social space much more extended. It happened that already in the following decade, the city of Avila refused to admit certain rights implied by the title, and on their part the four brothers (or at least some of them) proceeded expeditiously to falsifying the patent letter that emanated from the process. Where the document was limited with the word Aonly,@ that word was erased and substituted for it was the contrary term Aespecially.@ Some other retouches were introduced so that the copies of the patent letter that have reached us have alternatively one or other version: some tampered with, others correct. Obviously, the first were used more often.

6. It is interesting to ask ourselves what impact this family and

social episode had on Teresa, not only on her personal and family life, but also on her social life, on her spirituality or on her writings. Here it is only possible to respond in an outline:

a) It seems unquestionable that she knew about the episode involving the lawsuit, if not in its conceptual scheme, at least in its repercussions on the family;

b) But she never alludes to it in her writings. Nor is there a trace of any reference to the same in her biographical documentation. Nor is there any allusion to the episode of her family Jewish origins. In her writings there appears at various times the word Jew/Jews, always with a negative religious connotation.

c) It has been said that Teresa's harsh criticism of the Acult of honor@ or the show of lineage indicate her reaction to the problem of Apurity of blood@ (*limpieza de sangre*) or of the marginalization of the new converts. Likewise it has been insisted that Teresa's style (her humble speech) corresponds to a secret intention of hiding her Jewish origin. All these suppositions lack documental consistency.

d) Teresa on the contrary never presumes nobility or pure blood. On the other hand, she never manifests herself adverse to titles of nobility in other persons, although for spiritual reasons she despises and discredits them.

e) In Teresa's family life, there is a misunderstood episode. It happened in 1561, when she was sailing along in her high mystical life. It was her sending of the patent latter of nobility to her brother Lorenzo from Avila to Quito. She refers to it in Letter 2.13: "I mentioned that when Antonio Morán leaves I will send along for you a copy of the patent letters of nobility, which they say couldn't be better. I'll take great care in doing this. And if this time it gets lost on the way, I'll keep sending others until one arrives. For some foolish reasons it was not sent (it was the responsibility of a third party who did not want to B I'll say no more"*)*. That is to say, Lorenzo B then mayor in Quito B had requested the patent letter. Teresa did not possess this document among her papers. She had to solicit a copy of it from some one who refused her. She then got one in another way and is sending it to Lorenzo, at the same time disposed to try again if this one gets lost. The copy, according to her, couldn't be better. By necessity, this copy was of the one with the change to Aespecially@ instead of Aonly@ because only in this way would it be useful to Lorenzo. Did Teresa know about this falsification? We do not know. Only *a posteriori* does it result that a falsification like this doesn't fit, at least at this time, into the psychological context of Teresa.

f) In Teresa's biography there is another interesting fact, although late: informed that Padre Gracián was investigating the noble background of the Cepedas, Teresa reacted before what she believed to be a Aspiritual@ injustice., and she says so . . . did she fear that Gracián would uncover the Astain@ of being Anewly converted@ that weighed heavily on her lineage? From Teresa's words the contrary is what is actually deduced.

7. Attempting a balanced conclusion, Teresa as much in her social life as in her spiritual life B so carefully analyzed and described in its autobiographical notes B has no reference to any possible pressures on her because of her not being noble or of pure blood, despite the fact that in the social environment of the moment the harassment of the newly converted was on the increase. Teresa lived her social life with a free and ample breathing space, in intense and constant relations with the nobility. Freedom even more accentuated in the process of her spiritual life and in her activity as founder.

17. Lawsuit Within The Family Or The Disintegration Of The Home

1. The lawsuit within Don Alonso's family was not during Teresa's life a precise or marginal episode, but a prolonged process in the collapse of the family home. She had to attend to this from nearby while the events were destroying her sense of family. This lawsuit was begun in 1544 and was protracted at least until 1548. These were central years in Teresa's life. She had recently lived through a three-year period of suffering in the convent infirmary (1539-1542). She had undergone the death of Don Alonso at the end of 1543. In this same decade of the 40s., Teresa had to fight agonizingly against herself "struggling with a shadow of death" – she says – "but I had no one to give me life,"to redefine the meaning of her religious life and of her relations with God.

2. Well then, it was in this long journey when she had to be present at the mutual confrontation between her siblings over the sale and squandering of the paternal house and the storm that blew her three younger brothers still living in Avila toward the Americas. Here we recall only the scene of the family home, the chain of procedural events, and the devastating consequences of the lawsuit.

3. The family scene in this period was marked by the death of Don Alonso, at Christmas time in 1543. It left a great void in the home. Aside from the four sons living in the Americas (Hernando, Rodrigo, Lorenzo, and Jerónimo), there remained in the Avilan region two disparate groups: the daughter of the first marriage, María de Cepeda with her husband Martín de Guzmán y Barrientos and on the other side the younger sons (Antonio, Pedro, and Agustín) and the little Juana de Ahumada, who found shelter with Teresa at the Incarnation. Teresa was the possible connecting tie between the two rival groups.

In Don Alonso's will, Teresa remained as the executive along with her brother-in-law Guzmán y Barrientos, and with the uncle Lorenzo de Cepeda."Official" executive, but she does not appear in court even once in the painful acts of the lawsuit that was embarked upon among the two groups as soon as the paternal will was opened, because Doña Beatriz's four children, probably manipulated by the executor of the inheritance," repudiated the will" which favored ostentatiously the oldest daughter of Don Alonso, Doña María. With that, the scene remained in complete imbalance: the lesser in age against the two older who were much more powerful and shrewd. Guzmán y Barrientos had hurried on his own to make an inventory of the goods of Don Alonso and to auction off a part of the large, old family home "de la Moneda." It was normal for the four sons who were in the Americas to keep abreast of the lawsuit, but they did not intervene in it.

4. The events of the process followed their inexorable pace slowly and painfully. Hardly was Don Alonso dead when they proceeded to the opening of the will on 26 December 1543, and 2 February 1544, Guzmán y Barrientos formalized their denunciation of the "executor " of the deceased's goods, a certain Rengilfo, and against the four younger children. In the Avilan tribunal the witnesses from alternating sides confronted each other: they reviewed forty years of family life; the dowries and the jewels of Doña Catalina; the undertakings, expenses, the uses and abuses of Don Alonso; the death of Juan de Cepeda in Italy, the landed properties of Doña Beatriz in Gotarrednura, in San Martín de las Cabezas, in Nava de Arévalo and in Becerril; the festive days of the two weddings of almost a half century ago, and the gloomy days of the funerals of both wives, the mothers of the Cepedas-Ahumadas; the inventory, more or less slanted of the remaining family capital; the pending relatives and so on. A whole symphony of details in regard to the family history, which became sorrowful at only their remembrance. And between data and data the

ruinous decline of the two family estates of Avila and Gotarrendura.

5. Finally, after four years of litigation on 2 October1548, the judgment was given, in every respect favorable to Doña María, who had to surrender in the brief period of nine days, "half of the principal houses that the said Alonso Sánchez de Cepeda left in this city district of Santo Domingo that it seems were gained and acquired during the marriage of the said Alonso . . . and Doña Catalina del Peso . . ." But another huge amount of money (183,931 maravedis . . . and 110,000 maravedis more) . . . and so on . . . Against this judgment, "the adverse part" (the executor Rengilfo) appealed right away. And with the impossibility of their maintaining this appeal, on 15 January 1549 at the petition of the same Doña María de Cepeda it was declared void. In the meantime, the three brothers, Antonio, Agustín and Pedro, had abandoned the home and their land of birth and set sail for the Americas. The youngest of them all, Juana, continued living with Teresa in the Incarnation. After a period of five years (1553), she married Juan de Ovalle, and he intended to revive the lawsuit after the death of his brother-in-law Martín de Guzmán y Barrientos in 1557. It is good that Teresa managed to stop this new outbreak of family tensions.

6. The consequence the ill-fated lawsuit had was to demolish Teresa's old family home. They alienated and lost the family houses "de la Moneda," although they did save for the moment those of Gotarrendura. But the family, unity was split apart and almost pulverized. Years later, at the end of 1561, Teresa will engage in repairing this split. At Christmas time of this year, the most fortunate of her brothers in the Americas, Lorenzo de Cepeda, sent for the three brothers residing in Avila and the bordering areas a sum of gold pesos. It was a good remedy for stanching the family wounds. Teresa served as intermediary in the sharing of the gold. And at the same time she wrote in gratitude to Lorenzo for what he did: a settlement for the past and a preventive in face of the future. It is sufficient to reproduce here a frac-

tion of this long letter by Teresa written in the Incarnation on the eve of her departure for the palace of Doña Luisa de la Cerda in Toledo:

"Certainly all those to whom you sent money received it at such an opportune moment that I was greatly consoled . . .

Yesterday my sister María sent me the enclosed letter. When they bring her the other money, she will write again. The help came just in time for her. She is a very good Christian and undergoes many trials. If Juan de Ovalle initiates a lawsuit, it would destroy her children. Certainly he doesn't have as much claim as he thinks he does, even though the sale of everything went badly and proved a disaster. But Martín de Guzmán also had good intentions – God rest his soul – and the judge ruled in his favor, even though not well enough. I cannot bear that anyone should now claim what my father – may he enjoy eternal glory – sold. And the rest, as I say, would only kill María, my sister. God deliver me from the self-interest that brings so much harm to one's relatives . . .

I'm not surprised by Juan de Ovalle; rather, he has done well by setting this litigation aside for now out of love for me. He is by nature good, but in this case it would be unwise to trust in that. When you send the 1,000 pesos, you should ask him for a written promise to be given to me; and the day that he reintroduces the lawsuit, 500 ducats will go to Doña María" (Ltr 2, nos.1 & 7).

A selection of documents from the lawsuit may be seen in the *Espicilegio Historial: BNM, ms 8713*.

18. The Family Decline

1. The family decline of the Cepeda-Ahumada coincides with the days of personal decline in Teresa's story, the last six years of her life: 1576-1582. For the moment the group seems to blossom again at the fraternal level despite the paternal absence and the material loss of the large family house, which had been litigated over and sold at a cheap price, not without a certain sense of loss for Teresa. Throughout these six years there alternated moments of great rejoicing with high longings and unfortunate frustrations.

2. In the year 1576 the remains of the home in Spain were reduced to the two sisters, Teresa and Juana: close in affection, but different in all the rest. Teresa was a nun. Juana was the mother of a family. Juana lived in Alba (Salamanca), Teresa was living in Seville, struggling to found a new Carmel. Her brothers continued living in America, all but the two most loved by Teresa, Rodrigo, who died in the Pampas of Argentina, and Antonio who died at age 26 in the battle of Iñaquito (1546). The widower in Quito, another favorite of Teresa's, Lorenzo de Cepeda, had announced his imminent return to Spain. Teresa quickly found out about it when he and different family members landed in Sanlucar not far from Seville (F. 25.3). She received them happily in the improvised and very poor Carmel of Seville. There were five among the recently returned: Lorenzo with his three children (Francisco, Lorencico, and Teresita) and her brother Pedro de Cepeda, who was also a widower, sad, without children, and without money.

3. The joy of the encounter was marred by a shadow of sadness: on the return trip another brother, Jerónimo, lost his life, and a fourth child of Lorenzo, named Esteban, also died. Despite this, an overwhelming sense of fraternity and joy was felt by all. The family

Ovalle-Ahumada came from Alba to Seville: "Lorenzo is delighted with his sister and with Juan de Ovalle" (Ltr. 98,.5). The charming Teresita is enamored of her aunt the Mother Founder, and she finds shelter at her side in the monastery. Teresa becomes the accomplice. She has to consult whether a child 10 years old can be tolerated living in the monastery after the canons of Trent. The child's father, Don Lorenzo, places at the disposition of Teresa the *pesos* brought from America to speed up the foundation in Seville, even at the risk of falling into the hands of the law: "he helped us a great deal," Teresa sums it up (F. 25.3).

4. Having concluded the Spanish foundation, Lorenzo joined the group of founders on their return from Andalucia to Castile. He settles in Avila, but without any intention of recuperating the family houses from "de la Moneda." Yet in return, he intensifies to the maximum his intimacy with Teresa who for her part relives the moments of family euphoria as if she adopted her brother. There took place an intense correspondence between the two. They exchanged gifts and musical couplets, as well as accounts of spiritual experiences. Teresa reactivates her old family longing: "that we all be together here, to help one another so as to be together forever" (Ltr. 24.13, 16). In fact up to the last year of her life she insisted on the return of all her absent brothers to Spain.

5. Yet very soon this attempt to recuperate the fraternal home met with a bundle of shadows and frustrations that for Teresa turned into a fountain of bitterness and that will go on refining her until the eve of her death. First there arose the incompatibility between two brothers, Lorenzo and Pedro: Lorenzo's patience was exhausted; and Pedro was as mad as a hatter. Pedro, a vagabond and dying of hunger, sought refuge in Teresa, while passing through Toledo on his way to Seville. She acts as a mediator between the two: "And so I beg you for the love of our Lord, do me the favor of not bringing him back into your house

no matter how much he begs and how great his need . . . in this matter of wanting to stay with you, he is crazy" *(*Ltr 337.1); that Lorenzo seek to help him economically. Then after Lorenzo's death (June 26, 1580), Lorenzo's oldest son Francisco decided to become a discalced Carmelite. He went to Pastrana and was rejected without compromise by the prior Nicolás Doria. Teresa acknowledged the receipt of a blow, but she was powerless and did not intervene. And Francisco reacts by breaking with her and getting married against advice and distancing himself more and more."The story of Francisco," writes Teresa, "has astonished us all It would seem they undid him so as to remake him into a different person" (Ltr 359.2).

6. The pirouette by another nephew, Lorencico is not any better. He had to return to America to take charge of the estate left by his father, but before this he had left a natural daughter in Avila: *"for considering how you started out so early to go astray* Teresa wrote. The mother gave the child into the arms of Teresa. And she was moved to pity: "even though what you did was very distressing to me because of its being an offense against God, when I see how much this little girl resembles you I can't help but welcome and love he*r. . . "* And she asks for economic help for the little girl: "you could send a sum of money here from time to time . . .for her support" (Ltr. 427..4-5).

7. In the meantime Teresita continues as a Carmelite beside the Mother Foundress. But now she suffers the constant siege by her brother Francisco's mother-in-law who at all costs wants to get her out of the monastery so that she can renounce the paternal inheritance in favor of Francisco. Teresita suffers, secretly, the affective pull of her brother and a certain detachment of affectivity with respect to Teresa. With no end of aggravating problems and vicissitudes: even the Carmelite nuns wavered and took the side of the terrible mother-in-law and against Teresa. Teresa brought Teresita with her to the foundation in Burgos and Teresita accompanied her on her last journey (Burgos/

Alba/Avila) so as to place her there safely and allow her profession. (Teresita was only 16 years old.)

8. With this dose of bitterness in her soul Teresa made her last journey. The death of Lorenzo had produced a strong sensation of sadness and solitude "It has made me, more than anyone else, feel very sad" (Ltr 363.4)."The family unity recovered" had unraveled and been converted into a melting pot of fraternal love.

9. There remained standing Teresa's absolute fidelity to the memory of her brother. And at all costs she wanted to carry forward his will that had stipulated his wanting to be buried in St. Joseph's in Avila, so as to lie next to his sister Teresa's future (?) sepulcher. For a second time there occurred a family split. Teresa had lavished all her affection, yet this story of loves had ended twice in a being a story of frustrations.

19. The Cultural Level Of The Cepeda-Ahumada Family

1. Let us remember that in the Spain of the golden age the intellectual culture was normally reserved to a tiny minority. In that time the mass of illiterate people reached a very high percentage. And this percentage was worse in the feminine sector. Hence we have the normal question in the case of Teresa and her family. Up to what point did the family environment favor or serve as a prelude to Teresa's future mission as a writer.

2. The first bit of information in this respect Teresa offers us herself at the very beginning of her autobiography: "My father was fond of reading good books, and thus he also had books in Spanish for his children to read" (*Life* 1.1)."This is a witness not only to the cultural eagerness on the part of her father, but also to how he involved his children in it. And likewise her mother Doña Beatriz was involved as Teresa testifies in the following chapter" (*Life* 2.1). In this way, very probably, the family cultural level was a singular case – exceptional? – in that Castilian society. As we shall see in what follows, there were no illiterates in the family group Cepeda-Ahumada.

3. The first exponent of this family level, without doubt, is the head of the family Don Alonso. A merchant by profession, he passed his childhood and youth in Toledo and worked at collecting taxes and other dues, which certainly demanded an amount of juridical economic information. Yet we do not know the kind of formation he underwent. Still young when he married his first wife (1507), he redacted in his own hand, two copies of the inventory of his possessions, each one in twelve pages, the first copy of which has come down to us. In this he leaves evidence of having possessed among other things a dozen bibliographical titles of quality. To scholars today there remains the doubt

as to whether these books belonged to the merchandise he had for sale, or to his private family library. It seems more likely that the latter was the case. In this list, the following titles appear in order.

1. A Portrait of the Life of Christ by Juan de Padilla
2. *De Officiis* by Cicero
3. A Treatise on the Mass, anonymous
4. *The Seven Hundreds* by Fernán Pérez de Guzmán
5. *The Seven Mortal Sins* by Juan de Mena
6. *The Conquest Beyond the Sea*, a novel of chivalry
7. *The Consolation* by Boetius
8. *The Blessed Life* and *The Proverbs* by Séneca
9. *The Poems* of Virgil
10. *The Three Hundreds* by Juan de Mena
11. *The Coronation* by the same Juan de Mena
12. A *Lunario*, a kind of calendar used in households.

4. In sum: four or five Latin classics (in the vernacular), numerous Castilian poems; various Spanish spiritual writers; and one novel of a historical nature. In another inventory made at the death of Don Alonso there figured the book of the Gospels. And from Teresa herself we know (*L* 7. 10) that toward the end of his life she facilitated his reading of books on prayer. We don't know which ones "I loved my father so much, I desired for him the good I felt I got out of the practice of prayer . . . I gave him books for this purpose . . . within five or six years he was so advanced . . . that this gave me the greatest consolation." (Even in the case of the preceding list of books not corresponding to his own house library but to his merchandise, it will still indicate his literary preferences in that social context.)

5. This cultural panorama of the father of the family can be expanded with a simple look at the surroundings. We know that at

least two of Don Alonso's brothers were devoted to reading: the talkative priest Hernando de Santa Catalina and the spiritual Don Pedro who coached Teresa in the reading of Osuna (and who already before, in the lawsuit of nobility, appears using another popular book, *The Mirror of Conscience*). Among Teresa's brothers and sisters, we already noted that none of them were illiterate. Two of those who corresponded with her most assiduously are the youngest .Doña Juana, and her favorite brother Don Lorenzo. The numerous letters that have come down to us including the many that Teresa wrote to them, almost always in response to their letters, reveal a fluid dialogue between the three. Lorenzo, also, cultivated the cultural introduction of his three children. Two of them were sent early – at Teresa's suggestion – to the Jesuit college of San Gil (Avila). Teresita , the third of the three, will become a good secretary.

6. Yet perhaps the most indicative fact was the meeting of Lorenzo with Fray John of the Cross and with other theologians. When Don Alvaro de Mendoza challenged them to comment (and discuss) the famous Teresian motto: *"Seek yourself in me."* Each of the participants were limited to respond with a simple memorandum that then will become the object of the challenge. Lorenzo, for his part, answered with a poem, the stanzas of which were anything but common. Perhaps because Teresa had previously commented for him on her own poem: *Oh Beauty exceeding/ all other beauties!"* (Ltr 172 & 177).

7. In fact Lorenzo's poem (which begins "To give more heat to a dry response") merited the praise of M. Menéndez Pelayo, who considered him "the most ancient of the Spaniards we know that who passing through the kingdom of Quito composed some verses. . ." The distinguished writer judged the verses to be the equals of those Teresa composed on the same theme. And he recalls at the same time that he had composed "An account of the life and virtues of his wife" (*Obras Completas, t. 38,* Santander 1948, p. 8-10). In the above mentioned

response Lorenzo moreover made use of Latin, quoting from St. Paul.

8. Probably in the family home of the Cepeda-Ahumada, the mother, Doña Beatriz, carried out a special pedagogical function. Teresa as an adolescent owes to her mother her love for books of fantasy – the novels of chivalry – that doubtless stimulated her future literary inspiration. Recalling these days of Doña Beatriz, Teresa writes about herself the famous affirmation: "I didn't think I could be happy if I didn't have a new book" (L 2.1).

20. The Spiritual Life In The Family

1. We understand here by spiritual life the cultivation or promotion of the values of the spirit within the Christian context professed by Teresa's family and by Teresa herself. Did she who exercised so assiduously and intensely her mission as "Mother of Spiritual Seekers" as much in her lay surroundings as within Carmel, care or not for this aspect in the life of her family? This is the question which we now raise.

2. Let us remember that the history of Teresa's family unfolds at two different times. The first is the time of merchants under the paternal command: not only was Don Alonso a merchant by profession but the family houses of "La Moneda" served as a warehouse for the merchandise. Whereas the second period, marked by the sons, was dominated by the ideal of *conquistador*, shared by all of Teresa's brothers. Put simply, neither the profession of merchant nor the undertaking of the *conquistador* was the most favorable environment for feeding the project of the Christian spiritual life.

3. Nevertheless, the picture sketched by Teresa in tracing the family likeness in the opening pages of *The Book of Her Life* is clearly positive, well characterized, impregnated by a sound Christian humanism. The profile of Don Alonso is of an upright man, a friend of virtue, without excesses, socially well oriented, fond of reading, interested in the Eucharist (judging from one of his books, a *Treatise on the Mass*)."A man very charitable with the poor and compassionate toward the sick, and even toward servants." He was very honest. The feminine profile of his wife Doña *Beatriz* is very similar to his: long-suffering, retiring, "very peaceful and of a great intellect," inclined to cultivate Marian piety in her children and other Christian virtues. Teresa recalls repeatedly the interest in the poor."I gave what

alms I could." The family was a morally healthy group. In the light of Teresa's view we get a glimpse of a good humanist, Christian family. And this imprint is extended equally to the children and servants. Perhaps the most notable thing is the affective climate of the group: "the one I liked most." There are no perceptible breaks between the children of Don Alonso's first marriage and the second.

4. This was the human and Christian environment that one encountered in Teresa's family home when she was a child and adolescent. But what interests us more is what she promoted when she became a Carmelite nun and the distance that arose and the new environment favorable for the specifically spiritual. Let us turn our attention from the numerous episodes referred to by Teresa herself. Let us rather distinguish .two of her most defined and prolonged contributions. First as a simple nun she was interested in her father's spiritual life. And secondly as mystic she was interested in the spiritual life of her brothers and sisters.

5. The first coaching Teresa exercised when she herself was at a low spiritual level: they are the years when she was in the infirmary, followed by a period of uncertainty and struggle, 1539-1543. Don Alonso out of pure paternal love went down assiduously to the infirmary or the speak-room of the Incarnation to converse with Teresa. And she oriented the conversation to her spiritual concern, prayer, convinced that through it comes every spiritual good. She directs her father toward meditation and recollection: "since I loved my father so much, I desired for him the good I felt I got out of the practice of prayer. It seemed to me that in this life there could be no greater good than the practice of prayer. So in roundabout ways, as much as I could, I began to strive to get him to practice prayer. I gave him books for this purpose. Since he had such virtue, as I mentioned, he settled into this practice so well that within five or six years – it seems it was – he was so advanced . . . " (*L* 7.10). They were the five or six final years of Don

Alonso's life. Teresa had made of him an authentic spiritual person . As such he lived his last illness assisted by her. (In the house of Don Alonso there continued living three sons and the little Juana, yet only he and Teresa were involved in the end)."I cannot help but praise the Lord when I remember the death he died and his joy in dying . . . He looked like an angel. That it seems to me he was . . ." (L 7. 16).

6. Much more intense and interesting is the other chapter of Teresa's spiritual teaching office. She practiced it in the full phase of her mystical life (1576-1580), in profound empathy with her brother Lorenzo. It is impossible to enter here into all the details of this second picture. Lorenzo returned from America at age 56, a widower, with three children .with the difficult project of carving out in Spain a social position on the basis of a good economic backing. Yet from the first encounter he is fascinated by the personality of his sister (61 years old). Teresa made him change his plan of a project in life. From preoccupation with the household, his interest turns toward the spiritual life. Lorenzo becomes quickly and profoundly in tune with her, for at this period he sets out on the high sea of mystical experiences. And Teresa quickly involves Lorenzo on her own wavelength. She proposes to him the asceticism of mortification ("which is a great help in awakening love " Ltr. 177.13). She coaches him in meditation, until the first shoots of the prayer of quiet. In the dialogue with him, Teresa herself relives her former ecstatic exaltation: "You ought to know, she writes, that for more than eight days I have been in such a state that were it to last I would not be able to attend to so many business matters. From the time I last wrote you, I've begun to have raptures again . . . and in public . . .Trying to resist them doesn't help and, nor can they be disguised . . ." (Ltr. 177.3). Lorenzo also begins to have mystical experiences. He contacts St. John of the Cross who "understands him, for he has experience" (Ltr. 177.2). He makes a special promise of obedience to his sister. He gives her an account of his prayer, his

temptations, his life as a solitary in La Serna (Avila). He fell into the illusion of freeing himself from everything earthly and giving himself only to God like a monk. And Teresa had to remind him that no, that he is obliged to take care of his children's estate, that he has to keep his feet on the ground *"Jacob did not become less a saint for tending his flock, nor Abraham, nor St. Joachim"* (Ltr. 172 11). The two, Lorenzo and Teresa, have a taste for the verses of the poem "Oh Beauty exceeding/ All other beauties." Teresa transcribed for him and commented on them slowly (Ltrs. 172 & 177). When Lorenzo died at age 60 (1580) Teresa lived through a period of sadness similar to the one experienced at the death of her father (Ltr. 363.4). And how in this, she relived the sensation that Lorenzo ended his life "like a saint . . . he was in the end in such a way that he wanted nothing to do with anything earthly . . . If I were able to write some of the details about his soul . . ".(Ltr 363. 3).

7. Teresa was concerned likewise about the Christian life of her other brothers and sisters, residing in Spain or America. So for example, María (*Life* 34. 19), or Juana (in her letters to her). Of those residing in America, she took special interest in Jerónimo, and above all for the Benjamin of the family, Agustín de Ahumada, to whom she refers in one of her intimate testimonies: "I was in the hermitage . . . praying to God, I said . . . 'Why is my brother in a place where his salvation is in danger? Were I Lord to see your brother in danger what wouldn't I do to help him?' " (ST 16). For him she experienced great worries and hopes from the beginning ("I am very concerned about Agustín de Ahumada since I do not know how he is faring in his relationship with our Lord" (Ltr.24.19), up to the end of her life.)

III
Carmel, Teresa's New Home

When she was twenty years old, Teresa left her paternal home and entered Carmel. She will live in it for the rest of her life, forty-seven years. Carmel counted by this time several centuries of history. We will now present a brief summary so as to approach Teresa's vocation and her first years in the Carmelite life at the Incarnation.

21. "The Ancestry From Which We Have Come" What Is Carmel?

1. The "ancestors from which we have come" are the ancient dwellers on Mount Carmel (in Israel). Teresa evokes their memory especially in the *Interior Castle* in the fifth dwelling places where she begins her exposition of the mystical life: "all of us who wear this holy habit of Carmel are called to prayer and contemplation. This call explains our origin; we are the descendants of men who felt this call, of those holy fathers on Mount Carmel who in such great solitude and contempt for the world sought this treasure, this precious pearl . . ." (IC 5.1.2).

2. The origins: Mount Carmel is a biblical place, a small mountain (1,742 ft high) that lies near the Mediterranean sea behind the city of Haifa and extends for some thirteen miles to the east in the direction of Nazareth. As a biblical site, it is especially tied to the prophet Elijah, a figure charged with symbolism and seen in Eastern monasticism as the archetype of the monastic life. Here is where the family (Order) of Carmel began. Its birth is attributed to an anonymous group of Western (Latin) pilgrims and ex-crusaders who at the end of the twelfth century gathered together in one of the valleys of the mountain range (el Wadi 'ain es-Siâh), near the fount of Elijah, where they founded a small community of hermits. There then followed two notable events. In the first decade of the next century (13 c): around 1208 the Patriarch of Jerusalem, Alberto Avogadro, wrote for the group a "rule of life," which was the Carmelite rule that Teresa professed in the sixteenth century and that continues till today as the corner stone of all Carmelite life. And at the same time the hermits built in the middle of this place a chapel dedicated to the Virgin Mary in whose service they consecrated their lives. From this second event came the name that the group soon adopted.

3. The expansion: A military torrent of Saracens expelled the hermits from their solitude before the first half of the century, and before its end (1291) forced them to abandon definitively the Wadi and Carmel. They had to emigrate to countries in the West. The change in place imposed on them in turn a change of life, and the hermits settled in the European cities after the manner of mendicant friars. They spread through Cyprus, Italy, England, and France . . .a certain delay took place before they reached Spain. They founded monasteries at first in the Northeast of Spain: Huesca, Lérida, Sangüesa, Valencia. . . . In Teresa's time the Spanish Carmel was made up of four Religious provinces: Cataluña, Aragón, Castile, and Andalucia, with more than forty monasteries and about five hundred religious. Teresa belonged to the province of Castile. During her almost half a century of Carmelite life there were in Rome two General Superiors of great prestige: the Frenchman Nicolás Audet (1523-1562) and the Italian Giovanni Baptista Rossi, Teresa referred to the Italian as "Padre Rubeo"(1564-1578). Succeeding him was also an Italian Giovanni Baptista Caffardo. Teresa was affected especially by the General Chapter of Piacenza (1575), which dealt with her work and, with the Spanish, Carmelite provincial superiors of Castile, Angel de Salazar, and of Andalusia, Diego de Cárdenas.

4. The feminine branch: the Carmelite nuns in Teresa's time were considered "the second order of Carmel." Founded in France the previous century (1452, with the bull *cum nulla fidelium* of Nicholas V) by the superior general, Blessed John Soreth, they spread through Spain throughout the fifteenth and sixteenth centuries. In Teresa's time there existed two monasteries founded in the fifteenth century (Ecija and Avila) and another nine founded in the sixteenth century (Fontiveros, Valencia, Granada, Seville, Antequera, Piedrahita, Aracena, Paterna del Campo, and Onteniente). Three of them were in the diocese of Avila (Fontiveros, Piedrahita, and Avila itself). The

monastery of the Incarnation in Avila had the highest number of nuns. In Teresa's time the biblical site of Mount Carmel continued to be abandoned, in the possession of the Muslims. Only in the following century (1631) was it recuperated heroically by one of the discalced friars, Padre Próspero.

5. Within the order there had arisen movements of reform. Another singular happening at the beginning of the sixteenth century was the edition of the *Speculum* Ordinis Fratrum Carmelitarum (Venecia 1507, 111 folios), which had gathered the best of the Carmelite spiritual patrimony, for example: The ten books of *The Institution of the First Monks, The historical Speculum , The Treatise on the Rule,* The chapter on the way to respond to anyone who asks how and when our Order began and why we are called the Brothers of the Blessed Virgin Mary of Mount Carmel. *The Viridarium*, by the General Giovanni Grossi. A whole arsenal of spiritual traditions and mottos that allowed one to become aware of Carmelite spirituality. The only trouble for Teresa: it was all written in Latin.

6. The Carmelite Ideal: Alluding to this Carmelite patrimony from the past, Teresa exclaimed toward the end of her life: "How many saints we have in heaven who have worn this habit!" (F. 29.33). That is to say, the point of reference was not the physical place of Mount Carmel, but the life and the spirit of those who lived there. The reference to this glorious gold mine of models formed the nucleus of the Carmelite ideal. With the passing of time, to the historical figures were added a whole list of legendary ones. In the breviary Teresa had for her personal use (Venecia 1568), as with the liturgy of the whole order of Carmel, the Eastern rite of the Holy Sepulchre was followed. This rite celebrated many biblical saints from the Old Testament, not only the prophets Elijah and Elisha, but others as well, such as, David and Abraham. There were as many in the Missal of that time (León 1559). At the end of the *Speculum Ordinis* that was mentioned the

readers were offered a list "De *Sanctis Ordinis Carmelitani*" (The Saints of the Carmelite Order), in which after Elijah and Elisha were included other biblical prophets, such as Jonah and Abdias.

This hagiographical Carmelite panorama formed a part of Teresa's mentality which she spread through her Carmels. A record of this remains in the *Libro de Recreaciones* (The Book of Recreations) by María de San José. The fourth recreation proposes to the Carmelites three squadrons of martyrs, virgins, and confessors, 66 in all (although there is no feminine figure). It added to the first squadron a number of saintly biblical prophets. Teresa herself alludes in her correspondence to the saints of Carmelite legend. But for her the highest examples of Carmelite sanctity are the Blessed Virgin Mary, "whose habit we wear and whose rule we profess," and the prophet Elijah whom she mentions as a type of the mystical life at the end of the seventh dwelling places: "also that hunger which our Father Elijah had for the honor of his God . . ." *(*IC. 7.4.11).

22. Vocation And Entry Into The Incarnation

1. As a young woman Teresa lived through the process of her vocation between the years eighteen and twenty. She had to overcome the normal crisis of adolescence when she was around fifteen. She treats of two periods in her *Life,* chapters 2-4. The two stages are important for understanding her entry into Carmel. Let us begin by recalling some of the chronological milestones:
- Teresa resided with her family until she was sixteen (1531)
- She lived for a year and a half at Our Lady of Grace (until the end of 1532).
- A short stay of convalescence in Ortigosa, Castellanos (1533)
- She returned to her paternal home (1534-1535)
- She entered the Incarnation on 11 November 1535.

2. There precedes a period of resistance ." I was strongly against my becoming a nun*."* She is alluding to the first eight days of resistance in the school of Our Lady of Grace. The motives for this repugnance are varied. Teresa in her adolescence had indulged to excess in the reading of novels that took her away from "the truth she knew in childhood." She sought the favor of her cousins, male and female. Some of them were clearly out of harmony with the family morality. Because of them she eased up in her relations with her father or cast a shadow over them. She herself surmised the possibility that the friendship with one of the cousins was in view of a marriage This was a situation that was aggravated by various family happenings: María, her older sister, got married and left home (1531). Don Alonso decided to place Teresa outside the family atmosphere and enroll her in Our Lady of Grace so that she would break away from the network of her friendships. In the meantime, the first of her brothers, Hernando, leaves for

America (1532). In the school she continued to be opposed to religious life, yet a process of personal clarification began "I began to seek that all commend me to God so that he might show me the state in which I was to serve him. But still I had no desire to be a nun, and I asked God not to give me this vocation; although I also feared marriage" (L 3.2). This went on until she fell sick and had to return home from the boarding school. She convalesced in Ortigosa and Castellanos, and then returned to Avila. For Teresa's future vocation this state of battle against the current is highly important.

3. A period of struggle follows ."By the end of this period of time [a year and a half] in which I stayed there [at the school] I was more favorable to the thought of being a nun" (L. 3.2). She had established a friendship with an excellent religious, Doña María de Briceño. It was she who altered the course of her preceding repugnance. On leaving the school she passed some time in the house of her uncle, Don Pedro, on her paternal father's side, a widower with the vocation of a monk. He got her to return to the reading of good books and "to the truth she knew in childhood." Various decisive episodes followed: a/ Teresa had become friends with a nun at the Incarnation, Juana Juárez; b/ she read enthusiastically *the Letters of St. Jerome* which spoke to her forcefully; c/ she lived dramatically the departure of her preferred brother Rodrigo who had decided to go to the Americas and, after ceding to Teresa the right of his own inheritance (his share of the maternal estate), he passed between Seville and Sanlucar a long month of waiting (August-September 1535) before setting sail. Yet without a doubt the *Letters* of St. Jerome had a decisive impact on Teresa, especially the section dedicated to the contemplative life (Book Three: "Treatise on the hermit state. . . On the contemplative life or contempt of the world, or state of the hermit"); and perhaps the letter to Heliodorus, which speaks of overcoming the affection for one's father." I was engaged in this battle for three months, forcing myself" (L. 3.6).

4. The decision . *"* For without my desiring it, His Majesty forced me to overcome my repugnance" (L 3.4). The three months of struggle culminated in the decision to inform her father, Don Alonso, who was directly opposed first because of the love he had for his daughter, and then because of the family situation. We do not know to what point Teresa at this time functioned as the housewife. The picture at home is this: the father is a widower and the oldest son dead in Italy, the oldest daughter, María, married and absent, two older brothers, Hernando and Rodrigo, on course for the Americas; there remain at home Antonio age fifteen, Pedro age fourteen, Agustín age nine, and Juana age seven. Yet given Teresa's spirit, her decision is irrevocable. Without haste: certainly after "the three months" more than a year of waiting followed. She continued her conversations with her friend at the Incarnation. In the family she shared her project with the oldest of her brothers, Antonio and convinced him to become a friar, "I persuaded one of my brothers to become a friar telling him about the vanity of the world (L. 4.1). Teresa possessed then a rare persuasive force. And the morning of All Souls day, in the year 1535, very early the two fled from their home, and Teresa knocked on the door of the monastery of the Incarnation. To force herself to go, it was necessary for her to make a heroic effort ."I remember clearly and truly, that when I left my father's house, I felt that separation so keenly that the feeling will not be greater, I think, when I die. For it seemed that every bone in my body was being sundered. . . . the Lord gave . . . such courage against myself that I carried out the task"(L. 4.1). That is to say, one is not dealing with only a decision: Teresa had to use force with herself, to force herself for the love of God, who is the one who helped her to force herself. Her vocational process was not idyllic, but a battle.

5. The motivation: Why she became a Carmelite. This is probably the side that is most lacking in information in the whole process. Teresa, fundamentally, decides to be a Carmelite because she has a

friend in the Incarnation.''It was the convent I liked very much" (L 4.1), even though, once she had decided for the religious life: "I was determined to go where I thought I could serve God more or where my father desired" (L 4.1)). In Avila there were a number of monasteries to choose from (the Conception, Santa Ana, Our Lady of Grace, St. Catherine of Siena, las Gordillas). In Teresa's soul there were other motives, including the fear of hell, the love of Christ, her realistic prevision of the trials of religious life, for (I myself*)* "having been so favored." Essentially, she opted for the religious life. Her vocation, especially Carmelite, had precarious psychological motivations ."Oh, God help me! What means His Majesty was employing to prepare me for the state in which he desired to make use of me! For without my desiring it, he forced me to overcome my repugnance" (L 3.4).

6. The vocational endorsement. The only source we have to evaluate this vocational process is the account Teresa gave us in her *Life*. She wrote it at a distance of thirty years. She had lived through it in 1535. She gave her account in 1565. She recalled it with realism yet without hesitation. She is convinced that she was right and confident that her struggle ended in victory. And that this was definitive. These are her affirmations: "As soon as I took the habit . . . Within an hour, he gave me such great happiness at being in the religious state of life that it never left me up to this day" (L. 4.2). And she repeats it confidentially to the nuns at St. Joseph's: "May you be blessed my God . . . for my vocation to be a nun was a very great favor!" (W 8.2).

Teresa got it right about the path of her life. She never retracted.

23. The Monastery Of St. Mary Of The Incarnation

1. The monastery of the Incarnation is Teresa's new home. Here she learns how to be a Carmelite nun. She resided here over twenty-seven years (1535-1562). Here is where she began to have mystical experiences. From here she undertook her long journey as founder. She wrote: "I was so perfectly content in the house in which I was because it was very much to my liking and the cell in which I lived was just what I wanted" (L 32. 10, 12). Here we will treat briefly only three aspects: the monastery's preceding history, what it was like at Teresa's entrance, and what happened to Teresa during the time she lived there.

2. The monastery had a recent history, less than a century. It had been founded inside the walls of the city, near the gate of San Vicente, by Doña Elvira González de Medina, as a simple beaterio in 1479. In 1485 Doña Beatriz Guiera moved it to the Calle del Lomo. The beaterio was converted to a monastery, and quickly became too small. And the same Doña Beatriz built another completely new one outside the walls, in the place where it is now. It was inaugurated on 4 April in the same year of Teresa's birth, 1515, but its construction proceeded slowly. It is a large building, facing from a short distance the city walls, with a spacious church, having an upper and lower choir, and endowed with a good organ. It has a large garden. Water for irrigation. Community service was scarce, and occasioned lawsuits with the city. Initially there were forty nuns living there, but the number soon increased to one hundred, and in Teresa's time there were from one hundred eighty to two hundred nuns living there. They lived in extreme poverty. They sustained themselves economically on the basis of rents from properties (in Grandes, Mancera, Duruelo, Goterrendura, Grajos, and so on), the administration of the nuns'

dowries, and through work. In the city the monastery had a secular patron. Juridically, it depended on the Carmelite provincial. In making their profession, the nuns promised obedience to the Father General of the Order and to the prioress of the house according to the rule. They were ruled in addition by statutes that occasionally came from the provincial and probably by a text of constitutions which today we do not know exactly, but it depended on one used in the French Carmels in that century and inspired by the constitutions of the Carmelite friars. In their profession, the religious did not promise expressly the cloister. But in the visitation made by Padre Rossi (Rubeo) (1567), they testify to practicing it, although in very ambiguous terms. In fact, they went out of the monastery frequently.

3. When Teresa entered it, the prioress was Doña Francesca del Aguila. Because of the excess number of nuns, she demanded of each candidate before profession a considerable dowry for her food. Within the monastery there resided as well a number of seculars, some as students, others as servants. Teresa herself will have her sister Juana with her from age fifteen to twenty-five. The community nucleus was made up of choir religious (black veils) and of lay sisters (white veils). Only the choir Sisters have a voice and a vote in the chapter assemblies. In the community there existed the distinction of titles: Doñas, coming from noble families, and those without a title, non-Doñas. There was also the distinction in rooms: personal cells and common dormitories. Teresa had her personal cell, partially visible even today. The principal prioress of the monastery in Teresa's time was the one at her entry and profession, Doña Francesca del Aguila; she was succeeded by Doña María Cimbrón (1539) who will also be prioress in 1562 when Teresa had to return from her recently founded Carmel of St. Joseph. In being elected herself as prioress of the community, Teresa gave relief to her predecessor Doña Ana de Toledo (1568-71). Doña Ana was elected again in 1578 when the election of Teresa as prioress of the monastery was annulled.

4. During the twenty-seven years of her stay in the Incarnation, Teresa lived through intense periods impossible to enumerate in detail. She entered the monastery on 2 November 1535. Before her reception of the habit, Don Alonso, her father, had to formulate in writing Teresa's dowry (31 October 1536), in a solemn community act and before a notary. In it he grants "For her food and sustenance twenty-five bushels of bread for rent, half wheat and half barley . . . from the place and region of Gottarendura. . . . and in default of the said bread, that she give two hundred gold ducats . . ., and more, a bed for the said Doña Teresa which has bed curtains of quality and a bedspread and a blanket and six linen sheets and six pillows and two mattresses and one carpet and two cushions, and one curtained bed. And to clothe the said Doña Teresa with the necessary clothing and habit for her entrance and profession in which there must be given for all the habits one of common cloth and another of fine cloth, and two skirts, one of grana and the other of serge, and a sheepskin, and her toques and tunics and footwear and books, as is given to other religious . . ." (BMC II, p. 94). All of this is interesting in approaching Teresa's personal dowry and the customs of the monastery.

5. The most powerful event was without doubt Teresa's illness as a recently professed nun: the three months of absence in Becedas, the four days in a paroxysm during August of 1539, the grave in the monastery was open for a day and a half awaiting arrival of the body, the three months of paralysis followed by three painful years of convalescence in the infirmary ."when I began to go about on hands and knees, I praised God" (L 6.1-3).

6. But much more important are the events that sketch her spiritual growth: the reading of St. Augustine and the sight of the image of the much wounded Christ turned Teresa's religious life around definitively. Here in the Incarnation the mystical graces took place that are described in *The Book of Her Life*. From the Christological

experiences, passing through the favor of the transpiercing of the soul, to the charismatic graces that impelled her to found the new Carmel.

7. During the three-year period 1571-74, in which Teresa was prioress in the Incarnation, she associated intimately with St. John of the Cross. Receiving Communion from his hands, she was enriched with the mystical grace that introduced her into the seventh dwelling place (ST 31). During these same three years she received special graces referring to this monastery. To mention only the most explicit, it was then that she enthroned the Blessed Virgin in the prioress's seat in the upper choir and while the community sang the *Salve Regina,* the image seemed to take on life and told her: "You were right in placing me here; I shall offer these praises to him"(ST 21). This promise was ratified in a new vision in which "the Lord granted me a favor and gave me hope that this house would continue to improve, I mean the souls in it would" (ST 27). And still in a kind of endearing interchange between Teresa and the Lord: she asks the Lord to protect one of her brothers whose salvation was in America, and the Lord diverted the dialogue to the nuns at the Incarnation: "Oh, daughter, daughter! These sisters in the Incarnation are My Sisters, and you delay?" (ST 16). It was the critical moment in which Teresa accepted the mission of being at the head of the Incarnation, her former monastery. In fact she always considered herself a daughter of that house.

24. Carmelite Apprenticeship At The Incarnation

1. What kind of formation did Teresa receive at the Incarnation? We possess little data with which to respond to this question. Almost the only informative source would be the legislation then current in the Spanish Carmelite monasteries. And more concretely in the Avilan monastery of the Incarnation (apart from the Rule of which we will treat later on). To approach this possible informative fount, we have to answer first of all to a double question: 1) Did they have *Constitutions* at the Carmelite monastery in Avila? And 2) Do we know this text or at least the main aspects of its content?

2. To the first question there are those who answer negatively, deducing the negation categorically from the historian of the monastery María Pinel (XVII c.), who was sure that the Incarnation did not have *Constitutions* until they came from Rome in 1585. Nevertheless, this negative opinion is unlikely. St. Teresa refers to them repeatedly, comparing them with those of St. Joseph's. She herself had read them (*L 35*.2) with great interest. More than once she designates them as the ancient *Constitutions* on the basis of which she specifies something of her new constitutions of St. Joseph's (Ap 2). She probably copied literally from them the chapters on the faults and penalties, which initially were not incorporated into the text for St. Joseph's.

3. Still, do we know the text that was in force at the Incarnation? Up to this time we do not know it. The so called *Constitutions of the Incarnation* published by Padre Silverio (BMC, IX. pp.. 481-523) were not in force in the monastery, since in them is prescribed with all rigor and detail the observance of the cloister, whereas this was not in force in the Avilan monastery. Nevertheless this text – derived from the French monasteries of Carmelite nuns founded by Blessed

Soreth – contains the practice in force in the Spanish monasteries, with the exception of the problematic theme of the cloister. Of this Spanish adaptation of the original French we possess two manuscripts: the most ancient with the discalced Carmelite nuns in Seville, at the end of the fifteenth century or the beginning of the sixteenth. This is the one published by Padre Silverio. The other, very much later is found with the Carmelite nuns in Osuna, presented by Padre Balbino Velasco in *Carmelus* 88 (1991, pp. 155-208). Certainly Teresa knew in the Incarnation one of these Spanish versions and later she had it present when she wrote the *Constitutions* for her own Carmels. These texts that have come down to us were in any case siblings of the ones used at the Incarnation and through them we can follow in general the guidelines for Teresa's formation.

4. The stages in Teresa's Carmelite initiation were three: a year of postulancy when she was 20 years old; at 21 another year of novitiate that ended with her profession when she was 22 years old; and still four more years under the mistress of novices, a four-year period that was interrupted with the serious sickness that caused Teresa to leave the monastery at the end of 1538. After this Teresa's formation continued year after year in the community life, which helped her definitively to become clearly aware of her Carmelite vocation.

5. The year as postulant was a year of gentle and partial insertion into the religious life. Teresa practiced voluntary obedience. She was under the teaching authority of the mistress, Doña María de Luna (former prioress of the monastery) who trained her in the religious practices, and at the same time evaluated her vocation. At the end of the year as a postulant, Teresa had to dispose of the things she owned as "it seemed to her," and in agreement with Don Alonso she renounced the inheritance that Rodrigo had left her and gave it to her youngest sister, Juana (*BMC* II, p. 95). A few days later (2 November 1536) the solemn reception of the habit took place. Before the entire community,

the prioress asked Teresa:

- What do you seek?
- The mercy of God and the habit of the glorious Virgin
- Can you observe the Rule and our way of life?
- With the help of God I believe so (credo quod si).

This is the moment in which she was "flooded with such great happiness . . . that it never left me" (L 4.2).

6. There followed a year of intense formation. First came the insertion into community life, refectory, choir, chapter, the work room. Then the difficult apprenticeship in the singing and the psalmody, with the puzzling rubrics (in Latin). The teaching authority of the mistress was based on a twofold motto: to instruct them in the things of the order and in the doctrine of the Church: daily Mass, weekly confession or at least fortnightly. For this "she must be instructed to confess purely and with discretion." The frequency of communions was prescribed minutely. At the same time they were to be instructed with regard to silence, prayer, work, their life together with the other Sisters, the correction of faults on the occasion of the weekly chapter, and a rigorous asceticism of fast and abstinence. After precisely a year of novitiate Teresa made her profession (2 November 1537) with every solemnity: She repeated three times the formula of profession and received the black veil. A big celebration followed.

7. From this moment on Teresa was incorporated fully into the rhythm of community life. Yet the four-year period that followed her profession was interrupted by a serious illness that lasted three years (1539-1542). The infirmary was ruled with special norms. The rule of silence was loosened. At the times for the recitation of the canonical hours, a small group of nuns gathered to recite the hours in the presence of the sick. During the three years Teresa cultivated with special care not only patience ("all were amazed by my patience") but also the spiritual life. The evaluation she gives of herself in her *Life* is impres-

sive: "In that short time I saw some new virtues arise in me (although they were not strong since they were insufficient to sustain me in righteousness): not speaking evil of anyone, no matter how slight, but ordinarily avoiding all fault-finding. I was very much aware that I should not desire to say of another person what I would not want them to say of me. I was extremely cautious about this in the occasions there were . . . There remained in me the desire for solitude and a fondness for conversing and speaking about God. . . . I received Communion and confessed much more often and desired to do so. I liked to read good books very much, and felt the deepest repentance after having offended God. I recall I did not dare pray, because I feared as I would a severe punishment the very bitter sorrow I would have to feel at having offended God. . . . I became extremely vexed about the many tears I was shedding over my faults . . . They seemed fraudulent tears to me . . . I endeavored to go to confession right away . . . all these signs of fear of God came to me during prayer, and the greatest sign was that they were enveloped in love . . . this carefulness of conscience with respect to mortal sins lasted all during my illness" (L 6.3-4).

It would be more exact to quote this whole passage from the *Life* so full of details and so revealing of what Teresa was living through in the infirmary as the conclusion of her initial formation.

25. Teresa's Carmelite Formation And Readings

1. Thanks to the years of Carmelite initiation in the Incarnation, Teresa became aware of being enrolled in a spiritual tradition with secular roots. If the Carmelite nuns existed for hardly a century and the order itself for at the most four centuries and a half, the oral tradition dared to go back more than two thousand years and be inspired by the prophets of the Old Testament. This is what was inculcated in the young novices in the chapter about how to respond to anyone asking how and when the order began (*Speculum Ordinis,* f. 57). And a twofold response was proposed to them: the order began "at the time of the prophets Elijah and Elisha on Mount Carmel," and the name "The Order of the Brothers of the Blessed Virgin Mary" was due to "their successors, who after the Incarnation of the Lord . . . constructed there an oratory in honor of the Most Blessed Virgin Mary and adopted this title" (*Speculum Ordinis,* f 57*).* Certainly Teresa did not read the Latin text of the *Speculum Ordinis,* yet its content was without doubt the habitual topic of both the sermons of the confessors and the instructions of the Carmelite chaplains and vicars which they presented to the community of the Incarnation. Through these facts more than by historical information they inculcated a spiritual motivation in depth. There is little that the sources say to us in this respect. As we have noted Teresa liked to read the Carmelite *Constitutions.* Besides these, the two Carmelite texts she read assiduously were the *Rule* and the Carmelite *Breviary.* The first as a norm of life; the second as living liturgy.

2. *The Rule of Carmel,* after the Bible, was the text most often quoted by Teresa. Redacted as we know in the first decade of the thirteenth century, it was then retouched and approved during the pontificate of Innocent IV (1247), and it is this text that is designated

by Teresa as the first Rule or primitive Rule (*L* 36.26), which she believed was without relaxation. With regard to this last detail, we ask up to what point did she know the history or about the development of the text of the Rule. She read it obviously in its Castilian translation, in a manuscript copy, since it doesn't seem that at that time there was a Spanish translation in printed form. When at the end of her life, she insisted on publishing it after the chapter of Alcalá (1581), she arranged to have printed a beautiful Spanish translation, which comes in front of her *Constitutions* (Salamanca, 1581, pp. 1-16.). But the most important fact is that in the rule she saw expressed and endorsed the Carmelite ideal. And as such she took it for herself and proposed it as the fundamental norm of her Carmels. In the first pages of the *Way of Perfection*, she says to her nuns that she founded "this little corner, where I have also sought that this rule of our Lady and Empress be observed with the perfection with which it was observed when initiated" (3.5)

3. The aspects that stand out more among those proposed in the Rule are: evangelical poverty (L 35); prayer ("that we pray without cease . . . unceasing prayer is the most important aspect of the rule" W 4.2), solitude in the cell (Const 8; W 4.9), silence (IC 3.2.13), work and the example of St. Paul, and finally the traditional relation of the Rule with the Blessed Virgin as model, the motive for which Teresa calls it the "*rule* of the Blessed Virgin, the rule of Our Lady of Mount Carmel" (F. 14.5; L 36.26; WP, title, 3.5; M. prol. 1).

4. In the Carmelite biography of Teresa a late episode is interesting. After having lived nine years "according to the first Rule," in 1571 she had to renew her profession of the same rule and she did so in these words: "I Teresa of Jesus, a nun of Our Lady of Mount Carmel, professed at the Incarnation in Avila and now present at St. Joseph's in Avila, where the first Rule is observed, and until now I have observed here with the permission of Our Most Reverend Padre General fray Juan Bautista, and also with his permission that although the Superiors

gave me orders to return to the Incarnation I kept it there; it is my will to observe it all my life, and so I promise and renounce all the briefs that the Pontiffs have granted for the mitigation of the said first Rule, which with the favor of the Lord I promise to observe until death . . . *Teresa of Jesus , Carmelite nun"* (Ap n. 12).

5. The second Carmelite book more assiduously read by her was the *breviary.* We have one copy of the one she used, edited by P. Rubeo in Venice, "1568, conserved in the Carmel of Medina del Campo." It is valuable for its biblical and liturgical richness (the rite of the Holy Sepulchre). Yet it was difficult for Teresa to use since it was all in Latin and extremely complicated through its abbreviations and rubrics. Even so, Teresa nourished her life of piety by it and familiarized herself with the Carmelite sanctoral, and thanks to it she received the incentive for her Marian devotion, reciting each week the Office of the Blessed Virgin (pp 65-75), where she could enjoy numerous *verses* taken from the *Song of Songs,* which she would later comment upon in her *Meditations on the Song of Songs . "*Oh Blessed Lady, how perfectly we can apply to you what takes place between God and the bride according to what is said in the Song of Sosgs. And thus you can see, daughters, in the Office of Our Lady, which we recite each week, how much in its antiphons and readings is taken from the Song of Songs" (M. 6.8).

6. An important question remains. Did Teresa read or at least know the texts contained in the *Speculum Ordinis*? Did she read especially the book which transmitted the Carmelite ideal, the *De Institutione*? Frequently it has been supposed that she did. It has been insisted that in the remark made in the *Interior Castle:* "this call explains our origin . .. ' is a translation of "It is our first Institution." It seems without doubt that Teresa knew through an oral conduit the content of the book, even though she does not quote or allude expressly to any book of those contained in the *Speculum*, with the

exception of the *Rule.* There existed in her time a singular anthology recently discovered and highly interesting. It is titled "*Codice de Avila-Roma* (XV c). It is actually in Rome but was discovered in Jerez de la Frontera (Andalusia) and came from Avila. Here we can do no more than *highlight* two facts a) that the Avila-Roman manuscript contains valuable medieval Carmelite texts *(the* ancient *Constitutions* of the religious, three versions of the *Rule.* the *De Institutione,* the *Tractatus de Origine, the Viridiarum,* and so on),* and b) it offers the texts in a double version, Latin and Castilian. In the hypothesis of the reading on the part of Teresa, she will use the Castilian translation. Yet it happens that this translation is so deficient that it is practically unintelligible for anyone who does not compare it with the respective Latin passage. So for example, having read the three translations of the *Rule* contained in it she would have been not only mislead but also disconcerted by the foolishness in the Castilian text. All of this makes it unlikely that it was read by Teresa.

Yet this does not hinder the fact that Teresa through other conduits may have had a vast knowledge of the texts contained in the *Speculum* and that she incorporated into her life and her doctrine the corresponding Carmelite spiritual tradition.

26. A Period Of Crisis And Struggle In The Incarnation

1. In her autobiography Teresa dedicates to this theme two chapters: in the title of chapter 7, "how distracted a life she began to live, " and in contrast the following chapter title, "the great good it did her not to turn from prayer." An extended and detailed account of the crisis in the first; a more relaxed and pedagogical, yet no less dramatic, account in the chapter that followed. On the other hand it is difficult to determine the chronology of these two periods. Teresa speaks repeatedly of *many years*. But she is more precise with the crisis of the abandonment of prayer: it lasted "a year and a half" (L. 7, 11), or "I abandoned it for a year and a half – or at least for a year; I don't remember well about the half" (L 19.4). The terminal moment of this period would be the death of her father. It would have lasted, therefore, from the time she left the infirmary until the end of 1543. Whereas the years of struggle extended probably to the whole following ten years: 1544-1553. In her account Teresa describes these years with absolute realism. Yet now in 1565, with a retrospective gaze: from the new viewpoint of her mystical life. Here we are only interested in analyzing what these two periods consisted of. First the *crisis*, then the *struggle* and recovery. Both of them framed in the context of the Incarnation.

2. The crisis. When she left the infirmary, Teresa had overcome her physical sickness, the paralysis of her body and began to be sick in soul. In contrast to the virtues and graces received in the infirmary, she accuses herself of inconsistency and a lack of correspondence with grace. She abuses the freedom of her new community situation and opens herself up to an ambiguous familiarity with relatives and friends. Psychologically and socially she leans toward those outside the monastery. As a consequence she suffered a weakening in her spiritual life and

109

in her community sharing. Former friendships that she had abandoned surfaced again and prevailed. With three or four forceful facts she notes this weakening: a) a temptation to mediocrity, resigned to live, she says, like the many, without any urgency about her personal vocation; b) a loss of time in borderline conversations in the convent speak room; c) a pretense or a kind of duplicity, feigning to be what one is not without it becoming hypocrisy, as she adverts ("In this matter of hypocrisy and vainglory, praise God, I don't recall ever having offended him know-ingly" L 7.1); and d) above all the abandonment of prayer. Teresa is sure that she abandoned it out of "false humility" (L.19. 15) or a false sense of loyalty to God. She believed it impossible to engage in intimate friendship with him while she betrayed him with false friendships ("I was ashamed to return to a friendship as special as is that found in the intimate exchange of prayer" L 7.1). It so happened that this abandon-ment of prayer made her touch bottom in her spiritual life:"this was the greatest temptation I had" (L 7.11).

This low period had for its counterpoint three episodes that were a salutary shock: the moving vision of Christ who appeared with great severity in one of her friendships, . . ."I was left very frightened and disturbed" (L 7.6); the disconcerting (and symbolic) vision of the toad (L 7.8); and the prolonged episode of her filial relations with Don Alonso: first, sharing with him the ideal of prayer, and then his shock-ing death. This last episode was the final shock; Teresa passes from crisis to struggle (L 7, 10-16).

3. *A time of struggle.* This period lasted much longer and was more intense than the previous one of crisis. To begin again living an authentic life, Teresa began by going to her father's last confessor, the Dominican, Vicente Barrón. But already before there had burst forth in her interior gusts of powerful struggle. She tells us herself in her words to our Lord: "O Lord of my soul! How can I extol the favors you gave me during these years! And how at the time when I offended

you most you quickly prepared me with an extraordinary repentance to taste your favors and gifts! Indeed, my King, you as One who well knew what to me would be most distressing, chose as a means the most delicate and painful punishment. With wonderful gifts you punished my sins!" (L 7.19). Straining between two extremes, she spent a most laborious life, in such a way that the return to prayer was not in any way easy: "It is certain that so unbearable was the force used by the devil, or coming from my wretched habits, to prevent me from going to prayer, and so unbearable the sadness I felt on entering the oratory, that I had to muster up all my courage "(L 8.7). That is to say, she practiced prayer through pure force of will and against the watch: "very often for some years, I was more anxious that the hour I had determined to spend in prayer be over than I was to remain there . . . And I don't know what heavy penance could have come to mind that frequently I would have gladly undertaken rather than recollect myself in the practice of prayer" (L 8.7). Teresa had fixed a precise time for prayer in her daily schedule and she followed it despite all the mental resistance and all the external solicitations. Little by little she had become aware that prayer was her lifesaver. She had successfully obtained from herself a *determined determination*. And her narrative concludes with a powerful brushstroke: "I wanted to live (for I understood that I was not living but was struggling with a shadow of death), but I had no one to give me life, and I was unable to catch hold of it. He who had the power to give it to me was right in not helping me, for so often had he brought me back to himself; and so often had I abandoned him" (L 8.12). To sum up: Teresa had suffered a long and hard temptation to mediocrity. And her struggle not to succumb was filled with periodic interruptions and new crises.

4. *The field of battle, the Incarnation.* The two periods – of crisis and struggle – were framed within the Carmelite life at the Incarnation. With the recovery of her health, Teresa had recovered "voice and

vote" in the community. She had gone through the four-year period of the third formation stage. She enjoyed a prestige in the group. In reality when she said she was resigned to live like the many, she was accepting a common denominator of a mediocre level. There were so many who were open, as was she, to friendships from outside. In the same Avilan climate there were so many young men attracted by the American illusion that in the city there arose a morbid curiosity and a hidden flirtation with the aseptic world of the religious women. Yes, there was in the community someone who sounded the alarm for Teresa: "There was a nun there, a relative of mine, older, and a great servant of God and very religious. She also warned me sometimes. Not only did I not believe her, but I was annoyed with her and felt she was scandalized for no reason at all." (L 7.9). Yet the community background was harmless. Teresa defines it as between the indifferent and the ambiguous: "Oh tremendous evil! Tremendous evil of religious where there are two paths (one of virtue and religious life, and the other of a lack of religious life and almost all walk in like manner" (L 7.5). This kind of ambiguity enters the "to be or not to be.", it was the humus in which Teresa's crisis germinated.

5. On the other hand, in the subsequent period of struggle, she changed the lament: "A great evil it is for a soul to be alone in the midst of so many dangers. It seems to me that if I should have had someone to talk all this over with it would have helped me" (L 7.20). Or she also experienced her solitude in the midst of the crowd. She had to struggle and overcome alone. She lacked the sacramental help of a confessor: "The whole trouble lay in not getting at the root of the occasions and with my confessors who were of little help" (L 6.4). In spite of this lack of help on the part of the community and the confessor, Teresa probably was not aware that hers had to be a one-person battle waged alone with herself. She had to assume what was specific in her vocation and discover the profound meaning of her life.

27. The Decisive Fact

1. Also in the Incarnation of Avila there occurred the decisive fact that changed the course of Teresa's life. It was an exterior event but with its interior other side. It happened to her in 1554 after almost twenty years of Carmelite life. She refers to it in Chapter 9 of her auto-biographical account. It consisted, no longer in the overcoming of the struggle sustained in the ten preceding years, but in the openness of an horizon consisting of a new mode of relating to God and dealing with life each day. Here we sum it up in three moments:
   - the spiritual mental state of the last period;
   - two determining events;
   - this new horizon of her life, in what it consisted of..

2. The context of her spiritual life. Teresa herself sums it up with a couple of pen strokes "Well, my soul, now was tired; and in spite of its desire, my wretched habits would not allow it rest" (L 9.1). Let us underline two clarifying words: *tired*, yet incapable of rest. That is to say, a struggle for years without a psychologically acceptable outcome. The shadow of her wretched habits persisted on the ethical and ascetical plane. Yet no less important was the psychological substratum. Teresa was a woman of desires ."I have always had great desires," she assures us. The most constant note at the end of these years of struggle were her longings and plans for a better life. They were probably disproportionate because they were unobtainable: desires and plans that were beyond her strength at the time for putting them into effect. Thus Teresa psychologically lives in a state of frustration, incapable of obtaining what she proposes, because she proposes goals higher than her strength allows. Thus, in this mental state of frustration, some decisive events suddenly happen to her.

3. Two decisive events. She refers to them in continuing her account in the same chapter 9. The first was an unexpected and terrific happening . "It happened to me that one day entering the oratory I saw a statue they had borrowed for a certain feast to be celebrated in the house. It represented the much wounded Christ and was very devotional so that beholding it I was utterly distressed in seeing him that way, for it well represented what he had suffered for us. I felt so keenly aware of how poorly I thanked him for those wounds that it seems to me, my heart broke. Beseeching him to strengthen me once and for all that I might not offend him, I threw myself down before him with the greatest outpouring of tears . . ." (L 9.1). Looking not at the statue but at the Lord in a kind of loving ultimatum "I then said that I would not rise from there until he granted me what I was begging him for" (L 9.3). And she herself comments: "I was very distrustful of myself and placed all my trust in God" (L 9.1), yet centering it in a very human way in Christ in his passion. Probably it was not only her confidence that she centered in him but her own self, transferring to him her desires and plans that he might attain this goal that she found unobtainable. It came to be the point of departure for the whole history of love that supported Teresa's existence. Each time she became more enamored of her Lord.

4. The second event took place around the same time as the previous one. In the year 1554 *The Confessions of St. Augustine*, translated into Castilian by Sebastián Toscano, was published. Teresa read them enthusiastically for she was dealing with one of her own: Augustine–she knew it well– before becoming a saint had been a sinner. And he was converted only once (not as she, with all these highs and low, so many comings and goings). Reading it now produced in her a growing empathy with him ."As I began to read the *Confessions*, it seemed to me I saw myself in them. I began to commend myself very much to this glorious saint. When I came to the passage where he

speaks about his conversion and read how he heard that voice in the garden, it only seemed to me, according to what I felt in my heart, that it was I the Lord called. I remained for a long time totally dissolved in tears and feeling within myself utter distress and weariness" (L 9.8).

Total empathy by means of the book. The emotional release of tears repeats the religious emotion of the previous event. In continuation the voice of the mysterious child singing – "take up and read, take up and read"— surely caused Teresa also to continue reading the powerful words of St. Paul that pierced the soul of Augustine and threw him down on his own road to Damascus: "not in carousing and drunkenness . . . rather put on the Lord Jesus Christ" (Rm 13. 13-14). With an identical efficacy: "my soul gained great strength from the Divine Majesty for he must have heard my cries and taken pity on so many tears" (L 9.9). As if he was diluting the previous state of frustration.

5. The new horizon in Teresa's spiritual life. She describes this in a narrative connection between this chapter and the following with a total change of mentality and literary tone. She begins thus: "I sometimes experienced, as I said, although very briefly, the beginning of what I will now speak about. It used to happen, when I represented Christ, within me in order to place myself in his presence, or even while reading, that a feeling of the presence of God would come upon me unexpectedly so that I could in no way doubt he was within me or I totally immersed in him" (L 10.1).

It was simply the "beginning" of the mystical life; the experience of new life. (It is certain that there had preceded sporadic glimpses, only passing (see L. 4.7; 7.6). Teresa describes it as something that happened to her without her bringing it about: she sensed herself invaded from within, and immersed from without in the "presence of God." And it was an undoubted sensation.

Recalling her past experiences, she remembers that for many years before she slept she relived expressively the scene of Jesus in the garden of olives even to making the gesture of wiping away the drops of sweat. And that since she was so devoted to the Magdalene she also put herself in the scene of being at the feet of the Master in prayer. But now in this it was different: totally new. It was not she who did this. She had entered or she was introduced into the mystical space –"they call it mystical theology, she says - the intellect does not work, but is as though amazed by all it understands" (10.1).

It is effectively the *beginning* of a new manner of prayer and life, of unforeseen consequences.

28. Teresa's New Life In The Incarnation

We possess a living sketch of Teresa. It was traced for us by one of her first theologian assessors, the Dominican Pedro Ibáñez (d. 1565). First he was against her, but then he became her collaborator and admirer. He wrote it when Teresa was still residing in the Incarnation. And he destined it not for her but for his theologian colleagues who were wavering as to whether her presumed mystical experiences were being inspired by a good or bad spirit.

The brief text by Ibáñez was entitled traditionally *Dictamen*, because it contained a series of 33 statements in the manner of very brief notes meant to serve the group of theologians as they discussed and discerned Teresa's spirit. The central argument of the text would be her mystical graces and the repercussion they had on her conduct, on the community at the Incarnation, and on the many others she had dealings with. For the reader today they contain a series of snapshots of Teresa while she lives as a nun in the midst of a community.

We are selecting only the most relevant of these 33 notes (see the entire text in BMC II, p. 130-32).

1. All of these visions and other things that she experiences bring her closer to God and make her more humble, obedient, and so on.

2. She never experiences these things that she doesn't remain with great peace and happiness so that all the pleasures of the earth taken together seem to her to be much less.

3. She has no fault or imperfection for which she is not reproved by the one who speaks to her interiorly.

4. She never sought or desired these things, but only to do in all things the will of God, our Lord.

6. She has a very great purity of soul, great cleanliness, most

fervent desires to please God and in exchange for this to trample on all earthly things.

9. There is no one who deals with her, unless their intention is depraved, who is not moved to devotion by her conversation, even though she doesn't mention these things to them

13. So great is the benefit these things give her soul and the good edification she gives by her example that over forty nuns live in her house with great recollection.

14. These things ordinarily are experienced after a long period of prayer and of being very centered in God and burning in his love, or after receiving Communion.

15. These things give her the greatest desire to be right, and that the devil not deceive her.

16. They cause in her the most profound humility; she knows that what she receives comes from the hand of the Lord, and the little she has of herself.

18. They cause her to rejoice and be consoled with trials, slander-ous talk against her, and illnesses; and so she has terrible illnesses, of heart, vomiting, and many other pains, all of which leave her when she has the visions.

20. Both the things of earth that can give her some happiness and the trials, for she has suffered many, she endures with equanimity with-out losing her peace or quietude of soul.

21. She has such a firm proposal not to offend the Lord that she has made a vow not to fail to do anything she knows to be more perfect.

23. In hearing God spoken of with devotion and force, she is wont to go into rapture and in trying to resist she cannot, and she remains so for those who see her which gives them very great devotion.

25. With these things she cannot endure those who are in the state of perfection, yet do not strive to live it in conformity with their institute.

28. God has given her so strong and valiant a spirit that it frightens.

She was a fearful person; now she tramples on all devils. She is far from the dainty and silly ways of women. Very much without scruples. She is most righteous.

29. With this, our Lord has given her the gift of most gentle tears, great compassion for her neighbor, and a knowledge of her own faults; she highly esteems good people and lowers herself. And I say certainly that she has been of benefit to many persons, and I am one of them.

30. She has an ordinary remembrance of God and the sentiment of his presence.

31. Nothing was she ever told that wasn't so and that didn't come about. And this is a very great argument.

32. These things cause in her a clarity of understanding and an admirable light in the things of God.

33. They told her that she should examine the Scriptures and that she would not find that there ever was a soul who desired so much to please God who was deceived for so long a time.

(Other self-likenesses of Teresa in this same period – the last years of her life at the Incarnation – can be seen in her *Spiritual Testimonies* 1 & 2 written by her around 1560-1562. And also an extensive self-portrait referring more to her interior life in chapters 23-31 of *The Book of Her Life).*

29. Three Of Teresa's Carmelite Teachers

1. As we have already mentioned, a good part of Teresa's formation is due, more than to books, to oral teaching. This oral teaching came not only from the mistresses and the community of the monastery, but also more or less from the Carmelite confessors, chaplains and vicars. The confessor was to be a solicitous spiritual teacher: according to the Constitutions "the sisters should have a Father confessor assigned . . . whom in their dealings with and difficult matters should humbly call upon and without his counsel they should do nothing foolhardy." Teresa was moreover especially attached to the sermons, according to her own testimony: "I was very fond of sermons, so fond that if I saw someone preach well and with spirit, I felt a special love for that person . . . Hardly ever did a sermon seem so bad to me that I didn't listen to it eagerly" (L 8.12).

2. Among all her Carmelite teachers let us choose the three most esteemed by her. They correspond to the period of her spiritual maturity, when she had begun receiving her mystical experiences, when she was already a writer and founder. In chronological order they are:

The general of the order, P. Giovanni Baptista Rossi (Rubeo): 1567-1578.

The saint, Fray John of the Cross:1567-1582.

The provincial, P. Jerónimo Gracián: 1576-1582.

3. The father General P Giovanni Baptista Rossi (Rubeo). An Italian born in Ravenna, elected in 1564, General of the Order when Teresa had already founded two years previously the Carmel of St. Joseph. In February of 1567 he arrived in Avila and soon met with Teresa, who was prioress at St. Joseph. This first meeting between the two occurred in an atmosphere of anxiety on the part of Teresa because

of her juridically ambiguous situation. But she changed quickly thanks to the comprehending manner of Father General. The good relations between the two only degenerated in the last years (1576-78) because of incidents between Gracián and the Carmelites of Andalusia (see Ltr 271). Here we are interested only in the general's contribution to Teresa's person and project.

a) Avila, 1567: Rubeo approved Teresa's founding initiative. He affirmed his jurisdiction over her. And he authorized her to found new Carmels in Castile (MHCT I, 62). Teresa summed it up: "He rejoiced to see our manner of life . . . he gave me very extensive patent letters, so that more monasteries could be founded" (F 2.3).

b) Barcelona, 1567: A little before his return to Italy, Rubeo accepted Teresa's idea of beginning the foundation of discalced friars. He authorized her to found in Castile two monasteries. He wrote to her from Barcelona 10 October 1567 (MHCT I, 68). Hardly a month after this Fray John of the Cross enters the scene and soon makes a foundation in Duruelo (F 3.16-17).

c) Rome 1569: when back in Rome, Rubeo gave his warmest praise of Mother Teresa, "a stone to be highly prized for being a valuable friend of God: I give the divine Majesty infinite thanks for having granted so great a favor to this order, for the diligence and goodness of our revered Teresa; she is of greater benefit to the order than all the Carmelite friars in Spain . . ." *(MHCT* II. 317). He addressed this letter to the prioress in Medina. The praise reached Teresa soon after.

4. Fray John of the Cross. The collaboration of Fray John with Mother Teresa is well known. Here we will mention in a very summary fashion the most noteworthy events in the course of this development. When the two met each other for the first time in Medina (1567), she was approaching 52. He was only 26. Her contribution unfolded on three levels: that of her mission as founder; that of her interior (mystical) life; and that of her spiritual doctrine.

a) The first level occurred at the moment in which Teresa had decided to initiate the foundation of the discalced friars. She proposed this to Fray John who was about to function for the first time as a priest. He renounced his projects for the future and agreed to the proposal put forth by the founder. He agreed also to let himself be taught in a living way, within a Carmel, as she said "about our way of life so that he would have a clear understanding of everything, whether it concerned mortification or the style of both our community life and the recreation we have together" (F 13.5). In a certain manner he entered into mutual cooperation with Teresa. His contribution was something like the incarnation of her ideal of Carmelite life in the Carmelite masculine branch.

b) *In the second level,* when in 1572 Teresa brought him as the spiritual teacher for the community of the Incarnation where she was prioress: "The discalced friar who is confessor here is doing great good; he is Fray John of the Cross" (Ltr 45.4). He took part brilliantly in the last phase of Teresa's mystical life. He was present at the moment when she received the grace of mystical marriage (ST 31). And the two celebrate it, each with mystical poems: It is the *I live without living in myself* of Teresa's, which Fray John intones as *I no longer live within myself.* These two poems are a good exemplification of the mystical symbiosis of the two.

c) *In the third level,* Fray John contributed important data to the Teresian idealogy. Especially to the definitive codification of the spiritual life, realized by Teresa in her book *The Interior Castle.*

3. *Jerónimo Gracián.* He collaborated with Teresa in the last six years of his life, in her work as a founder as well as a writer, and also as the spiritual director of her soul. On the eve of his entrance in Pastrana he was interested in reading the *Speculum Ordinis* and he wrote for Teresa a little tract on *The Rule and the Prophets of the Order.* Perhaps this was what won Teresa's sympathy. From the first

meeting of the two in Beas (1575) she promised him special obedience (ST 35-36) and he professed a high esteem of her. On Gracián's initiative she wrote *The Interior Castle* and hardly had she finished when she submitted it to him for a kind of critical revision in dialogue with its author. At his request Teresa wrote *On Making the Visitation.* And she wrote to him more than a hundred letters, actually the largest section we have in her correspondence. To him she confided the re-elaboration and edition of the *Constitutions* for the nuns, which he dedicated to Teresa in a valuable introduction (Salamanca 1581)

30. Teresa Prioress At The Incarnation

1. Teresa is prioress of the Monastery of the Incarnation during the three-year period 1571-1574, from age 56 to 59. It has been pointed out that accepting this office was "the hardest trial of obedience that Teresa ever had to submit to." She had already founded eight Carmels and she had been prioress in all of them Yet at this time (July-October 1571), things had got complicated. In July, the Visitator, Pedro Fernández, had proposed to her the office of prioress at the Incarnation. Teresa resisted (ST 16). In the meantime the Visitator named her prioress of the Carmel in Medina, where a little before this she had to distance herself precipitously under threat of excommunication. Again in the morning of 6 October she traveled, out of obedience, from Medina to Avila. This same day, in Avila, the Visitator endorsed her new profession of the primitive rule. He designated her a member of the community of Salamanca, yet at the same time confirmed her as prioress of the Incarnation in Avila. Teresa took possession of her new office this day or the morning or the following day 7 October 1571. Here we recall briefly:

- Her being named prioress and her taking possession.
- Teresa, the mother and teacher of the community.
- The end of the three-year period and the new failed election.

2. Naming her prioress and her taking possession. Teresa was designated prioress not through the election of the nuns, but through her being appointed by the superior. Probably she was appointed by the Visitator, the Dominican Pedro Fernández, with the approval of the Carmelite provincial, Angel de Salazar (see this testimony *BMC* 19.3 and Teresa's words in F 21.1). Obviously the nuns at the Incarnation saw themselves as unjustly deprived of their normal right to elect the

prioress and they opposed this appointment with every effort. When the new prioress came down from St Joseph accompanied by the provincial, Angel de Salazar, and a great retinue, the nuns impeded them from entering closing the main door. The group, including Teresa, had to enter the monastery furtively through a little door in the lower choir. And even so they met with a strong and noisy opposition, perhaps not so much to the new prioress as to the offensive way in which she was being imposed on them. Everything calmed down when Teresa organized the solemn taking of possession in the community choir placing in her prioress's seat the statue of Our Lady of Clemency and directing to the community a very humble and peaceable sermon. It seems that this brought an end to the resistance.

3. Mother and Teacher of the community at the Incarnation. To be and exercise the role of mother and teacher made up Teresa's entire program as prioress of the community. She strove first of all to win the good will of the nuns. After exactly one month she already writes:" there is peace . . . they show me much respect" (Ltr 38.4). Among the 130 nuns in the community, at least 40, according to Padre IbáZez shared her ideal of prayer and the spiritual life. Yet the most serious lack in the house came from the economic poverty. The rents of the monastery were insufficient to provide a minimum of necessities. Even the DoZas suffered hunger. Teresa hastened to remedy the situation. She knocked on the door of her friends both male and female asking for help, including the doors of her own relatives: from her sister Juana she begs at the beginning of February 1572: "I need some reales," and when she learned that Juana was in the country house in Galinduste and had turkeys she wrote in a postscript to her letter: "Send the turkeys since you have so many" (Ltr 40.2). To her friend in Salamanca, "the very magnificent SeZor Maldonado Bocalán," while she thanks him for sending "sixty- two birds," she explains to him "the indigence of this house is so great and there are so many sick nuns that

we really needed them" (Ltr. 47.2-3; and cf. Ltr. 74). So until the end
of her term as prioress: on returning from Segovia in order to give over
her office, she writes to the prioress in Valladolid: "Do you know anyone there who could lend me some reales? . . . to go to the Incarnation
without a cent would be a mistake . . .Whether little or much try to get
something for me" (Ltr 71.5).

4. But more than anything else, she cares for the religious life
of the house. She began by getting rid of the numerous seculars who
were living in the house. She kept only those who were caring for the
sick. She was very careful about the liturgy and assistance at choir.
She herself gave the example, from the day of the great uproar, going
to Communion the next morning. She benefitted by the first Lent of
the triennium to safeguard recollection in the house, closing the speak
rooms and herself confronting some of the annoying visitors. Despite
the poverty of the house, she herself on occasion gave food to some
of the bashful poor. From the depths of her interior she heard the
encouragement of the Lord: "the Lord gave me hope that his house
would continue to improve" (ST 27), thus she assures some of the
benefactors. She benefits by the challenge of the hermits of Pastrana
to improvise a precious community dynamic.

5. Above all Teresa adopts an exceptional measure. She gives
special importance to the work of the confessors. She proposes to
bring for this ministry the best of the discalced, Fray John of the
Cross. To obtain this she sends her staunch supporter Julián de Avila
to solicit this from the Visitator. He agrees and Fray John of the Cross
accepts the appointment. He comes to Avila and from the Carmelite
monastery in Avila he descends almost every day to the confessional
of the Incarnation. Little by little his spiritual work becomes so intense
that Teresa prepares one of the little houses outside the cloister of the
monastery as a residence for Fray John of the Cross and his companion Fray Germán, and from there both of them exercise their service

assiduously and seriously ."The discalced friar who is confessor here is doing great good, he is Fray John of the Cross., " so Teresa writes in September of 1572 (Ltr 45.5). Fray John continues faithful to his mission as spiritual father even after Teresa finishes her term as prioress and leaves the house for Andalusia.

6. The new failed term of office. In 1576 Teresa returned from Seville and after a pause in Toledo she transfers to the little monastery of St. Joseph in Avila. Here while she is writing the pages for the sixth and seventh dwelling places of the *Interior Castle* – in the Autumn of 1577 – the three-year period of her successor, DoZa Juana del Aguila, as prioress at the Incarnation comes to an end. And this time the entire community reunites to elect a new prioress. The Carmelite Visitator Jerónimo Tostado presides over the election and there occurs once again the disturbance like the previous one although in reverse. The greater number of the nuns gave their vote to Teresa and the presider opposed each of these votes with a clear gesture and declared the votes null. It was the *hammering election* as Teresa called it. The nuns rebelled, the presider excommunicated them and they had to have recourse to spheres of higher influence . . . so as to initiate a lawsuit in self-defense.

7. Regarding this episode, we are interested only in the behavior of Teresa and John of the Cross. She has a maternal compassion for the poor excommunicated nuns, but in no way did she want to take on the charge of being prioress again. On the other hand, Fray John of the Cross, who had nothing whatsoever to do with the matter paid the consequences. On the night of 3 and 4 December he was kidnapped from his little house and confined in prison in Toledo. Teresa immediately had recourse to the king, seeking his favor for Fray John (Ltr 218). But she did so in vain. When, after eight months in prison, the prisoner reappears among the living, Teresa remarks: "God treats his friends terribly" (Ltr 233.3).

IV
Teresa Founder

After 27 years of Carmelite life, Teresa improvises her activity as founder. She obeys a mysterious order sending her out. In 1562, when 47 years old, she starts the Carmel of St. Joseph in Avila. In the following 20 years she founds another 16 Carmels. These years are at the same time the most intense of her mystical life. As founder, she travels in a covered wagon through Castile and Andalusia, she writes letters, she manages money, and mixes with people representing all the social classes. She herself tells the story in The Book of Her Foundations, written while she was on the march.

31.Teresa The Founder.
The Charismatic Send-Off

1. The title founder was bestowed on Teresa already during her lifetime by the nuns of her Carmels. She herself wrote some couplets, which they sang: *Mother Founder/ Is coming to recreation;/ Let's all dance and sing/ And clap our hands in jubilation.* This was sung by the child Bela Gracián in the Carmel of Toledo (Ltr 169.1). Sometimes she writes humorously of herself: *"What a brain for a founder"* (Ltr 172.24). Likewise that she is founder is acknowledged, in the first publications in print, even though these are her own works, or in books written by others about her. So for example, the first edition of her *Constitutions*, in the dedicatory letter by Gracián (Salamanca 1581); or the first edition of *The Way of Perfection,* or in Diego de Yanguas's dedication to her in *The Life of St. Albert* (Evora 1582), or the *edición principe* of her works prepared by Fray Luis de León (Salamanca 1588).

2. This title "Founder" involves a twofold reference: from the historical viewpoint it refers to the erection of new Carmels and Teresa's leadership in the group. But it has a more profound importance from the theological viewpoint. Teresa is a founder insofar as she is endowed with a special charism, which confers on her a mission within the church; a charism of which she herself has a clear awareness and testifies to expressly. Here we will sum it up in three points: the context in which her charism as founder arose; the testimonial account of Teresa herself; and the endorsement by means of the task of founding and of Teresa's mystical experience.

3. The religious context in which her mission of founder arose. This refers to a two-year period 1560-1562. Teresa is living at the monastery of the Incarnation. She is very happy there. Some forty

Carmelite nuns share her ideals about the spiritual life. The graces she received in this period place her so much in view that she planned to flee the Incarnation and find refuge in a Carmel far away where no one would know her (L 31.13). In the corner of her cell a group of enthusiastic nuns gather, most of them young. Personally Teresa has been receiving for at least six years mystical graces. The decree of the Inquisition in 1559 has decimated her little library of spiritual books, but the interior voice has promised her a " living book." Her confessors and theological assessors continued questioning the genuineness of her experiences presumably mystical. They oblige her to resist with grimaces of scorn (L 29.5). So as to submit her experiences to the judgment of Fray Pedro de Alcántara, Teresa spends some time in the house of the Avilan Doña Guiomar de Ulloa: "this holy man enlightened me about everything" (L 30.5). For Doña Guiomar she composed one of her first poems: "Oh Beauty exceeding/ All other beauties!" She is ignorant of the outcome of this whole process. At times she has the feeling that death is near (L 20.13).

4. In the context of this period and of the church at that time, one is living in an environment of religious reform promoted partly by the Council of Trent. Closer to her, she is assisted by the Franciscan movement of reform, in which the figure of Fray Pedro de Alcántara emerges and as a type for the feminine monastic life, the monastery for discalced nuns erected in Avila and transplanted to Madrid. In this same two-year period Teresa enlarged her horizon, from Avila to Toledo to the Americas (Fuentes documentales: (ST 1 & 2; L 23-31).

5. The charism of founder. We possess two original accounts of Teresa's: the letter to her brother Lorenzo (Ltr. 2), and chapter 32 of her *Life*. The letter to Lorenzo contains a simple allusion to the budding project, that is to say: "I have already written you a long letter about a matter that for many reasons I could not escape doing

since God's inspirations are the source. Because these things are hard to speak of in a letter, I mention only the fact that saintly and learned persons think I am obliged not to be cowardly but do all I can for this project – a monastery of nuns. There will be no more than fifteen nuns in it, who will practice a very strict enclosure . . .Their life will be one of prayer and mortification" (Ltr. 2.2). At this time she is ready to bring about the foundation of the Avilan Carmel of St. Joseph. What is important is that Teresa has a clear awareness of doing it "inspired by God."

      6. The account in her *Life* is much more explicit. After the obscure backdrop of the vision of hell, Teresa alludes to the two aspects of the project, the context of the monastery of the Incarnation and the mission from on high. In the cell of Teresa the group of companions continue to meet, nuns and young seculars, who recall the style of life of the discalced Franciscans and the possibility of doing the same. Teresa shares and supports the idea, but without any desire to bring it about, because "on the other hand I was so perfectly content in the house in which I was living because it was very much to my liking . . . I was still delaying" (L 32. 10). The decision came from on high: "One day after Communion, His Majesty earnestly commanded me to strive for this new monastery with all my powers, and he made great promises that it would be founded and that he would be highly served in it. He said it should be called St. Joseph . . . and that Christ would remain with us and that it would be a star shining with great splendor . . . and said that I should tell my confessor what he commanded . . . But often the Lord returned to speak to me about this new monastery . . . That I saw it was his will, and I could no longer help but tell my confessor. I told him in writing all that happened" (L 32. 11-12). This written report that was given to the Jesuit Padre Baltasar has been lost. Lost, too, are the letters, before and after, to Lorenzo. She will return to the theme in *Life*

33.14 (an endorsement of the Blessed Virgin!). What is absolutely clear in the detailed account is that if Teresa founded a monastery, she did not do it on her own initiative; she is one who is commanded or sent. This passage from her *Life* contains her charismatic patent as founder.

7. Endorsement of the charism. In the institutional aspect, Teresa after five years of life in St. Joseph's, has the approval of the Father General and begins new foundations, of nuns and friars. Here we are interested only in the interior endorsement, of new mystical graces. She testifies to it herself in scattered notes, whether in her *Spiritual Testimonies* or in telling the history of the foundations in *The Book of Her Foundations*. When she had founded a half dozen Carmels and the friars' monasteries of Duruelo and Pastrana, the interior voice told her "to hurry to establish these houses . . . that I should accept as many houses as given to me . . . and that I should write about the foundation of these houses" (ST 6). It was the year 1570. The following year it is repeated to her: "Take courage . . .In your days you will see the order of the Blessed Virgin flourish" (ST 11). This same year the interior voice supports her against those who complain about her, so as to discredit her work, using the saying of St. Paul about women (ST 15). Nonetheless a little afterward, Teresa notes down a personal awareness: "I understood that since our Lord desired to revive the original spirit of this order and in his mercy he took me as a means, His Majesty had to provide me with what I was lacking, which was everything, in order to get results and better manifest his greatness through so wretched a thing" (ST 30). Yet the fullest endorsement she consigned to her history of the facts in *The Book of Her Foundations*. It is enough to read her account of the last foundation (F 31).

32. The Charism Of The Teresian Carmel

1. The charism of Teresa the founder was not confined to her person, nor was it reduced to the founding of a series of Carmels and her consequent leadership at their head. Much more important and decisive is the spirit that she transmitted to them: the ideology, the objectives, the lifestyle. These were values present in germ in the first foundation, but that gradually evolved and were defined in Teresa's experience, in the contrasting and adverse alternatives, in the measure that Teresa continued rethinking and formulating them in her books and correspondence as well as in the legislation and life of the group, or in the official documents that sanctioned the onward march of her work.

2. In the Teresian ideology with respect to new discalced Carmels, from the beginning there stood out the principle of a double orientation: On one side there was a retrospective gaze toward the first Carmel of its origins; far from adopting an attitude of breaking with the Incarnation or with its Carmelite roots, she maintained intact her relationship with her community of origin (a transfer of many persons), and affirms insistently her will to remain connected with the ancient Carmelite spiritual tradition, the return to the primitive rule, the double model of the Blessed Virgin Mary and the prophet Elijah, the eremitic life of the ancient dwellers on the biblical mountain ("descendants of men of prayer and contemplation") and so on. And on the other side the sense of making something actual and new: the express will of insertion in the church of her times and the pouring out of her own religious or spiritual experience to the group of her followers.

3. In the retrospective orientation, there prevails the will to

connect with the origins (as with a number of the religious reforms of her times, or as in the humanism of the renaissance artists with their gaze always fixed on the classic greco-roman models). In the primitive rule, the ideal of evangelical poverty stands out without any lessening, and it states that it is basic "for continual prayer day and night. Our primitive rule states that we must pray without ceasing." (WP 4.2), The hermit life concretized by her in community cloister and in the personal cell, including hermitages constructed throughout the garden for a possible greater withdrawal (one of them Mt Carmel (ST 16) ." For the style of life we aim to follow is not just that of nuns but of hermits" (WP 13.6). Yet she did not conceive of the solitude as a flight to the desert: she always founded in an urban environment and within it created a community oasis.

4. Despite this will to be rooted in the past, in Teresa's ideology there prevails the will of insertion into the present church, and society. The idea of service of the church stands out. She mints for her first Carmel the fusion of contemplation and apostolate "the world is all in flames; . . they want to ravage his Church – and are we to waste time asking for things that if God were to grant them we would have one soul less in heaven? No, my Sisters." (WP 1. 5) . "Let us be the kind of persons whose prayers can be useful in helping those servants of God, that though enclosed we will be fighting in strict solidarity with the captains" (theologians and preachers) who defend the Church. In the first pages of the *Way of Perfection*, she comes to the idea of a Carmelite spiritual strategy necessary in the present setting of the church (cf the entire text of WP 3.1). Likewise her idea of founding the discalced Carmelites has its roots in the comprehension of what was occurring in America, "the millions of souls that were being lost there . . ." and once again a charismatic movement intervenes: "wait a little, daughter, and you will see great things" (F 1).

5. Yet what is first in this second orientation is the pressure that her own experience of God and of Christ exercised on Teresa. A pressure that in its turn reaches from Teresa to the group. Her whole activity as founder develops during an intense period of mystical graces. Overflowing . . . of the sort that Teresa's soul is like a fountain at the top of the experience of Christ and of ecclesial urgency. She needs to transmit them as an ideal and as life to the veins of Carmel. She herself empathizes with her followers. This is the dynamic experience transmitted in her writings. Teresa writes to entice or to empathize with her readers. A fount of empathy is simply her experience of God. For her nuns she wrote expressly *The Interior Castle* not only the first dwelling places but the sixth and seventh as she points out in the epilogue of the work. In such a way that when there come upon her Carmels moments of crisis, her writings will be the liberating force. They will likewise be a transmitting agent of the Teresian movement through the centuries. Without a living reference to Teresa of Jesus, to her experience, to her salvation history, to her written work, her work as founder, the ideal, the charism of her Carmel would be unintelligible. (Cf. The short text of *Foundations* 1.6 in regard to the intensity with which the new ideal is lived in the Carmel of St. Joseph's).

6. The elemental codification of the life in her Carmels was realized by her in a brief text of the *Constitutions*. Drafted originally during the first five-year period at St. Joseph's in Avila, they were retouched amply in the first draft of Alcalá (1581). These last were re-elaborated by Gracián and the chapter members on the basis of a number of suggestions by Teresa herself in her correspondence of those days and in fact accepted and spread by her. In the first text, apart from other numerous details, the work accentuates expressly one of the components of her ideal, what we could designate as Teresian humanism in the religious life: a high value placed on the person, the norm

of two hours of recreation a day (almost in parallel with the two hours of mental prayer). She had already insisted on the human virtues: "the holier you are, the more sociable you will be with your sisters," the intercommunion of persons and communities, the prescription of manual labor, reading as the nourishment of the soul, selectivity in regard to vocations, and the exercise of authority out of love. The text that was redacted by Teresa did not include the chapter on faults and penalties, which later they obliged her to insert and which she limited herself to copying word for word from a previous text.

7. These skilled lines Teresa thought out and wrote for the Carmels of nuns. Their transfer to the discalced friars, she did initially through Fray John of the Cross. Later, she proposed also the figure of Gracián as a model. To Fray John of the Cross, an expert in prayer and contemplation, she proposed the sisterly style and recreation in force in the group (humanism). And for the first opening of Duruelo she sets down the first *constitutions* of the nuns in Avila which the first friars transcribed almost literally adapting them to their own community of priest friars. In Teresa's esteem Saint John of the Cross, she wrote that he is "a heavenly and divine man, a man of so much grace, accompanied by so much humility, he is a saintly man . . . with the assets of a martyr": he incarnates the Teresian ideal. The Teresian charism among the discalced friars must be read and evaluated by means of the person and style of Fray John of the Cross.

33. The First Foundation: St. Joseph In Avila

1. In Teresa's history this is probably the most audacious and heroic deed she brought about. She herself refers to it three years later, reserving its telling to an entire section of her *Life* (chaps. 32–36), and begging the first reader-revisor of her work that in case he thinks it should be thrown into the fire, he "preserve whatever pertains to this monastery. And when I am dead, give it to the Sisters who live here that those who are to come . . . might be encouraged to serve God "(L 36.29). We have an unsurpassed account to which we now refer. In this present theme, we will synthesize the history of this foundation, filling in the founder's account with other contemporary Avilan sources, especially the acts of the city council and the pontifical documents that authorize the erection of the monastery.

2. The preparations. To set in motion her initial inspiration, Teresa solicits a multiple collaboration: above all the twofold support of Fray Pedro de Alcántara and the Dominican Pedro Ibáñez; two women friends Doña Aldonza and Doña Guiomar de Ulloa, who solicit the bulls from Rome; the presence, or the director of the work project, of her brother-in-law, Juan de Ovalle, who came from Alba, assisted by his wife Juana de Ahumada, Teresa's sister; in spiritual matters, her director, with his doubts and wavering, the Jesuit Baltasar Alvarez. One who is missing on the other hand is the Carmelite provincial, Angel de Salazar.

But the yarn on the skein becomes entangled: when the first brief that arrives from Rome is useless. Next because Ovalle buys houses for the future convent without being aware that they are buildings burdened with a city tax. Finally the small amount of money Teresa had to pay the work men, the pesos sent by her brother

Lorenzo from America (L 33.12; Ltr 2), were used up quickly. This is the time in which a new setback arose: the provincial gave Terersa orders to leave Avila and spend almost eight months in Toledo assisting Doña Luisa de la Cerda.

3. Erection of the monastery. The erection of the Avilan Carmel took place right after Teresa returned from Toledo. While she was at the palace of Doña Luisa, she met the Andalusian María de Jesús and the two exchanged thoughts about their projects and ideals. The little houses prepared somehow by Ovalle. under a personal title were ready ."The very night I reached this city our patent and our brief for the monastery arrived from Rome" (L 36.1). Fray Pedro de Alcántara accompanied by Salcedo traveled to El Tiemblo to present it to the bishop Don Alvaro ."Everything was done in deep secrecy" (L 36.3). The bishop resisted, but finally gave his assent and he came to Avila to get to know Teresa personally, who had gathered there for the purpose of the foundation the four young pioneers ("four poor orphans") and also a couple of nuns from the Incarnation. At the sound of the bell the inaugural Mass was celebrated by Teresa's cleric friend Gaspar Daza. He gave the habit to the four candidates in the presence of both Teresa and the future chaplain Julián de Avila. The cloister was established "behind some makeshift boards and matting, which at the time did not speak so much of cloister but that the house was very small and poor" (BMC 18. 384). All of this on the morning of 24 August 1562 ."Well with me it was like being in glory to see the Blessed Sacrament reserved . . . I was so intensely happy that I was as though outside myself, in deep prayer" (L 36.6).

But that same evening, Teresa suffered a profound interior crisis (L 36.7). There first arose an uproar in that section of the city. And the prioress of the Incarnation, Doña María Cimbrón, called for the immediate presence of Teresa to render an account. She abandoned the little convent and went down to the Incarnation.

Accompanied by Julián de Avila, she left the four novices alone and sad, yet determined, although totally inexperienced and hardly initiated into the new way of life.

4. The opposition of the city. The evening of the same inaugural day, there was heard around the little house the uproar from that section of the city. Two days before this (22 August), the quarryman and the overseer of the founts had presented before the council a sound of alarm against Ovalle for the houses of Valvellido constructed beside the city founts. And the day following the foundation, the chief magistrate Garcí Suárez Carvajal raised his voice in the council against the recently founded monastery.

In fact, because of the haste and inexperience of everyone, Teresa and her nuns got themselves involved in a tangle of problems which now came to light: a/ First of all the pontifical brief was accepted and executed by the prelate without a previous royal *placet;* b/ The houses bought by Ovalle from the Valvellido heirs were subject to a city tax, about which Ovalle was ignorant. c/ the restructuring of the buildings was done at the border of the aqueducts that provided water for the city. These amounted to three weak aspects which provided the motive for a multiple lawsuit. On the 30th day the council gathered a first large meeting of persons unfavorable to Mother Teresa: only in the gathering did the bishop's vicar-general present the pontifical Brief that justified the foundation. The following day another large meeting was held in the episcopal palace, questioning the admission of this brief. The theologian Domingo Báñez and the bishop who was present there supported Teresa. But they were not able to prevent the lawsuit from being transferred to the Court in Madrid, where it drew on until April 1564 with an incredible economic waste for the very poor Carmel of St. Joseph, which in the meantime had to send a large number of letters to the Council. They had to tear down a couple of hermitages in the garden, and they were at the point of pulling down part of their building. It was even proposed that they move the little house to another part of the city (see the respective documentation in the book by E. Ruiz Ayúcar, *El municipio de Avila ante la fundación de San José, Avila 1982).*

5. The first appearance of Carmelite life. The only sources of the life that was lived in the quiet of those first five years are the accounts given in Teresa's *Life ch.* 36 and in her *Foundations*, ch.1. Above all, this latter. There stand out in the two aspects: a great calm before the storm and harassment coming from outside (a); and within the empathy of the group with the founder's mystical life (b).

a) The peace of the house was in strong contrast with the racket that came from that *barrio* of San Roque, with the burden of the large meetings of the Council, and with the prolonged lawsuit before the Court in Madrid. Of the relations of the group with the council, we have only one letter, signed by the *poor Sisters of St. Joseph* a serene letter that didn't show the least amount of tension or strain, on the contrary it maintains a frank dialogue in submission and benevolence. (Something else were the summaries made by the council of other letters sent by the Sisters. . .)

b) Much more intense and revealing is the other aspect: a kind of idyllic view of contemplative life made possible through Teresa's presence. She is experiencing a torrent of mystical graces from the day of her return (*Life* 36.24; and chaps 37-40), graces at times uncontainable before the Sisters, at other times they were charismatic graces "for them." They were of the kind which made a strong impression on the little group of novices (that quickly reached the number of thirteen). The vibrant likeness Teresa draws of them makes up chapter 1 of the *Foundations*: "the five years I spent in St. Joseph's in Avila after its foundation seem to me to have been the most restful of my life." The thirteen Sisters were in the eyes of Teresa "angelic souls." (see. *Foundations 1).*

34. The First Exit:
The Carmel Of Medina

1. In Teresa's history her first exit as a founder takes on a special importance. The trip from Avila to Medina in the summer of 1567 marked a new call and a new style of life for her. The great expansion of her mission begins. The way was opened in an unfavorable social and ecclesial context having a twofold result. Teresa is a woman and more than that a cloistered nun. Soon she will be nicknamed the "restless gadabout," or as she herself notes down about this: "Of me they say that I am a restless vagabond" (Ltr 269.3) alluding to the sharp remark of the papal Nuncio Sega, but even before that there had reached her the suspicions of the nuncio Ormaneto and the rumors spread that she was exceeding the norm given by the Apostle Paul about the enclosure of women "of which I was recently told and had even heard before" (ST 19). Despite all this, Teresa traveled thousands of kilometers in covered wagon, or on the back of a mule or horse, or on foot, staying on the road until the eve of her death, on her last journey from Burgos to Alba. Before a fact of such magnitude a question imposes itself: why did Teresa a contemplative and mystic decide on this course of action?

2. The whys of the vagabond founder. Basically she refers to the whys at the time she is telling about her travels as founder in the *Book of Her Foundations*: a / the first impulse sprang from the life itself that the group of pioneers at St. Joseph were living: In considering the real value of these souls and the courage God gave them to serve and suffer for him, certainly not a characteristic of women, I often thought that the riches God placed in them were meant for some great purpose. What was later to come about never passed through my mind "(F. 1. 6). b / Then toward the end of the five-year

period the ardent words of the missionary Padre Maldonado, who had spoken to the nuns about the Indies and the millions of souls that were being lost there, came as a shock to the group, Words that gave rise to a special indecisiveness in Teresa's soul and were endorsed by an interior voice: "Wait a little daughter and you will see great things. Although I couldn't figure out how it would be possible, I remained very much consoled and certain that these words would prove true" (F 1.8). c / In the third place there came not only an endorsement but an express command from the general of the order, Padre Rubeo: "he gave me very extensive patent letters so that more monasteries could be founded . . . I did not ask for these, rather the thought seemed to me foolish because a useless little woman as helpless as I. . . But when these desires come to a soul it is not in its power to put them aside "(F 2. 3-4). Words that are foolish or crazy synthesize in Teresa's narration the uproar among the people and the opinion of the Bishop of Avila before the project of this first *exit*.

3. All of this created in the soul of the founder an option which she will hold firmly to the rest of her life and which she herself ratified various times in the account about her *Foundations*: "Fear of the hardship involved never prevented me from making a foundation even though I felt strong aversion to the traveling . . . And I considered for whose service it was made and reflected that in that house the Lord would be praised and the Blessed Sacrament reserved . . . This is a special consolation to see one more church, particularly when I recall the many that the Lutherans are suppressing. I don't know what trials, however great, should be feared if in exchange something so good comes about for Christianity" (F. 18. 5; cf no. 4). It follows clearly that her motive in depth is not merely Carmelite, but ecclesial and Christological and that Teresa feels herself exceeding and transcending herself by this impulse.

4. Getting Started. We have about this second foundation

two direct and complementary accounts: that of Teresa in her *Foundations, ch. 3;* and that of her collaborator, Julián de Avila (*Biografía de la Santa:* Madrid 1881, pp 249-257). Once she had decided to make the foundation, Teresa sent to Medina Julián de Avila to prepare the terrain. He got in touch with the Bishop Don Pedro González de Mendoza and organized in the town a solemn affidavit (a juridical statement, he calls it) in which important personages favored the foundation: the banker Simón Ruiz, three Jesuit Fathers, the merchant Diego de León , the governor of the town, and several more deponents. They are questioned as to whether the foundation of a monastery for nuns like these would be useful and beneficial to the city. Having obtained this affidavit, Julián rented some houses that were very expensive ("obliging me to pay for rent 51.000 maravedis a year. . . although the Mother did not have 50 maravedis when I took the houses"). Having returned to Avila he presided over the retinue of nun founders, seven in all: "three or four covered wagons with the nuns and clothing and other select things," and he on horseback. Halfway on their journey they were surprised by learning that the renter withdrew the house, and before the humiliating alternative of returning to Avila or continuing on at every risk, Teresa, with the fortuitous advice of Padre Báñez, chose to proceed; She avoided visiting the Bishop Don Alvaro and in passing she managed to rent another house in miserable living conditions. She set out again on her journey and arrived in Medina at midnight, she solicited help from the Carmelite friars and then the group of founders met the people "we were all so loaded down, that it seemed we were gypsies who had robbed some church, for certainly if we met the police they would have been obliged to bring us all to jail" (Julian de Aviila, p. 253). More details about how the enterprise unfolded can be seen in Teresa's account in *F. 2 and 3*.

5. An important detail: the Eucharistic episode. It is the most

pathetic moment in Teresa's account (nos. 10-12). It is situated in the full context of the times and highlights Teresa's exquisite Eucharistic sensitivity. The group of founders finds itself in the commercial Medina of that century, in its full mercantile and noisy festivity. Called together for the Medina holidays, there passed through the town merchants from places and mentalities antagonistic to each other. Only a few months after (January 1568), the profanation of the Eucharist in Alcoy stirred up a popular religious sentiment in the whole of Spain. In this social and religious climate, Teresa realized that she has enthroned the Blessed Sacrament almost in the street without any protective barrier. And so she keeps vigil day and night fearful that the guards she had hired to watch the Blessed Sacrament in the dilapidated entrance way that served as a church might fall asleep or become distracted ."When I recall this affliction and some others that I have had in the course of making these foundations, it doesn't seem to me that bodily trials, even though great, are anything in comparison" (F. 3.11).

6. A wave of expansion. It is here in Medina where the idea of completing her work as founder with a branch of discalced Carmelite friars took shape. This idea also germinated within her during the five years in Avila. From Avila Teresa wrote to the Father General– who was on his return trip to Rome – and on 10 August she obtained from him the license to start this new sector of her Carmel. The general Rubeo answered from Barcelona, directed the license, not to Teresa, but to the provincial and the prior of the Carmelite monastery in Avila. She received notice of this patent while she was in Medina. And so, in the recently established Carmel in Medina, she captured for her work her first great follower, the young Fray Juan de Santo Matía, the future St. John of the Cross: "I praised our Lord. And when I spoke with this young friar, he pleased me very much. . . . He promised me he would remain *"* [for he was thinking of leaving

the Carmelites to join the Carthusians] "as long as he wouldn't have to wait too long. When I saw that I had two friars to begin with, it seemed to me the matter was taken care of" (F 3.17).

Thus this first exit not only opened the way to her travels as a founder, but also brought the project to completion in the person of Fray John of the Cross.

35. Duruelo: The First Foundation Of Discalced Carmelite Friars

1. The successful completion of Duruelo, the first monastery for discalced Carmelite friars was due above all to Fray John of the Cross. Nonetheless it is not with his achievement that we are dealing with here. We are interested only in the intervention and contribution of Teresa, keeping in mind that her condition as a woman put a limit on her possibilities for action in the promotion of a monastery for friars. She gives an account of the entire episode, the project as well as the execution in the *Book of Her Foundations* (F 2 & 13-14). .Unfortunately, none of her letters to the pioneers of Duruelo have come down to us (see only Ltr 13).

2. Teresa's initiative. The original idea to found the discalced friars is due to Teresa and the bishop, Don Alvaro de Mendoza. It arose in the recently founded Carmel of St. Joseph as a duplication of St. Joseph's. Teresa had the idea that they would provide spiritual assistance to the thirteen pioneer Carmelite nuns and if there were more monasteries founded for nuns (F 2.5). And according to her, it was the Bishop of Avila, Don Alvaro who proposed the idea to the Father General, Rubeo, during his stay in that city. But the proposal was not accepted by Rubeo. He wanted to do it, but the idea would not be accepted by the order. And since the idea continued to boil in her head, Teresa wrote to the General in the first days of August 1567, repeating her request: "In the letter I begged him for this permission as best I knew how, giving him the reasons, even though he was anything but inclined to the idea" (F 2.5; 13.6).

3. But Rubeo answered right away (10 August) with a wonderful letter. He approved the project and appropriated the idea for the most part. He submitted the execution to the two provincial superi-

149

ors, the actual one and the preceding one. And at the same time he extended a lineal program for the two licit :monasteries: they will be and will be called contemplative Carmelites, they will live with complete reformation and a regular life consecrated to the divine worship, with prayers and meditations and other spiritual exercises and also helping their neighbor when the occasion arises (MHCT 1, 69-70). Rubeo's document was addressed to the two provincials. No mention is made of Teresa. But it reached her hands quickly ."From there [Barcelona} "he sent me the permission for the foundation of two monasteries"(F. 2. 5). And she obtained quickly the indispensable permission of the superiors of Castile.

4. Selection and preparation of the founders. In Medina where she received the patent letter from the General, Teresa then won over the two first candidates: the prior of the Carmel for friars in Medina, Antonio de Heredia and the young Fray Juan de Santo Matía, the future St. John of the Cross. She quickly appraised the two: she highly esteemed the first "although" [she was]"not completely satisfied." On the other hand, Fray John from the first moment they met pleased her very much. To Fray Antonio she proposed that "for a while he prepare by putting into practice the things he would be promising. " It was not so for Fray John of the Cross. She brought him with her to the foundation in Valladolid that he might learn from close up the way of life of the Carmelite nuns in that foundation ."He was so good that I, as least, could have learned much more from him than he from me." She taught him *"about our way of life so that he would have a clear understanding of everything, whether it concerned mortification or the style of both our community life and the recreation we have together "* And she stressed that the important thing was that he understand well "the style of life of the nuns "(F 13.5).

In the mind of Teresa, the style of life is precisely the point of connection between the two groups. With a clear awareness that what the friars were to learn from the nuns was that the grounds on which both friars and nuns were to base their lives was the rule, *"and if monasteries of nuns were to be founded that there be friars observing the same rule."*

5. The little place called Duruelo. Teresa visited Duruelo personally two times, without mentioning its name but referring to it as the *"little place of very few inhabitants."* So lost and so remote, that she and her companions on the trip spent a torturous, long and stuffy day in June of 1568 trying to locate it. In Duruelo she already had at her disposal a farmhouse that had been given to her by an Avilan gentleman Rafael Mejía. She arrived there accompanied by a Carmelite nun from St. Joseph and the chaplain Julián de Avila. The two remained almost terrified by the project of converting the miserable farmhouse into a monastery. Teresa, on the other hand, became an intuitive schemer "I figured out that the entrance way could serve as the chapel, the loft as the choir, which would adapt well, and the room for sleeping" (F 13.3).

6. She proceeded on her way from Duruelo to Medina, where she proposes to the two candidates the hard reality they were facing. And again her evaluation of Fray John of the Cross: "although he is small, I know that he is great in the eyes of God. . . . he is wise and just right for our way of life. I believe our Lord has called him for this task" (Ltr 13.2).

7. Teresa made a second visit to Duruelo three months after the foundation. It was founded on 28 November 1568. This new visit by Teresa was made at the end of February still in full winter. By this date Rubeo had already congratulated the prioress of Medina for the foundation: "I would like to know if the two monasteries of contemplative Carmelites friars have been founded to serve the needs of these houses" (Letter 1 August 1569). In her recent visit to Duruelo, Teresa noted the extremely harsh way of religious life recently begun

in the farmhouse, the two hermits in their separate corners, the snow on their habits at dawn, the good that they were doing in the surrounding villages: "I couldn't thank our Lord enough for the way they were living, I experienced the greatest interior joy, for it seemed to me that I saw a beginning that would be of much benefit to our order and service to our Lord" (F 14.11).

8. Did they live in Duruelo according to Teresa's constitutions? It is difficult to determine which statutes ruled the life of those first discalced friars. According to Teresa's initial project, they should be ruled by the primitive rule adopted for the monasteries of nuns (F2.5).Then when Rubeo granted permission for the foundation, he prescribed expressly for the future contemplative Carmelites that they live according to the ancient constitutions, without any further specifications. We don't know if this order took effect. On the other hand, the most relevant fact is that at Duruelo they had the constitutions of the nuns of St. Joseph, at least as a point of reference in organizing the life. One of the pioneers, probably Antonio Heredia, transcribed almost completely the text of Teresa's constitutions at St. Joseph, restyling them by changing the feminine gender to masculine and adapting them to the demands of his own clerical community. The new draft, improvised and full of corrections and hesitations reached the hands of the Father General in Rome, where it is still conserved. We don't know whether it was in force in the farmhouse in Duruelo. Yet it highly indicates the fact that its first dwellers not only connected with the legislation established for the Carmel of St. Joseph, but transcribed and worked on it in view of a possible adoption of the text.

With that, Duruelo connected with the very first Teresian ideal. Not only that, but it acquired a twin-like connection with the Carmel of St. Joseph.

36. Five More Foundations In Castile And La Mancha:

Malagón - Valladolid - Toledo - Salamanca - Alba de Tormes

1. In the year 1570 Teresa decided not only to continue making foundations but to write the history of each foundation. Three years later she began *The Book of Her Foundations*. Giving an account in writing of the beginning of each Carmelite foundation served to raise to a spiritual act her mission as founder. And this served as well to refer in detail and in chronological order to the milestones of this itinerary, in such a way as to give evidence of the unity and continuity of her work. She concludes them - the deed and the book - just a few months before her death. Reading the *Foundations* is indispensable for knowing about the work and thought of the founder. Here and in the following themes we are interested only in pointing out the specifics of each step and the growing process of experiences that were refashioning Teresa's thought as she went along founding.

2. The Foundation of the Carmel in Malagón. It was the same year as the foundation in Duruelo, 1568. Malagón was a town in Guadalajara. under the dominion of Doña Luisa de la Cerda in whose palace in Toledo Teresa had prepared and almost brought about her first foundation. Now it is the Toledan lady who urges her to make a foundation in a small and poor town like Malagón, not in a city like Avila or Toledo. In the palace of Doña Luisa, Teresa had previously met the Andalusian founder, María de Jesús, and for their future foundations both of them had opted for total evangelical poverty prescribed, according to them, by the Carmelite Rule. Teresa tells of this practice of poverty as an integral part of her new ideal in the account of her *Life* (ch. 35) and also in her *Way of Perfection* (ch. 2). She hastens to obtain a brief from Rome ratifying this addition of

poverty to her ideal.

3. Now, in her trip from Medina - Alcalá - Toledo - Malagón, Teresa makes a stop in Alcalá de Henares and visits the Carmel founded with extreme rigor and poverty by her Andalusian friend. It seems as though the rigor and style of poverty introduced in this Carmel did not convince Teresa. In setting up the program for her new foundation she changes her criterion, abiding instead by the orders of the Council of Trent and the council of theologians. In fact she founds the Carmel of Malagón with an income, expressly with a "comfortable income," so that it would be sufficient for the survival of the community. She formulates her new criterion: "I am always in favor of monasteries being either completely poor or maintained in such a way that the nuns will not need to beg from anyone for their needs " (F 9.3). This will be from here on Teresa's criterion.

4. The Carmel of Valladolid: 1568. A shorter and less compli-cated trip, Teresa accepted the offer of a brother of the bishop, Don Alvaro, and founded a Carmel in Valladolid on the outskirts of the city, "about four leagues." She hadn't changed her criterion about preferring the city to the open space. She made this foundation there with the hope of moving as soon as possible within the city confines. She brings about this move as soon as possible thanks to the donation of Don Alvaro's sister. She had made the foundation along the Rio de Olmos in August of 1568 assisted by Fray John of the Cross. The move to the city was made in February 1569. In Valladolid there entered the Carmelites a very young woman from the high nobility named Casilda de Padilla, the daughter of the governor of Castile. It was a vocation with a surprising twist. Teresa was blinded for a moment by the almost magical brilliance of the episode. She dedicated two chapters of her book of *Foundations* (10 & 11) to Casilda and mentions her numerous times in her correspondence. Yet she will have to become disillusioned when Casilda abandons Carmel for motives similar to those of her

entry. It was then that Teresa wrote: "God deliver me from those all-powerful lords with their strange reversals" (Ltr 408. 3).

5. The Foundation in Toledo. It was the year following Duruelo and Valladolid : 1569. Teresa knew well the city and its religious situation since 1561, although she never alludes to the noisy sequestration of Archbishop Carranza at the hands of the inquisition, a sequestration that happened only a couple of years before 1569. Teresa arrived in the city at the end of 1561, when he was already in prison, and thus the diocese went along without a head. Now when Teresa returned to the city in response to an invitation to make a foundation there, the diocese was ruled by a mediocre governor Don Gómez Tello Girón, who had to grant the necessary permission. Waiting for this permission, Teresa lived days of extreme poverty, despite the closeness of her wealthy friend Doña Luisa de la Cerda. And since Don Tello was procrastinating his giving of the license for a foundation, Teresa decided to confront him bravely telling him a few truths, as we would say today. She added the detail in her story of the foundation that it was the poor young man Andrada, dressed almost in rags, who found a house for her to rent and gave her the keys for the same.

6. Yet in contrast to the episode of the poor Andrada, there arose next another thorny problem. In the Spain of Teresa's century it was normal for a church or monastery to have persons of renowned lineage as patrons. And to them was granted the privilege of burial in the sanctuary. There were none of these people in this case who offered to be patrons for Teresa's future church and for this reason there were some who were embarrassed by her. Even to the extreme that she felt repercussions in her interior life: "the Lord said to me: 'You will grow very foolish, daughter, if you look at the world's law. Fix your eyes on me, poor and despised by the world . . . Are you to be esteemed for lineage or for virtue?" (This concerned the advice

they gave not to grant a burying-place in Toledo to one who did not belong to the nobility (ST 5).

7. Foundations in Salamanca and Alba: 1569-1571. The two poor foundations provided Teresa with new experiences and taught her some things. She refers to them in detail in her *Book of Foundations*. In the student environment of Salamanca, Teresa begins by renting a house in which students were living (it is not clear if they were tenants or just occupying the house), who when Teresa arrived were dislodged in bad humor. She entered the house on All Souls day: "It was the first monastery I founded without reserving the Blessed Sacrament, for I had previously thought that a foundation was not official until the Blessed Sacrament was reserved" (F. 19.3). But what was more serious is that afterward she bought for this Carmel a house from the touchy Pedro de la Banda (28 September 1573) that was an entailed estate and required royal permission for the sale. This was the beginning for Teresa of countless intrigues, abuses of authority, and delays. Nevertheless in 1582, when she is already on her deathbed, she had a long painful debate (lasting more than three hours) about the situation and future of the house (BMC 19, 174-175).

8. On the other hand, the Carmel of Alba was founded in 1571, also this time with the collaboration of Fray John of the Cross. It is the house in which Teresa's mortal remains rest. The money for this foundation was provided by the Salamancan Teresa Layz from the court of the Duke of Alba, a generous person but also stingy. She makes Teresa pay the typical tribute to the meddlesome benefactor. The interference and impertinent demands of Lady Teresa Layz cost Teresa innumerable hardships. Teresa Layz will show her presumed powers even during Teresa's last illness and even in the question of the burial place of Teresa's mortal remains.

37. From Pastrana To Segovia: Teresa And The Princess Of Eboli

1. This is one of the most intense periods in the experience of the saintly founder. A double foundation in Pastrana, 1569, and the erection of the Carmel in Segovia, 1574. A five-year period of full-ness in Teresa's spiritual life: prioress at the Incarnation; spiritual progress under the guidance of Fray John of the Cross, and entry into the highest stage of mystical experience: (ST 31).

2. From this height she had to deal with a woman of the court and of politics, perhaps the most intriguing woman of her century. It was precisely in her task as founder that the two met. On the literary plane, Teresa will dedicate some pages to capturing the entire scene front and back: chapter 17 of the *Book of Her Foundations* speaks of the foundations in Pastrana; chapter 21 refers to the foundation of the Carmel in Segovia. Both accounts were written respectively a short while after the facts, in the year 1576. Before resuming our account of this five-year period, we will refer to these fundamental pages of Teresa's

3. The two foundations in Pastrana. We must remember that in Teresa's time the title of "founder" was attributed as much to the lay person who financed the erection of the religious house as to the one who was its spiritual leader. In the case of Pastrana, Doña Ana de Mendoza, the princess of Eboli, was the financial founder. Teresa was the spiritual founder. They met each other in Toledo, in the palace of Doña Luisa de la Cerda in 1562. Now for a year, Doña Ana was insisting that Teresa come and make a foundation on her property in Pastrana. Knowing that Teresa had just finished a foun-dation in Toledo, she sent without any previous notice her carriage to Toledo so that Teresa might transfer then and there to the town of

Pastrana. Teresa refers to this discourteous episode in *Foundations*, chapter 17. She resists but finally accedes through superior motives. And sets out on the journey. In passing through Madrid she gets to know two Italian hermits and convinces them to join her to enter her Carmel and found a monastery in Pastrana for men at the same time as she is founding for the nuns. The two accept her proposal But once she has arrived in the town of Pastrana, Teresa has to spend a long time in the palace of Doña Ana, and there resist her demands. She is at the point of leaving without making the foundation. In the end the princess, pressured by her husband Ruy Gómez and Teresa, accedes to Teresa's demands. As the prioress of the new foundation, Teresa brings with her from Toledo an exceptional nun, Isabel de Santo Domingo.

4. A little afterward, the two Italians, Mariano Azzaro and Juan de la Miseria, erected the new monastery, not like Duruelo, but in an absolutely eremitical form. They inhabited some caves in a hill surrounding a little shrine to San Pedro. They lived a very austere life, to which unexpectedly they attracted a number of young vocations from the nearby University of Alcalá. Fray John of the Cross had to intervene them to get them to use moderation. The Dominican, Padre Domingo Báñez, also intervened with an urgent letter. Then Teresa herself intervened, imparting a refined lesson on spiritual humanism in her *Response To a Spiritual Challenge*. This challenge was sent by the hermits in Pastrana to the community of the Incarnation where Teresa was prioress at the time. For the moment it was all in vain. Only with the passing of years did this novitiate in Pastrana approach the good Teresian order.

5. The information that hit them like a bomb: the Princess was going to become a nun. On 29 July 1573, Ruy Gómez, Doña Ana's husband, died. And automatically the princess put on the Carmelite habit, got into her carriage and presented herself at the Carmel for

Teresa's nuns in Pastrana. Inevitably they had to open the doors to her. The death of her husband had left hanging financial and urgent family matters, and the princess now a widow and a Carmelite nun, domineering as ever, willingly leapt over every barricade the community had set up, and imposed her own will on the prioress, who for her part could not fail in the laws established by the Council of Trent or the norms of life established by Madre Teresa. Finally, the princess did not resist and returned to her palace in Pastrana not withdrawing in defeat but rather increasing her hostility toward the nuns in her former Carmel. Teresa did not accept this kind of declaration of war. Silently she arranged for a withdrawal and suppressed the foundation. She tells of it without any note of spite or resentment: "Even after the princess discarded the habit and lived in her own house, she caused them trouble. . . . I strove in every way I could, . . . to move the monastery from there" (F. 17.17).

6. The withdrawal to the Carmel in Segovia. It was then Teresa's last year as prioress at the Incarnation in Avila. Accompanied by Fray John of the Cross and the chaplain at St. Joseph's, Julián de Avila, Teresa traveled to Segovia and quickly inaugurated the new Carmel there. The excess of straightforwardness caused her to incur the wrath of the vicar-general, the supreme diocesan authority in the absence of the bishop. And the choleric canon prohibited her to have Mass in the house, suppressesd the Blessed Sacrament and was at the point of putting the good Fray John of the Cross in prison for having celebrated the first Mass.

7. When, finally, the last hurricane of the vicar-general subsided, Teresa sent a message to the prioress in Pastrana and immediately following this, Julián de Avila and Antonio Gaitán, arrived in the village, both gentlemen on horses. Padre Julián himself gives an account, for he acted as the strategist in the withdrawal: "We arrived in Pastrana in the most secret way possible and spoke to the

prioress, who . . . was not careless nor just a little desirous of seeing herself taken out of there. She arranged with someone to provide five carts for the nuns and some furnishings which they had to bring with them.. And having used every care the Blessed Sacrament was consumed by them and having agreed to depart at midnight without the princess knowing anything, although it wasn't kept so secret that it didn't become known that night and a servant or steward sent to tell many things . . .And as we had agreed, so we did, going out in procession climbing a hill until we reached the place where the carts were waiting for us . . ." (*Vida de Santa Teresa* . . . ed. De Lafuente, Madrid 1881, p. 275).

8. Opposite this picturesque account by Padre Julián, is the admirable measure with which Teresa refers to the facts, without a sour word for the princess. From woman to woman, Teresa is totally smooth, good, and restrained. It is sufficient to read the final numbers of chapter 17 of her *Foundations*, which in a few lines sums up what happened during these five years. The suppression of the Carmel took place at the beginning of April 1574.

9. The experience in Pastrana is unique to the life of Teresa. Painful yet enriching. Neither for the nobility nor for politics does Teresa bend her criteria. Not even when, a little afterward, the princess denounces *The Book of Her Life* to the inquisition does the slightest variation in Teresa's spirit show. The new problem of the book once sequestered by the inquisitors follows its course without disturbing the calm in its author's soul. And when the princess, after her last political intrigues, which land her in the prison of Santorcaz, the Mother Founder still remembers her with tenderness (Ltr 344.4).

38. Foundations In Andalusia

1. Two Carmels were founded by Teresa in the Andalusian lands: the first in Beas (Jaen), and the second in Seville. From Andalusia she organized as well the foundation of the Carmel of Caravaca (Murcia: see Ltr. 95), the first Carmel she founded without being present herself. And also at the end of her life, without being present herself, while she is preparing a trip to Burgos, she confided to Fray John of the Cross and Mother Anne of Jesus the foundation of the Carmel in Granada (20 January 1582).

2. But before her trip to the Andalusian lands, Teresa lived through two important events: a) In her admiration for the apostle of Andalusia, the master St. John of Avila, she submits for his approbation *The Book of Her Life*. She arranged for the autograph to be sent to him through her friend Doña Luisa de la Cerda. And she received from him a magisterial letter of approbation signed by him in Montilla, 12 September 1568; b) A little before this approbation there reached her also from the Andalusian lands an invitation to found a Carmel in Segura de la Sierra (Jaén) very much at the beginning of her foundational journeys, when she had still not founded Duruelo. Of the two events in the founder's life we are interested only in the second. We will deal then with:
- a failed foundation in Segura de la Sierra; 1568;
- the foundation of the Carmel in Beas de Segura; 1575
- sorrows and joys in the Carmel of Seville; 1575-1576

3. The effort to make a foundation in Segura de la Sierra: June 1568. It occurred as soon as Teresa returned from the foundation in Malagón. From the valleys of the nascent river Segura in the extreme northern part of the province of Jaén there arrived a formal request

161

from Cristóbal Rodríguez de Moya, a gentleman and merchant from the town of Segura de la Sierra, situated in Andalusia, but at that time under the jurisdiction of the Order of St. James, in the province of Castile. (Teresa did not have faculties to make foundations in Andalusia). Don Cristóbal had three daughters. When one died in May of that year, he proposed to found a Carmel of Teresa's in which the other two daughters might enter, who were actually at the time living a retired life in an improvised beaterio in the town. The Franciscan, Antonio de Segura, the guardian of the monastery of Cadalso de los Vidrios (Madrid) brought this offer to Teresa. But the monastery was to submit, oddly, to the obedience of the Jesuits. Teresa accepted the invitation enthusiastically. She even foresaw the possibility of erecting a house there for the discalced friars (Duruelo had not yet been founded). She accepted everything, except the clause that left the Carmel subject to the Jesuits (Ltr 11). This letter is very confusing though because of interpolations by a forger. In view of Teresa's response, Don Cristóbal changed his mind and decided to found a college operated by the .Society of Jesus.

Neither in the *Book of Her Foundations* nor in the Teresian correspondence does Teresa mention again this failed attempt at a foundation. One thing has remained clear: Teresa decided to found her Carmels only within the Order, as Father General had prescribed.

4. The foundation of the Carmel of Beas. Beas is also a town within the province of Jaén, a few miles distant from Segura. Both of them were very far from Avila, where Teresa resided. What is special about this case is that five or six years after the failure of Segura, the memory of Teresa and her Carmels remained alive. She refers to this in detail in chapter 22 of her *Foundations*. Reading this chapter is indispensable for getting an idea of the complexity of the foundation, the difficult situation in which Teresa found herself, pressured by the young women of Beas: the attitude of the Visitator, Pedro

Fernández, who was against new foundations; resistance by the hierarchy of the Order of St. James; personal recourse to the king, and so on. Let us separate out three details: a) while she was in Beas the hard news reached Teresa that *The Book of Her Life* was sequestered by the Inquisition; b) among all the actors in the foundational scene emerges the figure of the local founder, Catalina de Jesús, whose autobiography is so special that it was transcribed by St. John of the Cross; c) and here in Beas, Padre Jerónimo Gracián and Teresa met each other for the first time.

5. But the most notable feature in the foundation of the Carmel in Beas is the presence of Fray John of the Cross, exercising his ministry as spiritual teacher. Fray John arrived in Beas a little while after he had escaped from his cramped prison cell in Toledo. For the first time he undertook systematically the spiritual direction of a Teresian Carmel. He came weekly from El Calvario, and somewhat less often from Baeza. He quickly overcame the fears of the prioress, Anne of Jesus, who will become one of his most advanced disciples. But he took the responsibility as spiritual teacher for the entire community. He wrote spiritual maxims for them and wrote community letters to them, such as the two precious ones that have come down to us. It is the moment in which Teresa wrote of him; "He is a heavenly and divine man. I tell you, daughter, from the time he left and went down there, I have not found anyone in all Castile like him, or anyone who communicates so much fervor for walking along the way to heaven" (Ltr 277.1). In Beas, Fray John of the Cross was the first to realize Teresa's ideal of bringing together the two families of discalced nuns and discalced friars.

6. The Carmel of Seville. To the foundation of this Spanish Carmel Teresa dedicates four long chapters, 23-26, of her *Book of Foundations*, a good indicator of her predilection for this Andalusian Carmel. Moreover she includes here a biographical sketch of Jerónimo Gracián and an account of the reunion with her brothers

and the family members who had returned from America. For all of this we refer our reader to the delightful pages of her *Foundations*. Here we will recall only two of the most powerful experiences lived by Teresa in Seville.

A) She had to submit here to a face to face confrontation with the inquisition, which knocked on the doors of her Carmel. Apart from the nuisance the pompous show of the visitators caused the community, Teresa came out of the meeting in a cheerful manner. Rather, she quieted down the bothersome visitators. And on this occasion she left us two jewels from her pen, *Spiritual Testimonies 58 & 59*.

B) Much more painful was the other episode: the obscuring of her relations with the admired general, Rubeo. While she was in Seville, he celebrated in Piacenza the general chapter, from which there came to Teresa the categorical order to retire to a Carmel and not to make any more foundations. Unfortunately he was informed in a bad manner by the provincial of Castile, Angel de Salazar: who said that I came [to Seville] an apostate and that I was excommunicated (Ltr 102.15). From Beas and Seville she wrote to the Father General a half dozen letters. Without any response (Ltr 271.1), despite her repeated declarations of filial love and total submission. Yet she obeys. She returns to Castile, having decided to retire to the Carmel in either Toledo or Avila. From Avila she sent him nonetheless an extensive memorial (October 1576), which never reached Rubeo, who died a little before. In receiving knowledge of his death, she wrote to Gracián: "I greatly grieved over the news written me about our Father General. I feel deep sorrow, and the first day cried and cried without being able to do otherwise" (Ltr 272.1). It was, without doubt, one of the great sufferings of her life, not to have reestablished good relations with the Father General: "He was induced into becoming displeased with me, which was the greatest trial I suffered in the work of these foundations" (F 28..2).

39. The Foundations Cease: A Period Of Hard Trial

1. At the age of about 62 years Teresa goes through a dark night as a founder. She suspends her task as founder during four years: 1576-1579. Yet her inaction is only apparent. Apart from the mental torture during the cessation of her task as founder, Teresa lives an almost frenetic existence in putting the Carmels she had founded out of harms way. She recounts this in resuming her work in 1579, *The Book of Her Foundations*, chapter 28. 1-7. According to her the most intense moments of this period of true night happened thus:

- The foundation in Seville, made more than four years ago, was the last " because of the great persecutions that broke out unexpectedly against the discalced friars and nuns . . Now the whole undertaking was at the point of collapse" (F 28.1).

- These Fathers informed our Most Reverend Father General in such a way that even though he was a holy man and had given permission for all the monasteries. . . . He was urged to oppose strongly any new foundations among the discalced friars. Toward the monasteries of nuns, he was always well disposed. . . . [But] he was induced into becoming displeased with me" (F 28.2).

- " A holy nuncio [Ormaneto] died . . .who esteemed the discalced. Another nuncio [Sega] arrived who it seems had been sent by God to test us in suffering. . . ".(F. 28. 3).

- "The new nuncio appointed a superior from the cloth to visit the monasteries of our friars and nuns . . ." (F 28.5).

- "Since our Catholic king, Don Philip, knew of what was going on and was informed of the life and religious observance of the discalced, he took the initiative to favor us.. He did not want our cause to be judged by the nuncio alone but gave him four counselors, responsible persons, three of whom were religious, so that our rights would be carefully looked after" (F. 28.6).

   - Finally, in this storm at sea, Teresa feels herself personally implicated: "It seemed to me that I was the cause of this storm, and that if they would have thrown me into the sea, as they did Jonah, the tempest would have stopped" (F 28.5).

There were five persons, according to her, involved in this storm: Father General, Juan Baptista Rubeo, the two papal nuncios, the king Don Philip, and Teresa herself. One would have to add some more sufferers, such as Fray John of the Cross, Gracián, the Carmelite nuns.

   2. We can fill in this picture with some concrete chronological data. Only those that affect Teresa year by year.

   a) The starting point, 1575. Being already in Andalusia, Teresa in person and in the *Book of Her Life* comes under investigation by the inquisition. Almost at the same time the order's general chapter in Piacenza reproves and sanctions the discalced Carmelites. A little afterward the same general chapter notified Teresa of a double order: that she should cease making foundations and retire to one of her Carmels. On 18 June 1575, she wrote a long letter: it is an unblemished snapshot of the moment (Ltr. 83).

   b) Things get worse in 1576. Gracián is named visitator by the nuncio Nicolás Ormaneto. He convokes a chapter of discalced Carmelites in Almodóvar and he undertakes a visitation of the Andalusian Carmelites. With great (and well founded) fears on the part of Teresa. In Avila, the first imprisonment of Fray John of the Cross, who is quickly freed thanks to the intervention of the nuncio Ormaneto. Teresa also refers this matter to Father General (Ltr 102.16).

   c) The tensions increase in 1577: On 18 June the nuncio Ormaneto died. Foreseeing the imminent confusion and disturbance of her Carmelites, Teresa, on her return to Avila, turns the community of St. Joseph over to the obedience of the order (July-August). In October she was reelected prioress of the Incarnation, but she didn't take possession of the charge. At this same time, the first days of December, Fray John of the Cross was taken prisoner. Teresa wrote immediately to the king asking for his liberation (Ltr. 218). But in vain. Fray Juan will continue to be imprisoned until halfway through August 1578. This letter of hers to the king is symptomatic.

d) Extreme tension in 1578. The new nuncio, Felipe Sega, deposes and insults Gracián, knowing that he had been named visitator by his predecessor Ormaneto. In August Fray John of the Cross fled from prison. The following month, the Father General. Ruebeo, died. The discalced friars after receiving some bad counsel, celebrated a chapter in Almodóvar and elected Fr. Antonio de Heredia provincial (all contrary to the opinion of Teresa (Ltr 273)). As punishment the nuncio annulled what was done and submitted the discalced to the calced provincials. The Andalusian provincial, Diego de Cárdenas, deposed the prioress of the Carmel in Seville, initiated a process full of calumnies against Teresa, and sent it to the court in Madrid. It was a situation of the highest suffering for her because of the penalties endured by her Carmels in Spain, to which she sent maternal letters through different paths. At the end of the year, (December 20, 1578), the little tribunal set up by Sega and the three assessors appointed by the king, pronounced a sentence unfavorable to Gracián, confined him to the college in Alcalá, and prohibited him from communicating with Teresa. Sega knew about the activity of Teresa, yet he did not direct himself to her nor even mention her, rather he ignored her.

e) The final easing of tensions in 1579: Sega annulled his preceding decision and on 1 April named vicar of the discalced friars Padre Angel de Salazar. In April, two discalced friars traveled to Rome incognito for the purpose of promoting a solution (Ltr 290.4).

On 15 July the same Felipe Sega proposed the erection of a separate province for the discalced friars. This separation was decided in Rome the following year with the brief *Pia Consideratione* (June 22 1580). Teresa wrote:"While I was in Palencia, God willed that the discalced Carmelites be separated from the calced. This was done by letting the discalced form their own province, which was all that we were desiring for the sake of peace and tranquility" (F 29.30).

3. More interesting than this polemical crossword puzzle is Teresa's personal life and activity during these four stormy years :

a) She lives an intense spiritual life (SpT 34-64) and she traveled many kilometers, from Seville to Avila with stops in Malagón and Toledo.;

b) She suffered special attacks on her health: in February of 1577, she suffered a most serious crisis which prevented her from writing anything by hand. For several months she had to dictate her letters. At Christmas time of that year, she dislocated her arm and she couldn't use it until May when a bonesetter came from Valladolid to reset it. In the summer of 1580 she fell victim to the famous "universal flu" that left her without strength; this same year her brother Lorenzo died.

c) at the same time her activity with the pen is intense: during these four years, she wrote *The Interior Castle* and *On Making the Visitation;* she organized the *Spiritual Challenge,* she prepared the first edition of *The Way of Perfection,* she wrote an infinity of letters: 220 have reached us from this four-year period, some of which are of great value, for example, the three letters to the General, the ones addressed to Don Teutonio, or to the Jesuit Pablo Hernández expounding on the mess she got herself into, more than 60 letters to Gracián, and those addressed to the Carmel in Seville on the occasion of the absurd process.

40. Teresa Resumes Her Foundations. The Last Cycle: Villanueva De La Jara - Palencia -Soria -Burgos

1. In 1576 by order of her superior Teresa suspended the task of founding Carmels. She benefited by the pause to write the history of her recent foundations: Alba, Segovia, Beas, Seville, Caravaca: eight chapters (20-27), in all some seventy pages of manuscript of her *Foundations.* Three years later (1580) she resumes the double task of founder and writer. As she founded new Carmels, she wrote their history. It makes up the final sixty pages of her manuscript: four chapters, one for each foundation, drafted during the last three years of her life (1580–82). The reading of these last fruits of her life are indispensable. In this theme we will look closely at a handful of final experiences harvested by the founder.

2. The joyful experience of Villanueva de la Jara. She had never been so resistant to a foundation offered to her: almost four years of long requests arrived from the town. In compensation, the account of the foundation ends with a flaming doxology: "May it please His Majesty that he be always served in it, and may all creatures praise him forever and ever, amen."

3. The new foundation was made at the hermitage of St. Anne, built about twenty years before by a former Carmelite friar. Nine fervent young women from the town had withdrawn there. For more than two years they had persisted in asking Teresa to come and found a Carmel for them there. To their requests were added those of the lords of the town council, the prestigious Canon Ervías, and the discalced friars of La Roda, which was near the hermitage, among whom was the most insistent of all, one of the founders of Duruelo, Padre Antonio de la Heredia. But still Teresa resisted for a number of reasons

169

which she enumerated in detail: "It seemed to me that for the following reasons it would have been completely unsuitable to accept this foundation: First, there were so many women, and it seemed to me it would be very difficult for them to adapt to our way of life when they were used to their own" (F 28.9). In the end she conceded, pressured by an inner voice, which included the infusion of a desire to make the foundation personally. Accompanied by four nuns and a number of friars from La Roda, she entered the town in a procession, welcomed by all the people. Then she had the opportunity to verify the quality of the nine candidates who had been waiting and who quickly adapted to the lifestyle of her Carmels. It was the first time that Teresa had an experience of this kind. In a month she was able to return to Toledo leaving the new community in full splendor.

4. The initiative of two friendly bishops: the Carmels of Palencia and Soria. The two bishops were Don Alvaro de Mendoza and Don Alonso Velázquez the former had been the patron of the first Teresian Carmel having been bishop of Avila. Now he was bishop of Palencia (from 1577). The second knew Teresa in Toledo as master at the cathedral. There he was her preferred confessor (1576). Now he had been bishop of Osma (Soria) for about two years (1578), and soon he will be appointed bishop of Santiago de Compostela.

5. Invited by the bishop, Don Alvaro, to found a Carmel in Palencia, Teresa did not delay as she did in her recent foundation in Villanueva, and quickly set out on the journey. But in Valladolid, she was struck down by the epidemic of the century, the famous universal flu, which left her exhausted of energy and spirit: "When I reached Valladolid, I was struck down with so bad an illness that they thought I was going to die. I felt so listless and so unable even to think of doing anything . . ." (F 29.1).

It seemed she had become a complete coward. But the inner voice intervened as it did before so that it not only made her decide to go, but even made her desirous of going personally to Palencia. She arrived on 28 December 1580. There Don Alvaro awaited offering her every favor. And soon she discovered the quality of the people of Palencia: "The people are among the most gentle and noble that I have ever seen" (F. 29. 11) ."I would not want to fail to sing the praises of the charity that I found in Palencia both in general and in particular. Truly, it seemed like being in the early church " (F 20.27). She stayed only five months in the city and without giving herself any rest, she set off to found the Carmel in Soria..

6. Don Alonso Velázquez called her to Soria. For the new Carmel a distinguished lady of the Navarran nobility, Doña Beatriz de Beamonte, offered her palace. But it was the bishop who. programmed a journey like one Teresa had never before experienced. Five days in a first-class carriage, with a stop in Burgo de Osma and good inns. On arriving in Soria the bishop extended his blessing from the window of his house, and Doña Beatriz received them with all honors and offered them her own palace. Among the ladies in the family of Doña Beatriz there was another distinguished woman from the Navarran nobility, Doña Leonor Ayanz, who was immediately fascinated by Teresa and quickly entered the Carmel as a nun, in a gesture that still today leaves us perplexed, or really astonished. Teresa had to convert the palace into a monastery. It was impossible for her to do this in the few days she remained in Soria. She left it to the charge of another distinguished Carmelite, Catalina de Cristo. Before undertaking her return journey, she left a memorial in writing with precise counsels about the adaptation of the building even to the detail of the night lamp: "always after they leave Matins, they should light a lamp that will remain burning until morning for it is very dangerous to be without light . . . " In Soria she wrote a last and precious snapshot for us of the state of her soul (ST 65).

7. The final gesture: foundation of the Carmel of Burgos

(1582). The tables are turned. In Burgos. Teresa collides head-on with the opposition of the bishop. She arrived in the city in the midst of winter. It had been a long and difficult journey from Avila, where she said goodbye to Fray John of the Cross. On the outskirts of Arlanzón, they met with dangerously muddy roads. They paused out of devotion before the Santo Cristo of Burgos on the outskirts of the city. They received a cordial welcome in the house of Doña Catalina de Tolosa. This was followed by the painful lodging in the cramped quarters of the Hospital of the Conception. Yet the fatal counterproof came from the hostility of the archbishop, Don Cristóbal Vela, who was himself from Avila, from near the family of the Cepedas, a brother of Teresa's baptismal sponsor. Don Cristóbal saw no problem with his idea of Teresa, along with her nuns, returning as soon as possible to Avila. With empty hands ."And with such good roads!," Teresa exclaimed. Finally it seems the archbishop surrendered, but on the basis of economic conditions that Teresa had to rescind secretly rather than abandon the city. She had arrived on 26 January 1582 after traveling the entire month in a covered wagon. She left the city six months later 28 July 1582. In Burgos she received support from cordial and generous men and women friends. She continued to be seriously ill, but in her life she had the continual and self-sacrificing medical assistance of doctor Aguiar. Nonetheless, she needed the strength of the inner voice that spoke to her at least five times. Before leaving the city "forever" she enjoyed days of calm in which she wrote slowly and lovingly the history of the foundation, one of her most precious narrations, the last twenty-four pages of *The Book of Her Foundations.* In this her last foundation she experienced, as in the first, the force of adversity.

V
Cultural And Spiritual Formation

St. Teresa is a spiritual teacher and Doctor of the church. If here we are interested in her human and religious formation, it is as a premise to the exercise of her magisterial and evangelizing mission. To this end we survey the different stages of her formative process, from childhood to maturity.

41. Learning At Home: Reading And Writing

1. We have already explored the cultural atmosphere of her times (Theme 4 and 5), as well as the cultural level of the Cepeda-Ahumada family (Theme 18). Both aspects conditioned Teresa's formation. In the context of her century, she does not belong to the select group of *learned girls,* more or less concentrated around the court. Teresa belonged to a middle class social group of erudite merchants surrounded by illiteracy. Teresa's family did not belong to this group of illiterates. In the Cepeda-Ahumada family books were read.: "my father liked to read good books; and he had them in the vernacular so that his children could read them." Teresa stands out as the most cultivated of the group, not only by the fact of her literary production but for her doctrinal knowledge, literary and even artistic, and for her broad horizons, geographic and social. Nonetheless, Teresa is self-taught. She did not receive – as far as we know – an academic formation. Step by step she went about acquiring on the basis of reading and social contacts a specifically religious culture, although open to other horizons. In this present theme we are interested in the beginning of this training at the dawn of her childhood.

2. The first readings. In the Cepeda-Ahumada family this training was relatively precocious. We know of it because Teresa began to read at age six or seven, and because all of her brothers and sisters made able use of the pen, which was exceptional in that environment of a high percentage of illiterates. In previous themes we pointed out that the initiation of the child in well-to-do families, as was Teresa's family, had a twofold: basis: the primer and doctrine. As for the primer, she learned to read and write. These were small books for the teaching of a child and of elemental content. They were reduced to teaching the

alphabet, spelling and the norms of writing. On the other hand, the doctrine taught the rudiments of the Christian faith, the prayers, .the commandments, the sacraments, vices and virtues, the church, and the most elemental truths about the Christian life. At times they included the themes of the primer. Later all of this was, with the catechism, or with the art of making a good confession, explained in the so-called *Confessionals*. There is no doubt that these were the channels of Teresa's early Christian and human formation, probably at the hands of her mother and perhaps her older sister María. And since the texts of the *Doctrines* were usually expressed in musical verse, they were at the same time the occasion for educating the ear and good musical taste, even though the child Teresa made more progress in the art of versifying than in that of singing: she always preferred to listen to the singing of others.

3. Her first readings. It seems certain that Teresa's first readings – not those imposed but that were a matter of free choice – were encountered in the *Flos Sanctorum* of her time. The *Flos Sanctourm* was a late medieval book, written in Latin by Giacomo di Voragiine, translated frequently into the romance languages and edited very many times in the incunabular or post-incunabular series. The content was narrative, presumably historical, in reality legendary and imaginative, very widely spread among readers, dedicated to the saints whose lives were being narrated there. Definitely, for children, they were texts that seemed moralizing by our standards and for that reason suitable for reading by children. The copy used by Teresa was with all certitude printed in Seville in 1520, entitled: *Legends of the Saints (vulgarly called Flos Sanctorum) now newly printed and with much study and diligence explained for the perfection of the truth handed on, and even augmented with the following legends . . .* Among bibliographers of today it is known as the *Flos Sanctorum of Loyola*. It did not appear in the inventory of books drawn up by Don Alonso in 1507. He probably

acquired it around 1521/22 for the group of children that filled his home. It had been translated by the good Aragonese writer, Gaubert Vagad, and printed by one of the best Spanish typographers of the sixteenth century, Juan Varela of Salamanca.

4. Vagad had adapted the book for Spanish readers. He had placed at the beginning a translation of the Passion of Jesus according to the four evangelists (the *Monotéssaron* of Gersón: 16 initial pages). Then he added to the traditional hagiographical anthology some other popular pious pieces, such as the life of St. Anne or that of St. Joseph as well as some of a Spanish flavor, such as: "The history of how the chapel of the Blessed Virgin . . . Santa Maria del Pilar of the city of Zaragoza was built" or "The life of the glorious king Don Fernando that he lived in Seville" or "The history of the triumph and conquering by king Don Alfonso IX, of the moors in the Navas of Tolosa" or *"The life of San Juan de Ortega."*

5. For his part, the printer *Varela of Salamanca* disseminated alongside the book a series of xylographic sketches (no less than 223), which converted the work into a kind of comic book for children. We don't know which chapters or which biographies Teresa and Rodrigo read: the book consisted of 600 pages, with more than 230 biographies. The two children were certainly impressed by the sketches and the stories that were richly told about the martyrdoms of the saints. They had an impact especially on Teresa: "when I considered the martyrdoms the saints suffered for God, it seemed to me that the price they paid for going to enjoy God was very cheap" (L 1.4). Her reading influenced the effort the two readers made to run off to the land of the moors to have their heads cut off there. In fact, among the sketches in the book were numerous pictures of decapitated saints. Really striking. It is probable also that Teresa leafed through the first pages about the Passion of Jesus, illustrated with twenty wonderful pictures (among them, Jesus in the Garden of Olives), followed by a like portrait of

Jesus in the fantastic *Letter of Pontius Pilate to the Emperor Tiberias Ceasar.* Highly interesting for the children and no less for the adult Teresa.

6. The contribution of this reading to the formation of Teresa the child is without doubt. It was one of the intense memories she had when she wrote her *Life* at the age of fifty. It had motivated her first personal ideas, "the truth I knew in childhood." The work not only familiarized her with reading, despite the difficulty of the medieval style of the book, but introduced her to popular religion, which in her time granted so much importance to the Christian saints. And most of all from the stories of the martyrs she derived her concept of the heroic character of the Christian life, the importance of the *determined determination*, the normality of a possible martyrdom. Many years later she wrote in her own hand in the inside cover of her breviary a point taken from St. John Chrysostom: "It is not only a perfect martyrdom when the blood is spilt, but martyrdom consists also in the true abstinence from sin . . ." An echo of those first readings.

42. Readings In Her Youth

1. Among the characteristic features of Teresa's growth crisis in her passage through youth was the change in her reading. From pious books on the lives of the saints, she passed to profane reading, books of chivalry. Both types were books of phantasy, but much more so the latter, intertwined with arms and love affairs, dragons and knights. Even sometimes they repeat the accounts of the *Flos Sanctorum* such as the celebrated tale about St.Eustacius. Then the intensity and enthusiasm with which Teresa devotes her time to reading them is a good indicator of their influence on her literary formation.

2. The fact of these new readings. She herself refers to them in chapter 2 of her *Life*. "My mother loved books of chivalry . . . We used to read them together in our free time . . . Our reading such books was a matter that weighed so much on my father that we had to be cautioned lest he see us. I began to get the habit of reading these books . . . I started to grow cold in my desires and to fail in everything else. I didn't think it was wrong to waste so many hours of the day and night in such a useless practice, even though hidden from my father. I was so completely taken up with this reading that I didn't think I could be happy if I didn't have a new book '(L 2.1). In sum, her readings were hidden; clearly opposed by her father, not for reasons of swordsmanship, as later by Cervantes, but for moral motives. Teresa had done so with the connivance of her mother and with special enthusiasm day and night to the extreme that if she didn't have a new book she wasn't at rest. And as a final detail, not stated by her in the account of her *Life*, but in later confidences that those readings that she enthusiastically indulged in induced her to write herself a little novel in that style. (Her biographer, Ribera, testifies to this fact and then Gracián endorsed it

with the words: "she herself told me this.") It seems that she wrote this little novel in collaboration with Rodrigo, the same brother with whom she was motivated by her childhood readings to flee to the land of the moors. We are uncertain of just when she wrote her novel, either in the years that preceded the death of Doña Beatriz (d.1529) or that soon followed, sometime between the age of 12 and 16. She mentioned in her *Life*, when she bordered on 50 years old, looking then at this kind of reading through a negative lens: "I understood the harm they did me" (L 4.7).

3. We would be interested in knowing what the books were that Teresa read. Unfortunately, neither she nor the historical sources that we now have give us any title. We have only two clues. Don Alonso in the inventory of his possessions that he made in 1507 mentions expressly the *Gran Conquista de Ultramar*, a huge novel phantasized on an historical base, which begins with Islam and the crusades and introduces the beautiful legend of the *Caballero del Cisne* (*The Knight of the Swan*, one hundred chapters–notes Menéndez Pelayo– surely the most poetic and entertaining), and other interesting stories, such as *Charlemagne and the Sevilian Princesses* or *Baldovín and the Serpent*, and so on. We do not know if during the twenty years Don Alonso would have got rid of this later book or saved it so that it was in the reach of Teresa. This latter seems to be probable. Another clue, which we are offered in her *Life* (27.18), where she describes the ascetical life of Fray Peter of Alcántara: "so weak that it seemed he was made of nothing but tree roots." A similar descriptive touch is found twice *The Adventures of Esplandián* in order to describe an elderly woman, 120 years old in fact, sheltered in her cave in the mountains (chapter 101), "a certain indication of its being read by Teresa," notes M. Bataillon. Nonetheless and despite these two clues in the books of Teresa there is not a trace of the one or the other novel.

4. The insinuation of her words "I didn't think I could be happy

if I didn't have a new book" makes us think of the flood of novels of chivalry that in those years the Spanish press put on the market. According to the monumental *Bibliografía de libros de caballerías castellanos* by D. Eisenberg and C. Marín, there were twenty-one principal editions that appeared between the years 1515 and 1535. With titles as brilliant as *Floriseo;, Clarían de Landanis (*two volumes); *Floramente* de *Colonia; Caballero de la triste figura; Lisuarte de Grecia; Amadís de Grecia; Florambel de Lucea; Florisel de Niquea; Lidamor de Escocia; Ludidante de Tracia; and Tristán el joven.* Undoubtedly a good part of them passed through Teresa's hands. It is impossible to be any more precise.

5. Yet what was their importance in the literary formation of the future writer? Normally fifty or at least twenty of these books enthusiastically read by Teresa in her youth left a good deposit in her mind. It served as an adequate humus for the future sowing of the writer. Undoubtedly, the language as well as the plot of these novels passed into Teresa's mind. We have reliable proof of this in one of her minor writings, *A Satirical Critique*. It was written by her when the fashion was for books of chivalry to be interpreted in a divine mode or called "heavenly chivalry." The Carmelite friar novices in Pastrana, many of them from the university environment of Alcalá, tried a kind of competition in a divine mode. It was around 1572-73 while Teresa was prioress at the Incarnation. The friars in Pastrana sent her and the other nuns a challenge to measure their weapons in the practice of heroic penance. Teresa did not accept this kind of challenge. In her spiritual system penitential practices did not hold first place. But she does answer them in writing, giving a different version of the challenge. Entering the contest you have on the one side P. Gracián and on the other, Fray John of the Cross, a knight of the Blessed Virgin. The one acts as the presider and the other as the adventurer. Teresa herself wrote a response in which she figures moreover as a *master of*

the field and above all she adopts the style and imitates the gestures of the of the books of chivalry: the challenge, provocative voices, sharing the plunder, invitation to come out of the cave and into the field of the battle of life. . .: and as arms, piety and the virtues of the poor nuns in the convent infirmary, and so on. Whoever wins in this field of battle will pass on his victory to the defeated. A whole chivalresque landscape intentionally lowered in tone and given a divine interpretation.

6. It is a minute detail, lost in the forest of Teresian writings, yet it offers a good path for responding to our problem. Certainly those phantasy readings served as a stimulus to Teresa's literary imagination. They made her capable of recourse to images and a facile elaboration of symbols, as much in extending narrative texts as in redacting spiritual themes. Despite the monotony of the chivalresque scenes and settings, those novels were for the future writer a literary apprenticeship, which at the time culminated in the writing of a novel of that kind, but then turned into a latent seedbed for her way of thinking and writing. Details of concrete dependencies have been insisted on, such as those that allude to the great Teresian symbol of the *interior castle* that in depth bears a likeness to the outline of the novels of chivalry: in those novels everything centers around the knight, the lady, and the castle. In the book by Teresa: it centers around God, the soul, and the castle. Yet in reality, there is no likeness whatsoever between the three components of one and the other.

The real contribution of those readings to the cultural growth of Teresa consisted in having awakened her creative fantasy, which then favored the copious sewing of images, types, and symbols throughout the pages of her writings.

43. A Friend Of Good Books

1. "My fondness for good books was my salvation" *(L 3.7)*. The moment came when Teresa passed from novels to serious books. She was at the height of her teens around eighteen years old. Among her new readings a trio stands out, fathers and doctors of the church, St. Jerome, St. Gregory the Great, and St. Augustine. She knew of these three through their biographical sketches presented in the Flos Sanctorum. That Teresa as a young lady confronted the reading of these three giants is all a cultural event. With each one she was at a decisive moment. With St. Jerome she was dealing with the choice of a state in life. She was reading St Gregory the Great's commentary on the biblical book of Job when she was seriously ill. And she was reading St. Augustine during the difficult period of her definitive conversion. Here we are interested in just two facts: a) When did the young read*er* encounter each one? *And b) W*hat did the reading of each author contribute to her?

2. Reading the Letters of St. Jerome . In chapter 3 of her *Life* Teresa informs us of her encounter with the *Letters of St. Jerome*. She had recently come out of her stay at Our Lady of Grace. While she was staying in Hortigosa, her uncle Don Pedro had her read spiritual books to him, although she didn't like reading them. She continued to be sick with fevers and fainting spells. On the psychological plane Teresa was struggling to be gradually more open to a vocation. She engaged "in a battle within herself for three months, forcing herself in this business of choosing a state (L. 3.6), and little by little coming to a "fondness for good books ." The first of these was the *Letters of St. Jerome.*

3. The book bore the title: *Letters of the glorious doctor St. Jerome. Now newly printed and amended, 1532.* It was translated by the baccalaureate Juan Molina and printed in Seville. The translator translated

Jerome's letters in such a way that they constituted a real treatise on the different states of Christian life, beginning with the common and the ecclesiastical state (books 1 and 2), and concluding with the conjugal and the comfortable state (books 6 and 7). What above all interested Teresa probably was the third book on the eremitical or contemplative life and the fourth book which *treats of the virginal state, where the glorious Jerome, as an eye witness, clearly shows his talent.* His letters addressed to Eustochio, the daughter of Saint Paula, are among the most famous, with large autobiographical sketches of the saint, repeatedly alluded to by Teresa. Yet without doubt the letter that most affected her was the first of Book 3, addressed to his friend Heliodoro in a difficult period of being elected bishop. In spite of this, Jerome simply calls out to him to break with everything, that he leave—if necessary—his father and retire to the desert. It is the famous *perge per patrem calcatum* that Molina softens in his translation: "if it be necessary, trampling on all things fly to the standard of the cross." Teresa decides in a similar manner , she makes a choice not for the desert but for Carmel. She gently tells her father. Then in irrevocable terms: "I don't think I would have turned back for anything once I told him . . . I remember clearly and truly that when I left my father's house I felt the separation so keenly that the feeling will not be greater, I think, when I die"(l 4.1). Nonetheless St. Jerome had more influence on her life than on her thought.

4. A reading for her life: *The Morals of St. Gregory.* A total change in reading and scene. Teresa was now a Carmelite nun. She was twenty-four years old and in bed in the convent infirmary. She had been paralyzed for eight months. When she had gradually recuperated, she returned to reading. The *Morals* by St. Gregory the Great. She probably read the book between the ages of twenty six and twenty seven. The two volumes were given to her previously as a spiritual balm to help her support the unbearable sufferings brought about by the cures she underwent in Becedas. The book contained the biblical

story of Job, the saint of patience. It was precisely what St. Teresa needed at the time before she began "to go about on hands and knees" (L 6.2). Nonetheless the scene comes close to the improbable. *The Morals* consist of two huge volumes with a total of over a thousand pages .We can hardly see them placed in the hands of a sick person. To read them would require an enormous effort of will and an outstanding interest in the reading. In this case we are not dealing with a mosaic of letters or a book of fantasy. We are dealing with the first great doctrinal treatise read by her, a medieval book by Pope Gregory the Great (VI-VII c), translated by Alonso Alvarez de Toledo and printed in Seville by Jacobo Chromberger Alemán in 1527. It had for its title T*he Morals of St. Gregory, pope, doctor of the Church.* It contained a moral commentary on the biblical book of Job.

5. Teresa had already had contact with the New Testament in the first pages of the *Flos Sanctorum.* Now for the first time she could read an entire book of the Old Testament, since the commentator transcribes in outstanding characters each verse of the of the biblical text before commenting on it. Teresa recalls it thus: "It greatly profited me to have read the story of Job in St. Gregory's Morals. For it seems the Lord prepared me by this means together with my having experienced prayer, so that I could be able to bear the suffering with so much conformity to his will . . . I kept these words of Job very habitually in my mind and recited them: "since we receive good things from the hand of the Lord, why do we not suffer the evil things?*"* This it seems gave me strength (L. 5.8). The passage quotes to the letter the respective text in the *Morals.* This is a passage that centers on the theme in depth , the problem of evil in his relationship with God. We do not know if Teresa resisted the reading of these more than a thousand pages of the work. But it certainly helped her to think about and accept the suffering,: "all things are passing. . . . patience gains all." But much more than the theme of patience, the acceptance of the will of God will resonate for

Teresa, to which she dedicates entire passages in her *Way of Perfection* (ch. 31) and in the *Interior Castle* (6.9,16 and 7.3.5).

6. Reader and Disciple of St. Augustine. Once again we are in a total change of scene and reading. In the Incarnation Teresa was about to complete twenty years of religious life. She was about 39 or 40 years old. After a period of spiritual crisis, she embarked on a strong battle with herself and lived through the decisive event in her life (L. 27 and 28). A psychological climate highly receptive, when there falls into her hands the book, *The Confessions of St. Augustine* translated by Sebastián Toscano and printed in Salamanca this same year 1554 She refers to it herself: "As I began to read the Confessions, it seemed to me I saw myself in them . . . when I came to the passage where he speaks about his conversion and read how he heard that voice in the garden, it only seemed to me, according to what I felt in my heart, that it was I the Lord called. I remained for a long time totally dissolved in tears and feeling within myself utter distress and weariness" (L. 9. 8). Not only did St. Augustine have an influence on her vertiginous change of life, but he also influenced Teresa's profound thought. He is her teacher of interiority. From him she accepts and repeats the instructions *to seek God within herself.* Also the instructions of asking for him in all things, and those of seeking from him the means of love; "what St Augustine says helped me very much: give me, Lord, what you command and command what you desire" (L 13.3). Teresa will keep these thoughts present in almost all of her books. In her *Life* (40.6), in the *Way of Perfection* (ch. 28), in the *Interior Castle* (4.3.3 and 6.7.9). Apart from the *Confessions* she will find nourishment through other transmitters of the Augustinian thought such as the triptych, the *Meditations, Soliloquies, and* the *Manual. But* perhaps the data most relevant in Teresa's formation is that the account given in the *Confessions* served as a model of style. The evidence for this is in the account of her *Life.* Truly a copy of St. Augustine's autobiographical style.

44. Introduction To
Spanish Spitual Writers

1. St. Teresa fits into the literary current of sixteenth-century Spanish spiritual writers. A flowering *took* place at two different times: the one marked a free and abundant production *before Valdes's Index of forbidden books (1559)*. The other in the second half of the century, was conditioned by the catalogue of the Index. In general Teresa was a reader in the first period and a writer in the second. She was more indebted to Spanish writers than to translations from foreign books. That means that she was formed and grew in the setting of Spanish spirituality, which was plentiful in original works. She was interested above all in books about prayer, which constituted a strong part of this flowering. Here we will look only at those books Teresa cites or alludes to. Although she may have read many more, it is difficult to identify them. We will not follow the chronological order of their appearance in her biography, but will group them in families of writers. For reasons of space we will outline only the elemental date of each one.

2. *Franciscan Authors*

Francisco de Osuna (1492-1541). He was a contemporary of Teresa's. She read with special attention *El Tercer Abecedario (The Third Spiritual Alphabet)* (Seville1527) .This book taught her the prayer of recollection: "I was very happy with this book and resolved to follow that path with all my strength" (L 4.7: around the year 1538). "Taking that book for my master, " she attained to moments of quiet and even union. Thus Osuna was Teresa 's first teacher of prayer.

Bernardino de Laredo (1482-1540). Teresa read the best of his books *La Subida del Monte Sion (The Ascent of Mount Sion)* (Seville 1535 and 1538)* at the beginning stages of her mystical experience. He raised the concrete problem of *'no pensar nada' (not thinking of* *anything),* that is her manner of mystical prayer, beyond all meditation and discourse. Laredo's book clarified it for her. She underlined pages and presented them to her confessors that at the time acted more as her judges than as spiritual teachers (L 23.12). Laredo directed her along the path of the mystical life.

Bernabé de Palma (1469-1532). Teresa read his book *Via spiritus* probably at the same time as she was reading the former by Laredo. From him she cites the theory of *cuadrar la mente (*to adapt *the mind) so* as to arrive at the purely spiritual *(L 22.1).* Yet she doesn't agree with the idea that in order to reach this high degree you must exclude everything corporeal including the humanity of Jesus Christ. Christ is not only the way to the Father but his holy Humanity continues to be according to her the frequent object of the highest mystical contemplation (*IC 6. Ch. 7*).

Alonso de Madrid (1485-1579). In his *Arte de Servir a Dios,* he expounds in an original way the development of the spiritual life. Teresa read it and recommends it for beginners to awaken love in them and help them grow in virtue . . . "a very good and appropriate book for those who are in this state" [of beginners*] (L 12.2).* This is one of the very few instances in which she recommends *a book.*

Alonso de Guevara (1481 -1545), the bishop of Guadix and afterward of Mondoñedo. In his *Oratorio de religiosos (1542)* Teresa will complete her own religious formation, a very broad theme. It was so highly valued by Teresa that she includes him among the Spanish authors recommended in her *Constitutions (2.7).*

San Pedro de Alcántara (1499-1562) is without doubt the Franciscan who had the most profound influence on her. Above all, in an oral way, empathizing with her mystical experience *("I saw that he understood me through experience which was all I needed")* and with her ideals of poverty. Although she doesn't quote from the book it is certain that Teresa read his *Tratado de la oración y meditación (Treatise on prayer and meditation).* She refers in general to all his books in proposing them in her *Constitutions (2.7)* for the select libraries of her Carmels. Already in her *Life* (30.2) she had referred to some small books in the vernacular on prayer that are now popular. (Among the Francsican authors alluded to by her we would have to include St. Clare and Francisco Hevia).

3. Dominican Authors

St. Vincent Ferrer. Although of a previous time, his *Tractatus de vita spirituali* had been translated into Castilian at the beginning of the sixteenth century. Teresa knew the edition of León *(1528)*. She mentions it while lashing out against false raptures (L 20.23).

Domingo Báñez y Pedro Ibáñez. Known by their oral teaching of Teresa, they were also important authors read by her. Domingo Báñez wrote a valuable *Voto* favorable to Teresa's mystical life in the final pages of the autograph of her *Life*. And Pedro Ibáñez wrote two studies – *Dictoamen and Informe* – of which we already spoke in theme 29. Very probably read by her, these works are an endorsement of her mystical experience.

Luis de Granada (1504-1588). Teresa was an enthusiastic reader of many of his works *(Libro de Oración y meditación; Memorial . . ., Guia de pecadores . . .);* she writes to him in praise of his works *(Ltr 82),* and includes his work among those listed in her *Constitutions (no. 8)*.

Diego de Yanguas (1539-1607). Teresa read in 1579 *La Vida de San Alberto* written by him and sent to Portugal that it be published by Don Teutonio when he publishes for the first time the *Way of Perfection (Evora 1582)*.

4. Jesuit Authors

Baltasar Alvarez and Juan de Plaza. To this second we owe almost all of the *Counsels* attributed to Teresa and published among her works for the first time in front of *The Way of Perfection (Evora 1583)*. They had been given to Teresa by Baltasar Alvarez and constitute a series of ascetical counsels.

Rodrigo Alvarez (1523-1587). He is the author of a short but precious little tribute to Teresa's seven dwelling places. He writes it at the end of the autograph of *The Interior Castle*. It was probably read by Teresa in some copy made by María de San José *(Salazar)*.

St. Francis Borgia (1510-1572). It is only probable that Teresa read his book *Obras muy devotas y provechosas* . . . Perhaps it is one of the books sacrificed by her when the *Index of Forbidden Books* was brought out in 1559.

5. Other Authors

San Juan de Avila (1500-1569). As with the former book, it is probable that Teresa read him and had to sacrifice him in 1559. She does not quote him expressly. On the other hand she read his valuable evaluation of *The Book of Her Life* (in a letter written by him a little before his death). Later she became interested in promoting the reading of his *Sermons* (Ltr 380.4).

Carmelite Writers. Teresa knew the writings of Fray John of the Cross (the poem *The Spiritual Canticle)* and of P. Jerónimo Gracián. She doesn't quote any other contemporary Carmelites.

In conclusion: these books are but a small portion of the many read by Teresa. They were for the most part ascetical books. It has been said that in the Spanish religious literature the ascetical predominates enormously over the mystical (P Sainz Rodríguez). In Teresa's contribution a balance is achieved on both planes, although to her is due above all a strong dose of autobiographical mysticism, as for example the clear codification of the whole spiritual process, ascetical and mystical, not from theoretical premises but from empirical data. With that, she brought to Spanish spirituality a good basis for the construction of a spiritual theology.

In a final leap Teresa's contribution to Spanish spirituality is more than what she received from it. Nevertheless, the point of connection with the Spanish spiritual authors of her century was not realized through books and readings, but in an intense living dialogue with the theologians and spiritual writers. We will see this in the following theme.

45. Speaking With Theologians And Spiritual Persons

1. In the second period of her life (1554-1582) Teresa cultivates, more than the reading of books, a dialogue with masters. This dialogue represents the years of her mystical experience as well as those of her task as writer. For these two reasons she has recourse to theologians or *letrados (learned men)*, whether in universities or not, and she welcomes the help of *spiritual persons (los espirituales)*. These spiritual persons she needs to help her grow in her interior life. The theologians she needs to be assured of the authenticity of her experiences. She herself has a clear awareness of these two channels as part of the culture of her century. The theologians put her in contact with university thinking, above all at Salamanca. The spiritual persons put her in contact with the spiritual movements flourishing in Spain before and after Trent. Under this theme we will study the testimony Teresa herself gives regarding both sources.

2. The triple listing in *Spiritual Testimonies 58*. Teresa wrote this testimony in 1576 at the request of two consultors to the Inquisition of Seville, who had intervened in her appearance before the tribunal. They were both Jesuits, Rodrigo Alvarez and Enrique Enríquez. Looking back, she enumerates and qualifies the series of teachers that had assessed her and guaranteed the genuineness of her life and work. Among them, two groups can be clearly distinguished: one *spiritual persons* and the other *theologians*. Chronologically she had recourse first to the *spiritual persons*, but then she believed it necessary, indispensable we might say, to appeal to the knowledge of the second group.

3. In the first series she enumerates ten or eleven qualified Jesuits who assessed her first mystical experiences. She assigns to them by name the quality of honor or of service in the Society. Among them

were *Father Francis Borgia,* the Duke of Gandía, various provincials, and several rectors of colleges (in Salamanca, Cuenca, Segovia, and Burgos). The series culminates with "Doctor Martín Gutiérrez . . ., rector of Salamanca when I spoke with him, and who had died recently in France at the hands of the Huguenots." (There is no mention in the series of her two first assessors, Cetina and Prádanos, referred to in her *Life* chs. 23-24.)

4. In the second series she enumerates another nine Dominican professors. She begins with Padre Vicente Barrón with whom she spoke "before these things," *that is,* before her mystical experiences. And she introduces a series of Dominicans with a definite motive: With the intention (of not being deceived) she began *"*to speak with the Fathers of the glorious Saint Dominic," and she lists professors at Salamanca ("Master Fray Bartolomé de Medina who held the chair of prime at Salamanca and she knew that he had a bad opinion of her because he had heard of these things*").* She lists as well the rector of the college of San Gregorio in Valladolid, the rector of the college in Segovia, and the rector of Santo Tomás in Avila. She mentions especially Padre Báñez "who at the time was in Valladolid, regent of the college of San Gregorio. He was her confessor for six years, with whom she always kept in contact by letter when something occurred. . . (She submitted to him all that she wrote about in The Book of Her Life). He presented it to the Holy Office in Madrid" (ST 58. 8, 12).

5. And as a hinge between the two series, she gives the names of three exceptional assessors: "Fray Pedro de Alcántara, who was a holy man; the inquisitor Soto, then bishop of Salamanca; and Maestro Juan de Avila, a man who understood much about prayer." The list opened like a large fan with the greatest representatives of Spanish religious culture at the time, strangely coming together in it.

6. The list in this *Spiritual Testimony* nevertheless does not present a *closed number.* Unincluded in it, for example are assessors

like Fray John of the Cross (at the time chaplain at the Incarnation for a three-year period) or Padre Jerónimo Gracián, former student at the University of Alcalá, or the older confessors and judges of her at the Carmel of the Incarnation in Avila. With regard to all the Carmelites implicated in Teresa's life and work, there were no valid witnesses before the inquisitorial tribunal to which this list is addressed. Neither could one include in it important figures of the following five-year period, such as Doctor Alonso Velázquez from Toledo, who was aware of the theological currents at Alcalá, or to the former co-disciples of Gracián, Pedro Manso and Pedro de Castro y Nero. The latter was the assessor and last reader of *The Book of Her Life*, when it was still sequestered by the Inquisition. She does not mention in this account her relations with Cardinal Gaspar de Quiroga, the successor of Carranza in the diocese of Toledo. Nor does she mention her first assessors, Daza and Salcedo, or the Dominican Pedro Fernández, or the fiery defender of the American Indians, Alonso de Maldonado.

7. More implicated in Teresa's thought were the immediate destinees of her writings or people related to their composition. Meriting mention apart: a) She wrote *The Book of Her Life* in intermittent dialogue with P. García de Toledo, with whom she carried on an intense dialogue during those years (1561-67), as she herself testifies (L. 34. 6-11). This same P. García was a Dominican not listed among those given in her Spiritual Testimonies 58. b) This same P. García spoke with Teresa about, and was her censor, for the two successive redactions of the *Way of Perfection*, begun at the initiative of P. Báñez. c) On the other hand, a Jesuit named P. Jerónimo Ripalda proposed *The Book of Her Foundations* (Prologue 2), and insisted on her continuing (ch. 27.22 and ch. 29.4). d)Then she submitted this work to the Dominican Diego de Yanguas who previously had mediated in the bad fortune that the Teresian commentary on the *Song of Songs* underwent. e) *On Making the Visistation,* she wrote by order of P. Gracián.

8. Perhaps the most representative case of her relationship with the learned men is contained in the spiritual testimonies that include short accounts of her mystical experiences from 1560 to 1581. Teresa wrote many of them as a reminder for her personal use. On the other hand, others are destined for learned men, such as the two first addressed to the Dominican, Pedro Ibáñez. And S*piritual Testimonies 58 & 59 are addressed to* the Jesuit Rodrigo Alvarez; 36-38 were destined for the Carmelite P. Gracián. And the last of them all, ST 65, probably the most valuable, is addressed to Alonso Velázquez, at the time (1581) bishop of Burgo de Osma. Obviously none of these reports contain a contribution by the learned men or spiritual persons who received them in answer to Teresa. But they are clear indicators of the high level in which the dialogue between the two was carried on.

9. A last piece of information that interests us in the present exposition is that in our golden century Teresa's is the most representative case of the centrality of a person between the two groups, theologians and spiritual persons. We have here a relationship at a profound level, precisely in regard to the mystical fact lived by Teresa. In the multiple series of persons revolving around her were not only representatives of the various currents of spirituality then present in the peninsula, but also exponents of the university focus at Salamanca and Alcalá, and at other theological centers in Castile and Andalusia. For this reason Teresa's mystical life did not evaporate into an abstract or transcendent world, but was incarnated in that world that was most typical of the spirituality and theology of her time. Thus the literary personality and spiritual stature of Teresa cannot be understood without these two coordinate channels existing in her culture and epoch.

46. Christological Formation

1. Given The centrality of the mystery of Christ in St. Teresa's life and doctrine, it is important to highlight the most notable milestones in her Christological formation. Certainly the first seeds germinated in her early childhood. Among the household objects in the inventory made by Don Alonso was a larger-than- life oil painting of Jesus seated at the well in Sychar conversing with the Samaritan woman. After the death of Don Alonso, Teresa brought the precious painting with her to the Incarnation. From the time she was young – she assures us — every night before going to bed she spent some time thinking about the scene of Jesus praying in the garden. Probably this custom came from her first Christological readings in the *Flos Sanctorum*, which in the first introductory pages there was a translation of the gospels on the passion of Christ – Monotéssaron – and which were illustrated with a series of twenty drawings, among which figured one, really impressive, of Jesus praying in the garden. Yet even before these readings, Teresa was introduced to the most fundamental truths of the mystery of Christ through the primers and catechisms of her early Christian formation. In them she learned the fourteen articles of the faith, "the seven final ones pertain to the sacred humanity (of the Lord"). They made her memorize them, beginning with the first which is "to believe that the Son of God was conceived by the blessed Virgin Mary through the power of the Holy Spirit and not like us : more miraculously!" So they continued until the seventh article, on his return at " the end of the world." Highlighted in the third article is his passion and death, which Teresa from an early age celebrated with emotion in the Holy Week processions.

2. Nonetheless, the real manual of christological formation was

a book from the later middle ages translated from the Latin and known to her with the Castilian designation "the Carthusian." It was four large volumes written by the Carthusian Ludolph of Saxony with the title *The Life of Christ*. It spread throughout Europe from its numerous incunabular editions. It was translated into Castilian at the end of the 15th century and adapted for Spanish readers by the Franciscan Ambrosio Montesino, who published the four volumes in Alcalá at the beginning of the 16th century with a total of 1320 pages. The work consisted of two parts, the first of which presented the life of Jesus from his preexistence in the bosom of the Father to the healing of the blind man of Bethsaida. The second part , went from the messianic profession of Peter at Ceasarea Philippi up to the sending of the Holy Spirit. Teresa when already a Carmelite nun, had at her disposal in St. Joseph's the four volumes, and was accustomed to having them with her on days of retreat in the hermitage of Nazareth or that of Christ at the pillar. We do not know if she read the more than a thousand pages of the book by Ludolph-Montesino, but certainly, given the Casitlian structure of the work and given its precious content, *The Carthusian* was highly suggested by the contemplative sampling of Teresa the reader.

3. In her Castilian version the book contained a long exposition and meditation of the whole history of Jesus. Always for its basis it included the corresponding biblical text, highlighted by major type to differentiate it from the commentary. The most important section of the work centered on the steps of the Passion of the Lord (volume 4). The book presents them as a dramatic liturgical sequence, from what occurred at Compline on Holy Thursday, passing through Matins of that night, until what occurred at the hours of Tierce, Sext, and None and Vespers of Friday. Most important for a reader like Teresa was that each episode or each commentary concluded always with a touching prayer to the Lord for the purpose of reaching his person and entering into his mystery. It was the terminal contemplative moment of each section.

4. The entire book was preceded by a preamble of the author in which he imparted to the readers an introductory base with some keys for reading, meditation, and contemplation . These nineteen pages constitute a kind of little, introductory treatise not only for the comprehensive reading of the book but for access to the mystery of Jesus, based on eight premises, which are first stated and then developed at length. It is enough here to repeat this series of the eight premises.

- That in the practice of virtues, and in every perfect life, Jesus Christ alone is the true foundation.
- For people to exercise themselves in the life and contemplation of the Redeemer is something very beneficial for seven reasons.
- The preeminence of the life of Christ contemplated and lived. It is one of the great benefits that those receive who occupy themselves in the contemplation and guarding of it.
- An industriousness about contemplating without error the life of Christ.
- A brief summary of the exterior conditions of Jesus Christ and his properties.
- The perfection and beauty of the arrangement of the face and members of the Son of God.
- The excellence of the holy Gospels over all the other sacred scriptures.
- The discord and difference of some things present between the four evangelists is real concord.

5. We will highlight only a few of the data that undoubtedly influenced Teresa's Christological attitude. Above all, *the industriousness to contemplate,* proposed in the fourth premise. It is summed up in a precious instruction: "With all the affection of your soul, with diligent and delightful fervor, holding yourself in the contemplation of these mysteries with some delay, leaving aside all

other cares, be present to these things that were said and done by the Savior as though with your own ears you heard them and with your own eyes saw them; for they are very sweet to the one who thinks of them with desire and more to the one who tastes them. And therefore, even though many of them are counted as past, examine them as though you thought they were all present to you, because in that way you will undoubtedly taste a greater sweetness and read the things that have already taken place as though they were being done now; and fix your eyes on past facts as though they were present; and thus you will find the mysteries of Christ to be more pleasant." This was all a program of Christological prayer that Teresa put into practice in her own way of prayer.

6. The introduction insists especially on the beauty of the face of Christ: this is the theme of the sixth premise, which proposes to the contemplative " the face, form, and figure of our Redeemer (in a manner that] you can conjecture his acts deeds, and customs." And with true mime transcribe the portrait of Jesus, taken from the presumed letter of Publius Lentulus ad Tiberium Caesarem, which probably had already been read by Teresa in the preamble to the *Flos Sanctorum*. It is said that she transported it to her mystical experience: "The vision of Christ left upon me an impression of his most extraordinary beauty, and the impression remains today " (L 37.4).

7. Nevertheless, it was not the details but the mass of Christological data contained in the work that gave Teresa an incomparable Christological introduction. The Carthusian brought to the reader one by one all the biblical texts referring to Jesus. This book by the Carthusian is an immense Christological spirituality. Perhaps this is the reason why Teresa includes the book in the list of indispensable books for the libraries of her Carmels (C. 8).

47. Teresa's Biblical Formation

1. To obviate anachronisms in passing judgment on Teresa's biblical initiation in the middle of sixteenth_-century Spain, we must keep in mind the factors that at that time conditioned the access simple people had to the sacred books. Above all, we must keep in mind the tension that existed between theologians (letrados) and spiritual persons (*espirituales*). The theologians assumed a certain right to a monopoly on the Bible so as to base their theology on it. But this use was questioned by the spiritual persons, and especially by the simple people and women. Well known was the opinion of prohibition formulated by Melchior Cano: "Since women demand with an insatiable appetite to eat this fruit [reading the Bible], it is necessary to forbid this and place a fiery sword there to prevent the people from approaching it*"* (*Censura del Catecismo* by Carranza*).* And secondly, we must keep in mind the position adopted in mid-century by the inquisition in the *Index of Forbidden Books,* prohibiting practically all the biblical translations. It was suspicious of tendentious distortions of the sacred books . In Teresa's case, this is reflected in a doubly negative situation: first, it isn't obvious that she knew a complete translation of the Bible, although it is possible she had access to certain sacred books. In fact, in the household inventory made at the death of Don Alonso, among the books in his possession was a book of the G*ospels.* In Teresa's own confession, this was her preferred book, she found more recollection in the words of the Gospels than in very cleverly written books (W. 21.3). And, *secondly,* Teresa experienced another great restriction in the liturgical books which took shape from the biblical texts, but always in Latin. This forced the nuns – and among them Teresa – to read and

recite without understanding what was being read. Unless perhaps one surmised the meaning of the biblical text after its repeated reading in the breviary or the respective diurnals.

2. Reading and study. From a positive viewpoint, she had the fortune to read the text of three sacred books in other spiritual writings, that is: a) the first pages of the *Flos Sanctorum* include the entire text of the passion according to the four evangelists. It is sure that as a child or as a youth she read this. It proved to be a good introduction to the Gospels. b) Then in the fullness of her youth, Teresa was able to read integrally the biblical text of the *Book of Job*, although in the setting of its respective commentary spread out through the *Morals* of St. Gregory the Great. c) Later, when she was already in the monastery of St. Joseph she read the biblical texts referring to the history or mystery of Jesus, in the commentary on the *Life of Christ* by the Carthusian. There was always the inconvenience of a fragmentary reading immersed in the know-it-all embellishments of the commentators. Yet in the cases of b) and c) it was for her the equivalent of one of our intense biblical courses.

3. *A special book.* In the period of her mystical life, Teresa had the good fortune of a special reading and tasting of *The Song of Songs.* It was undoubtedly the Old Testament book most suited to the palate of a mystic. She herself asserts that "for some years now the Lord has given me great delight each time I hear or read some words from Solomon's Songs. The delight is so great that without understanding the vernacular meaning of the Latin my soul is stirred and recollected more than by devotional books written in the language I understand." And she specifies further: "For about two years, more or less, it seems the Lord has been giving me, for the sake of my purpose in writing this work, some understanding of the meaning certain words . . . "(M pro.)." I know someone [herself}who for a number of years had many fears, and nothing gave her assurance, but the Lord was pleased that she hear

some words from the *Song of Songs,* and through them she understood that her soul was being well guided" *(ibid. 6-9).* She wrote this in the years of her mystical plenitude: the decade of the 1570s. Coinciding with the years in which Fray Luis de León translated the S*ong of Songs* from the Hebrew into Castilian for a nun reader and suffered from envy and lies during those same years as a consequence for doing so. This coincided also with the period in which Teresa enjoyed the teaching of Fray John of the Cross who a little afterward – always in this decade – composed the stanzas of the *Spiritual Canticle,* a kind of poetic and mystical version of the biblical book. In the cited text, Teresa alludes to her readings of this book and the commentaries made of it: "each time I hear or read . . ." And she continues "even though at times – and these were few – I have heard explanations of some of these words and have been told their meaning when I asked . . ." *(*Ibid 1.9). But perhaps the most important thing is that she herself dared to put in writing her own *meditations* alleging expressly: " Nor must we make women stand so far away from enjoyment of the Lord's riches" *(*ibid 1.8). What is singular in this episode of the Teresian commentary on the *Song of Songs* is not that a theologian in turn caused the book to end up in the fire, but that in the daring of Teresa who with pen in hand tackled a spiritual commentary of the biblical book. We do not know whether she had a translation of the entire text or only a handful of select verses. What is special is that at that critical time she – a spiritual person and a woman – dared to put into writing a commentary just as previously she had done with the *Our Father*, precisely when the inquisition had forbidden those already in existence.

4. The presence of the Bible in her writings. More important than this episode is the verification of the intense presence of the of the bible in Teresa's writings. In fact Sacred Scripture is the book most often quoted by Teresa. With concrete references to the greater part of the sacred books: a/ from the Old Testament 23 books, and from the

New Testament 20 books; b/ and this latter referred to about 400 times; c) the highest number of references is from the *Gospels* and *St. Paul*; d) among the Teresian boo*ks,* the most packed with references is the *Interior Castle,* with at least 130 references; following closely is the *Book of Her Life,* with some 120 references, and the *Way of Perfection,* with 105; e) among her minor writings the *Soliloquies* stand out with 17; which frequently consist of short prayerful commentaries on a biblical text. See, for example number 17; it shows a special sensitivity to the doctrinal acceptance of biblical types, which in her writings ascend to at least 60, with special representative force in the whole process of *the Interior Castle.* From all this it may be deduced that Teresa had not attained to a dominion of the sacred text, but yes to a deep biblical mentality.

    5. Most notable is the impact of the bible on Teresa's experience. There are biblical texts and persons who penetrate the fabric of her mystical experience. The most singular case is her empathy with St. Paul or the personal reliving of certain Christological experiences of the Apostle. For example, that which is testified to in Galatians 2.20: "I have been crucified with Christ and the life I live now is not my own; Christ is living in me" (Gal 2.20). She refers to this text for the first time in her *Life*: "It seems to me that with your favor and through your mercy I can say what St. Paul said, although not with such perfection, that I no longer live but that you, my Creator, live in me," and she repeatedly gives testimony to this (*Life* 6.9; 21.6; ST 3.10; W 19.11; IC 7.2.5; and the poem " I live without living in myself"). With identical intensity she relives the Pauline alternative of Philippians 1. 23-25. And the same must be said of her reliving of the words of Jesus promising the indwelling of the Trinity in the one who does his will (Jn 14;23; ST 65. 9; 13.1).

    6. The main value of the biblical data. – Teresa accepts the Bible as the highest criterion of truth: "All the harm that comes to the world

comes from its not knowing the truths of Scripture in clarity" (*Life* 40.1). She appreciates the knowledge of theologians insofar as it is derived from the sacred text: "In Sacred Scripture, which they study, they always find the truth of the good spirit" (ib. 13. 18). And of herself she gives testimony: " I would die a thousand deaths for the faith or for any truth of Sacred Scripture" (Ibid 33.5).

48. Liturgical Formation

1. We lack data about Teresa's introduction to the liturgy in her first years. In the diocese of vila it was prescribed that girls receive Communion at age twelve (for boys at age fourteen).

The celebrations in the city parishes were excellent, above all the Cathedral parish, which disposed of a numerous chapter and an exceptional choir with musicians of great quality, such as T.L de Vitoria and S. de Vianco. For the choir there were precise norms in vigor. The diocese had its own breviary, called the Avilan. The procession for *Corpus Christi* was most solemn and popular; also very popular was the procession for Holy Week and for other rogation days that took on prayer in great social calamities and for urgent causes of the citizens. They exercised a kind of intermediary between the liturgical church and popular religion.

2. Yet the real liturgical introduction for Teresa took place at the Incarnation where she was incorporated into a contemplative community which gave the highest importance to liturgical prayer and disposed of a good, young choir to solemnize it. (It was the beginning of the XVII century when the celebrated case of the sisters Eugenia Clara and Clara Eugenia, artists in the use of the harp, organ, and bassoon). The liturgical recitation was the main occupation and around it revolved the other ordinary duties that one might have. Care was taken also of the sacraments—number of Communions and the frequency of confessions — just as the community celebrations of the Eucharist: the entire community attended the sung High Mass; separately they attended the low Masses.

3. Teresa, nonetheless, made progress in the liturgical spirit, above all when her mystical experience began. This will be the mystagogical

truth, which makes her deepen in the mystery of church prayer, as much in the liturgy of the hours as above all in the great mystery of the Eucharistic celebration. The daily recitation of the divine office and the daily Eucharist were the two cornerstones of her spiritual life. Let us look at both the one and the other.

4. The Liturgy of the Hours. Teresa learned to recite the Divine Office at the Incarnation when about 20 or 21 years old in a very numerous praying community, under the direction of the Mistress of Novices. The *Constitutions* imposed a special care about this: "with much diligence the novices will strive throughout the year of novitiate to study and be instructed in the chanting of the psalms and divine office, and they will be instructed in the rubrics of the *ordinarium* and most suitable institutions" (BMC 9.949). The rubrics of the breviary constituted an authentic puzzle since they were in Latin filled with abbreviations. The Mistress would necessarily have recourse to the help of the chaplain or another competent Carmelite. The Hours that were recited in choir were distinguished as night hours and day hours (in the infirmary only the day hours were recited, for which they used a special diurnal breviary). At night there was Matins and Lauds, which were recited before dawn. For daily prayer there was: Prime, Terce, Sext, None, Vespers and, to end the day and begin night silence, Compline, which ended with the sung *Salve Regina*. As an absolute guide for all of this was the *Carmelite breviary*. It is interesting to know from up close. Teresa, like the rest of the Carmelite nuns, had for her personal use the breviary of the Jerusalem rite: *Breviarium Carmelitanum secundum usum Ecclesiae Hierosolymitanae et Domminici Sepulchri*, which further on specified: *extract de approbato usu dominici sepulchri ecclesiae Hierosolymitanae, in cuius finibus dictorum fratruum religio exordium*. There is conserved in the Carmel of Medina a copy used by Teresa from 1568-1569. It was edited by *R. P. Jo. Baptista, ipsius generali, solerti cura editum et emendatum* (Venecia 1568). It was all

in Latin, text and rubrics with an introduction which reproduces the pages from Augustine "de laude et utilitate psalmorum" and after the daily psaltery and feasts of the saints, it concluded with special offices of the Blessed Virgin (Assumption and Immaculate Conception), of the Crowning with Thorns, etc. and numerous blessings for daily use. The central nucleus was constituted by the biblical texts: psalms and select readings from almost all the sacred books, minutely distributed in the different offices and liturgical seasons. Moreover there was an extended sanctoral, much to Teresa's liking, frequently illustrated engravings that corresponded to the text and occupied a whole page. This breviary not only gave direction to Teresa's prayers but was converted into a companion book of hers: in the choral recitation of the Office at St. Joseph's, in the celebrations in the covered wagons of the founder, or in stops along the way without strain, in a woods in Andalusia accompanied by the trilling of the birds and the flowers, in any country shrine, or in some little shanty to protect them from the wind where the founders spent the night and joined together for prayer. Many times she recited alone or with companions Matins at midnight after struggling for long hours with pen and paper. Teresa uses a special effort to penetrate the meaning of the psalms. She frequently asks a learned friend to explain to her a certain text that interests her. But, above all, it was this humble breviary that incorporated her mystical experience of the liturgy. Numerous are the profound graces received (and noted) by her while reciting an Hour or when she recites at Prime the trinitarian *Quicumque*, or a very devout prayer for the deceased, which were included at the end of the breviary, or when she sings unusually the calenda of Christmas. No one or anything was her companion the way her breviary was.

5. Her Eucharistic liturgy. It was incomparably more intense than the previous. We also have exemplars of the Carmelite missal used by the Carmelites. It was, with every probability, the missal edited by

Rubeo's predecessor, the General N. Audet (Lión 1559). It doesn't seem that Teresa had any special Eucharistic formation comparable to that of the recitation of the Office. It was her mystical experience that provided the great door of entry into the mystery of the Eucharistic liturgy.

6. The little story of her Communions is significant: the *Constitutions* of the Incarnation (the ancient *Constitutions*) strictly prescribe a limited number of Communions. In such a way that during the brief period of young Teresa's spiritual lukewarmness, the frequency of her Communions was also less, and when she recuperated she began to communicate every fifteen days (L 7.17). In the Constitutions of St. Joseph's, Teresa doubled the prescribed number of times. Yet in her personal life, she invariably practiced daily Communion. And with careful fraternal sense she strove that insofar as possible at least one of her nuns would receive Communion at her side. Habitually she wanted the community to participate actively in the celebration of the Mass. She herself usually made use of a little Missal to follow the rite. She gave special importance to everything referring to the celebration at the altar; the corporals, the flowers, cleanliness of the place, even to the extreme of cleaning the occasional little shrine where the caravan of the founders stopped for the celebration. With her entry into mystical experience, the Eucharist became the support of her whole life. The most intense graces she received on the occasion of receiving Communion. In one of these moments, she received the charism of founder. The mystical graces documented by her as being given during the Mass or after Communion are numerous. Very special is the Eucharistic grace given on Palm Sunday or that of the spiritual marriage after receiving Communion at the hands of Fray John of the Cross, or those others she received at decisive moments in her foundations.

7. Yet, in her writings, the text that best documents the depth of her Eucharistic piety is the improvised anaphora with which she ends

in the *Way of Perfection* her commentary on *panem nostrum*: Teresa prayed in the name of all the contemplatives in the house, presented to the Eternal Father the sacrificial Bread of Jesus, and offered it for all the Church as the unique sacrifice or the unique valid offering to put an end to the evils that at this moment afflicted humanity. (Cf. Theme 74).

49. Humanistic Formation

1. *Although she was a citizen of the golden age*, Teresa did not have any humanistic formation strictly speaking. This was reserved for a select group of *puellae doctae* of the higher class. It consisted above all in the study of good letters, the classical languages (Greek and Latin) and skill in certain arts, such as poetry, music, and painting. Neither Luis Vives in his *De Institutione feminae christianae, nor* later Fray Luis de León in *La perfecta casada* alludes to these aspects In the formation of women. Nevertheless, yes, they are relatively present in certain comfortable families. In the Castilian environment, this partial educative complement is patent, for example, in the case of Teresa and of her friend Doña Juana Dantisco, the mother of Jerónimo Gracián. In Teresa it doesn't seem that she had any introduction to classical literature. We only ask ourselves to what degree she had an introduction to the three arts mentioned above.

2. *Teresa's introduction to poetry.* We will allude later to Teresa's poetic production. It was not very copious, but varied enough with regard to quality, a variety of stanzas and poetic arguments. Perhaps the most relevant data is her attachment to popular carols destined for singing. In the Christmas season she exchanged these carols with not only the nuns of her Carmels but with Fray John of the Cross ("a little song for Fray John of the Cross they sent me from the Incarnation," (Ltr. 171). She composed one of her mystical poems in concurrence with Fray John on the basis of the same mystical experience of both and commenting on the same line "I live without living in myself." Surely Teresa's poetic knowledge did not proceed from a previous academic formation but from its insertion in the life and soul of the people, sharing in the songs, the couplets, and the little dramas of the street. She translated them

spontaneously to the religious life in its double manifestation, personal and communitarian: with a series of poems celebrating the interior feast of her mystical experience; others she composed to celebrate the feasts of the community: Christmas carols, ballads for the profession of nuns, songs for the feast of the saints. Both series show that Teresa's poetry did not proceed from something cultivated but was popular in nature. All of this does not prevent some of her compositions from being masterpieces.

3 Beyond the popular influence, it is possible that in her poetic work she was influenced by the frequent reading of certain psalms, true Hebraic poems. In fact, Teresa is aware that she is not a poet, but she perceives at the same time that, as does the author of these psalms, poetry overflows in moments of strong mystical impulse: "I know a person who though not a poet suddenly composed some deeply-felt verses well expressing her pain. They were not composed by the use of her intellect; rather, in order that she enjoy the glory so delightful a distress gave to her, she complained of it in this way to God. She desired all her body and soul to break in pieces to demonstrate the joy she felt in this pain" *(L.* 16.4). She writes in commenting on the psalmist; "this joy is seems to me must have been what was felt in the admirable spirit of the royal prophet David when he played on the harp and sang the praises of God." When she wrote this she didn't yet know Fray John of the Cross or his poetry. She had already written her poem: *Oh, beauty exceeding all other Beauties.*

4 Her love of painting There has been insistence on relating Teresa to the brushstrokes of El Greco or better in relating the two to each other. Nevertheless and despite chronological and Toledan coincidences, Teresa did not live in this connection nor did El Greco suffer the impact of her mystical dramatizations, although it is possible that he read her works toward the end of his days. She, on the other hand, had a most modest introduction in the apprenticeship of embroidery. We don't know when since we lack concrete information. We can only enumerate some

isolated facts that give witness to a progressive pictorial sensitivity: a) for her ability in embroidery we are left today with some skilled and delicate works: in the Carmel of Medina: a vestment and some corporals exquisitely embroidered by her; in the Incarnation in Avila they also have conserved a towel for the washing of the feet on Good Friday, which was embroidered by her; b) her esteem for good painting is manifest through the paintings done at her request for the hermitages of St. Joseph or of the Incarnation, or the two modest oil paintings purchased for the altar in Toledo, for which she invested all the capital that the group of founders disposed of, or the oil painting done under her direction in Salamanca as her biographer Ribera states (I, c. 11, p.88). c) In the covered wagons on their journeys she brought with her a precious tryptich of the risen Christ who with tender eyes and hands outstretched giving his peace, of which two exemplars still exist, one in the Carmel of Toledo and another in that of Burgos. d) We know some of the holy pictures that Teresa carried in her breviary. Ribera writes: "I have seen two small holy cards that the Holy Mother carried with her, one of the risen Christ and the other of our Lady (ib). And in the margin of this text Gracián notes: "the Mother gave to me this image with another two, of the Eternal Father and of the Holy Spirit, which she carried in her breviary because they were of the size of a little holy card, . . . the one of Christ looked in his eyes like the Veronica that is in Jaén. That of the Holy Spirit was represented in the form of a young man wrapped in flames to the waste, an image that was widespread and had an adventurous history until the 18th century when Pope Benedict XIV, prohibited its reproduction because there was no foundation for it in the Bible or in the Christian tradition. e) In her breviary she also carried another symbolic holy picture, of Italian origin, which represented the Infant Jesus enthroned on a human heart, and that still is preserved in the Carmel of Tarazona. f) In chapter 14 of her *Foundations* she explains her great her great admiration for an image brought from Flanders, "I haven't seen anything better in my life*"* (no.

9), placed in an altarpiece in the church in Mancera: probably it was not a painting but a sculpture. It is not the only case of her admiration of Flemish art. What stands out in Teresa's pictorial taste is that her attachment to images is simultaneous with her profound mystical experience. Nonetheless, in her pictorial taste the religious aspect prevails over the aesthetic value of the painting.

5. The problem of music. Music and song are a true problem in Teresa's case. From the beginning of her religious life she had to consecrate long hours to training in the choral chant, without obtaining great results. In the Incarnation the constitutions prescribed it specifically. In the monastery there were nuns who were professional musicians. Still there exists in the monastery museum the remains of the song books of that time as well as an excellent organ of the time. Teresa sums up her case with a stroke of the pen: "I didn't know how to sing well!"

6. There are numerous testimonies of her recourse to festive songs in the extra-liturgical community life. A good indication of this is the impact that Sor Isabel de Jesús (Jimena) had on her in recreation during the Easter days (1571) when she sang the song about "how hard it is to endure life without God." It was the song "Let my eyes behold you." It seems that on different occasions Teresa asked her to sing it again. It is symptomatic that the theme of the song was converted for her into a doctrinal symbol. Writing on the harm done in the spiritual life by concern about the point of honor, she presents it as one of her topics: "I often say that however small the point of honor may be, the concern for it is like that of sound coming from an organ when the timing or measure is off: all the music becomes dissonant" (L 31.21 and also 22.12). In fact, popular music was one of the elements introduced by Teresa into her Carmels in order to foster joy during recreation.

Despite everything, Teresa's true problem arose in the option for liturgical chant. A complicated problem that doesn't fit in the present theme.

50. Experience, The Wisdom Of Life

1. Generally, when teresianists investigate the founts of Teresa's magisterium or of her knowledge, they insist on the readings and contribution of scholars. Certainly the books and the learned men are affluent in their cultural abundance. But these are not the founts of her thought. It is Teresa herself who maintains insistently that she speaks or writes from experience: "I shall say nothing about things of which I don't have much experience" (L. 18.8); and *"afterward I understood that if the Lord didn't show me, I was able to learn little from books, because there was nothing I understood until His Majesty gave me understanding through experience"*(L 22.3); or: "I have very little or almost no need for books. His Majesty had become the true book in which I saw the truths" *(L 26.5)*. Numberless times she endorses her saying with the guarantee of knowing it through experience "Many, many times have I perceived this truth through experience"(L 22.6); "I see clearly that it is not I who say what I write; for neither do I plan it with the intellect nor do I know afterward how I managed to say it. This often happens to me" (L 14.8). These assertions are repeated like a refrain in the first of her books when she is starting her work as a writer. She repeats it in beginning her pedagogical lesson in the *Way of Perfection*: "I shall say nothing about what I have not experienced myself or seen in others" (W Pro. 3). And in writing her last book, the *Interior Castle*, the theme is converted into an axiom: "one cannot be sure about what one has not experienced" (IC 6.9.4). An axiom formulated in the mystical context of the sixth dwelling places. She is convinced that if she knows how to speak of it, it is because she had been able to experience it (W 23.4). With pen in hand she dialogues from experience to experience, from her own to that of her readers: "Those of you who know it by experience, through the goodness

of God, can be my witnesses" (W 23.6), convinced that many of her teachings readers will not understand but through their own experience, since it is very important, she writes, "not only to believe these truths but to strive to understand them by experience" *(W* 28.1). Hence her interest is not only to explain and make herself understood but above all to entice and to promote in the reader an empathy for her experiences. In sum: a) in her writing, books did not serve her; b) she writes from experience (her own and that of others); c) readers will only understand certain things (above all the mystical), if they experience them; d) she writes about them to entice, not so as to inform but to stir in the experience of the reader an empathy; e) She, finally, was understood through experience by people like Fray Peter of Alcántara, Fray John of the Cross, and Francis Borgia.

2. Obviously, we stand before the reading of a contemplative. The words of St. John of the Cross are valid for Teresa, according to whom contemplation is "the loving wisdom of God." In Teresa, contemplation is the experiential wisdom that makes her taste the transcendent mystery of God, and that at the same time makes her sensitive to the small details of life (a little ant, she will say) to see them and to feel them in the light of the transcendent one. In the present theme, we are interested in two things: to get to the bottom of what she understands by experience and the extent of her own experience.

3. In Teresa's acceptance, the word "experience" maintains its usual and current significance. Experience is the opposite of theory. Theory is the doctrine of books or of the discourse of learned men or the thought that she herself came up with. Experience, on the other hand, is to know something for having lived, felt, or gone through it. But "having gone through it" does not refer to the experiment in a laboratory, but to a living experience, either empirically with the senses or in one's own life. From the common, multiple life experiences: lights and shadows, victories and defeats, successes and disappointments, a good direction along the way or losing one's way. Even to the experience of profound friendship or the

highest experience of the mystery of God. Also the doctrine in books in
the field of experience when it has the confirming refrain of what is lived.

4. Teresa had a double scale in her experiences. A first series that
brought her to human maturity. And another that came upon her in midlife
and brought her to Christian plenitude. In books of spiritual theology
the first is usually referred to as "ascetical," and the second "mystical."
Between the one and the other, in Teresa's case, there came a dividing
boundary. It was the moment in which the interior voice guaranteed "I
will give you a living book." With a kind of devaluation of printed books
("very little or almost no need did I have of books") and the placing on
the first plane of a "living book" the transcendent knowing, "the true
book in which I saw the truths" (L 26.5). Her literary work all followed
after this unequalled boundary. When she writes, she refers more than
once to the first class of experiences. But the highest percentage of all
allusions refer to the second share. Teresa is a writer on the basis of her
mystical knowledge. The fact itself of writing is due to this second class
of experiences; a triple grace made it possible (a triple component of the
experience): to experience; to understand what is experienced; and to
be able to express it (which in our psychology corresponds to the triple
endowment of the normal person:: to perceive or sense; to understand;
and to communicate. We are interested in diagramming briefly: a) which
are Teresa's experiences that promote her human maturity; b) which
decide her ascent to Christian maturity and, consequently, to her spiritual
teaching authority.

5. *Her human experience.* It corresponds to the strata of her
biographical curriculum: experience of family, experience of the religious
community, and experience of society. They are experiences placed on
each other as constructive strata in Teresa's feminine personality. It is rich
in affective content, the experience of the multiple family that welcomes
her: infancy, childhood, orphanhood and youth. Deeply soaked physically
and psychologically, her passing through three years of sickness, which

left chronic effects in her life, with daily vomiting and the demands of daily Communion and her travels as founder. In the experience of the religious community, it is noteworthy that Teresa was not subject to a crisis of adaptation, but, yes, to growth. And finally the experience of so multiform a social life enters now into the sphere of her mystical life.

6. Much more important is the large quantity of experiences constitutive of her mystical life. Contemplation changed her gaze and the value of things, happenings, and persons. It is now that Teresa has the living experience of prayer. Prayer becomes easy, as a normal dimension of her life. She speaks to God or with God while she writes or when she works or when she dedicates herself to prayer. To pray is to share with him in friendship. The same, and much more so, as with human friends. For this, the face of God has changed (L. 4.10). Christ passes from the historical plane to that of present realities. Really present in so many ways, in the Eucharist, in the Gospels, in the images done by artists, in her brothers and sisters, at her right side. Within herself, Teresa has the experience of her own soul: she doesn't experience it as she does her own hand when she touches it, but, yes, much more deeply and in it she perceives the Holy Trinity. From these boundaries she sees the world in a different way, in another light. She evaluates differently what is fallen and what is sound. Friendships rise again but clothed in another visual light. Within them emerge the great earthly realities, the Church, Carmel, exceptional persons, Fray John of the Cross, Fray Peter of Alcántara, any of her novices. It provides above all a way of facing the ending of the present life. Teresa lives in hope and sings of it. *I live but not in myself. . .*" I am consoled to hear the clock strike, for at the passing away of that hour of life, it seems to me I am drawing a little closer to the vision of God" (L. 40. 20). The doctrinal synthesis of the *Interior Castle* will be a codification of her experience.

VI
Teresa The Writer

Teresa had an elemental literary formation. Despite the illiterate environment, she possessed her own unmistakable handwriting and style. She wrote thousands of pages. Still today 2,000 of her autograph pages are conserved. A writer but not a publicist, all her writings were published after her death. At present, published again, including facsimile editions, and translated into numerous languages, they have become classics of universal religious literature.

51. Teresa Learns To Write

1. In our total lack of information, we have to refer to the primers used in Teresa's time for children's learning. Nonetheless we do not know which of these primers was used by Teresa. We don't possess any notes or notebooks as we do with Thérèse of Liseux or Elizabeth of the Trinity. She would have learned to read and write when about seven years old. Probably without going to school. As in other well-to-do families, she had the help of some young teachers, a friend of the family, or that of her own mother, or her older sister. Although the primers of the first stage used gothic characters, she instead always employed the normal Latin alphabet in cursive writing, with great security and agility. She must have had a rigid training, since she maintains a firm and constant handwriting style — without any wavering of the pen – in all her writings, books, letters, poems, and notes. Her handwriting style has no likeness to that of her brothers. It in no way resembles Lorenzo's nor her niece Teresita's.

2. To facilitate for students the reading of any teresian autograph some elemental signs can be of use to them.

- Teresa knows and uses all of the Spanish alphabet, except k and w; and rarely does she use h or x.
- She doesn't punctuate except rarely; she does so with the slash (/) generally at the beginning of a new paragraph; she uses the same slash to spell out words of mistaken reading, such as v/e/s/o/, v/y, v/y/a for hueso (bone), huid, huia (run away, flee)
  - Without a fixed norm in the division of terms she elides: soyo, doyo (soy yo, doy yo) [I am; I give].
  - To enumerate she uses Roman numerals; never Arabic, although she knew them.

- She has an original way of writing: a double rr, in the manner of a capital H.
- She usually places a bracket before the o a [ora; [obras (now, works).
- For the phoneme "I" she uses the signs i-j-y.
- She writes distinctly b/v; also v/u.
- She wavers in the use of labials b/p, also in v/f (puscar, falladolid) (buscar to seek, Valladolid).
- She is clear in the use of use of the uvular g/i: the g is always with sound (gerra, gidsar) (war, to cook); the "j" is always quiet (jente, imajen)(people, image), after the manner of Juan Ramón Jiménez.

Other characteristics can be seen in our introduction to the facsimile edition of the autograph of the *Way of Perfection* (Rome, 1965). As an introduction to the reading of the teresian autographs you can use the teresian alphabet that we propose in that edition, p. 143.

3. Another characteristic of the teresian writings, that confer fluidity to the writing is the abundant recourse to abbreviations. The most frequent are the particles *para* and *que,* abbreviated pa and *q* (in the habitual form). She abbreviated in a flowing way the n at the ending of a word or syllable (*so, tabie*; for *son tambien*). I reproduce in continuing the table of abbreviations in the introduction mentioned to the facsimile edition of the *Way of Perfection*, p. 149, adverting that in addition to the abbreviations recurring in this book, there are many others frequently used, above all, in her letters, for example: v.m. (*vuestra merced,* your honor), v.p. (*vuestra paternidad,* your paternity), s.s. [*su señoria)/*[your lordship; or ladyship*], vra mag (vuestra majestad)* [your majesty], s.m. (*su majestad)* [his majesty*], -s- (señor)* [lord], ssto (*espíritu santo)* [Holy Spirit], gra (gracia) [grace], m/p (*madre/padre)* [mother/ father], etc.

4. A sketch of the abbreviations (taken from the *Way of*

Perfection p. 149, facsimile edition)

5. A specialist in graphology (G.M. Moretti) has defined Teresa's writing: *a fluid writer methodically irregular, sinuous, with choice letters, austere, clear, clean, winding, dilated in letters and words*" (The Saints in Their Handwriting). Another French grapholiogist, Suzanne Bressnard, wrote: *The writing of St. Teresa, of expressive relief, appears as put down with vigor. Its form is incisive and original; she reveals a personality of a powerful will and thought. How has one been able to treat as an hysteric a woman so present, so lucid, and so strong. There is in that an ignorance of psychological realities unacceptable to a graphologist. (L' Espagne Mystique au XVI siècle, Paris 1946, p. 35).*

52. Teresa's First Writings

1. Teresa is a belated writer. The writings of hers that have reached us pertain to the last quarter of her life. She wrote her first great work – *the Book of Her Life* – when 50 years old (1565). And she finished the last chapter of her *Foundations* in July of 1582, a few months before her death. Nevertheless, paradoxically, Teresa is a young writer. When she wrote her first book, she had been reborn to a "new life" – as she says – only ten years before on the wings of her mystical experience. All her writings were set in the mystical climate. They are youthful, with a fluid, rapid, and agile thought, dense with images and symbolism.

2. Nonetheless before this literary period, Teresa had occasion to sketch various choice writings. Although many are lost, they merit a simple review. Let us begin by recalling the first appearance of her young pen on the basis of books of chivalry. It is then – as we already pointed out – that she wrote, in probable collaboration with Rodrigo, a novel of chivalry for the recreation of a group of friends. We do not know if she composed it during the life of Doña Beatriz, another impassioned reader. It seems more probable that Teresa wrote it in the days that preceded her entrance into our Lady of Grace. As a result, toward the age of 16 (Rodrigo was almost 20). Of this her first writing not a trace remains. We have only the testimony of its existence in the biography of Teresa by Ribera: "within a few months she and her brother Rodrigo de Cepeda composed a book of chivalry with its adventures and fabrications; and it came out in such a way that there was much to be said for it." Gracián marked this passage: "she herself told me this" (Ribera 1, 5, p. 56). The episode presaged in Teresa a thoroughbred writer.

3. The first note from her pen to reach us is a modest one – we would almost say ordinary – a note that acknowledges the receipt of the tax of ten bushels of wheat, which obviously was the simple share of her nun's dowry, at the same time that she solicits from the one in charge of the dovecotes in Gotarrendura to do her the favor of sending some little pigeons. The date is 12 August 1546. It is the first autograph of Teresa's that we possess. Signed: Doña Teresa de Ahumada.

4. There follow her first spiritual writings, all of them lost. There were at least five small autobiographical accounts written for her confessors after the outburst of her mystical experience. A first account she destines for her first assessors, Gaspar Daza and Francisco de Salcedo with unfavorable results (L. 23. 12-14); there follows another account with "my general confession and I put down in writing all the good and bad things—as clear an account of my life as I knew how to give, without leaving anything out" (L 23.15). Destined for the young Jesuit Diego de Cetina, it was her first autobiographical account: a little afterward she wrote for the Jesuit Baltasar Alvarez, an account of the inspiration to found the new Carmel:" I told him in writing all that happened" (L 32. 12); and still another account, much more delicate, about her Christological experiences destined for the Dominican García de Toledo "when you insistently ordered me to do so" (L 28.3); finally an exposition of the problem of poverty planned for the new foundation, sent to the Dominican theologian Pedro Ibáñez who did not share her opinion (L 35.4).

5. Despite the lack of the these lost pieces, there has reached us the choice collection of her first *Spiritual Testimonies* (ST 1-3), three authentic jewels from the year 1560-1563, anterior to the *Book of Her Life.* The most extensive and unpretentious, the first of them, which contains an instantaneous, introspective view of her soul's landscape is probably from 1560 and is directed to the Dominican theologian, Padre Ibáñez, who during these years outlined, from an exterior point

of view, this same landscape in the 33 points of the *Dictamen* (see *Theme 28)*. *These* two pieces – *The Spiritual Testimonies 1* and the *Dictamen* – are like the *two* sides of the coin of her soul. Together with the *Spiritual Testimonies 2 and 3,* something later, they formed a kind of treatise, utilized by her confessor for discerning, in such a way that in presenting them again in 1565, when Padre Ibáñez was already dead, she adds to them a clarifying note: the account "that is not in my own handwriting, the one at the beginning, is the one I gave to my confessor, and without subtracting or adding anything he copied it for himself [and for] other learned men." And she adds a final warning: "Remember that all of this must be kept under the secrecy of confession, as I begged your Reverence" (ST 3.13), an indication of the intimacy and absolute reserve of the writing. We do not know who this last confessor was. Yet these three *Spiritual Testimonies* constitute an anticipation of the future *book of Her Life*.

6. A first poem. Belonging to this triennial is the poem Teresa wrote to celebrate the beauty of God "O Beauty exceeding [dialogue] all other beauties." It is poem no. 6. She wrote while in the company of Doña Guiomar de Ulloa (1560 - ?). Teresa seems to have memorized it and later transcribed – from memory – the three first stanzas for her brother Lorenzo, who was touched as she was with the sickness of love. Only three stanzas: "I don't remember any more" – she says – "what a brain for a founder" (Ltr 172. 23). We still have not recovered the rest.

7. A letter to the same Lorenzo. She wrote on Christmas eve (Ltr. 2) 1561. Another letter had preceded this one that is lost today. When she had already begun the project of her Carmel of St. Joseph, Lorenzo had sent her money through three men returning from the Americas. One of them, Alonso Rodríguez, seems to have demanded the corresponding receipt and she wrote it very willingly, with the date 22 November 1561. Signed by Teresa de Ahumada.

8. Petition to the Council of Avila. It is a request made to the gentlemen of the Council of Avila. In the most difficult stage of the lawsuit set up against the new Carmel and carried to the Court by the said Council, the placid and submissive trait of Teresa's plea regarding one of the points raised in the litigation: the city water and the edifice of the founts was obstructed by the hermitage that was built in the garden of St. Joseph's. It was dated 7 December 1563. And signed by the poor nuns of St. Joseph, yet the autograph is in Teresa's handwriting. Insofar as we know, it was the first document to emanate from the nascent teresian community.

9. Finally, a spiritual book, the first redaction of the *Book of Her Life*. Written by Teresa in the Toledan palace of Doña Luisa de la Cerda, when she interrupted the process of her foundation of the new Avilan Carmel. Having terminated before her return to Avila, as she noted in finishing the second redaction of the work: "This book was finished in June 1562." This first redaction of the work is not conserved, which probably did not go beyond one half of the definitive text. It was a purely autobiographical text, more unitary than the present text. It consisted of the first ten chapters of her life at home, and her struggles at the Incarnation (1-10) followed by another nine chapters about her mystical experiences (23-31). It was her first great literary and spiritual work. She probably destroyed it in 1565, after elaborating the second redaction.

To sum up: Teresa had a good literary training, from a little novel to the sketch of her first book, passing through letters, poems, and autobiographical sketches.

53. The Problem Of The Redaction

1. We shall see further on about the redaction of each teresian book. In the present theme we will treat only of the literary posture adopted by Teresa In confronting the task of composing a book. For her, to write a book was not something very different from redacting a long letter, an identical dialogIcal posture, the same spontaneity, equal interest in connecting with the problems or supposed queries of the ones for whom she is writing. Like the letter, the book is a communicating vessel for the display of convictions and experiences. Yet Teresa, who had no academic formation, nor had she practiced through exercises of redaction, met with concrete problems, in planning a book, that didn't arise in the writing of a letter: should she approach the theme, directly or on the basis of jotting down notes, what should be the title of the book, or how to present the preface in order to connect with the reader; should she structure the text into chapters or proceed in a continuous discourse, how should she conclude it, is an epilogue enough or does she prefer to have recourse to a letter of dispatch? These are aspects that we will pass over one by one.

2. Previous notes? She does not know, or practice, the normal technique of taking notes or elaborating previous outlines so as to establish ideas. Yes, it is certain that more than once she took notes. Yet without any connection to a future literary project. For example, in the initial pages of her breviary she notes various thoughts. On the title page she writes with a trembling hand a word of Jesus (Mt 11: 29) "learn from me for I am meek and humble." And in other of these initial pages – today conserved in the Carmel of Medina – she notes various sentences of St. John Chrysostom about perfect martyrdom. But neither the text of Matthew nor those of Chrysostom appear again

in any of her writings. There is conserved a copy (not autograph) of another series of notes with texts from the Bible or from Cassian (a saying of Abbot Sereno) or allusions to Elijah and Elisha or to the 24 elders of the Apocalypse. Nevertheless nothing of all this is reflected in her writings. They are devotional notes for remembering, not in preparation for a book. If she had sketched some preparatory outline – for example of the redaction of the *Interior Castle* – certainly her nuns in Toledo or those in Avila would have handed on to us some remnant – relic. On the contrary, Teresa wrote directly. She did not use note cards or notes. A case apart will be some chapters of the *Foundations* as we shall see further on.

3. Must she give the work a title? Teresa does not usually give her book a title, neither before nor during the redaction. Even today the greater number of her autographs are without a title. Years after writing *The Way of Perfection*, she gives it for the first time a title in which she dedicates it to all her Carmels. "This book deals with the advice and counsels Teresa of Jesus gives to her religious Sisters and daughters who live in the monasteries she founded." Yet when she refers to it in her letters she calls it "the little book on the Our Father" (Ltr. 190.4; 172. 8). Equally, without a title is the *Foundations*. The only one titled in her own hand is the *Interior Castle*.

4. How to articulate the text. At first Teresa extends the text as a conversation, without breaking it into chapters or setting apart points. This is how the text appears in the writing of its first redaction. Only the *Foundations* constitutes a special case, well structured from the beginning. The most significant is the *Way of Perfection* in its first redaction. Having finished it, Teresa returned to the first pages and attempted to break the text up and give titles to the chapters. Yet in the presence of the difficulty of the undertaking, she had recourse to the help of a Sister who, while Teresa revised the writing, wrote the titles of each chapter in the style of an index at the end of the book (only a

couple of times did Teresa take her pen to assign a title to a chapter (chs 56 & 57). Yet the breaking into chapters made them so small that the result was 73 chapters. This was done in such a way that when Teresa redacted the work again, she reduced them so that there are only 42 chapters, this time assigning them a new title in the respective place within the text.

5. On the other hand the *Interior Castle* did not have a second redaction. She strives to structure it while she is writing, but afterward after having concluded the book, she had to enumerate the series of dwelling places and the respective chapters, drawing a little box in a corner of the page to assign the number of each chapter. And as she had done in the redaction of the *Way of Perfection* she opted to add on separate pages the respective titles. Since these choice pages have been lost, it was Gracián who transmitted them for us in his copy of the work. The only section not an autograph.

6. Epilogue or letter of assignment? Teresa ends her books accentuating the dialogical tone. The case in the *Life* is typical, with a double conclusion. First she sums up the narration in finalizing chapter 40. Dialoguing in intimacy with the main person for whom the work is intended, García de Toledo, she states: "this is the way I now live, my lord and Father. May your Reverence beg God that he either take me to himself or show me how to serve him" (L 40.23). Yet in view of the fact that this "my lord and Father" solicited the book with every urgency, Teresa refers in this same folio a pleasant charming letter of consignment with some final recommendations and some late commissions.

7. Also she concludes The *Way of Perfection* with a simple word of farewell to her Carmelite readers of St. Joseph's, at the same time she submits it for approval to the Dominican *presentado* Fray Domingo Báñez "who is my confessor" (WP 42.6). Yet it happened that the ones for whom the work was destined heard rumors about

another book by their Mother, which was secret, that of the *Life*, and Teresa did not find it inappropriate to refer to it and propose it as an ulterior approach to the "fount of living waters"; "You may get it, for Padre Fray Domingo has it. If this one (*The Way of Perfection*) is all right for you to see and he gives it to you, he'll also give you that other one"(W 42.7). It was a way of insinuating the doctrinal unity of the two works and to propose them as such to her nuns. But this was not the opinion of Padre Fray Domingo. And Teresa had to suppress these words in the second redaction.

8. Like the double epilogue of the *Life* is the conclusion of the *Interior Castle*. First she bids farewell to the readers at the end of the seventh dwelling places. "In sum, my Sisters, what I conclude is that we should not build castles in the air." But then she adds a folio apart, a kind of letter of consignment, showing humor to the readers, a folio whose location Padre Gracián will change to the beginning of the book. Here Teresa wrote the colophone of her work: "This writing was finished in the monastery of St. Joseph of Avila in the year 1577 . . . for the glory of God who lives and reigns forever and ever, amen."

9. The case of the Foundations. Teresa wrote the book while on the march, with long intervals in between. Due to these intervals she thought she had concluded at least three times: at the end of chapter 27 when she believed her task as founder had terminated through a counter order by her superiors: "I have finished today, the vigil of St. Eugene, the fourteenth day of the month of November in the year 1576" (no. 22). She takes the work up again and closes in receiving the information about the erection of a separate province of discalced Carmelites in the chapter of Alcalá: a moving conclusion (29.33). And, finally, after the foundation of Burgos, she writes again in a kind of appendix on the transfer of obedience of the Avilan Carmel of St. Joseph to the order.

Teresa always terminated her written conversation without need of adding an index as was the use in current books.

54. The Problem of Style

1. In what style to write. It was no problem for Teresa. It was for her students. She, in her writing, attained to a more precise norm than Valdés. "I write as I speak": she speaks in writing She assures us of this at the beginning of the *Interior Castle*. The book will adopt the language used between women : ". . . and so I will be speaking while I write." In fact, in the text there usually occur words to speak or to say instead of to write or I will write when she refers to what has been said before or what will be said further on. Including the chapter heading, for example in the *Way of Perfection*, chapter 9. "Speaks to souls unable to reason with the intellect" or the heading of chapter 23 "Speaks once more of the great value that lies in beginning with determination," or toward the end, chapter 41: "Speaks of the fear of God." Or when in the *Life* the impulse of ecstasy breaks the thread of the account: "Alas, I don't know what I'm saying to myself, because almost without my uttering this I'm already putting it down in writing" (33.22). It is certain that Teresa complains about her bad style: poor style, or heavy style or crude style, and this she anticipates at the beginning of each work. Yet without getting a complex about it, convinced that "what I say in this imperfect and bad style will be more acceptable" to her readers than books very well written.

2. Among students, the problem of the teresian style arose because of the presence of presumed and repeated barbarisms in her texts. Or, it has been insisted, for the uncouth manner – they say – of certain expressions – that indicate an intentional lowering of the pen of the author that deliberately makes her language boorish. The presence of barbarisms seems obvious. Then she herself avoids them in successive pages. Or uncouth expressions on the same page. The more abundant examples are

233

an, anque (for *aunque*), *naide, niervos, indino, pusilámine, yproquita, ylesia, relision* (for *iglesio or religión), perlados, carrastolendas (*for *carnestolendas*) . . . It has been noted that in the current books used by her one reads *iglesia, indigno, aunque, etc.* It is impossible that she was ignorant. Wasn't there in this a secret intention of lowering or making her style sound rustic. In any case, to what do we owe these lexical anomalies of Teresa's or what is the explanation for them?

3. Hypotheses of the scholars. Let us remember first of all the most frequent explanations from the philological or historical viewpoint: a) Teresa opted intentionally for an eremitical style in accord with her Carmelite kind of life.: "For the style of life we aim to follow is not just that of nuns but of hermits." (WP 13.6). This thesis was held by the great philologist, Ramón Menendez Pidal. According to him "the renunciation of the precise voice we must explain as an act of humility. Teresa was embarrassed to employ a technical style, she doesn't want to appear learned." "She herself," continues Don Ramón, "would have forbidden it for her nuns": "In the manner of speaking, they should be simple, plain, and religious, who live more in the style of hermits . . . not using the latest fashionable expressions or sweet talk" (*Visitation,* 42). b) another explanation more historical told about the family origins of Teresa, arising on her father's side from being a neo-converted Jew. Now truly, for most readers, it was proper for the Jews to use a correct and elegant style. For Teresa her interest would have been to hide this stain of her origin, and for that reason she would choose a grammatical rusticity in her writings. Or again, in the misogynist ambient of her times, she would have done so to hide her condition of a "woman writer." In any case her lowering her style would have been a stratagem of hiding. In both hypotheses, Teresa would write not only with a secret intention in her style, but with a dose of simulation, as if in the depth of her spirit as a writer she needed to feign what was not or hide what was, spilling a drop of fiction into the undercurrent of

each page. Precisely for this reason the two explanations are not very likely. Without need to argue against them, it is enough to think of the univocal linearity of her style according to the criterion of "truth and plainness" so often formulated by her. (Recall the conclusion of her first book: "I have dared to recount this dissipated life of mine, . . . to put it in writing and record as clearly and truthfully as I could what has taken place in me" (L 40.24).

4. Before all, what are we to say about Teresa's supposed lexical barbarisms. They are such only from an anachronistic view of the idiom. Teresa wrote from popular speech. She wrote as an Avilan woman at a moment in which the evolution of many words was fluctuating in form. When Fray Luis de León edited her works and had to reduce them to the cultivated usage, using himself more than once very cultivated Latinisms, he equally maintained so many other times the popular word used by Teresa. As it is known, at the time the idiom had frayed edges and diverse peculiarities in the speech of León, Avila, and Toledo. And it was normal that Teresa's speech would reflect her city. It is enough to compare it with Avilan writers, contemporary friends of Teresa, like Anne of St. Bartholomew or Julián de Avila (Ana, for example writes : *anque, nayde, ylesia, nenguno, entramas, cuntino, yndina, milaglo, perlada . . . cay, trayo, quijerey,* like Teresa. Somewhat less, Padre Julián de Avila.) In Teresa's pen, these words are not barbarisms but usual and normal in the popular dialect.

5. Counterproofs. There are reliable indications that Teresa wrote *plainly* without second intentions of stylistic degradation:

a) Teresa wrote her letters in an identical style as in her books. Especially long, intimate letters (to Lorenzo, María de San José, and Gracián) in those in which the hypothesis of lowering her style or simulation does not fit.

b) An equal lexical identity in the writings with a double redaction, for example, *The Way of Perfection* or the *Spiritual Testimonies* (no.

58): the author's intention of lowering her style would be manifested in passing from the first to the second redaction. A meticulous comparison of both cases shows the non-existence of such lowering. (one test alone: in the five first chapters of the first redaction of the *Way of Perfection* the incorrect word *ylesia* recurs five times; in the second redaction the word is always transcribed correctly *yglesia*. A total absence of the process of stylistic lowering; maybe an inverse process.

c) Teresa revised and amended personally the copies of the *Way of Perfection*. Made by her nuns, for example the copy of Salamanca. She introduces retouches on every page (79 folios). Not one emendation is made for the sake of lexical or stylistic lowering. On the contrary.

d) At the end of her life, Teresa decided to edit the *Way of Perfection* and far from trying for the slovenly character of the text, she takes pains to improve it. She gives it to a learned Toledan who makes a clean copy (codex of Toledo) and polishes it. Then she herself revised the copy and introduced hundreds of retouches, always positive, never for the sake of making the text more rustic. She is interested in sending the book to the editor, Don Teutonio, in the best condition possible. For this she has another copy made from the Codex of Toledo and sends it to Evora. It is well corrected. without any indication of lowering the style in the whole process.

6. On this basis you would have to define the characteristic note of the Teresian style: above all her instruction is valid, "writing smoothly." She writes "with all plainness and truth" (a binomial of teresian stamp); with spontaneity, without upsetting the rhetoric (as she says); without aesthetical pretense, an aestheticism that on the other hand springs forth from her naturally. With freedom of pen, she is interested in the content much more than in the garb. Yet at the same time, her "Castilian is elegant," according to Fray Luis de León, "with delicacy and clarity, with purity and facility of style, with grace and good composition of words, with an unaffected elegance that is extremely delightful" (Fray Luis).

55. The Persons Ordering the Teresian Writings and Those for Whom They are Destined

1. Among Teresa's works, only a small group of minor writings were written by her without a previous command from another: only the *Constitutions* for her first Carmel, the *Soliloquies*, and the *Meditations on the Song of Songs* were written without a previous order to do so. All the rest of her major works depend in their origin on someone else, a friend, a confessor, or superior, who motivates her to write. We recall these persons who gave the orders, not only for their motivating or authoritarian function but because in almost every case they enter into the core of the respective book and are important for a comprehensive reading.

2. Let us see first of all who these persons who induced Teresa to write were.

a) Life. Who ordered her to write it? First came various commands that she write small accounts of conscience. They were given by her confessors. The *Life* also was born by order of her confessors: "this account that my confessors ordered"; "since my confessors commanded me," she says in the prologue. But not as a confession (recall the warning of Teresa at the end of ST 3). This time they assigned her the theme of prayer and the graces the Lord gave her, leaving in the shadows other aspects of her life. Probably one of those giving the orders was Padre García de Toledo, who in the definitive redaction becomes the person who keeps the dialogue alive. He tells her to resume the mystical account (L 37) and once the writing is finished, he urgently wants it. Nonetheless, the book has a deeper source than this external command: "I know the Lord wants it" [that she write]. "And I know, too, that even the Lord has for some time wanted me to do this, although I have not dared" (Pro 2). Or, the book arose from a deeper and secret fount.

b) The command to write the *Way of Perfection*. This time a command from outside does not intervene, but the petitions come from within the Carmel: "The Sisters in this monastery of St. Joseph . . . have urged me so persistently to tell them something about it [prayer] that I have decided to obey them" (Pro 1). That is, she writes under pressure from her daughters. And those who begged her or urged her were not left outside in the antechamber of the book, but they become her indispensable interlocutors within the writing. It is impossible to read the book without keeping them in mind or making oneself a part of the group.

c) The *Interior Castle* arose from a painful command. "Not many things that I have been ordered to do under obedience [by authority?] have been as difficult for me as is this present task of writing about prayer," she says in the beginning of the prologue. Teresa obeys but with strong feelings against doing so that arose from her nature. This, despite the fact that the two persons giving her these orders were dear to her: her confessor, Dr. Velázquez, and her most admirable superior, Jerónimo Gracián. But the command took away the lack of inspiration that the author underwent at the moment, for immediately she shaped the basic symbol. Yet neither of the two ordering her to write will penetrate into the castle, the dwelling places within.

d) The *Foundations*. Again a command goes against the grain. It is given when she is in Salamanca in the year 1573 by "a Father Rector from the Society, whose name is Maestro Ripalda" (Pro 2). Teresa resists, "It seems impossible [to write this book] . . . the Lord said to me: 'Daughter, obedience gives strength.'" It was again the mystical endorsement of an external command.

e) The Manner of Making a Visitation. It was in 1576 during a painful pause for the founder in her fifth foundation, Padre Gracián ordered her to write it. He testifies to it: "She wrote it at my request." Teresa had to use force with herself to take up the pen: " beginning this work has been the greatest mortification for me, and I have felt a strong repugnance toward doing so." She trusted in God and "in the humility of the one who ordered me to write." This time Gracián will be the one for whom she is writing.

It is easy to confirm that in the majority of cases, Teresa began her books by an imposition and not by a literary inspiration. This second force, inspiration, yes, decides the birth of the *Life* and the *Way of Perfection*. In the remaining cases it comes when Teresa takes up her pen.

3. *Importance of the persons for whom the Work is destined.* In flagrant contrast with the spacious horizons of teresian readers today, the number of person's Teresa had in mind when she wrote her books is highly reduced. This means the number is important: from it depends in great part the micro-climate created in each book.

a. *For whom does she write the L*ife? She wrote it above all for the Dominican García de Toledo. The *Life* is a book of intimacy. Then, she has no problem with it being read by her twelve nuns at St. Joseph's. If Báñez would decide to burn it, Teresa wanted chaps 32-36 to be saved for her nuns because it tells the history of the birth of the first Carmel. Afterward she sends it to the Master St. John of Avila. Later, we do not know when, she herself is open to the possibility that the writing goes beyond the circle of intimates and passes into the hands of others. She didn't exclude its being published.

b. *The Way of Perfection* is also an intimate book written for the little familiar world of her Carmelite nuns. Very few nuns at this time. Yet also she is open soon to an expanded space, first putting it in the hands of her brother Lorenzo and then deciding to have it published and then launching it in printed form.

c. Those for whom *The Interior Castle* is destined were expressly her nuns. The book dialogues with them. It seems to her even that "it's nonsense to think that what I say could matter to other persons" (Pro 4). This as she started to write. Later, she became aware of its universal value. She believes it to be superior to her *Life* (Ltr. 219.8). As soon as possible she puts it in a place safe from possible confiscation, sending it to Seville to María de San José. Did she sense its possible entry into the world of theology?

d. Again the ones for whom the *Book of Her Foundations* was destined was fluid. She wrote it for the historical memory of her nuns. But as she writes the pages, she opens the horizon, dialoguing with the discalced friars and sends them the continuation of the work. In fact, Gracián, the friar deeply involved in the book, will receive Teresa's suggestion and himself continue the history.

e. A case apart is the one for whom her *Meditations on the Song of Songs* is destined. Teresa wrote it because the verses of the biblical poem had been a fount of consolation for her soul. Now she wants to communicate to her nuns this fountain of joy. The little teresian book was destined, therefore, to a reduced world of Carmelite readers. Until the theologian censor burst in from outside and disapproved of this "feminine" project. And Teresa threw it into the fire.

Another special case is *The Soliloquies*. It is perhaps her most explosive and unidirectional book. Written in closed circuit, in soliloquy. Teresa dialogues with the deepest part of herself, with her soul and her life. "Oh life, life! How can you endure being separated from your Life?" (1.1). Beyond the soul itself, the one for whom the *Soliloquy* is destined is God. "why have I said this, my God? To whom am I complaining? Who hears me but You?" (1.3).

4. If the one for whom a book is destined in part decides its tone and internal makeup, for Teresa the one or ones for whom a book is destined is very defined and determined. Without keeping them in mind we would hardly get it right in reading her pages. Without

doubt the one for whom the *Sologuies* are destined is most precise and definite. Teresa directs herself to God, and without diversifying or digressing. In all Teresa's writings God is present, in a hidden way, as the one for whom she destines her work. He is, for this reason a good key in reading all her books.

56. The Stumbling Block
Of Censorship And Censors

1. As was normal at the time, Teresa in writing keeps the censors present. Censorship was an obligatory frontier to pass for every book that aimed at being presented in society in printed form. There was an official censorship that imparted approval before passing the text to the press and after being printed, on occasion, a further confirmation was demanded not only to fix a price for the book but also to check the corrections if there were any. It was the censor's task to examine the orthodoxy of the writing as far as faith and customs go, and evaluate the book's public usefulness. The censor did this for the Royal Council in the name of King Philip II. He had inaugurated a strict program of rules on the theme in Teresa's time.

2. She did not reach the point of presenting any of her books to the official censor. Not even the only one published in her lifetime, *The Constitutions* (Salamanca 1581); although, yes, the *Constitutions* for the discalced friars needed this approval of the censor the same year. Yet the diffusion of a manuscript also needed the signature of a learned man who endorsed the text. The episode occurring for one of her audacious books is revealing, *The Meditations on the Song of Songs*. Judged badly by the theologian censor, Diego de Yanguas, Teresa herself threw it in the fire. Despite this, the little book continued to be spread around in manuscript copies, one of which reached the hands of Báñez in Valladolid, precisely the same year in which Fray Luis de León got out of the Vallodolid prison. And Báñez makes haste to shield the teresian manuscript with a pair of approbations, one at the beginning of the text and the other at the end of the text. "I have read over with attention these four notebooks and I have not found in them anything that would be bad doctrine, but rather good and ben-

eficial doctrine. In the College of St. Gregory in Valladolid 10 June 1575. Fr. Domingo Báñez." So the manuscript remained protected from painful denunciations.

3. In the presence of revisions and censors Teresa adopted a characteristic attitude. Not one of fear, but of positive desire. Not through a feminine complex but from a most normal sensitivity before the social and religious nervousness of the moment. For her the intention of the censor is a doctrinal safeguard as much in favor of the text as of the readers. Yes, it was also a kind of safe conduct for the entry of the book into society. In any case, this desire of hers that a competent scholar review her book was filtered spontaneously into the interior of the book, even in forming part of its textual fabric. If in it there is anything mistaken, the censor will set it right, or, if the case warrants, burn it. It is not certain that fear of the censor silenced her pen. Among her major works only the *Foundations* was exempted from this confrontation with the censor. The lot of the other three will be very different. Let us see this one by one.

4. The case of the *Life* is complicated. Although she at the beginning wrote it more as a simple account than as a book, in the measure that it grew in her hands she is convinced that the first reader, the Dominican theologian, García de Toledo, will revise it. "And in the case that the book goes beyond bounds, he will tear up or burn whatever he finds to be outside the rule: as to its conformity with the truths of the holy Catholic faith. And if it should not be in conformity with them, your Reverence may burn it immediately for I will submit to its being burnt" (L 10.8). It was a pact between the two. I did what your Reverence commanded me and enlarged upon the material. I did this on the condition that you do what you promised by tearing up what appears to you to be bad" (epil 2). To burn and tear up were clear allusions to the inquisitorial practice of expunging or burning. As is known, after the approval of Padre García, the work was not free of

being sequestered at the hands of the Inquisition, for it was submitted for a statement by the censor of the office, P. Báñez. And although his decision was favorable ("this woman, although she is mistaken in something, at least she is not a deceiver"), he did not think the book should be allowed out of prison but only later, after the death of the author, provided the inquisitorial censor should then give a favorable judgment.

5. As for her second book, *The Way of Perfection*, Teresa writes it trusting in the immediate revision on the part of her preferred theologian, Padre Domingo Báñez. Instead Padre García de Toledo reviewed it and found in it dangerous allusions to the Inquisition and to the Index of Forbidden Books as well as some daring commentaries on some psalm or the Our Father. Padre García began his work applying to the book the technique of inquisitorial expunging, but then he considered the writing inadmissible and limited himself to marking large sections, proposing to the author a new redaction of the work. He also reviewed the second redaction, crossing out long paragraphs and obliging her to cut out entire pages. When, in the end, she decided to publish the book, she herself placed before it a statement of submission: "In all that I say in this book I submit to what our Mother the Holy Roman Church holds. . . ." Nonetheless and despite the superb declaration, the teresian text before being published for the first time in Evora, underwent again the normal censorship of the Portuguese inquisitors, who demanded the suppression of the entire chapter that dealt with the prayer of quiet (W. 31) and granted their approval on this condition that they *tirad as clausulas que estao riscadas. Et antes de corer, tornara a esta mesa hum dos liuros impressos con este original, para se cotejar el hum com outro. (Remove the clauses that are crossed out and before proceeding, return to this assembly one of the books printed along with this original, so that they can be compared with each other).* All this happened during Teresa's lifetime (7

October 1580). Yet these transactions slowed the book down for three years. After the final check demanded by the censors (Paulo Alonso and Antonio de Mendoza) it was published on 8 February 1583 after Teresa had already died. We do not know if in her life she knew about what took place.

6. What happened with her third book, *The Interior Castle,* was very different. Teresa incorporated into the prologue the mood expressed in the anterior declaration of the *Way of Perfection,* that is to say, "In all that I say, I submit to the opinion of the ones who ordered me to write, for they are persons of great learning." One of them had been Padre Jerónimo Gracián who submitted the teresian manuscript to an attempt at scholastic correction in the presence of Teresa. He himself tells us about it. "We read this book in her presence, Padre Diego de Yanguas and I, I arguing about many things that in saying them were bad sounding and Fray Diego responded to them, and she said that we should take them out and so we took some out" (Glanes 61). The series of interlinear or marginal corrections introduced by Gracián in the autograph of the book can give an idea of the uncalled for criterion operating for those gentlemen censors that well reflected in its turn the censorial mentality of the period.

7. We arrive thus at the great official censure imposed on the three books in projecting their first editions. The censor was designated in Madrid, an exceptional theologian, Fray Luis de León, to whom was entrusted the Salamancan edition (1588). In the hands of this distinguished professor, the censorship was converted fortunately into an apology of praise: "I have seen the books that the Mother Teresa of Jesus composed that are titled *Life, The Dwelling Places,* and *The Way of Perfection,* and everything related to them; they are of very sound Catholic doctrine and in my opinion of the greatest usefulness for all those who read them, for they teach how possible it is for human beings to have a close friendship with God, and uncover the steps by

which one ascends to the this good . . . and all of this with such facility and mildness on the one hand and on the other, with words so alive that no one who reads them, if he or she is spiritual, will not find great profit, and if they are not spiritual, at least they will admire the compassion of God for men who seek him and the sweet conversation that he has with them. And so for the praise of God and for the common benefit, it is fitting that these books be printed and published. In San Felipe in Madrid, 8 September 1587, Fray Luis de León."

57. The Teresian Autographs

1. Teresa has been especially fortunate in the passing on of her writings. The autographs of all her major works have reached us. *The Book of Her Life*, *The Foundation* and the first redaction of *The Way of Perfection* (CE) are conserved in the Library of the Escorial. The second redaction of the *Way of Perfection* (CV) is conserved in the Carmel of Valladolid. The precious autograph of *The Interior Castle* is conserved In the Carmel of Seville. Of her minor works there has reached us the entire work *On Making the Visitation* conserved also in the library of the Escorial. Various autographs of *The Spiritual Testimonies* are found dispersed through Mexico, England, Italy, and Spain. Autograph fragments of her poems survive in Italian Carmels of Livorno and Savona. And of her letters no less than 240 autographs have reached us, dispersed through Europe and America.

2. A global stocktaking of this teresian treasure of autographs is illuminated by the following statistics:

—   autograph pages of the *Life* 409
—   autograph pages of the *Foundations* 259
—   autograph pages of the *Interior Castle* 222
—autograph pages of CE 306
—   autograph pages of CV 404
—   autograph pages of On the Visitation 43

The total comes to 1643 autograph pages that taken with her *Letters and* Spiritual Testimonies surpass the number 2,000. Much more than any of our classics.

3. Let us make an elemental presentation of only the major autographs, the most important. (For a more technical and detailed

description we refer the reader to the Historical Note that accompanies the respective facsimile editions).

— Autograph of the *Life*. It is the most precious of all. A large codex of 225 folios. The format is 295 by 210 mm. Transcribed by her with every care from the previous draft. Written more than once in a charismatic trance. Preserved in the Library of the Escorial, where it has been guarded on both sides for various centuries by two presumed autographs, one by St. Augustine and the other by St. John Chrysostom. Without an original title, the title was placed there at a later date by the librarian P. Sigüenza: "The Life of Mother Teresa of Jesus written in her own hand, with an approbation by Padre M. Fray Domingo Báñez her confessor and professor of Prime at Salamanca." On the second page of the cover, a slip of adhesive paper informs us about what happened to the book during the 1936 war: "The central assembly of the artistic treasure: Deposito de Perelada Procedencia Escorial FN° de procedencia: E. N° 55." The note refers to the abandonment or risky destiny of the book during the civil war; a paper that was omitted in the recent restoration of the text. And at the end, there are three folios with the statement of approval by Báñez, signed and dated "seventh day of July 1575." In the interior of the text there are marginal notes, some autographs of Teresa (folio 91v and 92 r), others of Báñez (folio 169r), or by a third hand (folio 127v, 138v, 180v). A brilliant penmanship, pages full and well framed, with very rare erasures (folio 107r, 115r). At the end, the letter of dispatch incorporated in the middle of folio 250r keeps the date of the first redaction: "This book was finished in June, MDLXII."

— *The first autograph of the Way of Perfection (CE)*. It had the most ephemeral public life. It passed directly from the Carmel of St. Joseph to the large container of the Escorial. It consisted of 155 folios; the last two were blank. A minor format 220x155 mm. The title is by a strange hand: "*A treatise on the Way of Perfection*. In a second moment the author adds two folios (146-147) "in which she treats of the prayer of quiet in which she says this "and there follows the celebrated comparison to the baby nursing." It will be inserted in chapter 31.9 of CV. The text was retouched very often by the author and corrected by the censor, Padre García de Toledo, who after crossing out numerous pages (62v, 113v, 121v) gives orders that it be redone. To him is due the great smudge on folio 9s 11-12v. which contains the famous apology for women. At the end (folios 148-153, not numbered) another hand writes the titles of the 73 chapters into which the text is broken up (Teresa wrote the title of chapters 56 and 57). In short, a text badly treated, reduced to a simple draft.

— The second autograph of the *Way of Perfection* (CV) is conserved in the Carmel of Valladolid. Format 212 x 116 mm. The folios are numbered by Teresa (I-CCVII). Many of the numbers cut off. The title on the autograph was added later: "this book deals with the advice and counsels Teresa of Jesus gives to her religious sisters and daughters . . ." On the contrary, another hand hesitatingly titled it: "The Book called *The Way of Perfection.* On the first page beneath the title given by Teresa, one of the censors wrote the approval of the book. Pages filled with underlinings, marginal notes by a stranger, crossed out paragraphs, pages torn out and rewritten . . . with marginal annotations by various different hands. To one of these is due the fact that Teresa tore out the eight pages that contained the comparison to the game of chess (folios LIX-LXIII). In such a way that the actual text is in part a third redaction.

— Autograph of the *Foundations.* Also conserved in the Escorial. It consists of 133 folios, numbered by another hand. In major format: 303 x 200 mm. the autograph lacks a title. In the middle of the 17th century, another hand labeled it: "The original book of the foundations of her reform which the glorious Virgin Saint Teresa of Jesus made in Spain, written in her hand." Like the other teresian autographs in the Escorial, this one also bears the certificate of its being in Perelada during the three years 1936-1939. With numerous corrections and marginal notes by Padre Gracián in the first folios (1-18). With a most varied teresian handwriting, according to the different stages in which she is composing the manuscript: 1573-1582. At the end of chapter 27 (folio 100v), Teresa inserted a half page with the four counsels, a fragment which after its being stolen and restored was glued to the other side of folio 100. *The foundations* are the most varied and detailed of the teresian autographs.

— The autograph of the *Interior Castle*: a manuscript begun in Toledo and concluded in Avila and guarded in the Carmel of Seville. It is a notebook of 310 x 205 mm., with a total of 115 folios, numbered by Teresa in the margin of the top right (I-CX) and by Padre Graciǎn at the bottom "1-224." Entitled by Teresa: This treatise, called the *Interior Castle* was written by Teresa of Jesus, a nun of Our Lady of Mt. Carmel, for her Sisters and daughters, the discalced Carmelite nuns." In the top margin of each page she notes the corresponding dwelling place. In a second moment she inserts in the text the numbering of chapters, but without headings. The respective headings she will write down on separate folios, lost today. The text is written in a strong, fluid handwriting. It is perfectly framed. In the final part of the manuscript the ink begins to run out. The book was approved by Padre Rodrigo Alvarez who wrote a warm praise at the end of the seventh dwelling places (folio CX). It is without doubt the great jewel of the teresian autographs.

4. To sum up: among Teresa's autographs there are first and second redactions; they reflect the different moments and situations of her soul; they document the process of composition; they offer to students direct access to the text, limpid and clear and avoid the problem of textual criticism for editors.

58. Pseudo-Autographs And Spurious Writings

1. The proliferation of spurious teresian writings is a baroque phenomenon difficult to explain. Also for Teresa as for the great Fathers of the Church the falsifiers followed close behind. Under the shelter of her name and fame, apocryphal writings infiltrated the editions of her works. They plagiarized her handwriting for the sake of spreading pseudo-autographs in a teresian garb. They even cut off the letters from her own autographs for the sake of recomposing with them her signature or to counterfeit some of her spiritual sentences or to include in dozens of reliquaries of baroque taste and devotion. In this series of spurious writings attributed to Teresa, we can distinguish three categories:

— works falsely attributed to her
— false letters and poems
— pseudo-autographs.

2. Among the works falsely attributed to Teresa, we only recall the three most important, which managed to filter into the editions of Teresa:

a) The *Seven Meditations on the Our Father* had a small diffusion in manuscript, yet made a triumphal entry into the *Works of St. Teresa*. It was first published by Gracián in Valencia 1613 and 1615 and then with all honors in the Plantinian edition (Antwerp 1630, t. II pp. 585- 620) guaranteed with a preamble that said: "these Meditations are from a notebook of the works of the Holy Mother Teresa of Jesus that Doňa Isabel de Avellaneda had in her possession . . . in which notebook was present what the same Holy Mother wrote of the *Song of Songs*. It was then circulated in Castilian in a little notebook of 102 pages (ed. Plantinian, Antwrp 1656). It was a precious writing. The seven petitions of the Our Father were divided into the seven days of the week on the basis of the "names or titles of God. . . . which are Father, King, Bridegroom, Shepherd, Redeemer, Physician, and Judge." In such a way that each title corresponds to a petition and a day of the week. All of this refined affectation is incompatible with the teresian simplicity. Already in the prologue it begins by quoting Leviticus in a form thoroughly well known: "the Lord himself commands in chapter six of Leviticus so that the fire on the altar not go out, that each day the priest would fill It with new wood." And in continuation the biblical texts are brought forth in brilliant Latin. The fortunate little book had numerous teresian editions until a very recent date. Today no one doubts its spurious origin.

b) The *Ordinances of a Confraternity*. It is a very short text of only ten numbers destined for the confraternity of the Rosary for the people of Calvarrasa de Arriba (Salamanca). It was called the *Ordinances* that have to be kept in the confraternity of Our Lady, made and arranged by Teresa of Jesus in the year 1571." It had the honor of being judged authentic by the great teresianist of the 18th century Andrés de la Encarnación, who transcribed them although he did not get to publish them. In the following century Vicente de la Fuente rejected them as spurious (*Obras* ed. Rivadeneyra t.1, 1877, p. 532). But recently another distinguished teresianist, Pedre Efrén de la Madre de Dios published them as authentic (*Obras* T II, Madrid BAC, 1954, p. 984- 987, and again Otger Steggink in *Obras Completas*, Madrid 1962, p. 840-841, although they were omitted in the following edition). Today everyone judges the teresian attribution as inadmissible.

c) The fortune of *Avisos* (Counsels) has been greater. Found in Seville by Padre Gracián after Teresa's death, they were in front of the *Way of Perfection* (Evora 1583) with the title *Counsels of Mother Teresa of Jesus*. They followed constantly included in the editions of the works of Teresa until the end of the 20th century. They had reached the height of fortune with the two enormous commentaries that saw in them the quintessence of the teresian doctrine: the first was the Jesuit Diego de Andrade (Barcelona, two volumes, 1646 – 1647) and then the Archbishop of Burgos, J.J. de Arellano, in three volumes (Burgos, 1777-1786). Only recently we have discovered that before Saint Teresa they were written and spread by the Jesuit Padre Juan de la Plaza for his novices, among whom was Baltasar Alvarez, Teresa's future confessor. In reality the *Counsels* were a connecting link between Teresa and the Ignatian spirituality, although there is not any trace that she spread them in her Carmels (N.B. Another spurious document that continues to be included. Teresa's work is *Relacion 38,* certainly neither an autograph nor authentic).

3. Apocryphal Letters. Already before the first edition of her *Correspondence* by Palafox (Madrid, 1658) there were spread in print letters falsely attributed to Teresa. Here we recall only the most famous: a) Before all one in which is imparted a long lesson on prayer written to a bishop ("to a most serious prelate of the church," the title was given by Francisco de Santo María in inserting it in his Historia, vol 1, 865-868. According to Palafox. The one to whom it is addressed would be the Bishop of Osma, Alonso Velázquez). A text having a self-sufficient tone, not at all teresian. b) the letter in which Teresa tells her friend Inés Nieto about the encounter with Philip II ("look your honor, Doňa Inés, what this little woman felt when she saw herself before so great a king. . . his penetrating gaze . . . seemed to wound me . . .") c) a dozen or so letters edited by the teresianist Marqués de Piedras Albas in the *Boletín de la Academia de la Historia* (years 1914 -16), and reproduced in facsimile with some fragments of the *Way of Perfection*; d) Letters to Fathers Ambrosio Mariano and Juan de Jesús Roca) motivated by the attitude of the nuncio Sega against the discalced friars; e) a hybrid letter, half authentic and half rigged, still today inserted in her *Letters* (Ltr 11), falsified to obtain the praise of

Jesuits; f) also sadly made famous formerly were different prophecies of Teresa: about Portugal, the Society of Jesus, etc. (Of the spurious poems we will treat in another theme).

   4. Teresian pseudo-autographs. They are an unfortunate kind that closely accompany Teresa's genuine autographs. A strange phenomenon that was produced in the baroque ambient of the century. In part they reproduced pages by Teresa, in part they just downright invented them. They were disseminated throughout Europe and America. They are of two classes a) spurious that imitate Teresa's handwriting; so, for example, the series already mentioned of 13 manuscripts published by the Marquis of Piedras Albas; or those that reproduce the text of the *Spiritual Testimonies* 13-14, or the teresian book of poems reproduced in facsimile edition by Vicente de La Fuente (Madrid, 1884); or the spurious *Four Counsels* also edited in facsimile (Alicante 1963); or the most extensive of all, which reproduces the *Soliloquies* . . . b) Very lamentable is the second series : pseudo-autographs elaborated on the basis of letters cut from genuine teresian autographs destroyed for that purpose: with this material they composed fragments of the *Soliloquies and four counsels, the Spiritual Testimonies 14 and 19,* the already mentioned letter to Padre Roca, etc. More than once these pseudo-autographs served for the graphological analysis or to show the superior quality of the teresian pen.

   Fortunately between the authentic writings of Teresa and the false ones, a clean line separated the unmistakable teresian handwriting and her very distinct literary style from the spurious writings.

59. The Teresian Legend

1. This theme is certainly not about Teresa's writings. Yet next
to them the same as next to her biographies, legends have contributed
in a special way to give shape to the popular image of Teresa and
have influenced not only its iconography but also the merely artistic.
Opposite the version of scholars and painters employed in presenting
her as the seraphic Saint Teresa or as the saint of ecstasies or the writer
inspired by the mystical dove, the popular imagination has inclined to
see her simply as a realistic, human being, with a sense of humor, with
the salt of her sayings, wandering about on the roads, a dweller in poor
Castilian inns, a nun for whom God walks "among the pots and pans."
The legend from its first stages in the 17th century a little after her canonization, was diffused by Italian, Flemish, and French engravers in the
customary representations of that time. For the first time in print Roque
Fazi (O. Carm) put it down in his book *Gracias de la gracia* (Zaragosa
1757). Fazi noted the anecdotes and historical maxims and in a section
apart the bunch of legends that passed around through the mouths of
the people (pp. 330-336). In our time this same guideline is followed:
on one side the teresian anecdotal material is spreading (for example,
Alfonso Ruiz: *Anécdotas Teresianas,* or J. Gicquel in his *Les Fioretti
de Sainte Thérèse de Avila;* or much before *El polvo de sus sandalias,*
by S. Albarran); and on the other side, the flowers of the imagination
run wild, for example the precious book by Otilio Rodriguez: *Leyenda
aurea Teresiana* (Madrid 1970) or the amusing one by J. C. Cortés,
Teresa la de Jesús, or so many other amusing ones, without there being
any lack of coarse versions like that of C Bretécher.

A good collection of samples of this variety of legendary flowers,
with the respective bibliographical documentation can be seen in the

book by Otilio Rodríguez already cited in which no less than 34 legends are referred to.

2.. With the impossibility of undertaking here the presentation or the simple enumeration of the same, we can diagram them by their content with a half dozen shadings

a) There are legends that propose to highlight Teresa's sense of humor: so, for example the four or five staged by Maribobales, a Portuguese lay sister who disguises herself as a bishop so as to give a pontifical blessing to the sick Teresa, who doesn't understand the Trinitarian prayer, and who begins to dance with the basket of crockery on her head so as to get a smile from Teresa, etc. There is the undercurrent of name changes in her letters: *Mathusala, Melchisedec, el Pausado . . ., that of obedience with slices of bacon . . .,* the saying so often attributed to her *"a sad saint is a sorry saint."* Or her reaction at seeing herself badly painted by the lay brother Fray Juan de la Miseria.

b) There are those that underline the humanism of Teresa in her realism in daily life. *So, the La Manchan episode:* "when I eat partridge, I eat partridge, when I do penance I do penance," which the German theologian Karl Rahner thought so highly of; and the emphatic sentence that Jacques Maritain commented on in the mode of a philosopher (that "life would be intolerable if there were no poetry"), and the most celebrated of all: "Teresa alone is worth nothing; Teresa with God and a ducat can do all things" (rendered in French, Italian, and in English thus: "with God and two ducats I can do anything").

c) There are others that interpret the household of Teresa with her nuns: for example: the episode of the mentioned Maribobales, charged by the holy prioress to preach a sermon in recreation; or her praise of her nurse with whom she was so close: "Ana, Ana, you have the works, I have the fame; or "a nun badly dressed is like a woman badly married."

d) There are those that underline her sense of transcendence, beginning with the legendary episode of her going up the stairs and midway meeting the Child Jesus coming down and they dialogue: "who are you?" "I am Teresa of Jesus and who are you" "Jesus of Teresa." In reading this the Catalán poet Mosén Cinto was so enchanted, and the same for the author of the humorous *Teresa of Jesus*. More beautiful is the other dialogue with someone who tells her that in heaven she will meet saints a thousand times higher than she, in that case what will you do? And her answer was: "that in heaven there are saints higher than I, I see as normal, but that there are those who love more than I, I will not be able to bear," a little scene engraved in a beautiful French painting that had the good fortune of presiding in Lisieux at the bed of the sick Thérèse, and the same in Dijon in the room of the sick Elizabeth of the Trinity. Then the episode of the three lies (beautiful, discreet, and holy); the one of St. Joseph the squealer, the story of the group of founding nuns praying at the sound of the bell in the covered wagon and meditating on the Our Father; and the legend engraved in the roman church of Our Lady of Victory above the painting of the Transpiercing by Bernini; this time making the Eternal Father intervene: " If I had not created heaven, I would have created it for you alone." The Story was spread by Saint Josèmaría Escrivá in *Camino* (no 761). The legend also of the quarter of an hour, so much spread about by St. Enrique de Ossó: "give me a quarter of an hour of prayer and I will give you heaven." Of a more theological nature is the sentence according to which God has no other hands but ours: St. Teresa is much more pedantic in the English version: "Christ has no body on earth but yours, no hands but yours, no feet but yours. Yours are the eyes through which Christ looks out with compassion on the world. Yours are the feet by which he is to go about doing good. And yours are the hands by which he is to bless now." It's precious, but. . .

e) There is another series of legends that are used to confront Teresa with St. John of the Cross.

Among the most celebrated is that of the two founders eating in an inn while on the road: when the generous innkeeper offered each of them a pastry as a gratuity. Fray Juan abstained from trying it; on the other hand Teresa eats hers heartily and comments: "If the pastries of earth are so good, what will those of heaven be like." Or also, the two holy founders being on the road, Fray John of the Cross began to blush at the flirtatious remarks that were given them by a group of lads, she comments jokingly: "Fray Juan, Fray Juan the lady doesn't blush and the gentleman becomes embarrassed?" Equally celebrated is the legend of the covered wagons stuck in a sand trap, and when she complains to the Lord, he responds: "Teresa. This is how I treat my friends." And Teresa answers: "for this reason you have so few." Perhaps this is a mere resonance of what she actually wrote—this time historical—when Fray John escaped from the Toledan prison: "God treats his friends terribly" (Ltr 233.3).

f) There remains another series that highlights the femininity of Teresa.

3. In a consolidated summary, the features emphasized about her by the popular fantasy can be summed up in a few brushstrokes:

- Teresa has a special and original sense of God;
- She equally has a singular sense of humor;
— Teresa is a great realist and has a special mode of facing life;
— When compared with Fray John of the Cross she comes out the winner in charm and in the sense of daily reality.

60. Teresa's Body of Writings

1. Teresa wrote books with various titles and arguments. We ask ourselves about the thematic unity: are we dealing with a heterogeneous conglomeration or is there some type of unity that would be shown in a special organizational chart or a reading in depth? A first answer is that her writings, including the humorous ones, the poems and the letters, are written with a religious content. Varied in form but one in depth. Even in the form, it is characteristic of Teresa's style to refer – implicitly or explicitly – to the theme of God. We have no trace of her one profane writing, the first "novel of chivalry." In this present theme we will cover first the series of her writings in their chronological order so as to analyze next their thematic coherence.

2. The Chronological Sequence of Teresa's Writings:

a) As a point of departure, before looking at the redaction of her first book, Teresa finds herself immersed in full mystical experience, adorned with the characteristic phenomena. These experiences will provide the background for her first writings: special Christological graces (L 26.5; 27.2, 37.4); a mystical glimpse of the ecclesial landscape (WP 1); anthropological graces that grant her a new comprehension of self and of the soul's landscape (L 40.9). Yet above all there is a fundamental experience that permits her to go beyond the ineffability of these living experiences, what she designates as "the grace of the three favors" (L 17.5). This communicative endowment was received only a short time before and according to her permits her for the first time to speak and write about the mystical experience. Typical of this contemplative panorama is also its impelling dynamic character: from her contemplation she is impelled to found a Carmel, for which she risks acquiring a house, although she has no money, and for which she has recourse to Rome for the license, to resolve family problems, and finally she is impelled to write. This last impulse will be in its root her first writing (L pro 2) and will also impel her to complete it (L 37.1).

b) The immediate effect of this mystical dynamism on her writing style lies in her first books. She wrote the *Life* in 1562 and 1565. She wrote the *Way of Perfection* in 1566 and 1567. In deciding to write the first, she receives the order to do so from her assessors who were very much involved in her mystical experiences, yet at the same time she herself says that she is moved by one of these interior impulses to write. The *Way of Perfection* she writes because of the intense urgings of the group she had recently brought together in St. Joseph's, who knew of her mystical experiences and in a certain way wanted to empathize with her.

c) Five or six years afterward (1573), she undertook the redaction of the *Book of Her Foundations*. She writes again for her nuns, that is, so that they will be aware of the happenings: to give them a sense of the foundational process. She continues the account she had begun in her *Life* (chaps 32-36), because her confessor Padre Ripalda had ordered her to, yet the mystical impulse had also intervened (F pro. 2). She wrote the book in installments, as she continued to make foundations, until a little before her death in 1582. As a result, the book has at times the character of "memoirs" of what had been happening.

d) Finally in 1577 she composes the *Interior Castle*. As with the *Foundations* this last book also connects with the *Life*, not in the account of the work (L 32-36) but in the account of her mystical experiences (L 22-31; 37-40). She wrote it in case the *Book of Her Life* had been lost, and to complete the panorama of her interior experiences, codifying them in such a way that they serve as a paradigm of the process of every Christian, spiritual life. It is a book having an autobiographical undercurrent, written anonymously, and at the same time it is a treatise on spiritual theology.

e) Alongside these major four books, Teresa was composing minor works: *The Spiritual Testimonies,* the *Constitutions, On Making a Visitation,* the *Soliloquies,* and *the Meditations on the Song of Songs.* And as a substrate to all of this, the work that went on from day to day, hundreds of letters.

It seems clear that the conducting thread of the series has its roots in the *Life,* which offers a first synthesis of ascetical struggle and of mystical experience. Joined to this is the foundational account of St. Joseph's given in that book. Also a first effort to codify the spiritual process with the four ways of watering a garden. From all this was born the pedagogy of the *Way of Perfection* and the theology of the *Interior Castle.*

3. On the basis of this chronological process, it is easy to obtain a unitary vision of Teresa's literary production: using the teresian symbol of the castle, one could say that the corpus of her writings is a building with various dwelling places.

a) At the base we would have to place the huge support of her correspondence, an expression of her realism, of her social openness, of her emotional and relational balance: something like the cement that holds together the building or the humus on which it is established.: the letters make up almost half of her writings.

b) In the second place, Teresa thinks about and presents herself with a pair of narrative writings: first the introspective account of her personal life and her intimate or mystical experiences in the *Book of Her Life*; then, the extended account of her work as leader of a group, in the *Book of Her Foundations.*

c) As the crown of these narrative accounts, Teresa writes two doctrinal books: strictly pedagogical in the *Way of Perfection*; and of a theological bent in the *Interior Castle.* Both of them expressly bound to the group of followers referred to in the two anterior works. Yet she does not theorize in the abstract, but she teaches from her experience.

d) For this same group she writes here and there other minor pieces, now serious, now humorous, now mystical introductions: to the first group belong the *Constitutions* and *On Making the Visitation* in order to govern the life of the group; among the humorous writings are *A Satirical Critique* and a *Response to a Spiritual Challenge*; belonging to the mystical introductions would be the *Spiritual Testimonies, the Meditations on the Song of Songs* and the *Soliloquies.* As the culmination and reflection of all of this would be her *Poems*, which celebrate in part her interior feast and in part the feasts of the group.

4. *In summary:* What stands out above all is Teresa's mystical legacy , which, beginning with her personal experiences, moves on to the codifying synthesis of the *Interior Castle*, passing through the pedagogy of the *Way of Perfection*, always in dialogue with the select group of her Carmels, yet without losing contact with "the reader," with the society of the times, or with our fundamental human experience.

VII
Two Narrative Books:
The Life And The Foundations

Among Teresa's narrative pages two of her major works stand out. The Book of her Life, which sketches bits of her autobiography, above all her interior and mystical life. It was written in 1565. And The Book of Her Foundations, which tells about her work as founder. It was begun in 1573 and finished after her last foundation was made a few months before her death.

61. The Book Of Her Life And Its Two Redactions

1. Fortunately we possess even today the autograph manuscript of *The Life* just as it was when it came forth from Teresa's pen. If perhaps with some small modifications in its external vestment and in the marginal trimmings of the guillotine. In this present theme we are interested in establishing the act of its birth, in explaining the why of its two redactions, and in pointing out some small incidents of its historical trajectory.

2. The first redaction and its context. Teresa wrote her *Life* for the first time at the age of 47 in the Toledan palace of Doña Luisa de la Cerda, which is presently the Royal Academy of Fine Arts and Historical Studies in Toledo. She writes it thus not in the severe, walled precincts of the Carmelite cloister but in the magnificent surroundings of a noble palace. She finishes it probably in the spring of that year; "this book was finished in June of the year 1562" (a final note from the second redaction, yet referring to this first). The text has been lost. We do not know its dimensions or its plan. With all probability it consisted of two sections: one to recount her early life (her sins) and the other to tell of her mystical experiences (the "favors" of God). Certainly the narration did not reflect the external magnificent surroundings of the palace, but the extreme internal situation of the author. She was pressed to discern her mystical experiences by two urgent facts of the moment. On the one hand the fact of the foundation of the Carmel of St. Joseph, which was interrupted on account of the trip to Toledo, and then she felt urged to continue with it by the visit of another Carmelite founder, the Andalusian María de Yepes; and, on the other hand, an increasing wave of mystical experiences that forced her to write in order to understand herself. Among

these mystical graces was a recent one that gave her the capacity to overcome the mystical ineffability. Now she is able to speak and write about what was happening in her. And when she was about ready to finish the writing, there took place the decisive encounter with the Dominican Padre García de Toledo, for whom she wrote the second redaction of the book.

3. The second redaction. This is the only one that has reached us. She writes at the command of her confessors, but at the same time through an interior impulse of mystical origin. Among those commanding her to write, two stand out of a different stripe: on the one hand is the Inquisitor Soto, who suggested that she write the book and submit it to Master John of Avila. Soto did not command this under pressure or fearing some sinister plot; he suggested it to her since he saw her so anxious and that she might be at rest (ST 58.6). On the other hand, among those who ordered her to write was an intimate, theologian friend of hers, García de Toledo, who empathized with her and her living experiences, and who not only ordered her to write but pressured her and closely followed the process of the redaction and took possession of the writing as soon as it was finished. But his was a pressure from "outside"; he pressures her because he longs to see the writing. He needs to know from within about the mystical experiences that the author is undergoing and there was raised up in his soul a surge of expectation. At the crossroads of these two personages – the inquisitor and the mystical neophyte — a new book is born which at the same time will come to end up first in the hands of the neophyte Padre García, and then in the hands of the Inquisitor Soto, in the exercise of his inquisitorial function, but equally benevolent toward Teresa. So, by somewhat torturous paths, the Teresain autograph was kept in the inquisitorial caverns and then in a chamber of the Escorial.

4. The first steps of the manuscript of *the Life*. Teresa wrote it

not in Toledo but in Avila, on the poorest writing desk of her cell in St. Joseph's. She wrote it, according to herself, with many breaks little by little, stealing the time "because it keeps me from spinning" (L 10.7). She was 50 at the time. Probably throughout the year of 1565 when she and the new Carmel had overcome the tensions with the City Council (L 36.23). As soon as it was finished, the manuscript passed into the hands of García de Toledo and those of Domingo Báñez who did not think it should be published and warned about throwing it in the fire. In 1568, Teresa gave it to her friend in Toledo, Doña Luisa de la Cerda so that she might bring it to Montilla and give it to Master Juan de Avila. But Doña Luisa delayed her trip and Teresa feared the reaction of Báñez (Ltr 8.9; 10.2). This is probably the time in which the existence of the manuscript became known by the Princess of Eboli. In September of that year, it had already been read by the master John of Avila and was on its return to St. Joseph's. Yet a few years later (February 1575) it was requested by the Inquisition, and the Bishop, Don Alvaro, had to send it to the tribunal in Valladolid, from where it passed quickly to the supreme tribunal in Madrid. In May of that year, Báñez was charged by the inquisitors to examine it. He did so at the College of St. Gregory in Valladolid and gave a favorable opinion, signed 7 July 1575. Yet the teresian autograph – "my soul" Teresa calls it – was strangely kept by the Inquisition, until after Teresa's death. Anne of Jesus got it back in 1586 and placed it in the hands of Fray Luis de León, who edited it for publication two years later (Salamanca 1588).

5. The autograph in the Escorial. The manuscript of the *Life* reached the Escorial passing through the court. The published edition of 1588 was dedicated to Our Lady the Empress ((Madrid, 10 April 1588) and a little afterward Philip II let Doria know of his desire to keep in "San Lorenzo el Real the original books of Mother Teresa" (3.6. 1592). Doria quickly solicited it from Fray Luis's successor,

the celebrated Agustín Antolínez, and he gave it to the prior of San Lorenzo, who at this time was a former confessor of Teresa's, Fray Diego de Yepes. Thus the autograph entered into the collection of the royal Library at the end of 1592 and was granted the great honor of being kept between two presumed autographs, one of St. Augustine and the other of St. John Chrysostom. It is precisely the time in which De Yepes had to defend the book and the author against a flood of denunciations sent to the tribunal of the Inquistion (letter from Diego de Yepes of 7 June, 1594). There followed for the autograph years – centuries – of peace. In 1773, after a terrible fire in the Library, it was kept apart in the "room of St. Teresa." At the beginning of the 20the century, it was on exhibit again in a special showcase in the exposition room. At present it is in the reserved section.

6. We will sum up with two serious incidents in the history of the autograph at the Escorial. The first occurred during the War of Independence. In 1809 by order of the French government, the *Life* together with other precious manuscripts of the Escorial was brought to Madrid destined for France. Fortunately, the manuscripts were deposited in a chapel of the convent of the Trinity, beneath a mountain of printed paper, where their trip to Paris was frustrated. The second episode occurred in regard to the teresian manuscript during the Spanish civil war of 1936. Taken precipitously from the Escorial destined for some outside country, it ended up on the frontier, retained — no one knows how — in the warehouses of Perelada (Gerona), from where it returned, safe and sound, in 1939 to its precious case in the Escorial, where, thanks to its guardians, today enjoys good health.

62. Structure And Content Of The Book

1. *The Book of Her Life* both in the history of spirituality and as literature is generally known as Teresa's autobiography. Nonetheless it is not strictly speaking an autobiography. It doesn't comprise in its complexity the history of the author. Its autobiographical content is partial and only in sections. It leaves many threads barely mentioned without development (Rodrigo, her becoming an orphan, sickness, friendships). Other important aspects she doesn't mention (the introduction to the monastic life, her Carmelite formation). Its plan develops only the thread of Teresa's relationship with God, yet giving more space and relief to God's relations with her. She is interested, above all, in resolving a pressing problem that underlies the whole narration: what meaning does this intervention of God in her life have. Why does it always increase until taking complete possession of her.

2. For this reason precisely the heart of the account is constituted as "the mystical fact" lived by her, which is not an exact fact but a radical, global, all-enveloping one. In relating her account Teresa wants to clarify for herself – and for those ordering her to write — the meaning of her life: not only by referring to it but by understanding and interpreting it. Hence the introspective and univocal force of the narration. The other biographical data or incidents remain outside the focus, or they are referred to insofar as they contribute to the focus and clarification of the given nucleus: God and herself. From the viewpoint of the narrator this relationship between God and herself is concentrated on prayer as a sharing in friendship. For this reason there is interpolated in the account a long parenthesis on the degrees of prayer, which in the autobiographical key is translated into the

degrees of life or degrees of the relationship between the two.

3. From this thematic focus of the account it is easy to follow the plan of the book in four or five related sections.

a) Teresa begins by recounting her life and prayer in her home environment (how the Lord began to awaken this soul – the first chapter title), and the following highs and lows of her conduct that frames her prayer, or abandonment of it, or the recovery of the "truth I knew in childhood," the family, the readings, the vocation, the Carmelite life, the illness, the decisive fact . . . The story of her infidelities, that she believed incompatible with the mystical graces which came upon her. All of this she covers up to chapter 9 inclusive. Chapter 10 connects with a change of direction in the account: from here on the matter must be kept secret.

b) But before dealing with these mysterious, secret happenings, Teresa feels the need to set forward first a key to the reading with an outline of the degrees of prayer. She introduces them with the symbol of the garden and the water wheel, not in a narrative but in a theoretical key. Yet very gently she returns to the autobiographical element: these degrees are the ladder of ascent that she will then narrate. And from chapter 16 we have the degrees of prayer that she is experiencing at the time she is writing her account, her mystical journey: chapters 11-21. And again she changes with the interpolation of chapter 22 on the humanity of Christ, for without taking this into account the mystical facts that ensue in the third section of the book will be hardly intelligible.

c) Section three, chapters 23-31. Now she tells of the most burning facts of the mystical life in the relations of God with her. Gradually, before all, Teresa has entered experimentally into the mysterious sphere of the presence of God. First she listens (locutions) and then she sees (visions). She doesn't understand. There follow two powerful episodes: the first to center her scattered affectivity

"No longer do I want you to converse with men but with angels" (L 24.5; see the context, nos 6-7); and then to illumine the mind and disengage if from human theories: "I shall give you a living book" (L 26.5; see again the context). Then Jesus Christ becomes present and installs himself in her life (L 27-28), as a mysterious companion along the way: "It seemed to me that Jesus Christ was always present at my side" (l 27.2). But all of this did not remain in a closed interiority or in ecstatic contemplation: the mystical contemplation turned into a an imperative and impelling call to action with regard to others, as will be seen.

d) There then came an absolute novelty for her life. Teresa receives orders to found. She had before this gathered around about 40 nuns in her monastery. But now the novelty consisted in that she received a commission to erect a house-monastery. This was seen as the wrong thing to do by almost all the surrounding learned men and by her superiors. It was In contrast also with the peacefulness of her life in the old monastery. With a complete lack of means. It went almost against the common sense of Teresa herself. And the book centers on the execution of the commission, with the foundation of St. Joseph. An account characterized by a double component: mystical-interior life and social-operative-exterior life. All of this goes to make up chapters 32-36; the only ones that should be saved, she says, in case the manuscript is burned.

e) Her account ought to end here. Yet Teresa's mystical life continues increasing with new interior happenings and to them she dedicates the last part of her account (L 37.1), which nevertheless remains in suspense pending the sound of the clock. "I am consoled to hear the clock strike, for at the passing away of that hour of life it seems to me that I am drawing a little closer to the vision of God"(L 40.20), with a last flash on the present moment: "This is the way in which I now live, my Lord and Father" (L 40.23).

4. The Life is an unconventional religious narration. Frequently God is the subject of the action. The narration itself culminates so many times in a religious act of doxology or of adoration or of petition, or bows before the mystery of his presence in her life. Besides the strictly thematic content expounded in the previous number, the entire book is impregnated with mystagogical intent. Teresa does not write for literary reasons or with an aesthetic objective. She is convinced of the religious undertone of her case. And she proposes to testify to it, not as a model (she is convinced that her life is not a model) but as a communicator. For that reason she makes use of a certain lyrical vibration incorporated into the account, yet above all she utilizes the inherent force of the mystical fact in itself, which more than once puts her into an intense trance while she writes. For example: "in writing this it seems to me that . . . I can say . . . that I no longer live but that you, my Creator, live in me . . . for some years now" Or also "nor since this morning when I received Communion do I think it is I who am speaking [writing]. It seems that what I see is a dream, and I would desire to see no other persons than those who are sick with this sickness I now have. Or breaking the account: "Alas! I don't know what I am saying to myself, because almost without my uttering this I'm already putting it down in writing. I find I'm disturbed and somewhat outside myself since I have brought these things back to mind (L 38.22). For this reason, *The Book of her Life* demands a religious reading. Only when read in this key can it be understood. Teresa did not give a title to her account. Only many years later (1581) did she give it one: 'So this book is entitled 'On the Mercies of God'" (Ltr 415.1).

63. Why Anonymity?
Is The Life A Secret Book?

1. *The Life* is an anonymous autobiographical narration. It is so programmed by its author that it states neither the name nor the title of the book. She presents it in sum as a "relation that my confessors commanded me to write" (L. Pro). She doesn't ever give the name of the city ("this place") nor does she give the name of the monastery in which the scenes are framed, nor does she give the names of her companions along the way. Of the half hundred persons who populate the account, only three appear with an uncovered face: Fray Pedro de Alcántara, Father Francisco, "who is the Duke of Gandía, and Father Master John of Avila. When she has finished the account, she writes a letter of consignment (also without mentioning the name of the one for whom it is destined). She beseeches this unnamed person to arrange to have a copy made if they are going to bring it to Padre Master John of Avila since someone might recognize her handwriting and thus identify the author. And this desire for anonymity was not due – as has been often said — to her intention of being silent about her condition as a woman; on the contrary, she does not hide this fact from the reader, that the one writing is "a little woman, wretched, weak, and fearful like myself" (L 28.18), " a woman and wretched . . . and without learning, without instruction from a learned man," normally obliged to "spin for this is a poor house" (L. 10.7). She gives an account, for example, of her trip from Avila to Toledo and in return from Toledo to Avila and was careful not to give the name of either of the two cities. Nor does she mention the name of Becedas or of the quack.

2. What is the motive for this anonymity? Having finished the first part (chapters 1-9) and before taking up the narration of her

mystical experiences, Teresa gives the title of the new chapter thus:
"Asks the one to whom this is sent to keep secret what she writes
from here on, for they commanded her to speak so personally about
the favors the Lord grants her." (L. 10. title). And in the body of the
chapter she formulates categorically the petition: "As for what I say
[= write] from here on, I do not give this permission; nor do I desire,
if they should show it to someone, that they tell who it is who has
experienced these things, or who has written this. As a result, I will
not mention my name or the name of anyone else, but I will write
everything as best I can so as to remain unknown, and this I ask for
the love of God" (L. 10.7). That is to say, not only anonymous on
the part of the author, but secrecy imposed on the reader. And the
motive that she brings forth is not "the secrecy of confession" as she
had asked for a little before in writing her *Spiritual Testimony 3.
13*, but a certain caution, so that the book does not lose its authority
by being known as written by a person "without learning or having
lived a good life." She repeats this more expressly, distinguishing
the two strata of the narration, the sins and the favors. "Neither in
the one instance nor in the other would there be any gain in my telling my name. It is clear that during my life no good should be said
of me. After my death there should be no reason for doing so, but
rather goodness would lose prestige, and no credit would be given to
it for being said of so wretched and base a person" (10.7). In such a
way that the desire for anonymity is concentrated especially on the
person of the author. The reader should not identify her. Hence the
desire that a copy of the manuscript be made before its journey to
Andalusia to place it in the hands of Master John of Avila, lest it pass
into the hands of others and they recognize her handwriting.

　　　3. Yet in spite of the fact of this systematic concealment as
much of the author as well as of other persons in the drama, it happens that the book itself is inhabited by a group of select persons –

also with their faces concealed— with whom she dialogues intermittently, until establishing with some of them a permanent dialogue in the manner of empathy from within the mystical experience. This is an important data for a comprehensive reading of the book. We recall only the three most important cases.

a) First of all, those who ordered her to write. They are an imprecise group, with a scarce presence in the book. In the first place, the Dominicans, Báñez and Ibáñez. Especially, the second is the great theologian of the city. He enters the book only in the second half of the account. In dealing with Teresa, the theologian is changed into a spiritual person. He begins a life of prayer. He renounces his chair and retires to a solitary monastery, from where he maintains his relationship with Teresa, under the contagion of her mystical experiences. And finally he dies (2 February 1565) while she is still writing the book. In the last episode that takes place between the two she writes: "He wrote to me a little before he died asking what he should do, because when he finished saying Mass he often went into rapture for a long time without being able to prevent it" (L. 38. 13).

b) Also there is another heterogeneous group that finds lodging in the book, "the five persons who at present love each other in Christ" are not easy to identify. With them Teresa strikes up her strongest dialogue in full mystical trance: "Nor since this morning when I received Communion do I think it is I who am speaking. It seems that what I see is a dream, and I would desire to see no other persons than those who are sick with this sickness I now have." And she directs to them her shout: "may we all be mad for love of him who for love of us was called mad" (L 16.6-7). An intense flowing of the mystical current passes among the five. A current much more intense would be with one of them, namely:

c) The third Dominican who would be the greatest inhabitant of the book, Padre García de Toledo. There had preceded a decisive episode during the first redaction of the book. Teresa encountered this old friend on his return from his conquering adventures in Mexico, and she connects with him in depth. So much so that immediately she presents him to her great Friend in a mystical trance praying: "Lord you must not deny me this favor: see how this individual is fit to be our friend" (L 34.8). Now during the second redaction of the book, Padre García, already in full mystical empathy, is the object of an intermittent yet constant dialogue, from the first allusion (L. 7. 22), repeated each time the author goes out of boundaries and speaks foolishness or when she succumbs to this holy heavenly madness (L 16.4) of the mystical trance. There are moments of stirring emotion, he is "my son and my Father," which sometimes Báñez can't stand and crosses out (L 19.9). She asks him to cry out in her place: "Your Reverence ought to cry out these truths, since God has taken from me the freedom to do so" (L 27.13). There are entire chapters written in the mode of a letter to him: "Let some of these things which Your Reverence sees I go to excess in, be for you alone" (L 16.6). I ask you to tear up or burn it (L 10.7; 13.22; 14.12); "tear this up if it sounds bad to Your Reverence and believe me that I would say it better in person if I could (21.4)... and even the entire book: "I beg your Reverence for the love of God that if you think you should tear up what else is written here you preserve whatever pertains to this monastery. And when I'm dead, give it to the Sisters who live here that when those who are to come see the many things His Majesty arranged for its establishment . . . they might be greatly encouraged to serve God" (L 36.29). She expresses the highest confidence in him: "since your Reverence says that you love me, prove it to me by preparing yourself so that God may grant you this favor" (L 16.6). For his part Padre García every time he writes to her insists that she write without drawbacks or restrictions: "Since your Reverence again sent me orders not to worry about enlarging this and not to omit anything . . . (L 30.22). Thus we owe to

Padre García not only the existence and great detail of the book, but also the emotive and effusive character or mystical tension found in the most intense pages.

4. In conclusion, within the book the author has created a space for confidentiality. She has dialogued at different levels with various groups of intimate friends. She wrote especially "to attract souls to so high a blessing" (L 18.8) or to empathize with them. An empathizing provocation that persists with every reader that they may enter the interior space of the book. Without the flow of this mystical emotion, we would have only empty pages, as if the batteries were to run out on the mystical current. For all of this, the initial intention of anonymity is quickly diluted like a lump of sugar. Even the inquisition quickly found out that the author of the book was Madre Teresa, a nun at St. Joseph's in the diocese of the Bishop of Avila, Don Alvaro, from whom they demanded surrender of the book.

64. The Treatise On
The Degrees Of Prayer

1. Unexpectedly, Teresa interrupts her narration and introduces a treatise perfectly articulated on the degrees of prayer. Why this doctrinal interpolation in the middle of her account of her life? The author limits herself to announcing this in the title of chapter 11, the first chapter of this treatise: "Begins to explain through a comparison four degrees of prayer." Let us underline the three points of the epigraph: "Begins the theme / it is based on a comparison /she will expound the four degrees of prayer." This means that she will abandon for the moment the narrative thread and open a new section. She opts for a literary change not stylized until the present: she will develop the theme in the framework of a comparison. A comparison in the teresian lexicon has a polysemantic value, equivalent to a simile, image, allegory, or symbol. In fact she will find support initially in an elemental simile; then she will go on enriching it and converting it into a true symbol. Yet we note above all the third point: she will treat only of four degrees of prayer, as the reader will later see. She doesn't announce generically a treatise on prayer and its degrees, as had been repeatedly said, but only of "four degrees of prayer in which the Lord in his goodness has sometimes placed my soul" (L 11.8).

2. And let us note, finally, that the new treatise begins at the turn of the page with a categorical demand for secrecy, imposed on the reader. "As for what I say from here on" (L 10.7), a demand that doesn't make sense in the doctrinal pages of the treatise, but refers rather to the account of the great mystical graces, which will appear again when she resumes the narration (chapters 23-31). It proves that the treatise on the four degrees of prayer is an addition to the second redaction of the book: Teresa believed it necessary to place it before

the narration of her great mystical graces so as to offer the reader a doctrinal key that will permit the reader to understand them as a unitary process and not just a series of unconnected episodes.

3. It has occurred, moreover that at this time there arose the great friendship with Padre García de Toledo, quickly begun through mystical experiences similar to those of Teresa and to teach him she introduces the comparison of a garden and its development, which "will provide some recreation for your Reverence, I will be pleased if you laugh at my manner of explaining if it seems foolish to you . . . given that your garden is watered with all these four degrees, although the last is still not given except in drops" (L 11. 6-8). Thus the little treatise has a twofold reason for being: it serves as a premise that will facilitate the understanding of what follows in the mystical narration and as an orienting introduction for the neophyte mystic who is the first reader.

4. The comparison. As we have indicated the image of the garden serves Teresa as a means of articulating the doctrinal treatise. The "garden of the soul" is a frequent topic in spiritual literature, from" the enclosed garden" in the *Song of Songs (4.12)* or the "watered gardens" in Jeremiah 31.12. Yet in her pen it acquires original nuances and shades of meaning at the same time having a broad reach in symbol, because as Teresa herself assures, the image of the garden has passed previously through her experience: "This comparison has its charm for me because often in my beginnings . . . it was a great delight for me to consider my soul as a garden and reflect that the Lord was taking his walk in it" (L. 14.9).

5. Let us highlight the elements that are incorporated into the symbol and have a doctrinal value: *the garden* is the soul of the one who prays; the *water* is the life or the grace; the *irrigation,* the prayer; the *flowers and carnations* are the aroma of good that impregnates the life of the one who prays; the *fruits* , the virtues

(fruits which nourish the one who prays, who in her turn shares the fruit and gives it to others to eat); the *gardener,* the one responsible for the garden and its irrigation, charged with uprooting the weeds and distributing the fruits; finally. The absolute owner of the garden and of the gardener is the Lord, from whom proceeds the water for irrigation and for whom the aroma of the flower and the fruits of the orchard are destined.

6. The treatise distinguishes four ways of watering the garden: *the well, the water wheel, the stream, the rain from heaven.* These ways refer to four degrees of prayer: meditation, prayer of quiet, sleep of the faculties, and union. With a clear diversity of participation on the part of the gardener and of the Lord of the garden: only one degree for the first (ascetical prayer), and three for the full initiative of the second (mystical prayer). Each degree is thus developed: first we are told what it consists in, and then its influence on the life of the one praying. Let us sketch this in outline:

— the first degree: prayer of the beginner, discursive meditation, intertwined with reflection and affection, on different themes from the gospels or other occasions, especially the Passion of the Lord. To the beginner are given practical instructions: determination to persevere in prayer at every cost, to pray one's life, to love very much the Humanity of Christ. Above all not to practice false mystical flights, which are unattainable through one's own efforts. Teresa is not a partisan of mental emptiness.

— the second degree: the first mystical experience in prayer is a pure gift from God; quiet of the will, fascinated by the mystery of God, yet without the submission of the remaining interior functions: wandering of the fantasy occurs, but one is to pay no attention to this mad woman in the house. In the prayer, there is the first experience of the action of God, "who finds his delight in being with humans." This is the fruitful experience of his evolving presence. Loving is the principal and delightful exercise, with a great influence on a change of life.

— the third degree: the experience of the presence and action of God is extended to all interior activity, to all one's being. "she would want to be all tongues to praise the Lord. All of her body and soul would want to break into pieces to show the joy that with this pain she feels." Pure doxology. A total change of life. An irradiation on others. Prolonged, pre-ecstatic high spirits. (The term "sleep of the faculties" she took from Laredo, *The Ascent of Mount Sion.* II. 19)

— the fourth degree: experience of full union with God. Prayer of total conformity with the divine will. The one who prays has surrendered herself to the overflowing action of God. It is like being possessed by God. In poetry: "Yours I am, for You I was born . . ." : a clear awareness and experience that the one praying is of God and for God."Multiple mystical episodes, of ecstasy, flight of the spirit, and raptures.

7. *The four stages* are a process that begins with human action and ends in the divine action. Yet the one praying doesn't grow in the sense of action but in that of relation. The prayer is not established on a relationship between equals, even though God abases himself to find his delights among humans (Prv. 8.31). On his side the relationship has infinitely higher possibilities. Hence the preponderance of the mystical degrees. The treatise reflects directly the evolution of Teresa's prayer, which doesn't correspond necessarily with anyone else's prayer.

65. The Mystical Fact

1. The first redaction of the *Life* is reduced to the alternative narration of "Teresa's sins and God's favors to her." Yet this second theme was the whole reason for her writing the account. The book in fact expounds the mystical fact as it happened to Teresa in the last decade of her life. It was a new life she lived from then on. "This is another new book from here on—I mean another, new life. The life dealt with up to this point was mine; the one I lived from the point where I began to explain these things about prayer is the one God lived in me" (L. 23.1). This is the data with which the narration of this great adventure of her life opens. The mystical fact becomes the powerful contribution of the book, all of its reason for being, what keeps it actual and its pages still speaking to readers today. In this regard, we have three questions.

— In what context did her mystical life arise?

— What is the structure of the teresian account?

— What was Teresa's mystical ascent?

2. The context. A theme of special importance. The mystical element related in the *Life* comes about, beginning when Teresa was 39-40 years old: 1554-1565. Mostly all of it took place in Avila. The external mark of the city at this time is that it suffers from a double hostility – social and religious –toward the mystical phenomena in women visionaries, whether from the pseudo-mystical episodes that had recently occurred in Spain ("Since at that time other women had fallen into serious illusions and deceptions caused by the devil." are Teresa's immediate words) (L 23.2), or whether through the iron attitude of the inquisition with regard to the illuminists ("severe

times!'"), or whether from episodes of the famous Avilan Maridíaz, an exceptional woman who, nonetheless, had nothing of these illusions. Hence the two hostile forces that frame from nearby Teresa's mystical experiences: on the one hand the permanent harassment of her religious assessors, inclined to fear hidden demons in these events; and on the other hand, Teresa herself, who far from welcoming them in the psychological context of favor, cedes to the alarm and is frightened by what is happening to her. She is systematically on guard against herself. And when the interior fact becomes public (raptures), not only does she blush, but would prefer to be buried alive (L. 31.12), and even thinks seriously about flight to another far off Carmel where no one would know her. That is to say, the teresian mystical fact does not arise in an environment of favor; and neither is it applauded or magnified by the chorus of spectators, nor does Teresa herself have the least temptation to histrionics or exhibitionism. In her the mystical fact goes against the grain, as does the prophetic mission for certain biblical prophets.

3. *The structure of the mystical account in the Life.* The mystical account occupies three fourths of the book, from chapter 14 to 40. Nonetheless, the nucleus of the testimony is concentrated in chapter 23-31. To this nucleus account is added two successive complements. First, to refer to the mystical origin of the foundation of St. Joseph's (chapters 32-36), and then to tell about the experiences she had in the new Carmel (chapter 37-40). When taken together the account becomes a complicated mix of experiences and interior phenomena and of a whole exterior undertaking dense with consequences, yet of an origin and depth as mystical as the interior phenomena. For the moment we are interested only in the central chapters (23-31), which probably correspond to the original account. In them Teresa tells of the intersection of interior mystical graces and the rejection (permanent or intermittent) of her immediate surroundings, she inter-

twines her account with the two components: idyllic on the one side, dramatic and almost tragic on the other ("there were enough things to drive me insane," she notes in the middle of her account L. 28.18). She writes it without a pre-established plan. Narrating and reasoning. In a general line, she follows the chronological order of events, in such a way that she permits us — the reader and the student – to catch a glimpse of the ascending and undivided process of her mystical experience, beyond the narrated episodes. We will propose, in continuing, the stages of this process.

4. The ascent of mystical experiences. Before all, the mystical fact in Teresa is not the result of a preparatory process, nor of personal asceticism, nor of a technique or training induced from outside oneself. Nor does it arise from thinking of God in a general way or through yoga. The mystical experience breaks forth in Teresa's psychological space as an unexpected fact, unforeseen, not desired, neither procured nor known.

— The first episode recorded by her is the fundamental fact of her entrance into the presence of God, consciously experienced as something absolutely new: "I sometimes experienced, as I said, although very briefly, the beginning of what I will now speak about. It used to happen, when I represented Christ within me in order to place myself in his presence, or even while reading, that a feeling of the presence of God would come upon me unexpectedly so that I could in no way doubt he was within me or I totally immersed in him" (L 10.1). These episodic beginnings soon became stable and permanent, a substrate of the new interior activity of joy and quiet, "not thinking of anything" an affective overflow.

— The second stage follows when this mysterious presence turns into a communicating presence, with the giving of occasional and incisive messages, not heard with the ears but understood in the depth of her being. These words are what unleashed in Teresa a first

series of raptures (L 24.5), not only intimate but public. There follow
both locutions and raptures of a profound and unknown psychological mechanism. One would call it subjugation, as though she felt supplanted or misplaced before this impelling grace.

— In the third place. There happened to her an advance in
the basic fact of the presence of God. Teresa experiences the presence of Christ. She doesn't perceive him through the senses, but
yes localized on the right side as a stable witness to her daily tasks,
and it would go on for years (L 27.2). In a crescendo: first it is an
experience purely spiritual – from spirit to spirit —; then it takes on
concrete forms, the hand, the face, the risen humanity. (Adopting
the lexicon of her times, she designates the first experience as an
intellectual vision; and the second as an imaginative vision). Christ
is the supreme beauty: he is impressed and engraved in the profound
depths of her being.

— In the fourth place, an overflowing increase of her interior
activity: great impulses of love, impulses that are so great it is impossible to be able to understand them . . ."there increased in me a love
for God to such a degree that I didn't know where it came from (for
it was very supernatural) . . . I saw that I was dying with desire to see
God." To see God is now the terminal reason for every mystical fact.
Among these loving impulses, the grace of the dart that transpierces
the heart has a special place (a grace essentially spiritual – although
with reflections in her whole being – yet which does not have anything to do with the alleged bodily wound – heart attack – of the
physical, incorrupt bodily organ).

— Finally, perhaps the most characteristic aspect: the operative
tension. In Teresa the mystical fact does not terminate in contemplation but in action. In two fundamental actions: writing and founding.

66. The Denoument Of The *Life*

1. As we have already noted (Theme 62), the *Life* is an account to be given to others. To the central chapters that narrate the mystical fact, Teresa adds five other chapters to tell the story of her first Carmel (chaps. 32-36). And having finished this, she returns to the account of her interior life ("the favors the Lord has granted me") during the first three years of her life in this first Carmel (chaps. 37-40). These four chapters are a separate literary piece, a kind of instantaneous finale about her soul. For marginal details of the account, we know that she wrote them in the third year of this three-year period; that she wrote them at intervals ("I've returned so often to write these three folios and so many days have passed . . . (L 39.17); and sometimes she needs to suspend her pen in the presence of a mystical trance coming on her ("Alas! I don't know what I'm saying, because almost without my uttering this I'm already putting it down in writing. I find I'm disturbed and somewhat outside myself" (L 38.22). Thus at the end of her account she can endorse it with the assertion:: "this is the way in which I now live," the final measure in the score of her life. In this account we are interested in three things: the space in which she lives and writes; the sequence of the "great mystical favors"; the final gesture of waiting and hoping.

2. The context: the idyllic environment of the Carmel of St. Joseph. It serves as a link with the preceding chapters. Teresa grants herself a pause to sketch the life that was lived in "this little corner," in the midst of a group of young and enthusiastic warriors: " I now see some young girls entering this house; because God has touched them and given them a little light and love (I mean that after a short

while he gives them some gift), they do not wait for him, or suffer any obstacle in their path, or even remember to eat. On account of him whom they know loves them, they close themselves up forever in a house without income, like someone who doesn't esteem her life. They give up everything, neither do they want their own will . . . together they all offer themselves as a sacrifice to God" (L 39.10). The emotion of this love affair lived by all together is so intense that Teresa will give another report about it eight years later at the beginning of her *Foundations*: she sees herself as a "wretched one among these angelic souls . . ." What interests us is finding her in this little world of contrasts: extreme poverty of the house and the literary and spiritual euphoria of the author.

3. The great favors of the moment. Never had the *Life* been so detailed and overflowing. The recollections are so alive, so copious they come crowding in on one another in such disorder that it is hardly possible to highlight in this kind of mystical upsurge what the great favors are that are enunciated in the headings of chapters 38, 39, and 40.

a) Above all, the Christological experiences emerge. Christ contemplated in the bosom of the Father is according to Teresa the most sublime favor of all that she has received (L 38.18). Christ is beauty that is engraved and impressed indelibly on her soul. He is majesty in itself. Just recalling this majesty at the time of Communion made her hair stand on end. His beauty and his love had emptied the depth of her soul of all its old human affections.

b) She likewise lives her own personal Pentecost: while she celebrates the liturgical feast and is reading from the pages of Denis the Carthusian, a dove of mother-of-pearl whiteness flutters over her head and causes her to go out of herself. Very great was the glory of this rapture (38.11).

c) The experiences of the divinity and of the Trinity are

redoubled: "I was given so clear an understanding of how there is only one God and three Persons that I was amazed and greatly consoled. It was extraordinarily beneficial ' (L 39.25). In the divinity lies all of creation and the world clearly reflected as in a mirror.

d) Also as in a mirror she has the experience of her own soul in which is perceived and reflected the splendor of the divinity. (L 40.5).

e) She has a singular experience of the Blessed Virgin in her Assumption into heaven, always from the springboard of the liturgy (L 39.26).

f) She feels herself invested with a supplicating priesthood, with the absolute security that her supplications are always welcome in the bosom of God (L 39)

g) All of these experiences seem to reach their culmination in the last chapter registered and commented on at length: Teresa experiences the truth of God, "the height and summit of all truths and the love of all loves: "This truth, which I say was given to my understanding, is in itself truth, and it is without beginning or end; all other truths depend on this truth, just as all other loves depend on this love and all other grandeurs on this grandeur . . ."(l 40.4). "all the harm that comes to the world comes from its not knowing the truths of Scripture in clarity and truth" (L 40.1).

In sum, the accumulation of mystical experiences leaves her transposed; it causes her to "look from on high," with the soul transferred to the world of the transcendent, yet at the same time with her feet well planted on the ground, attentive to the friend who suffers an illness of the eyes, or to one who suffers from stone, or another who is tempted (L 39); she is the first to take the broom or to work in the kitchen, where "the Lord walks among the pots and pans."

4. The ending, between tension and hope. When she writes the last pages of the book, Teresa was 50 years old. She found herself "in this little corner so enclosed, where according to what I thought,

I would, as one dead, no longer be remembered" (L 40.22). She is at the head of the community of St. Joseph. She and her nuns live in absolute poverty. Recently (1564) the painful lawsuit with the city Council had ended. Personally, she had to suffer the weight of her own body, the daily vomiting, many ailments. At times she suffered a momentary blackout of all the tensions: "At other times I am in such a condition that I neither feel like living nor have I any mind to die, but I experience a lukewarmness and darkness in everything, with many trials, as I've said I often do" (40. 21).

5. Yet spiritually she lives in a situation totally new, in a zone on the frontier between life and death. Without any fear of death, "which I always feared greatly" (L 38.5). "She observes as though from up high" the mechanisms of social life, the farce over money and honor (L 40.22), "all things seemed to me like an ant-hill" (L 39.22). "Everything I see with my bodily eyes seems to be a dream" (L 38.7). "Merely to look toward heaven recollects the soul" (L 38.6). She is secure in thinking that "never does he neglect me" (L 40.19). Likewise she is convinced that "there are few who have who have arrived at the experience of so many things" (L 40.8). As a result in the depths of her psychology there prevails the gesture of amazement expressed with her typical words to be "frightened or amazed" (repeated with different nuances 22 times in these chapters).

6. The most determining factor in this amazement is the dynamic of the desires and the attitude of hope. She lives against the clock: " I am consoled to hear the clock strike, for at the passing away of that hour of life it seems to me I am drawing a little closer to the vision of God" (L 40.20). The hour of seeing God is now measured by the parameter of death. Hence her classic motto: "Lord, either to die or to suffer; I don't ask for anything else for myself." Another alternative meaning is: to die is to see him; not to die is to work for the good of others for his glory. "I would like some soul

to profit a little by all that can be said about me. Since I have been living in this house [St. Joseph], the Lord has been pleased that all my desires converge upon this one. And he has given me a kind of sleep in life, or it almost always seems to me that I am dreaming what I see" (L 40.22). The final balance: "this is the way in which I now live my Lord and my Father" – she sums up this strong tension between the eschatological (to die in order to see God) and the ecclesiological (to live serving others). It is the classical Pauline dilemma in Philippians 1.22 ("I do not know which I shall choose.") At bottom Teresa is convinced that the end is near (L 20. 13). Yet she will have to traverse an extended period of life in permanent service.

67 The Autograph Of The Life Before The Inquisition: To Publish It Or Not?

1. The *Life* is Teresa's only autograph sequestered by the inquisition. Confiscated by the inquisition of Valladolid in 1575, when Teresa was in Andalusia founding the Carmel of Beas (Jaen). It doesn't seem that she had expected this outrage. In the redaction of the book the inquisitor Francisco de Soto y Salazar had intervened. At his suggestion, Teresa had submitted the work to St John of Avila for his approval (1568). The book counted in its favor moreover exceptional theologians, like Domingo Báñez and García de Toledo. The Bishop of Avila, Don Alvaro de Mendoza, possessed and read a copy. They were guarantees more than sufficient for Teresa not to suspect the painful incident. Although in previous notes we already alluded to this, it is necessary to tell this story apart, given its importance and the effect it had on Teresa's soul.

2. The Cross of Denunciations. During the ten years from its redaction, the manuscript of the *Life* had been spread in a strange way: "the reason for its having spread" – notes Teresa in 1575 – is that since she had gone about with fear and communicated with so many, some told others: "because of the great fear she was undergoing, she consulted many and so many of these experiences were told around, which was for her an extraordinary torment and cross and cost her many tears" (ST 58.13). It is not easy to document the different sources of the diffusion alluded to by Teresa. We do know, on the other hand, two channels of denunciation linked to two adverse readers. From Andalusia, the Blessed María del Corro, an ex-Carmelite novice, denounced her to the inquisition in Seville. And from Pastrana the fearsome Princess of Eboli, also an ex-Carmelite novice seems to be the author of the outrage alluded to by Teresa.

Certainly the denunciations to the tribunals in Castile and Andalucia took place almost simultaneously. In Castile, after the denunciation of the Princess of Eboli, the tribunal in Madrid solicited from the tribunal in Valladolid information about Teresa (29 January 1575) and solicited from the bishop, Don Alvaro, surrender of the *Life* (1 Febraury 1575). Don Alvaro obeyed with a letter 27 February 1575, and the following month the teresian autograph was in the hands of the Madrid tribunal (2 March 1575). In Andalusia the tribunal of Córdoba already in March of 1575 alerted the tribunal in Madrid against Teresa and the 12th of that month formalized the denunciation against her. In the following May Teresa arrived in Seville, and at the end of the year she was denounced by María del Corro to the inquisitors of Seville, which quickly presented themselves at the Spanish Carmel and discussed the denunciation personally with the founder. In a following Act the Sevilian inquisitor informed the tribunal in Madrid and solicited the *Book of Her Life* that they might examine it (23 January 1576). Yet the tribunal in Madrid refused to send the book, because at that time they had received a favorable opinion of it from Domingo Báñez.

3. The course of both denunciations flowed from different sources. In Seville Teresa wrote tranquilly the *Spiritual Testimonies* 58 and 59 to give an account of her life and of her way of prayer to two consultors for the Inquisition, the Jesuits Rodrigo Alvarez and Enrique Enríquez, who are absolutely favorable. In Castile, on the other hand, everything is for the time being settled because of the favorable opinion of Padre Domingo The vote of Báñez.Báñez , dated 7 July 1575.

4. In Madrid the Inquisitor Soto – who himself had induced Teresa to write the book — is now the one who confided the teresian autograph to Domingo Báñez so that he could give an opinion of it. Báñez received the book in Valladolid. Evidently in Madrid and

Valladolid there blew winds favorable to Teresa and her work. Báñez benefited by the occasion to show the worth of his competence as a theologian. He knew the book for a long time. He had certainly read the laudatory letter of St. John of Avila. He agreed with him in that the book was not meant for the public. He wrote: "The book should not be let into the hands of many, because it is necessary to polish the words in some parts and explain them in others." Báñez in his opinion imitates this: "I have decided that this book is not to be communicated to everyone, but is for learned and experienced men and of Christian discretion" (BMC 2. pp. 208 & 213). That is to say Báñez is opposed to the publication (including its diffusion), but he does defend Teresa: "this woman, as her account shows, although she may be mistaken in some things, at least she is no deceiver, for she speaks so openly, the good things and the bad, and with such desire to be right, that her good intention is not in doubt" (ibid 212). (Báñez, always informed of the things having to do with Teresa, must have probably known that the hypothesis of publishing her *Life* had passed through Teresa's mind. Still she was told to do this and tells about it in the prologue (no. 2) of her *Foundations*. But certainly Báñez did not share this opinion.)

5. The book remains in prison. The censure of Báñez dated July 1575. The book remained under lock and key by the inquisition at least until 1586. Was it influenced by Báñez's reserve that it was not a book to be communicated to everyone? In 1577 Teresa and Padre Gracián asked for it through the good graces of the Inquisitor, Cardinal Quiroga, a good friend of both of them. Yet with no result. This took place in Toledo where the Cardinal was Archbishop, successor to the famous Carranza. And out of fear that the book might have been lost, Gracián induced Teresa to recuperate what she had said by writing another book, *The Interior Castle*. Fortunately. The strange thing is that the retention of the book in the prison, while

copies of it were spread everywhere through the Duchess of Alba, or through Bishop Don Alvaro and his sister, or transcribed by Gracián. In fact, Teresa obtained for a short period of time the autograph in 1581, something from which she benefitted by having a copy made in her own monastery of St. Joseph. It is during this period that copies of the work penetrated the halls of the University of Salamanca and Professor Céspedes gave public praise to it before his students. A copy of the *Life* had reached the hands of the Empress, Doña María, and she will be Mother Anne of Jesus's best advocate in rescuing the work and placing it in the hands of Fray Luis de León (1586).

6. From the Inquisition to the printing press. Suddenly there arose an exceptional promoter of the edition. Fray John of the Cross, in his commentary on the *Spiritual Canticle* said this: "the Blessed Teresa of Jesus, our Mother, left writings about these spiritual matters that are admirably done and which I hope will soon be printed and brought to light" (SC 13.7). A little later (1 September 1586) the discalced Carmelite superiors decided in favor of the edition and a year later (8 September 1587) Fray Luis de León decided in favor of its printing and diffusion. Despite the reservations of St. John of Avila and Báñez, Fray Luis de León didn't see any problem whatsoever with its being in the hands of all: "it is in my opinion of great usefulness for all those who read it," without any need whatsoever of changing or purging words. According to him: Teresa wrote "with such ease and sweetness on the one hand and on the other hand with words so alive that no one will read it without benefit." Thus the problem of the publication of the *Life* was settled, for in little more than a year it was published three times (Salamanca-Barcelona 1588-1589).

68. *The Book Of Her Foundations*: The Autograph And Its Printing

1. Among the teresian writings, *The Life* and *The Foundations* form a diptych in contrast: the landscape of the soul in the first; the roads and landscape of a "gadabout" in the second. This latter work Teresa wrote during the last decade of her life between the ages of 57 and 67, the years 1573-1582. She writes it as she goes on making foundations. Frequently she brings the manuscript with her in the covered wagon. She pauses in the writing in Salamanca, Avila, Toledo, Palencia, Soria, and Burgos. Through the book there passes by some one hundred important persons, colorful adventurers, Castilian and Andalusian landscapes, social classes and religious hierarchies, muleteers and bishops, mystical ecstasies and financial problems.

2. The autograph. It is the first of Teresa's autographs to reach the hands of Fray Luis. After his death, it passed directly from his trustee, Doctor Sobrino (Valladolid), to the royal Library of the Escorial (1592), where it was assigned the catalogue number Nº *158 – B. Escorial*. Preserved today in the section of *Reserved Books*. And as Teresa left it without a title, it was given one at a later date by one of the librarians: "The Original Book of the Foundations of the Reform / that the glorious Virgin Saint Teresa of Jesus made in Spain, written by her hand. . ." It is a notebook of 303 x 210 mm. With a total of 135 folios, numbered by another hand: 1-133, to which were added various folios in blank at the beginning and end of the manuscript. A handcrafted codex that groups together two series of little notebooks well differentiated. The first series (folios 1-100) is integrated by sets of five sheets of paper registered by Teresa in the lower margin and chapters correctly numbered from I to XXVII. The second series consists of little notebooks without any registration in the lower margin

and unnumbered chapters, but simply attached to the preceding series: folios 101 – 131. Between the two series, Teresa included a half folio as part of the book with the *Four Counsels to these discalced friars.* This did not originally form part of the book and that is actually pasted to folio 100v. From the viewpoint of graphology the manuscript is splendid. It reflects the changing states of soul of the last ten years of Teresa's life. On the pages of the first series a foreign hand rode rough-shod over the autograph text, smudging it with crossed out words and marginal and interlinear notes. All of these are done through the hand of Jerónimo Gracián, crossed out in turn by a second corrector. Whereas the pages in the second series (chapters 28-31) are unpolluted. At least one time Teresa ceded her pen to one of her nuns, María Bautista, prioress in Valladolid, who wrote the whole title of chapter 12 (f 38v) the biographical sketch ("life and death") of Sister Beatriz de la Encarnación.

3. Redaction of the book. According to Teresa, she wrote the *Book of Her Foundations* by orders of her confessor, the Jesuit Jerónimo de Ripalda: "when Ripalda had seen the book about the first foundation, it seemed to him that "it would be of service to our Lord if I wrote about the other seven monasteries that were since founded" (F pro. 2). But in reality already before this Teresa had been asked by an interior voice that she write the history of the foundation of her Carmels: "that I should write about the foundation of these houses" (ST 6). In fact she began the redaction of the work in August 1573, and she went on writing in stages. In the first days:

— The first period, 1573. Teresa was prioress at the Incarnation, yet she was in Salamanca, negotiating badly with Pedro de la Banda the acquisition of the new house. A painful situation because she had still not been able to install the Blessed Sacrament in the old house of the students. There she wrote chapters 1-9: about the foundations made in Medina and Malagón, and various doctrinal chapters. A total of 29 folios.

— The second period, 1574. At the end of the year, Teresa alternates her residence between Avila and Valladolid. There happened three episodes that unsettled her spirit: the stunning entry of Casilda de Padilla in the Carmel of Valladolid; the exit of the Princess of Eboli from the Carmel in Pastrana; and the end of her term as prioress at the Incarnation in Avila. She begins with the account of the foundation in Valladolid, yet before this she has to eliminate three preceding written folios. We don't know why. She rapidly fills 66 pages, up to folio 65 in the notebook. The foundations of Valladolid, Toledo, Pastrana, and Salamanca and moreover the beginning of Duruelo by Fray John of the Cross.

— The third period, 1576. The trip to Andalusia imposed on her pen a long parenthesis. On her return to Toledo, between August and November 1576, Teresa wrote the foundations of Alba, Segovia, Beas, Seville, and Caravaca. They make up chapters 20-27 and occupy 34 folios (from 55v to 99). Yet she writes them while she is going through the most critical situation of her life. Not only does she consider the foundation of her new Carmels as concluded, but she also figures that her book is done. For this reason she closes chapter 27 with two emotional epilogues .

— The fourth period, 1580-82. Four years of interruption took place. In the notebook there are two blank folios: 99-100. Here she places in 1579 *The Four Counsels to these Fathers.* There follows the account of the four final foundations, folios 101-131. The history as it is going on in 1580, the foundations of Villanueva de la Jara and Palencia (chapters 28-29). In 1581, Soria (chapter 30). And in 1582, Burgos (chapter 31). She concludes the account of Burgos in July. The 26th of that month she undertook her last journey. During a pause on this journey she redacted as an appendix, folios 132-133. Without an epilogue, as she had done on finalizing the first series (chapter 27).

4. Edition of the work. The first editor of Teresa's *Works,* Fray Luis de León, did not think it fitting to include the *Foundations* in the Salamancan edtion of 1588. He was preparing its publication in a separate volume, when in 1591 he was surprised by death. The first edition of the book took place years later in Flanders through the initiative of Mother Anne of Jesus and through the work of P. Graciǎn. The book was printed in Brussels in the house of Roger Valpio in the year 1610 with the title *The book of the Foundations of the Discalced Carmelite Sisters, that the Mother Foundress Teresa of Jesus wrote.* To the teresian text Graciǎn added a pair of pontifical documents and after the foundation of Burgos added the history of the foundation in Granada, written by Mother Anne of Jesus. In his exile far from Spain, Graciǎn did not have access to the teresian autograph. He made use of a copy made in the Carmel of Valladolid, which suppressed – for obvious reasons — everything relating to Casilda de Padilla (chapter 11-12), and incorporated into the text the erasures and amendments made by Graciǎn in the autograph. Because of this and above all because it reproduces the fabulous praise that Teresa gives to Graciǎn in chapter 23, the Brussels edition met with a disparate reception in Spain, reviled and repudiated by the male superiors and the Carmelite friars, but celebrated joyously by the Carmelite nuns. Gracián's edition served as the text of the *Foundations* in the editions and translations for almost three hundred years.

69 The Structure Of
The Book Of Her Foundations

1. To tell plainly the history of the recently founded Carmels was the norm for the redaction assigned by Padre Ripalda in his command to Teresa to compose the *Book of Her Foundations*. Perhaps she could confine herself to the model followed in her *Life* for the account of her first foundation: inspiration, difficulties, and the final success. From the first moment she avoided the formalism of the old chronicles of Religious Orders, the tone and intention of giving examples. In the new book she will adopt a plain style and freedom of narration, without omitting pauses to offer warnings and counsels to her Carmelite readers or to present to them model types that arise along her march. In any case, she writes for the internal use of her Carmels.

2. Yet the characteristic of the book results in the interweaving of two planes In the narration. Teresa is a founder and a mystic. In the account she brings together spontaneously mysticism and history. She presents in the length and breadth of the narration a microhistory of nuns, travels, and nascent Carmels. Yet all of this is seen with a mystical gaze and focus. She doesn't allow this singular focus to empty the facts of material realism or let them get out of focus in the least way. Thus the roads continue to be dusty, the young lads who care for the mules continue to become muleteers, and the quagmires of Arlanzón continue to be full of mud and cold. Yet it results at the same time that what is mystical is also an historical, well dated and contextualized. From the first chapter, the supernatural voice that intervenes – "wait, daughter, and you will see great things" – initiates the narrative suspense that is prolonged throughout the book, up to the last chapter, that of the dramatic narration of Burgos. Here there are intermingled no less than five mysterious words, as for the

first foundation. The whole account is impregnated with a breath of transcendence that sustains the attention of the reader and raises the question "why and for what reason is this course of action, or what is the ultimate reason for the adventure related in the book. This intertwining of mysticism and history is perhaps the most outstanding note of this literary and spiritual teresian writing

3. The historical framework. As we have seen, the book has a chronological development, by narrative and steps and layers. Its themes are multicolored. Three motives in the storyline take precedence: a/ before all the Carmels that were founded; b/ then, the group of founders among whom is Teresa the author; c/ and finally, the emerging types or models. Mixed with all of this are the copious anecdotes.

a) *The Carmels*: There are 15 Carmels founded, with their respective outlines and adventures. Before all, the strong group of nine Castilian Carmels. Then three foundations in la Mancha (Malagón, Pastrana, Villanueva), two Carmels in Anadalusia (Beas and Seville), and one, that of Caravaca, in the Murcian landscape. And moreover, there were several Carmels of discalced friars. The most intense and extended accounts Teresa dedicates to Valladolid, Seville, and Burgos: to each 19, 31, and 23 folios respectively. She has a special interest in presenting Duruelo (14 folios) and in connecting the narrations at the beginning of the second series with the foundation of Villanueva and the situation of calm after the chapter of Alcalá: "Now we are all at peace, calced and discalced; no one can hinder us from serving our Lord" (F 29.32).

b) In the groups of founders, we find special coloring, the remembrance of the mother community of St. Joseph in Avila (chapter 1). Pages further on, she presents as a singularly hardened and enthusiastic group of Andalusian founders: "the six souls who were with me were of the kind that made me think I was daring enough to go off with them to the land of the Turks" (F 24.6). The most desolate group was the one for the foundation in Salamanca: only one nun accompanied Teresa and the two passed the night of All Souls in the large house that had recently been abandoned by students. In contrast, there were nearly triumphal groups like the ones for the foundations of Villanueva or Soria.

c) Finally, the models of a Carmelite. Teresa outlines them with special relief only in the first series of the book. There is above all a little gallery of friar-types: first of all the general, Giovanni Baptista Rossi, who for Teresa was a real discovery for a superior, learned and a model Carmelite (chapter 2). And also even in difficult hours further on in the book "I love him much" (F 27.19). Almost in the following line but not in second place is outlined the figure of Fray John of the Cross "he was so good that I, at least, could have learned much more from him than he from me" (F 13.5). And the third, Jerónimo Gracián: to him she dedicates the longest, most extended, and laudatory likeness (F. 23). Throughout the book she will present sketches of other types of discalced friars. Yet much more copious, although less certain, is the gallery of Carmelite nuns. Teresa was not certain – she will find out later — in her praises of the sketches of Casilda de Padilla (F 12), of Beatriz Chaves (F 26.3) and of the eccentric Catalina de Cardona (F. 28.21-36). On the other hand there are certain and even delightful portraits of Beatriz de la Encarnación in Valladolid (F 12); and Petronila de San Andrés in Toledo (F 16.4). And among the prioresses, María de San José (Seville), María Bautista (Valladolid) and Anne of Jesus (Beas and Granada).

4. A Retinue of personages and a collection of stories. A numerous entourage enter rapidly on the scene of persons that flow by fleetingly in the narration, yet with well defined profiles and characteristics. It is impossible to record them all. Among the most noteworthy there stands out the profile of her faithful chaplain and squire, Julián de Avila; a noble lady, the Toledan Dona Luisa de

la Cerda; and another lady even more distinguished Doña Beatriz de Beamonte y Navarra, a descendant of the kings of Navarre (F 30.3); an impressive poor man, yet an unconditional servant, the Toledan Alonso Andrada, in strong contrast with the governor of the diocese, the braggart Don Tello Girón (F 15.5); Teresa's bishop, Don Alvaro and his two sisters: another three bishops of drastically different outlooks, of Seville, of Soria, and of Burgos. Of an almost interminable series, let us select three contrasting profiles: The distress of the boatman's son in making the dangerous crossing of the Guadalquivir, "which I never forget" (F. 24.11). A distinguished example of a woman, Doña Catalina de Tolosa, "a holy widow, a native of Vizcaya. I could go on at length telling about her virtues" (F 31.8). And the unequalled portrait of Philip II, "so fond of favoring religious who he knows are faithful to their profession" (F 27.6).

5. Throughout the book there pass as well the representative institutions of the Spain at that time: the inquisition; the Royal Council and the Council of Religious Orders, the stores and little inns along the way, the Hospital of the Conception in Burgos, the guilds for clerks and notaries . . . even to the corralling of bulls on the night in which the group of founders passed through the streets of Medina (F 3.7).

There are also portraits done in chiaroscuro. These are the hostile persons. Teresa treats with greatest delicacy the Princess of Eboli (F 17.16). With equal respect for the vicar general in Segovia, who almost imprisoned Fray John of the Cross and placed a guard at the door of the church (F 21.8). There is total silence with regard to the Spanish ex-novice who denounced her to the *inquisition*.

(See the outline of the book at the end of the next Theme)

70. Doctrinal Digressions In The Foundations

1. A good proof of the freedom with which Teresa undertook the writing of *The Book Of Her Foundations* is that she had hardly finished the narration of the first foundation of the series when she changed course and dedicated five chapters to giving advice and counsels to her readers. First she does so on her own initiative: "Since I do not know how much time on this earth the Lord will still give me, or how much opportunity to write, and since now it seems I have a little time, I thought that before I go further I should give some counsels to prioresses that they will learn how to guide their subjects so that the souls of these latter might receive greater benefit" (F 4.1). Then within this very digression she introduced another long parenthesis—the famous chapter on melancholiacs – to second the express petition of the nuns in Salamanca. The digression revolves about themes already treated in her *Life* and *The Way of Perfection,* yet with a different focus: the longest is the theme of prayer; somewhat quickly, that of obedience and authority in her Carmels; and in the middle between both the psychopathological theme of melancholia.

2. Counsels in the matter of prayer. She deals now with an aspect which she had avoided in the pedagogy of the *Way of Perfection*: the attitude one should have with regard to visions and revelations (see the titles of chapters 4, 5, and 8). First she recalled what the substance of perfect prayer consists in, in outline form, that it doesn't consist in long periods of concentration, or in much thinking, but in loving much and the disposability for service and obedience: for not everyone is able by nature to think much, but all souls are able to love much (F 5.2, 8, 15); and then she deals fully with the

theme of revelations (mystical and pseudo-mystical), without getting lost in studious efforts. It was a phenomenon, that of apparitions, that was spreading in the religious psychosis of her times, as in ours. In her critique, Teresa devalues them: holiness does not consist in them. And continuing she judges and discerns them from the conduct of the visionary, the works and virtues that accompany the phenomena.

3. Equally original is the focus given to the theme of obedience. It is important, according to her, in the religious life to imitate Christ, *obediens usque ad mortem* (F 5.3). She refers to concrete episodes drawn from the daily life in her Carmels (F 6.9). And before a certain pseudo-asceticism regarding the practice of obedience, she warns prioresses in the use of authority to be alert to the presence of this type of irrational obedience, inspired perhaps by reading anecdotes in the desert fathers.

4. Yet the strongest counsels fall to the theme of melancholia. She deals with this theme because the nuns in the Carmel of Salamanca asked her to, for they knew she was deeply engaged in the task of writing: "These Sisters of mine at St. Joseph's in Salamanca, where I am staying while writing this, have repeatedly asked me to say something about how one must deal with the nuns who have that bodily humor called melancholy" (F 7.1). Under the name melancholy/melancholics or melancholia/melancholiacs, Teresa is referring to a complex phenomenon, perhaps frequent in the little religious world of her time. It was a phenomenon in part pathological and in part poor conduct, through defeatism and demoralization before the ideals of community life, using one's own depressions as a pretext for a comfortable self-marginalization within the religious community. She who had dealt with many persons having this affliction (F 7.4) diagnosed it with medical competence. And she resolves it with careful pedagogy. She desires the prioress, responsible for the sick person and the community, to act as a doctor for the one and a

mother for the other. And she analyzes the case with the subtlety of a psychiatrist of today.

(We offer in continuation an outline of the book: the plan of the autograph; the series of foundations; and their chronology.)

The Prologue: folios 1-2; number of pages: 4; theme treated: Introduction.

Chapter 1-2: folio 3r-7r; Preambles; 9 pages.

Chapter 3: folios 7r-11v; Medina del Campo; 10 pages; 1567.

Chapters 4-8: folios 11v-28v; Advice and Counsels; 35 pages.

Chapter 9: folios 28v – 32v ; Malagón; 3 pages; 1568.

Chapter 10-12: folios 32v-41v; Valladolid; 19 pages; 1568.

Chapters 13-14: folios 41v – 48r; Duruelo; 14 pages; 1568.

Chapters 15-16: folios 48r – 54v; Toledo; 14 pages. 1569.

Chapter 17: folios 54v – 58v ; Pastrana; 9 pages; 1569.

Chapter 18 – 19: folios 58 -65 ; Salamanca; 15 pages; 1570.

Chapter 20 : folios 65 – 70; Alba de Tormes; 10 pages; 1571.

Chapter 21: folios 70 – 77; Segovia; 5 pages; 1574.

Chapter 22: folios 77 – 81; Beas; 12 pages; 1575.

Chapter 23 – 26: folios 81 – 92; Seville; 31 pages; 1575.

Chapter 27: folios 92 – 99; Caravaca; 14 pages; 1576

Counsels: folio 100; Counsels for disc. friars; page 1

Chapter 28: folios 101 – 109; Villanueva de la Jara; 18 pages; 1580

Chapter 29: folios 110 – 116; Palencia; 13 pages; 1580;

Chapter 30: folios 116 – 119; Soria; 7 pages; 1581

Chapter 31: folios 120 – 131; Burgos; 23 pages; 1582.

Epilogue: folios 132 – 133; Avila; 2 pages.

VIII
Doctrinal Books : The Way Of Perfection And The Interior Castle

St Teresa wrote for her nuns two books on formation. The Way of Perfection, she wrote only after she had founded her first Carmel , St. Joseph in Avila. The Interior Castle she wrote after she had founded eleven Carmels. In the first book she proposed to form the nuns in the life of prayer. In the second, she offered them a compendium of the spiritual life. The two books exceed the initial objective. They have become two classics of universal spirituality, and they are found even beyond the frontiers of Christianity.

71. The Way Of Perfection: Autograph And Redactions

1. As with the *Life* the *Way of Perfection* was also redacted twice by Teresa. We conserve both redactions. The first autograph is conserved in the Library of the Escorial and is usually referred to as *Way E*. The second autograph is conserved in the Carmel of Valladolid and is referred to as *Way V*. This second redaction had a wide manuscript diffusion in Teresa's contemporary Carmels. She personally corrected several of the copies made. The two autograph codices were reproduced in facsimile, which makes them accessible to today's reader. The facsimile *Way E* was edited in Valladolid in 1883 by F. Herrero Bayona.. *The Way V* was edited in Rome 1965 (The Vatican Library) by Tomás Alvarez and Simeón de la Sagrada Familia.

2. The first autograph: Way E. Teresa wrote it at St. Joseph's in Avila for the nascent community of ten or twelve nuns, of whom she was the prioress and director of formation. She wrote it around 1566 at the request of those for whom it was destined, dialoguing with them as "daughters, friends, and sisters." The Carmelite nuns, who had known that their prioress had written T*he Book of Her Life* for certain learned men, had insisted ("have urged me so persistently") that she put in writing the lessons she imparted in words to them daily. The book was born in this climate of reciprocal confidence, intimacy, and love testified to in the prologue. Today, the autograph is conserved in the reserved section of the Library of the Escorial.

3. The autograph is a notebook of 210 x 175 mm. It consists of 147 folios, numbered by a strange hand. All of the folios are autographs of Teresa's, except the table of contents. In a first moment she tried to break up the text and insert in it the titles of each of the chapters. Later she stopped doing this and redacted the book as a

313

prolonged conversation. Having finished the writing (f. 145), she annexed a double addition: first, four pages (ff. 146-147), which were to be inserted in the chapter on the prayer of quiet: they contained the delightful comparison to the nursing child; and then the titles of the 73 chapters of the book. Teresa dictated them to a nun who served as secretary (except for chapter 56 and 57, written by Teresa herself). The six final folios are not numbered. The autograph is filled with erasures and emendations by the censor, who obviously did not grant his approval of the manuscript, and perhaps suggested to Teresa to write a completely new text. Despite these blemishes, the pages of the autograph are of a handwriting that is fluid and vigorous, without any hesitation, of a splendid presence, with the most personal and courageous handwriting of all the teresian autographs.

4. Autograph of the Way V. It was written also at St. Joseph's in Avila, probably at the end of 1566 or the beginning of the following year, without any interval after the former redaction. From time immemorial it was conserved in the Carmel of Valladolid. It is a codex of 210 x 155 mm. It contains 207 folios numbered by Teresa, plus another two at the beginning not numbered. In one of these Teresa wrote at a later date the dedicatory title of the work: "This book deals with the advice and counsel Teresa of Jesus gives to her religious sisters and daughters . . ." Another hand wrote a new title on the reverse side of the folio intermingled with erasures and hesitations: "Book called the Way of Perfection" and in continuation Teresa wrote herself: "This book is intended for the discalced nuns who observe the primitive rule of Our Lady of Mount Carmel." The codex lacks a table of contents. Incorporated into the text are the titles of the chapters, reducing them to 44, even though in fact there are 42. All of this was revised by the censors with erasures , underlining, and marginal notes which obliged Teresa to tear out various folios (ff. 19, 32, 59-64). Among them were the four folios that developed the comparison to the game of chess. Thus in the notebook there are pages of a third redaction (for example, those that treat of pure love (ff.19, 32-33)). In redoing the text in this second redaction, Teresa abided by the corrections made by the censor in Way E: she retouched the suspect passages, inserted the pages that contained the comparison to the nursing child and omitted the passages that were crossed out in such a way that there did not pass into Way V the bold defense of women (W 3.7). The notebook is in careful handwriting and the pages perfectly centered, framed by a vertical line on the left margin. But there are a number of paragraphs that have been crossed out by the censor.

5. Copies. Already in Teresa's time, T*he Way of Perfection* had a normal diffusion in the Carmels founded by her. It was the book of formation in the spirit and style of Teresa. She herself frequently took an interest in reviewing , done at times quickly, these copies, regretting the lapses and errors incurred by the impromptu copyists. (cf. BMC 16, 484). Among these there are three that have been retouched by Teresa herself. They are the copies of Madrid, Salamanca, and Toledo.

a) The first of the three is preserved in the Madrid Carmel of St. Teresa (calle Ponzano). It is a precious codex, bound in silver sheets, in neat handwriting, very suited to community reading, with numerous corrections in the text made by Teresa, who on the final page authenticated the copy in this way: "This book has one hundred eighty-three pages [in reality, only 83]. It is copied from one that I wrote at St. Joseph's in Avila and for the truth of this, I sign my name: Teresa of Jesus, Carmelite nun."

b) Slightly later is the copy of Salamanca ("this copy made in the year 1571" was noted beneath the book's colophon). Revised and corrected in its entirety by Teresa , who wrote beneath the colophon: "I have examined this book: it seems to me to be in conformity with what I wrote and was examined by learned men . . . In this Carmelite monastery of our Lady of the Annunciation , in this town of Alba de Tormes, 7 February 1573. Teresa of Jesus Carmelite nun."

c) Yet the most interesting copy among those corrected by Teresa is the one conserved by the Carmelite nuns in Toledo. It was copied at the beginning of 1579 by a learned secretary who took great liberties in the literary manipulation of the text. This same year it was meticulously corrected by Teresa, who introduced into it hundreds of retouches and annotations so as to prepare the first published edition of the book (Further on we will return to this theme.)

In conclusion, no other teresian writing was followed so closely by Teresa, so often re-elaborated and retouched by her. It was diffused by her in her Carmels until she decided to have it printed, a good indication of the importance that she bestowed on it *a posteriori,* as well as the interest she had in both its presence and its being read in the Carmels of her day.

72. The Way Of Perfection: Composition Of The Book

1. *The Way of Perfection* was written spontaneously and rapidly. Yet at the same time the writing of it was demanding and prolonged, due to the interference of Teresa's censor friends. In her mind the first redaction of the book (*Way E*) had the trait of a rough draft. The text remained without division into chapters and with a final complement of four pages preceded by the warning: "in that which deals with the prayer of quiet [cross out: 'I forgot'] I failed to say that this is very important." That is to say, these four pages should be inserted in the context of the prayer of quiet (ch. 53, folio 102), something that will be possible only in the following redaction.

2. But there then followed a double setback. Teresa proposed as censor the Father *presentado* Fray Domingo Báñez. And since she thought that the best complement to the reading of the *Way of Perfection* was the reading of *The Book of Her Life*, which at the time was in possession of Báñez himself, she invites the nuns to ask him for it: "You may get it from Fray Domingo Báñez, a presentado of the Order of St. Dominic . . . the one to whom I'll give this book. If this one is all right for you to see and he gives it to you, he'll also give that other one" (W 42.6). But Báñez did not submit in the case of the one or the other. He did not act as the censor of the *Way of Perfection* and he opposed the diffusion of the *Life,* or its reading by nuns who were beginners. In such a way that Teresa gave up on both books. She will give the book to another assessor. And insofar as the reading of the *Life goes (CV 42.6)*, she does not repeat in the new redaction the invitation to get it from Fray Domingo , although inevitably she had to follow referring to the *Life* because it contains the best complement to the thirst coming from the living water of

which she speaks here in the *Way of Perfection*. (On the double attitude of Báñez, see BMC, 18.10, where he himself affirms of the *Way of Perfection* that "he had not read it either in printed form or in manuscript." And of the *Life*, he said that "it was not suitable that writings by women be published.")

For the indispensable approbation of the book, Teresa had to have recourse to another Dominican more friendly and accessible, Padre García de Toledo, who had a good knowledge of the preceding B*ook of Her Life*. Padre García accepted for love of Teresa the commission of being assessor and censor of the *Way of Perfection*.

3. The revision of the book. Padre García went over the first 20 pages without any problem.

But when he came unexpectedly to the passage in which Teresa gives her defense of women (folios 11-12) with clear allusions to the Inquisition ("Since the world's judges are sons of Adam and all of them men, there is no virtue of women that they do not hold suspect, " W 3.7), the assessor- censor frowned and decided to do away with this whole passage as being dangerous. He leaves it unreadable, but without any marginal note to say why. Only that from this moment on he remains alert and burdens the book with notes and scribbles – entire pages crossed out with an x – he corrects Teresa when she tries to comment on Psalm 88 ("this is not the meaning of this psalm!"). Before the allusions to the index of forbidden books he seriously warns her: "It seems she is reproving the Inquisitors for forbidding books on prayer," and erases the dangerous allusion (f 72).

4. There is no point in enumerating one by one the interventions by the censor. They all reflect the hypersensibility of the theologian before Teresa's ingenuity. His probable note that went along with the supplement of warnings made to Teresa has not reached us. We add only two data: that she complied with all the insinuations of Padre García in her second redaction. And also that Teresa never

had the intention of dealing editorially with this first redaction of her book. For her it was simply a draft.

5. A new redaction and a new censor. Despite the many things she had to do in the Carmel of St. Joseph, Teresa took up immediately the new composition of the *Way of Perfection* , which in part remained a copy of the previous one and in part a completely new redaction. She wrote careful pages, with a serene and clear handwriting, the titles of the chapters within the text, without a final table of contents and with the insertion of all the corrections made by Padre García in the previous notebook. Teresa persisted with her idea that Báñez would go over the writing (W 42.6-7). But she didn't succeed with this desire. The revisor and censor of the new notebook was Padre García himself, to whom were added other censors of less caliber. On the Teresian text there came a new mangling of censorship with more strictness than on the first. Padre García crossed out thoroughly no less than nine passages of the autograph, almost always out of pure theological meanness. He erased Teresa's allusion to the troops of Philip II in Europe (f. 8r). He crossed out an entire page on the mysterious presence of God in the Eucharist (f. 130). He did the same with a critical allusion to the devil (f. 121), and on and on. He finds it strange that the apostle Bartholomew is presented as the son of a king (f. 122). He alerts the author to a previous note he made (which is now lost) when she speaks on the theme of pure love ("take care to be in conformity with the note" (f. 32r). At least once he gives in to a certain male chauvinism: that the nuns "should not preach at the grille but be silent, for being silent will do them more good" (f. 20v). More than once he is prodigal in his praises of Teresa : "this is good, because there are some spiritual masters who, so as not to err, condemn many spirits as being influenced by the devil" (f. 23v).

6. Probably , it is due to the warnings of Padre García that Teresa tore out and redid various pages that spoke of pure love, or

likewise cut out four pages that treated of humility and the game of chess (f. 59-64). Fortunately all the other passages crossed out by the censor in the autograph have been recovered by the editors. Thus we can read them in their original integrity despite the strength of the smudges that were intended to expurgate what was crossed out.

7. After these painful episodes of the censor and the consequent meddling of the theologian in the text of the *Way of Perfection*, the question spontaneously arises: Didn't Teresa succumb to outside criteria? Didn't she have to renounce her own ideas? To what degree were the ideas in the book or Teresa's original thinking contaminated by foreign ideas or theses. The answer is in the negative. It is certain that the crossings out and smudges in the text made the author tone down her expressions and even her thought. Yet it doesn't seem that even one of the numerous notes of Padre García in both autographs or of the other censors of the second autograph had any impact or distorted even so much as one of the ideas expressed by Teresa or made her retract. Yes, certainly her idea about whether or not the mystical graces can be given to a sinner so that she might be converted (ch. 16) underwent a development, but this change was not due to the censor but to the later influence of St. John of Avila.

8. The most negative aspect in passing from the first redaction to the second is literary. We don't know if this is due to pressures by the censor. What is certain is that between the two redactions there takes place a literary descent: the draft is more spontaneous and brilliant, also it is more clearly dialogical. Images so typically teresian do not pass into the definitive redaction, such as those of the beggar and the emperor, the bull fighter and the spectators, the unskilled horseman who always goes about in danger , or that of those who argue over points of honor which is the equivalent of debating whether the earth is good for mud (she had written dust) or for sun-dried bricks. Nor did she give way to occasional caustic

expressions, such as in her allusion to complaining nuns: "it seems to me to be an imperfection, my sisters, to be always complaining about light illnesses. If you can tolerate them don't complain about them " (W. 11.1). Nor in the use of diminutives exquisitely teresian, such as agravuelos (little wrongs), hombrecillo y mujercilla (little men and little women), simplecita (little simpleton), and so on. In a global balance one would have to say that in the second redaction the teresian writing acquires a bookish adornment and is enriched doctrinally, but it loses points in literary charm.

73. The Plan Of
"The Way Of Perfection"

1. The initial project of the book did not arise from a proposal made by Teresa. It was rather an idea agreed upon between her and the group of young Carmelite nuns, members of the community in St. Joseph's in Avila. Probably it was one of the topics of conversations in the community recreations. The sisters kept begging her to write. And she gave in ("I have decided to obey them"). The proposal by the nuns was generic: "that I write some things about prayer." Teresa specified more at the beginning of the book: "that I manage to say something about the mode and manner of life proper to this house." ("Something that will be of benefit to them" written first in CE). Obviously, the manner of life lived in St. Joseph's was a life of prayer. Teresa excluded the use of strange books, although she is aware that there are those that are very well written for whoever knows what the author is writing about. She will write whatever she will be thinking as she goes along, without order she assures us. She prefers to pay attention to a model that keeps her away from theories, and she approaches what is experienced: "I shall say nothing about what I have not experienced myself or seen n in others."

2. Further on she will include in the project an important double commentary: she will comment on the Our Father and the Hail Mary. In fact she does comment on the Our Father, but then she gives up on her promise to comment on the Hail Mary: "I have also thought of saying something about how to recite the Hail Mary. But I have been so lengthy that I have to let it go." This is in the last chapter or epilogue of the first redaction (WE 73.2). Likewise in passing on to the second redaction, she had to retouch the initial criteria of not writing except what she experienced. In the first redac-

tion she had formulated it in more compromising terms: "I shall say nothing that I haven't experienced . . ., or was given to understand in prayer by the Lord." That is to say, the source of the writing will also be her own mystical experience. Yet this last aside did not pass into the new redaction. She will attend to this norm as she goes along in the book: she will reduce the references to her mystical experience. Perhaps it was one of the guidelines suggested by the censor: not too many personal allusions, or comparisons to games (for example the bull run or the game of chess).

3. The plan of the text. The structure of the book does not respond to a pre-established plan. She had already warned of this in the prologue. She will deal with the themes as they come to mind (Pro. 2), giving free course to her pen. She, nevertheless, keeps in order some convictions and the corresponding set of ideas that serve her as a basis for what she writes. She knows well the style of life that she has established in St. Joseph's for the group of Carmelite nuns for whom the book is destined. In such a way that the work is articulated in two parts, almost halves. The first part deals with the education for prayer. The second part deals with prayer itself, which is the reason for the life in the house and the principal objective of the book. The conducting thread of her thought is simple: to live a life of prayer (2nd part), one must previously base it on daily life (1st part).

4. This is the focus that she follows in its development from the beginning. The book starts off with what is most fundamental: why and for what are we here in such strict enclosure (title of the first chapter). And the response is almost disconcerting: because in France or in Europe and in the church terrible things are happening: wars of religion, the breakup of Christianity, things that affect the entire world: "the world is in flames . . . . they want to ravage his Church" (W 1.5). We are here for the purpose of being such that by our manner of living and being Christians we will carry some weight

in the conflict. The contemplative life must have an apostolic function and reason for being. And immediately she specifies concrete aspects: evangelical poverty, pure love for each other, detachment from all created things, and humility that puts a seal on the truth of what we live. Virtues that configure the manner of life in this house: love will create the unity of the group. Detachment will facilitate freedom in its depth. Humility will authenticate everything, it will be the truth along the way. The second part of the book imparts a strong reading about prayer. To decide for it with a radical "determined determination." Prayer is learned by practicing it. Teresa teaches it by praying herself before her readers. For this she prays with them the Our Father. And with Jesus and like Jesus, she assumes the sentiments he directs to his Father. For this reason, her treatise on prayer will be a free commentary on the Lord's prayer.

5. The allegorical support of the exposition. Accompanying the two extreme themes of the book, Teresa introduces two images which serve as a literary and symbolic support. In the ascetical part she uses the image of struggle or militancy. On the other hand in the contemplative exposition she illustrates it with the image of the fountain of living water. The image of struggle is supported by the initial chapters of the book; the readers are in Carmel because in Europe and in the Church they are in a ferocious struggle, "the world is on fire," and the nuns cannot be soldiers as the legions of the king by the "force of arms" (alluded to in W 3.1). They will fight in another way, not through an assault but by being such that through their prayers and life they have an effect in favor of the church and the captains who defend it. "These are the insignia that must be on our coat of arms" (W 2.8). "even though very enclosed, we shall be fighting for him" (W. 3.5). The Carmel of St. Joseph is a "little castle of good Christians" (W 3.2). As a strategy she proposes to them the tactic of the king who withdraws within a bulwark with a

handful of select soldiers: "since they have no traitor they cannot be conquered" (W 3.1). Nevertheless, in introducing the symbol of the fount she will say that after the battle the living water is the reward (W. 19.14). Effectively, the new symbol of the fount of living water of which the Lord spoke to the Samaritan woman arises as the final aim of the struggle, after conquering the first enemies, without backing down from the second or the third (W 19.2). And she develops as she goes on the little symbol of the biblical origin ((w 19.6; Jn 7. 37), expounding on the three properties of water (prayer): that it refreshes; it cleans dirty things; and it satisfies to the full and takes away thirst (W. 19). The book is the way to this fount of living water.

6. The polemic tension of the book. Teresa composed this work when in the Spanish religious environment there was a strong confrontation between theologians and spiritual persons. The inquisition was on the side of the theologians and painful episodes occurred on the side of spiritual persons. Although Teresa is a spiritual person, she doesn't belong to either faction. In her *Life* she proclaims that she strongly favors the theologians. On the theme of evangelical poverty she opposes the opinion of her theologian assessor Pedro Ibáñez (L 35.4). Yet at the same time she opposes the opinion of the spiritual person Fray Pedro de Alcántara, who has an opinion contrary to the theologians in matters of poverty and of the evangelical counsels. On the other hand, in the *Way of Perfection* she argues hard and fast against the learned men who were in opposition to mental prayer. She especially opposed those who prohibited it for women. She opposed the thesis that challenged the way of prayer as a way of danger: "But that the way of prayer be a way of danger – God would never will that. Pay no attention to the fears they put before you or the dangers they paint" (W 21). She assures her readers that even though their books about prayer are taken from them, no one can take from them the book *par excellence* the *Our Father*. And she concludes the first

redaction of the *Way of Perfection* branding as false prophets those who oppose prayer: "For no one can take vocal prayer from you or make you recite the Our Father hastily and without understanding it. If some person should take it from you or counsel you to give it up, do not believe him. Believe that he is a false prophet and consider that in these times of ours you don't have to believe everybody. Even though there is nothing to fear from those who can counsel you now, we don't know what will come in the future" (W 42.4). And because this was too daring, she omits this passage in her second redaction. Yet the entire book is impregnated with tension.

74. The Lesson Of The "Our Father"

1. In the second part of the *Way of Perfection* – 21 chapters – Teresa proposes to present her teaching on prayer. To do this she concentrates on the prayer Jesus taught us, the Our Father. She doesn't intend to write either a treatise on prayer or a systematic commentary on the words of the Our Father. She goes about it freely. She interweaves her convictions and ideals with intervals of spontaneous prayer, directed to God, but lived before her readers without any disguise. She will try to empathize with them. For Teresa it is impossible to speak of prayer without praying. She will comment one by one on the petitions of the Our Father teaching her readers to be in tune with the sentiments that seized upon the soul of Jesus when he pronounced them. From his manner of saying the first word, *Father*, until "forgive us . . . as we forgive ," he includes us always in this plural , in which he (and she) intermingle their sentiments with ours.

2. Previous observations. Her teaching about prayer she draws out in chapter 22 of this book. The title of the chapter is: "Explains what mental prayer is." Before praying the Our Father, Teresa wrote various introductory chapters. She knows books written on the Lord's prayer. But she prescinds from them. They have been recently included on the Index of Forbidden Books, among them the famous works, now in the vernacular, by Erasmus and Savanarola, both with the title of "Exposition of the Our Father." (Catalogue, 1559, pp. 40-41). For Teresa, the Our Father is a point of reference in a double sense: as a prayer and as a teaching apprenticeship. It is the prayer of the Master who not only prayed this prayer at the moment in which the apostles asked him to teach them how to pray, but continues to pray it with us as often as we recite it in prayer. To affirm this she

establishes it on her basic idea that prayer is a relationship between two subjects (a sharing between friends), between God (or Jesus) and ourselves. Without realizing this relationship there is no prayer. There is no prayer, she says, only words. We will expound in no. 3 the content of these introductory chapters. Let us give the outline of the last 21 chapters:

Commentary on the Our Father (chaps 22-42)

Chapter	Text of the Our Father*	Theme of the Commentary
22-25	What is prayer, vocal, mental-contemplation	Introduction to the Our Father
26-29	Our Father who art in heaven (ch 27)	prayer of recollection
30 – 31	Hallowed be thy name/ they kingdom come	prayer of quiet
32	Thy will be done on earth as it is in heaven	perfect contemplation
33 – 35	Give us this day our daily bread	Eucharistic prayer
36	Forgive us our trespasses	
37	The excellence of the prayer the Our Father	to go about in the love and fear of God
38 – 41	And lead us not into temptation	
42	But deliver us from evil. Amen	

*In the titles of the chapters Teresa transcribes in Latin the invocations of the Our Father. She recited it in Latin in the liturgy of the Mass and in the Hours of the Breviary. For Carmelite nuns who could not recite the divine Office, the Rule of Carmel prescribed the recitation of the Our Father a great number of times. In the text of the chapters she transcribed the invocations as she recited them into Castilian.

3. Previous instruction, chs. 22-25. Before beginning her recital and commentary on the Our Father, Teresa pauses so as to inculcate in her readers her own convictions. The first is her idea of prayer as a pure relationship of friendship with the God-man and the man-God. Yet within this relationship the one praying should be interested more in the persons than in the possible relational contents: according to her, the prayer should take into account who she is and who God is. And this as much in vocal prayer as in mental prayer, or in pure contemplation. She diligently takes up the question of prayer with words alone. (She alludes perhaps to the risk of choral recitation in Latin, without understanding it.) The recital of words only is hot air. Yet at the same time the recital done well can develop normally into perfect contemplation (mystical). Only that in this the words have the Other, who is converted into a fountain of living water from our interior activity. In any case "do not think that he is silent."Even though we do not hear him, he speaks well to the heart when we beseech him from the heart (W 24.5).

4. The first invocation of the Our Father, chs. 26-29. The word Father in the mouth of Jesus has a profound echo in Teresa's soul. It places her in recollection: "O my Lord, how you do show yourself to be the Father of such a Son; and how your Son does show himself to be the Son of such a Father! May you be blessed forever and ever! This favor would not be so great, Lord, if it came at the end of the prayer." And immediately she initiates the readers into this form of praying: the recollection, according to her, consists of two components. Psychological, the first component, enter into your own interior, calm as much as possible the inordinate siege of the senses. Silence them. The second component is Christological: center the attention on Christ, and make all our attention converge on him. The prayer of recollection is something intimate and profound. (Teresa will repeat many times the Augustinian datum: "in the intimate part

of the soul, in the deepest and most intimate part of the soul"). The more personal and intimate this mutual relationship may be, the more it will overflow to others. This includes perfect contemplation — the mystical – it is impelling, never inactive, according to Teresa.

5. *Chapters 30-31.* They deal with entry into this mystical prayer. They call it the prayer of quiet. In the relationship with him the noise of the will quiets down: there arises another form of love that helps to silence the "madwoman of the house." It is the passage cut by the censors in the first editions of the book. This chapter is entitled: "Explains the nature of the prayer of quiet. Gives some advice for those who experience it."

6. Chapter 32 follows : "Discusses the words of the Our Father, Fiat voluntas tua sicut in caelo et in terra; the great deal a person does when she says them with full determination; and how well the Lord repays this." It indicates the arrival at the fount of living water: "Drinking from it is perfect contemplation, that which you told me to write about (W 32.9)." It is the point of connection of the present lesson in the *Way of Perfection* with what she imparted in another book, which was half secret, *The Book of Her Life.* Teresa, despite the resistance of the theologian assessor, Padre Báñez, not only referred to this book, but actually invites her readers to procure it . . . but only those who have reached this fount of living water, and only after her death (W 25.4).

7. There follows the petition for "our daily bread," chaps. 33-35. Teresa moves to the Eucharistic Bread so as to impart to her readers a lesson on liturgical prayer. She not only prays and teaches in the act of Communion or before the Real Presence, but she feels herself clothed with priestly unction and breaks forth in an ardent Eucharistic prayer. She ends with the petition for pardon and reserves one of the last chapters to proclaim the excellence of this prayer, the Our Father (W. ch 37).

75. The First Edition Of "The Way Of Perfection"

1. An important episode in the history of the book and in that of Teresa the writer is that the *Way of Perfection* was the first of her works to be published . Certainly the publication of her *Constitutions (Salamanca 1581) came before it. But* those constitutions were not the ones written by her but the ones elaborated by the chapter of Alcalá. On the other hand, the publication of the *Way of Perfection* was a special undertaking, although the venture was wrapped in a tangle of setbacks. We will expound first Teresa's preparation of the edition, then the setbacks of the *Way of Perfection* between Evora and Lisbon, and finally the printing of the book after Teresa's death. In all of this, the most important thing is the treatment to which Teresa submitted her work in face of the first edition.

2. The preparation for printing. Written between 1566 and 1567, the book had been diffused in copies that were not always faithful to what she had written, as we have already noted. For this reason Teresa decided to have it printed, when she was far into the next decade. She and her Portuguese friend Don Teutonio de Braganza, Bishop of Evora since 28 June 1578, had agreed on this. The book would be published in Evora at the expense of the bishop. Teresa writes to him on 22 July 1579: "Last week I wrote you a long letter and sent you the little book, and so I will not be lengthy. I am only writing because I forgot to ask you to have printed along with it the life of our Father Saint Albert, which is in a little notebook enclosed with the other" (Ltr 305. 1). That is to say that in the first fortnight of July Teresa had sent to Don Teutonio in one packet the text of the *Way of Perfection* and the biography of the Carmelite St. Albert, composed by the Dominican Diego de Yanguas. Now she

proposes the printing of both in one volume only.

3. Yet Teresa noted with time that none of her autographs could be given to a printer since they lacked punctuation, capital letters, separation into paragraphs and so on. And for this she had recourse to a competent secretary, totally reliable, — a learned person – to transcribe the entire manuscript of the book in good handwriting, and the due pre-editorial requirements. We do not know who this secretary was who made the precious copy. Yet he sinned by doing too :much: not only did he polish the handwriting and the writing from a literary point of view, but he manipulated Teresa's text to his own taste and talent. In such a way that when the brand –new copy reached Teresa's hands, she found no other remedy than to undo the injustice page by page.

4. We nonetheless possess the notebook done by the secretary in what is called the Codex of Toledo. Teresa revised and corrected it in her own hand from the first page to the last. In the first page she added the Protestation of submission to the Church, written in another hand. In the last page she crossed out entirely the colophon, which enumerated the monasteries founded by her. And on pages within the text she crossed out words, introduced corrections, added marginal and interlinear notes . She even added some at the foot of the page. In all, hundreds of retouches and corrections, which in part restored the text to its original purity, but the copy was left damaged and unpresentable to the typographer. She herself had to procure a third copy to send to Don Teutonio. We do not know who this last copier was. We only know that a young Carmelite nun in Salamanca collaborated in the task. For the Portuguese printer this third copy served for the final text, the first edition of the book. (Centuries later, the codex of Toledo was published by BAC II, 1954 as the definitive text of the *Way of Perfection* according to Teresa.)

5. Between Evora and Lisbon. As was the norm in those times,

Don Teutonio submitted the teresian text for the approbation of the ecclesiastical authority of Lisbon. They were difficult times and the procedures were slow and troubled. Only after a year (7 October 1580) did the two censors in Lisbon, Paulo Alfonso and Antonio Mendoza, grant their approval: "seen and reviewed by Padre Bartolomeu Ferreyra, it can be printed once the crossed-out clauses are removed," yet with the condition that before putting it before the public one of the printed copies be presented to this assembly to be compared with the approved text." That is to say, once more the censors questioned the orthodoxy of the vocabulary employed by Teresa and, above all, they imposed a suppression on chapter 31 of the book, in which Teresa explains the nature of the prayer of quiet. Probably they were wary of quietism. Between this hair-splitting approbation (7 October 1580) and the approval of the crossed-out clauses and the chapter that was cut down three years passed by. The two censors noted on the front page : "it can be published. In Lisbon, 8 February 1583. Four months before, Teresa had died, and so she had not seen her book in print.

6. The edited text. It happened however that immediately following the death of Teresa, Father Gracián sent to Don Teutonio the famous pseudo-Teresian Counsels to add to the *Way of Perfection*. In such a way that the edition consisted of a multicolored hybrid: First an introductory letter of praise, signed by Don Teutonio (nine pages without numbers); in the second place, the *Counsels* of Mother Teresa of Jesus (another nine pages without numbering); in continuation the text of the *Way of Perfection* (folios 1-143) and finally, *the Life and miracles of the glorious Father St. Albert*, another 44 folios, preceded by a charming "Prologue to the very religious Lady and our Mother Teresa of Jesus," published probably while Teresa was still alive, since this last piece carries as the date 1582.

7. The book was entitled: "The treatise that Mother Teresa of Jesus wrote. For the Religious Sisters of the Order of Our Lady of

Mount Carmel of the Monastery of St. Joseph. In Avila where she was at one time the prioress and the founder. The present work was printed in the very noble and always loyal city of Evora, in the house of the lady widow mother of Andrés de Burgos, may he be in glory. 1583."

8. The Evoran edition imposed the text of the *Way of Perfection* on those that followed, that of Graciấn (Salamanca 1585), and that of San Juan de Ribera (Valencia 1587). Both of them reproduced, with slight modifications, the text of Don Teutonio and suppressed chapter 31, precisely the one that had been enlarged upon by Teresa with a the delightful comparison to the child at the breast.

9. Only in 1588 did Fray Luis de León return to the autograph text and reincorporate into it this suspect chapter 31, although he also intermingled the two redactions of the book. Fray Luis justly warned under the title of the work: "Printed in accordance with the original manuscripts, amended by the hand of the Mother herself and not in conformity with those that are printed, in which many things are missing, and others that are very corrupted." In his edition Fray Luis, from the first chapter, sprinkled apologetic notes in the margins of the text, yet he didn't add any note to the suspect chapter on the prayer of quiet.

10. Undoubtedly the most notable thing in this whole editorial process of *The Way of Perfection* is the care with which Teresa handled her text, making it better, even from a literary point of view, without ever incurring the intention of lowering her langauage or use of rusticity for the sake of style as some of her modern critics have claimed.

76. A New Book: The Interior Castle

1. *The Interior Castle* is the last doctrinal book written by Teresa. She began it in Toledo in June 1577, when she was 62. At least five years previous to this, her mystical experience had entered the stage of fullness. She explains it in a new and better book in a more ordered way than in any of her previous books. On the basis of an autobiographical framework half veiled, she elevates the Christian spiritual life to a most original synthesis. Not only is this the best achieved book of Teresa's but a classic of spiritual theology.

2. Situation of the author. Apart from her human and spiritual maturity, she is living at this moment through one of the most adverse periods of her life. She had returned to Toledo from Anadalusia, having been chastised and confined there by the supreme authorities of the Order (in the chapter of Piacenza 1575). In the first months of 1577, she had suffered from a crisis of psycho-physical exhaustion, so grave that the doctor forbade her to write in her own hand except in cases of extreme necessity. Here in Toledo the autograph of her *Life* continued to be sequestered by the inquisition: in a moment of favor, she and Padre Gracián dared to solicit its return from the Gran Inquisitor, Gaspar de Quiroga, but with a negative result. Teresa has the feeling that in the book her soul had been captured. Perhaps the most aggravating circumstance was that after she began the book, the nuncio Ormaneto died in Madrid and she had to interrupt the writing for months and was awaiting the feared harassment of the new Nuncio Sega, who arrived in Madrid at the end of August. The positive factors at this moment are the more decisive in the composition of the new book. Teresa had recently expressed the desire to complete the account of her *Life* which had been sequestered by the

inquisition. She wanted to add the final experiences of her mystical trajectory. This was undoubtedly the germinal seed of the new writing. In Toledo, moreover, Teresa had an exceptional spiritual director, the biblical scholar Alonso Velásquez (ST 60), a good friend of Gracian's. The two of them encouraged her to take up her pen and write. Yet there was above all a third factor more valid: there was the accumulation and quality of ideas that had matured in her mind: above all the idea of the soul indwelt by God, the most special mutual relations between God and the soul, that had become clearer and more pronounced in these last years after the order "to seek yourself in Me." These will be the stone blocks of the *Interior Castle*

3. The decisive episode. It was a conversation between three parties: Teresa, Gracián, and Alonso Velázquez. Gracián refers to it repeatedly: "what happened with regard to the *Interior Castle* is that while I was superior and once speaking with Teresa about many spiritual things, she said to me: "Oh how well this is written about in the book of my life which is in the hands of the Inquisition!" I told her that since we cannot get it she should try to remember what she said there and other things and write another book, but put down the doctrine as though for everyone without naming who experienced what she is explaining. And so I gave her orders to write the book of the *Interior Castle*, telling her so as to persuade her more that I would speak of this also to Doctor Velázquez who had been her confessor at times. And so I ordered her to do so." *(*Scholias . . ., p. 428. This was told also by Gracián more extensively in his Dilucidario . . . BMC 15, p. 16).*

4. This mandate she records on the first page of the book, the *prologue*. (Let us recall that Teresa usually begins her works by writing a prologue.) In acknowledging the precarious state of her health and the suggestions made by Gracián, above all to connect it with the *Book of Her Life*, which will culminate now in the seventh

dwelling places. Herein lies the originality of the work: it elaborates a spiritual theology, not from theory but from the living experience of the author.

5. The composition. She had the good fortune, or better, the literary inspiration, to consider the book from the viewpoint of the symbol of the castle, which arose ("there came to my mind") in the first lines of chapter 1 and that finds support on the firm columns of three biblical texts that serve as a support to the exposition. The symbol of the soul/castle/interior, takes up again one of the most persistent ideas of her previous books. *Life* and *Way of Perfection:* that the human person consists in, grows, and becomes strong through the interior life. Yet not isolated within itself but in its double relational dimension: openness to the divine transcendence from the most interior depth of oneself and the operative tension that determines its relation with others. Each of the others is a castle like herself, with an identical vocation to transcendence. Becoming aware of this is the primordial act of knowing oneself so as to arrive at transcending oneself.

6. The steps of composition. Teresa begins the book on 2 June 1577. In a month and a half she writes the first four dwelling places. With a brief pause while working out the fourth dwelling places: "God help me with what I have undertaken! (IC 4.2.1). Yet she continues the task until entering the fifth, a total of 46 complete folios. With very few spaces for divisions into paragraphs or dwelling places. But on the 18 of July the death of the nuncio Ormaneto upset her plans. She interrupted her work and undertook a trip to Avila. She had reached the second chapter, inclusive, of the fifth dwelling places. In a pause — we don't know where – she redacted the third chapter of the fifth dwelling places. Yet there follow two months of interruption. When finally she takes up her task again at the end of October, she has to reorient herself because as she says "About five months have passed since I began (5.4.1). Yet at this moment she

introduces into the exposition the bridal symbolism (5.4.3), and here in Avila in a month the most profound and delicate section of the work: the last 66 folios: "this writing was finished in the monastery of St. Joseph in Avila in the year 1577, the eve before the feast of St. Andrew (29 November). This had been one of the most hazardous months of her life: re-elected prioress of the Incarnation and rejected by the one in charge of the community assembly. She shares the difficulties of Fray John of the Cross who was immediately taken prisoner and entered the little Toledan prison cell. We could say that they were her harshest months, in which she wrote the mystical dwelling places of the *Interior Castle.*

To sum up, the book, begun in Toledo and finished in Avila, was written in two stages: the first until half way through the fifth dwelling places; the second from chapter four of these fifth dwelling places until the end.

7. In the shadow of the writer. While Teresa was writing she permits one of her nuns to keep in her possession the first quinternions and transcribe them. First a nun in Toledo. Then after the Toledan secretary she gives a turn to a Carmelite nun in Avila. In this way there arose almost at the same time the autograph and its first copy. From the prologue, the book was destined for Carmelites ("So I shall be speaking to them while I write") and they corresponded with all haste. Perhaps they already knew Teresa's intention to send the autograph to the Carmelite nuns in Seville and they were not resigned to remain without it. This copy has reached us — *ms de Toledo* – dated "the year 1577." Yet we are much more interested in Teresa's autograph itself. The following theme will speak of it.

77. The Autograph Of The Interior Castle

1. The autograph has been conserved in the Carmel of Seville for four centuries. And it is in good condition. It is a codex of 310 x 210 mm. The autograph title on the first page reads: "IHS this treatise called *The Interior* Castle was written by Teresa of Jesus, a nun of the order of Our Lady of Mount Carmel for her discalced Carmelite Sisters and nuns." It is bound in red velvet with 210 folios numbered by Teresa, plus three others unnumbered: the initial page and two of the epilogue. The margins slightly cut off by the knife of the binder, who more than once trimmed the autograph annotations in the exterior margin. The pages are full: they oscillate between 24 and 30 lines for each one. The writing is fluid, with letters as though engraved and separate, there are abundant abbreviations, in lines perfectly parallel, slightly elevated at the end. The white spaces are very rare. There are ample margins that frame well the box of writing (26 x 16 cm). Quality paper is used, with three different kinds of watermarks, although the ink used by Teresa is so strong that frequently it has gone through the page darkening and making it difficult to read.

2. She herself revised the writing. Before giving the manuscript to the expectant Padre Gracián , Teresa revised and completed the work. It is then that she added the initial folio, with the title of the work. She numbers the folio with Roman numerals in the right hand of the upper margin. She inscribed the headings of each page: on the left, the abbreviation for moradas (dwelling places): and on the right the number of the respective dwelling place (also in Roman numerals). She looks for a blank spot in the text to fit in the number of each dwelling place or of each chapter. At times she adds it in the margin (cf. f. 46 r). She also adds numerous marginal notes, always interest-

ing. She will write as well in a separate notebook a table of contents, lost today, with 27 chapters of the book. And above all she decides on two important corrections, that is:

a) At the height of the seventh dwelling places, she notes in the margin (f. 103 v): " when it says and what he asks of you, read this paper." And she attached a piece of paper that contained about fourteen lines, today lost, yet known through the copies and incorporated into the text by Luis de León in the edition of 1588. It was a matter of specifying the compliments or requests of the Lord from the depths of the soul in the state of union (7.3.10).

b) In the second place, she herself tore out folio 97 and does it over integrally. This folio comes in the seventh dwelling place, at the end of chapter one and the beginning of chapter 2. We do not know why she removed the one and did a second redaction. They are the passages in which she refers to the difference between the soul and the spirit (IC 7.1.11), and the first time that God gave to this soul (Teresa's) the favor of the divine and spiritual marriage (IC 7.2.1). Perhaps this removal and revision of the text had been done after the input of Gracián which we will indicate as we go on.

3. The Interior Castle before the tribunal of the theologians. Teresa's autograph of the *Interior Castle* is infested with corrections and marginal notes, which in turn have been crossed out by a second or third corrector. This sad misfortune began in the summer of 1580 in Segovia, where the theologians Gracián and Diego de Yanguas (the one who opposed the fact that a woman, even though it was Teresa, should do a commentary on the *Song of Songs)* feigned a tribunal of orthodoxy in which they questioned Teresa on passages in her book. Gracián gives an account of this: "We read this book in the presence of Padre Fray Diego de Yanguas, and I arguing many things with him saying they were *m*ale sonantes (bad sounding), and Padre Fray Diego answering me about them and she saying that

we should remove them. And so we took out some, not because the doctrine was bad but because they were lofty and difficult for many to understand. . ." (Es*cholias.* . . p. 429).

4. The corrections of Padre Gracián were not so gentle and scarce. The teresian autograph is sprinkled with them from the first chapter. At times it is a matter of pure lexical trifles (for example when Teresa brands as beastly the fact of the Christian speaking to God as to a slave." Gracián erases the word, with its moralizing connotations, and substitutes it with "abomination." At other times, he introduces large corrections and interlinear or marginal annotations (for example in f. 9 v: IC 1.2.14) either for literary or for theological scruples.

5. It happened nonetheless that a little after Teresa's death, the autograph fell into the hands of her first biographer, Padre Ribera, for whom these corrections were intolerable and he erased them one by one. Finally he returned to the first page and wrote a long tirade under the title of the work: "In this book many times what the Holy Mother wrote is crossed out, and different words added or comments made in the margin. And ordinarily they are badly crossed out and it was better the first time, as she wrote it. And it will be seen that in the sentence it was better stated . . . And because I have read and looked over everything with some care, it seems to me right to advise anyone who reads it that they should read it as the Holy Mother wrote it, for she understood and said it better . . . And I ask that out of charity whoever reads this book reverence the words and letters made by that saintly hand." Fortunately Gracián made his corrections with extreme delicacy, in such a way that beneath what he crossed out the Teresian original remains legible.

6. Yet the autograph fell into the hands of a theologian of the inquisition. Teresa had sent her writing to the prioress of the Carmel in Seville, María de San José. When the Jesuit Rodrigo Alvarez heard of this, he begged Teresa, "with much restraint" to know its

contents (Ltr 412.18). And she gave orders to the Spanish prioress
that rather than give him the book she read to him personally the seventh dwelling place, and "tell him that that person reached that point
and that she lives in that peace." Padre Rodrigo listened attentively
to the reading, he begged to have the autograph for a moment and on
the reverse side of the last folio (110 v) and much moved wrote: "the
mother prioress in this monastery in Seville read to me this seventh
dwelling place . . ."May all the saints give praise to God's infinite
goodness, who communicates himself so much to those who seek his
greater glory and the salvation of their neighbor . . ." It was the first
testimony to the impact produced by the book on readers.

    7. The first editors. Two involved according to the anterior
episode: Gracián and Ribera. Each made a personal copy — elegant
and luxurious – of the autograph, with the intention of immediate
publication. Failed projects. Fray Luis de León brought it out for
the first time, who fortunately did not introduce into the text any of
the emendations to the autograph. This book had the good luck of
being reproduced twice in facsimile. In 1882, by the Carmelite (O
Carm) Archbishop of Seville, Cardinal Lluch, who had an autograph
reproduction made. In the following century a photo type reproduction was made with the corresponding paleographic transcription by
Tomás Alvarez and Antonio Mas, in Burgos 1990. It was made in
such a way that the autograph of the *Interior Castle* is accessible to
any reader, just as it came from Teresa's pen.

78. Basic Essentials Of The Interior Castle

We are referring to the theological and literary essential points of the work.

1. The theological essential point. In writing the *Interior Castle* Teresa proposed at the outset to compose a treatise fundamentally theological. Not a devotional or superficial writing. Already in her *Life* the little treatise on the degrees of prayer aimed at basing it on the truths of sacred Scripture. "May God deliver us " — she said – "from foolish devotions" (L 13.16). Thus now, from the first part of the *Interior Castle* (IC 1.1.1) she quotes three biblical texts that have a high resonance in her thinking: a/ that the human soul has great beauty and capacity, since it was created in the image and likeness of God (Gn 1. 26-27); b/the soul has many dwelling places just as in heaven there are many dwelling places (Jn 14.2); the basic theme that she will develop in remembering that Jesus fulfills his word that we will come (the three) and make our dwelling in the Christian; c/ and that God finds his delight in the children of men (Prv 8. 31), which always had a great resonance in Teresa's soul and that will determine the development or the framework of the book.

2. There are three basic theological particulars in Teresa's thinking. They had been present from the time of her first mystical experiences when "a feeling of the presence of God would come upon me unexpectedly so that I could in no way doubt that he was within me or I totally immersed in him (L 10.1). This experience made her aware of the mystery of the presence of God in things, so different from his presence in the depths of the soul in grace. Rooted in this fact is her comprehension of the capacity of the soul, the human soul is capable of God, that is to say, from the depths of its being it is open

345

to transcendence, it is not locked up in itself, but has a primordial call from God. She does not recall in the *Interior Castle* – as she did at other times — the Augustinian motto "you have made us for yourself . . ." (*Confessions 1.2),*which she had recently celebrated in a poem: "I am yours and born for you . . ." Yet on the other hand the motto from *Proverbs* — that he found his delight in the children of men (Prv 8.31) — served her as the basis for developing the ascending, relational process of the dwelling places, which will be the steps of this process until in the final dwelling place the relation is converted into an inseparable union . . . as two drops of water fallen into the sea, or two rays of sunlight illuminating the same room.

3. From these three theological presuppositions, the two that most serve to establish the exposition of the *Interior Castle* are the fact of the presence of God and the truth gotten from *Proverbs* , that is, the delightful relationship of God with humans or better, the interrelationship between the two, not only on the loving-affective plane, but even more so in the depth of the human being: the human is a paradise for God. The seven dwelling places are not seven rooms but seven degrees of life or of communion of the human with the divine.

4. Literary foundation. Teresa bases her exposition on a multifaceted symbol, the *castle*, which is at the same time a castle-diamond jewel or very clear crystal, and the castle as a warrior's dwelling place, with battlements and walls and ditches: these are susceptible of a twofold symbolism, either of light and illumination , or of struggle and victory. In the development of the work she super-imposes a series of symbols that stake out the steps of the process at the same time as they assume the basic theological themes. In such a way that the symbols carry out a double function, literary and theological. In outline they are the following:

1. The Castle of the soul: the first dwelling places (IC 1.1.1).
2. The two founts of life for the soul: the fourth dwelling places (IC 4.2.2)
3. The silkworm reborn as the butterfly: fifth dwelling places (IC 5.2.2)
4. The biblical bridal symbol: fifth dwelling places (IC 5.4).

We will highlight the most important semantic aspects of each of these four symbols.:

1. The castle of the soul is an anthropological symbol. The underlying image of the whole exposition. It determines the structure and the figured language of the book. It serves first of all to give a sketch of the human being — body, soul, spirit — center of the soul, transcendent relationship of the human person with God. It comments as well on the gospel text about the indwelling and the mystical Trinitarian experience. Perhaps the most relevant point in the symbolism of the *Interior Castle* is the openness of the human being to the divinity, the radical vocation to transcendence.

2. The two founts: one is artificial and far away, which brings the water through a series of aqueducts; the other from a trough over a spring that flows from the deepest and most secret place of the human being, to symbolize the contrast between human effort – the asceticism of bringing water through aqueducts – and the divine gift, the trough that fills with water." For Teresa the water is always an image of life ("I don't find anything more appropriate to explain some spiritual experiences than water" IC 4.2.2). The two sources symbolize the two forms of life: natural and supernatural. (In the teresian lexicon supernatural equals "mystical.") Already previously she had spoken of the soul immersed in the divine as a "sponge which absorbs water" (ST 40).

3. The silkworm that is reborn as a butterfly. A symbol that for

Teresa has a Christological sense. The metamorphosis of the worm symbolizes our transformation into Christ that develops along the three final dwelling places, so as to highlight the arrival at freedom in Christ, as the flight of the butterfly that has freed itself from the sheath of the worm until the definitive mystical transfiguration, the fire that burns up the butterfly (IC 7.2.5; 7.3.1) or the phoenix bird (IC 6. 4.3).

4. *The nuptial symbol,* which serves Teresa to articulate the three last dwelling places (meetings, betrothal, marriage). It has the appearance of a sociological image but in reality it is inspired by the symbolism of the *Song of Songs*, which she does not interpret in an ecclesiological sense but in an individual sense as the process of love between God and the soul, until culminating in the mystical union of the two, as the supreme milestone of the Christian life, understood as a process of love in which the determining factor is the divine love.

5. A third basis of the Castle: experience. The same as for the *Way of Perfection* the *Interior Castle* is also inspired by Teresa's own living experience. The trajectory of the seven dwelling places has an autobiographical undercurrent. They are above all the seven dwelling places lived by Teresa. To her personal experience she joins many other experiences of life, known by her, above all the experiences themselves of her immediate readers. And in the full mystical exposition, there emerges a reference to Fray John of the Cross and his experience, which matches Teresa's: "I know a person or two persons — one was a man — to whom the Lord had granted some of these favors who were so desirous of serving His Majesty at their own cost, without these great delights, and so anxious to suffer that they complained to our Lord because he bestowed these favors on them, and if they could decline receiving these gifts they would do so." (IC 6.9.17). It is easy to glimpse the Fray John of the Cross in this anonymous person. From all these experiences she rises to the universal landscape of spiritual theology.

79. The Seven Dwelling Places: The Plan Of The Spiritual Life

1. Teresa is conscious of writing a treatise on the spiritual life. She gives it this designation in the title of the work. In the process of writing, the contrast between the two extremes is symptomatic, the beginning and the end: She begins fearful that she won't know how to do anything but repeat what she has already written and accepts the order to explain "some doubts about prayer for the sisters. In ending the epilogue, she is pleased with the writing, literarily and with humor: she revalues and universalizes it. "Now that I am finished I admit the work the work has brought me much happiness . . . although no more than seven dwelling places were discussed, in each of these there are many others, below and above and to the sides, with lovely gardens and fountains and labyrinths, such delightful things"(IC epil. 3). It is then that she gives it the title of a treatise. And she expresses the same satisfaction in the correspondence of these days, after having finished the book. Although Báñez doesn't think it is so good (Ltr 324. 9), she is convinced that it is superior to the *Life*. She writes to another theologian: "if Señor Carillo were to come here, he would see another jewel which – insofar as one can tell – has many advantages over the previous one [the *Book of Her Life*]. It deals with nothing else but who he is; and it does so with more exquisite enameling and decoration. The jeweler did not know as much at that time, and the gold is of finer quality, although the precious stones do not stand out as they did in the previous piece [the *Life*]. It was done by order of the Glassmaker, and that is evident according to what they say" (Ltr 219.8, written ten days after finishing the book).

2. About spiritual theology (or "mystical theology" : cf *Life*

chaps. 10,11,& 12), she knows not a few things. She knows above all, the traditional structure of the treatise into a trilogy of three ways (purgative, illuminative, and unitive), but she sets them aside (cf *Life* 22.1), although her *Interior Castle* will be structured in three sections, yet with a different meaning. For her book she prefers a sevenfold scale, founded on diverse theological reasons. She knows and utilizes the concept of perfection, but she does not use it as a criterion for growth. Love expands the castle. The measure of the seven dwelling places is both anthropological and theological. It is inspired by the lofty concept of the human being and the level of reciprocal relations between "God and humans": degrees of presence and love of God. In the measure that the dwelling places advance, the love received in the castle of the soul will be more and more the determining factor of growth. Love enlarges the castle. Teresa does not conceive states or gradual stages as something static or merely of one person. Prayer (an intimate sharing between two friends) as well as perfect contemplation are overflowing, essentially urging: "I believe that , since our nature is bad, we will not reach perfection in the love of neighbor if that love doesn't rise from love of God as its root" (IC 5.3.5). "Works are what the Lord wants" (IC 5.3.11).This is the reason for prayer, my daughters, the purpose of this spiritual marriage; the birth always of good works, good works." (IC 7.4.6).

3. The three sections into which the book is structured. In the process of the Christian life, Teresa highlights three steps different in character but continuous:

— above all as a point of departure, the anthropological basis: affirmation of the human being and its dignity, its spacious interiority: within the soul, capable of God; in its deepest part, the spirit, the seat of the Holy spirit and dwelling place of the most Holy Trinity; this not by reason of its structure, but as a supernatural gift. The first dwelling places.

— the central phase of the process is Christological: plenitude of the mystery of death and resurrection in Christ: "my life is Christ." To live in the depth of the Christian life is to develop the process of transformation in him. The fifth dwelling places.

— the point of arrival is Trinitarian: the highest realization of his presence, the indwelling of the Trinity in the soul. In the personal case of Teresa, she experiences the main mystery of the Christian life and the fulfillment of Jesus' words "we shall come" . . . Lived as a radical dynamic of service to others and to the church.

4. Each dwelling place. In the theological symbolism of the castle, each dwelling place denotes a degree of interiorization or humanization of the person and, at the same time, a level of intensity in the relationship between God and the human and vice versa. Although it is risky to reduce to an outline the rich content of each one, it is possible to attempt it.

— First dwelling places: enter the castle of oneself; the door of entry is prayer, to have an awareness of one's own interiority and personality and to begin the personal relationship with God; primordial vocation of transcendence; what is called "teresian socratism" consists in knowing oneself in relation with God. To be converted and to recover the spiritual sensitiveness progressively. As biblical types: "St. Paul and the Magdalene," or the paralytic of the Gospels (IC 1.1.8), or Lot's wife who did not turn her gaze to look at herself (IC 1.1.6). "Let us set our eyes on Christ" (IC 1.2.1. & 11).

— Second dwelling places: "to struggle," to confront the tensions of disorder existing in oneself and in the disordered exterior dynamisms: fidelity to prayer; the necessity of becoming strong in the radical option: "a determined determination." Biblical types: the prodigal son (IC 2.1.4), or the soldiers of Gidion (IC 2.1.6): "be determined to fight with all the devils and realize that there are no better weapons than those of the cross." (IC 2.1.6).

— Third dwelling places: culmination of the ascetical effort. To submit to the trial of love. Establish a program of life, yet submissive to the plan of God. There will come periods of dryness and powerlessness, as states of trial: "Test us, Lord, — for you know the truth – so that we may know ourselves" ((IC 3.1.9). Three biblical types: the rich young man of the Gospel and the two contrasting figures of David and Solomon: the one who overcomes risk; the other, who succumbs to it.

— fourth dwelling places. Period of transition: entry into the mystical experience, but intermittently; moments of infused light (recollection of the mind), and of mystical-passive love (quiet of the will). Newness of life: as though an interior fount were rising. There prevails in the soul his initiative. Biblical types: the day laborers of the parable or the bride of the *Song of Songs.*

— Fifth dwelling places. Symbolism of the silk worm that dies and is reborn , "our life is Christ." The phase of union begins, with either the "mystical union" experienced in the depths of the soul, or the "non-delightful union, through conformity of the wills, manifest especially in the love and service of neighbor: "works are what the Lord wants!" Multiple biblical types: the fathers and prophets of Mount Carmel or the bride of *Song of Songs,* who has already purified her love ("He put charity in order within her") and the antitypes of Judas or of Saul, called to love but failures.

— Sixth dwelling places: *s*tate of mystical betrothal; the crucible of love; ecstatic period and eschatological tension. New mode of feeling sins. Christ becomes present "in an admirable manner in which the divine and human joined is always its companion" (the soul's). A profusion of mystical phenomena. The wounds of love. Transpiercing of the soul (IC 6.11.4). Biblical typology: Jacob and the ladder; Moses and the burning bush; St. Paul raised to the third heaven, the Samaritan woman invited to the living water, the bride of the *Song of Songs.*

— Seventh dwelling places: the mystical marriage; "here all three divine Persons communicate with it . . . they never leave the soul." A full insertion into ecclesial service: "hunger to bring souls to God." Biblical types: the soul is like Solomon's temple; it receives the kiss of peace like the bride in the *Song of Songs;* like Paul and the Magdalene, who attained the madness of love.

80. Sanctity

1. Sanctity is the central idea presented in the last dwelling place, the final end of the process and objective of the book projected from the first dwelling place: Teresa's final experiences, not told in the *Book of Her Life* since it was happening to her only in the last five years. They were precisely the experiences of her present situation and those that explained the reason for all the anterior experiences. For this reason in the seventh dwelling places she will deal with the theme from a clearly autobiographical perspective: not from some theoretical premises, but from sanctity as it was realized in her; from her own peephole she extended her gaze to the mystery of Christian sanctity in itself.

2. The theme of sanctity. Teresa does not use this word in the abstract in her entire exposition (seventh dwelling places). She takes as her aim, above all, a "model sanctity," that is, the sanctity incarnated in the biblical types or in the models of sanctity such as Paul or the Magdalene, or in the symbol of the bride in the *Song of Songs*. They are the ones most often recurring as the archetypes of the highest love of God. There will appear also in these dwelling places, St. Elijah – the one who hungered for the glory of God — St. Peter in Rome, saints closer, such as, St. Francis and St. Dominic, or Father Ignatius, the founder of the society (the fifth dwelling places). She is far from the gallery of heroes presented in the *Flos Sanctorum*, as though they had been surpassed by the new teresian vision of sanctity. There emerges above all Christ, as the absolute model: she repeats her initial watchword: "Fix your eyes on the crucified!" (IC 7.4.8)

3. The exposition. Rarely has she been so systematic and well ordered. She analyzes the theme and expounds it in four chapters

perfectly organized, with the four fundamental components of Christian sanctity as a base. That is:

Chap. 1: Sanctity is above all Trinitarian and Christian

Chap. 2: Departing from the Christological fact: the spiritual marriage

Chap. 3: It realizes the human plenitude of the new human being

Chap. 4: It is an ecclesial fact that situates the Christian in full service.

In such a way that the four components of the mystery are superimposed one by one: the Trinitarian with the indwelling; the Christological with the full configuration to Christ; the anthropological with human fullness as a basis for the supernatural gift; and the ecclesial, with the total service of the Church. Teresa develops these four aspects of sanctity, evoking how they have happened in her personal experience. That is:

4. The four themes:

Chapter 1 : How she experienced the Trinity in her soul: "In the seventh dwelling place the union comes about in a different way: our good God now desires to remove the scales from the soul's eyes and let it see and understand. . .; brought into that dwelling place, the Most Blessed Trinity, all three Persons, are revealed to it in an enkindling in the spirit in the manner of a cloud of magnificent splendor . . . Here all three Persons communicate themselves to it, speak to it, and explain those words of the Lord in the Gospel: that he and the Father and the Holy Spirit will come to dwell with the soul that loves him and keeps his commandments" (IC 7.1.6). " Oh, God help me! How different is hearing and believing these words from understanding their truth in this way! (IC 7.1.7) "You may think that as a result the soul will be outside itself and so absorbed that it will be unable to be occupied with anything else. On the contrary, the soul is much more occupied than before with everything pertaining to the service of God . . ." (IC 7.1.8).

Chapter 2: The Christological fact. "with other persons the favor will be received in another form. With regard to the one of whom we are speaking, the Lord represented himself to her, just after she had received Communion , in the form of shining splendor, beauty, and majesty . . . and he told her that now it was time that she consider as her own what belonged to him and that he would take care of what was hers (IC 7.2.1). It is the fact of the spiritual marriage, referred to in *Spiritual Testimony,* 31 on receiving communion at the hands of Fray John of the Cross, that gave rise to the strongest tension of theological hope: a longing for the final parousia

Chapter 3. Treats of the great effects caused by this prayer. To the preceding words of Christ, she responds as does St. Paul: "What would you have me to do, Lord" as in her poem "what do you want of me?" And she enumerates the four features that characterize the new self:: a/ a forgetfulness of self that makes it truly seem that one no longer is (no. 1); b/ a great desire to suffer, but not in a way that disquiets as it did, for the desire is extreme that God's will be done in it . . .; c/ these souls also have a great interior joy when persecuted . . .without any hostility toward those who do them wrong; d/ the strong eschatological tension ceases (longing for the parousia), and like St. Paul prefers service (no. 6: this is what amazes it most of all).

Chapter 4: Again the model figures appear. Above all, Christ crucified; his glorious Mother and the apostles; St. Paul, with his most severe trials; St. Peter . . . the Magdalene, our father Elijah . . . (nos. 4-5. 11)The hour has arrived for a sacrificing and unconditional work for the Church.

"What do you think is the reason for these inspirations . . . and other messages the soul sends from the interior center to the people at the top of the castle . . . that those outside might fall asleep? No, absolutely not! . . . the company it has gives it much greater strength than ever. Do you know what it means to be truly spiritual? It means becoming the slaves of God. Marked with his brand, which is that of the cross, spiritual persons because they have given him their liberty, can be sold by him as slaves of everyone, as he was. He doesn't thereby do them any harm or grant them a small favor (IC 7.4.8). And again: fix your eyes on the Crucified and everything will become small for you. (IC 7.4.8)

5. Is there security of life in the seventh dwelling place? Teresa is a daughter of the tridentine Church. She lives intensely the problem of the certainty or uncertainty of the state of grace." She records her anguish in one of her Spiritual Testimonies 24 "with regard to the fear about whether or not I was in the state of grace." She had already stated this equally in her *Life* (38.9). Personally she heard the words absolutely comforting: "don't fear, daughter, for no one will be a party to separating you from Me" (ST 31), remembered here in the seventh dwelling places. (IC . 7.2.1). Nonetheless, there persists in her the realism with which she ends the *Way of Perfections* : to live in love and fear. At the summit of the seventh dwelling places she raises the theme again and answers it thus:

"It seems I'm saying that when the soul reaches this state in which God grants it this favor, it is sure of its salvation and safe from falling again. I do not say such a thing, and wherever I so speak that it seems the soul is secure, this should be taken to means as long as the divine Majesty keeps it in his hand and it does not offend him. At least I know certainly that the soul doesn't consider itself safe even though it sees itself in this state and the state lasted for some years. But it goes about with much greater fear than before, guarding itself from any small offense against God "(IC 7.2.9).

IX
Minor Writings

We are dealing with a cluster of small writings: opuscules, humorous pages, poems, laws, selected thoughts, and several hundred letters. In Teresa's complete works, they make up more than one half of her writings. Some of them are very important in order to know her thought or her biography, whether from the mystical aspect or from that of her duties as founder. In both aspects the richest and most varied are her letters.

81. Spiritual Testimonies

1. The *Spiritual Testimonies* are not a treatise but an anthology of heterogeneous pieces: autobiographical accounts of interior experiences; spiritual consultations at times sealed with secrecy (in one case she writes: "Remember that all of this must be kept under the secrecy of confession: ST 3.13); select points in an instantaneous manner for strictly personal use; formulation of the vow of obedience to her spiritual director; counsels for the discalced Carmelite friars, and so on. There are 67 pieces in all. Padre Silverio in his critical edition (BMC, 2) distributed them in groups, 6 major pieces, which he called *Relations*; and 61 minor pieces, which he called *Favors* . The first group were detailed, introspective expositions, in which she presents a panoramic view of her soul, always destined for one of her directors. The sixty remaining are smaller in size, some for an imprecise person, others strictly intimate are reserved for Teresa herself. Some are so intimate that she is embarrassed to put them in writing: "there is no need to put here in writing" (ST 13.3).

2. Composition of the series. The composition of this anthology extends over a period as long as 21 years, which covers almost Teresa's entire literary period: the first Testimony was written in 1560; the last in the series in 1581. We don't have a precise date for any of them. Putting them in order we can divide them into four groups:

-The first group was written in the years of the foundation of St. Joseph's in Avila, 1560-63; *Testimonies* 1-3, the first writings from her pen were contemporary with *The book of Her Life*. Destined for her first Dominican confessors, Ibáñez and García de Toledo, they are all that remains of her first introspective attempts (all the others have been lost).

- The second group is made up of numbers 7-36. They are Testimonies written in the intense period of mystical experiences, from 1569 to 1573. In the last of the series, she is then under the direction of Fray John of the Cross. Beginning with number 25, she writes them at the Incarnation. The central and most important one is Testimony 31, which refers to Teresa's entry into the seventh dwelling places, at the reception of communion at the hands of Saint John of the Cross (1572).

- The third group corresponds to the years of conflict: the denunciation of Teresa to the inquisition of Seville, the denunciation and sequestering of the *Book of Her Life,* the journey to Seville, confinement to Toledo 1575-77. This series is made up of three small groups: nos. 35-36, the vow of obedience to Padre Gracián (1575); nos. 58-59, written n Seville for the consultors to the inquisition (1576), highly interesting are nos. 33 and 37-66, notes on the mystical graces she received during this period, in preparation for the synthesis of the *Interior Castle.*

3. Autograph*s.* There are only a few autographs that we possess of these Teresian writings. Around 1572, Teresa had heard an interior voice that ordered her: "don't fail to write down the counsels I give you" (ST 24). It seems that from this moment on she wrote down her experiences in a notebook. She indicates this herself: "Now in turning back to read this little notebook (ST 55.3), a notebook of which no trace can be found. Nonetheless, she at times noted these experiences on loose pieces of paper, so as to submit them to one of her directors. For example, after narrating the famous ecstasy in Salamanca, she notes in sending it to her confessor: "Your reverence can tell me when you see me whether pain can cause suspension. . ."(ST 12.2), and a little after: "Will your Reverence write me your opinion . . . and send this paper back to me" (ST 25.4). In some cases she herself makes two copies, one to send and one to keep, for example, she did this with Testimony no. 58 and with the vow of obedience to Padre Gracián (ST 36). The little notebook that contains the autograph of the "Four counsels" which she inserted in the *Book of Her Foundations* (folio 100) when she thought she had finished the book.

Actually the most important are the precious Testimony 12, which is conserved in the Carmel of Locarno (Switzerland); the extensive Testimony 58 in the monastery of Discalced Carmelite friars Caprarola, Italy, and Testimony 36, divided between the Carmels in Consuegra (Spain), Terre Haute (USA) and the Carmelite Friars in Puebla (Mexico).

4. Content and quality of the text. The *Spiritual Testimonies* have, before all, an historical, autobiographical value. They are not an intimate diary, yet they contain bits about Teresa's interior life: sometimes, great panoramic views of her state of soul; at other times, simple instantaneous accounts of a mystical moment or grace. There is a long series in which she records a word of the Lord's, within her mystical experience, so for example 23-32; 37-39; 45-54; 55-57; 60-64. This record is due to the order given by the Lord: "Don't fail to write down the counsels I give you" (ST 24). Especially interesting are those of Trinitarian content (ST 13, 14, 29), the swoon in Salamanca (ST 12); the Eucharist on Palm Sunday (ST 22); the grace of the spiritual marriage (ST 31).

5. One of the Testimonies – St 58 – served as the occasion for Teresa to put in order her own ideas about the mystical experiences: written in 1576. It was an immediate preparation for the codification of the dwelling places of the *Interior Castle* the following year. These ideas are of a clearly Carmelite content; for example the numbers 6; 10; 11 ("in your days you will see the order of the Blessed

Virgin flourish"); 16 (in favor of the Incarnation); 18 (regarding the Carmel of St. Joseph in Avila); 21 (the Blessed Virgin in the prioress's choir stall at the Incarnation). Interesting is the approbation of the activity of a woman founder (ST 15; 30) or the one that dissolved her scruples concerning affection for family members (ST 41). Without doubt the most important are the ones referring to her own spiritual life: the already mentioned grace of the mystical marriage (ST 24; 25). Finally, there is a little series of graces alluding to Gracián (ST 36; 38; 39; 54; 55).

6. From all of these Fray Luis made a selection, which he published for the first time (1588) at the end of *The Book of Her Life* with the statement: "With the original of this book there came into my hands some pages written by the holy Mother Teresa of Jesus, in which for her own remembrance or so as to give an account to her confessors, she had written down things that God had said to her or favors that he had given her in addition to those contained in this book. It seemed to me good to include them here since they are very edifying. And so I include them in the very way the Mother wrote them down". The series concludes with signature of Teresa of Jesus, at the end of Testimony 64.

82. Meditations On The Song Of Songs

1. *Meditations on the Song of Songs* is a singular little work among the writings of Teresa. We do not possess the autograph ., nor do we have the entire text composed by Teresa. We have only fragments, authentic ones, but we do not know how they correspond to the original plan of the work. It is also a singular work for her audacity in writing a commentary in that historical moment on the biblical poem *The Song of Songs* and for her original focus in commenting on it: a lover who appropriates the biblical poem of love.

2. Historical context. Although we are not sure of the date or place of composition, it is probable that Teresa wrote it during her three-year period as prioress at the Incarnation (1571-74). It was a time of actuality for the biblical poem in its Castilian version, despite the distant condemnations in the *Index of Forbidden Books* of Valdés (1559). They are the years in which Fray Luis de León was imprisoned in Valladolid because of his translation of the *Song of Songs* into Castilian. Among his opposing and denouncing theologians were some personal friends of Teresa's , such as Báñez, Medina, and Pedro Fernández. It was the period also when Teresa was under the direction of Fray John of the Cross, who was called by her to be the spiritual director of the community of the Incarnation. It seems normal that Fray John in his conferences would comment more than once on the biblical poem. Only a little after he will compose his *Spiritual Canticle* in the prison of Toledo almost as a poetic alternative to the *Song of Songs.* Yet more important is the contextual date: it is the time when Teresa has entered into the mystical phase of the spiritual marriage (November 1572), a happening that literally determined her recourse to the nuptial symbolism (made use of especially

in the *Interior Castle*, much less present in the *Life* (L 27.10; 36.29).

3. Composition of the little work. Teresa herself supplies us with clues: a/ She writes the book because "For a number of years now the Lord has given me great delight each time I hear or read some words from Solomon's *Song of Songs*. The delight is so great that without understanding the vernacular meaning of the Latin my soul is stirred and recollected more than by devotional books written in the Language I understand"((M. Pro. 1)). b/ she asked theologians what the Holy Spirit meant in the vernacular and the true meaning of the poem, and they answered her with evasive words: that " the doctors wrote many commentaries and yet never finally finished explaining the words fully"(M. 1.8). c/ Nevertheless we have more autobiographical data: "I know someone [referring to herself] who for a number of years had many fears, and nothing gave her assurance, but the Lord was pleased that she hear some words from the *Song of Songs*, and through them she understood that her soul was being well guided." (M 1.6). d/ "For almost two years , more or less, it seems to me the Lord has been giving me , for the sake of my purpose in writing this work, some understanding of the meaning of certain words" (M pro 2). e/ She desires to share these sentiments with her Carmelite readers: "I think these words will bring consolation to the sisters that our Lord leads by this path" (M pro 2). That is, she wrote it out of her personal tasting of the words of the poem and she destined her writing for those who have a similar taste. f/ She knew that the theological interpretation of this poem was something for learned men to do, but neither "must we make women stand so far away from enjoyment of the Lord's riches" (M 1.8).

4. She as a result wrote the book on the basis of personal experience of the words of the poem. She kept away from all intention of literal exegesis. And, although she comments on the words of the *Song of Songs* as alluding to the soul and not to the church, she

does not attempt an allegorical exegesis. She simply appropriated the words of the poem out of her own experiential perspective. From the time of the episode related in *Spiritual Testimony 35* (November 1572), she felt herself to be the "true bride" of her Creator, King , and God. It was easy for her to identify with the bride of the biblical poem, without playing her role. She already sang it in the poem "I am yours and born for you." She celebrated it in another poem Dilectus Meus Mihi: "Myself surrendered and given, / The exchange is this: / My beloved for me, / And I am for my Beloved." Only in this bridal and mystical key does her commentary make sense.

5. There occurred, nevertheless, an unexpected fate. Informed about the writing, one of the theologian assessors, expressed his total dissent: according to him "it was not decent for a woman to explain the *Song of Songs*. . . I don't know, Mother , why you tire yourself doing this." This was enough of a warning to prompt her to throw the manuscript into the fire. All that remains for us are fragmentary copies made by the nuns. The theologian who was opposed was the Dominican Diego de Yanguas, a professor in Segovia. It is probable the episode occurred in 1574 on the occasion of the foundation of the Segovian Carmel. (Fray John of the Cross was also there).

6. The biblical verses commented on in the book. In the fragments saved from the flames there remains only a commentary on a half dozen verses. First of all the one that had the most impact on her. "Let him kiss me with the kiss of his mouth" (S. 1.1): she dedicates to it the first three chapters "O my Lord and my God, and what words are these that a worm speaks them to its Creator (S. 1.10). In the following chapters she quotes the verses:

    - "Your breasts are better than wine, and give forth the most sweet fragrance" (ch . 4).

    - "I sat down under the shadow of him whom I desired and his fruit is sweet to my taste" (ch 5).

-" The King brought me unto the wine cellar and set charity in order within me" (ch 6).

-"Sustain me with flowers and surround me with apples, for I am dying of love" (ch. 7).

7. Within the commentary she will add other verses. It is probable that Teresa took them from the Little Office of the Blessed Virgin, which she recited each week. She recalls this in ch. 6.8. In any case, she is interested especially in the verses of the bride, which she can repeat as her own. As for the other one in the dialogue of the poem – the bridegroom – she was interested in the words "You are all beautiful, my love" and "Who is this that is as bright as the sun?" (6. 9,11). Yet the verse most frequently commented on is Dilectus meus mihi (My beloved is for me) (Sol. 16).

8. Transmission of the text. In salvaging the little book after the autograph had been thrown into the fire, a singular episode occurred. One of the various manuscript copies of the text arrived soon into the hands of Padre Báñez, who perhaps was ignorant of the disastrous intervention of his Dominican brother, Padre Yanguas, but who gives his unconditional approbation: "Having seen with due attention these four little books, which in all have eight and a half folds, I did not find any bad doctrine, but rather good and beneficial doctrine. In the College of San Gregorio in Valladolid, 10 July 1575. Fr. Domingo Báñez." The one who signed knew well who the author of the manuscript was , for he had noted on its first page: "this is a reflection by Teresa of Jesus. I haven't found anything in it that offends me. Fr. Domingo Báñez (the actual manuscript copy is in the Carmel of Alba de Tormes). It is probable that one of these copies reached the hands of Luis de León in 1588. But he preferred not to include it in his edition of Teresa's works. Padre Gracián published it

in his Brussels edition of 1611 with the title "*Concepts of the Love of God*, written by blessed Teresa of Jesus , on some words of the Song of Solomon." It was reproduced in facsimile by Tomás Alvarez, Editorial Monte Carmelo. Burgos 1979.

83. Soliloquies

1. This is a little book of prayers. It has been called the Teresian psalter and it has been published in the form of psalms. The prayers are intimate and at the same time they cry out. They are without an original title and without an addressee other than the author herself. In his first edition (1588), Fray Luis de León placed them after the *Interior Castle* and labeled them *Exclamations or Meditations of the Soul on God, written by Mother Teresa of Jesus, on different days, in conformity with the spirit that our Lord communicated to her after Communion, in the year 1569.* But the last affirmation is not very certain, since in no Soliloquy is there any allusion to the Eucharist. Neither does Teresa allude to this little work in any of her writings or in her *Letters.* Nor is any autograph of the work conserved although there are pseudo-autographs. As the transmitting text we make use of the one published by Fray Luis.

2. *The Soliloquies* were written in the form of the soliloquy. This was a literary form known by Teresa not only through the recital of certain psalms or what she had read in the *Soliloquies* attributed to St. Augustine, but she had also encountered this form fervently in the typical monologues of Denys the Carthusian in his *Life of Christ* and above all in the *Confessions of St. Augustine.* All of her works are permeated by this form. Perhaps less so in the *Interior Castle.* Much more so in her *Life* and *The Way of Perfection.* So for example at the end of the introductory chapters in the *Way of Perfection* , she finishes with an exclamation (W 3.8-9). She does the same at the end of the Eucharistic theme (W 35.5). In writing her *Life* she would like to cry out (L 25.17) or like "St. Francis, when the robbers struck him, ran through the fields crying out and telling the robbers that he was the

herald of the great King" (IC 6.6.11). (She did not know, however, the cultivated word "soliloquies." She prefers words like "crying out, exclamations, shouting.")

3. The internal plan. The 17 Exclamations or Solilioquies that make up the little book do not respond to a pre-established plan. They are spontaneous and irruptive. Written, according to Fray Luis , "on different days." They begin with a cry directed to her own soul or to her own life: " O life, life! How can you endure being separated from your Life? . . . with what are you occupied? What are you doing?" (she uses the familiar you, something exceptional on her pen!). Yet this initial sentiment of the absence of God serves only as a detonator that sets in motion a huge range of uncontainable sentiments. In going forward she alternates between the words to herself and cries to the Lord will alternate. (To him she uses the unfamiliar Vos (you): rarely does she use "Your Majesty"). And more than once, to an unnamed listener: "O Christians, Christians! Behold the communion you have with this great God" ((S 14.2). O mortals, return, return to yourselves (S. 12.4).

4. Starting from the third *Soliloquy*, the flow of sentiments revolves almost always around a biblical theme. In such a way that the little book is filled – more so than any other of her writings – with biblical references, not cited but incorporated into or assumed by the exclamation. They are never quoted out of erudition, but as a supplication coming from within. The book that she turns to most is the *Book of Psalms*. Then next are the *Gospels*. these are followed by the *Letters o f St. Paul* and *St. Peter*, the *Apocalypse*, the prophets *Isaiah* and *Ezekiel* and the *Wisdom Books*. She thrills at the words of Jesus: "come to me all you who labor and are heavy burdened . . ."(S 8.2), or "come to me all you who thirst and I will give you drink" (S 9.1), or the words of the Blessed Virgin: "My soul magnifies and praises the Lord"(S 7.3), or the exclamation of the psalmist "How sweet is the Lord!" At other times , the word produces amazement in her such as

the word of Proverbs: "When I consider how you say that your delights are with the children of the earth, my soul rejoices greatly . . . what words are these" (S 7.1). Finally there appear with the supplications of the *Song of Songs :* "My Beloved is for me, and I for my Beloved and my Beloved for me" a cry by which she quickly appropriates them to herself: "the faculties and senses . . . go out into the streets and squares entreating the daughters of Jerusalem to tell of their God " (S 16. 3). This supplication of the *Song of Songs* rises in tone to a final exclamation: "Love is as strong as death, and unyielding as hell. Oh, that I might be slain by him and thrown into this divine hell where there is no hunger where there is no longer any hope of coming out"(S 17.3). She associates with only one other non biblical prayer, a master as she was with the soliloquy, St. Augustine, to find solidarity with her sentiments: "Oh, how late have my desires been enkindled . . . Well, when, Lord, when? How long?" (S 4, 5, 6).

5. *Themes and motives for prayer.* This constant reference to the Bible permits us to verify the extent to which the prayer of Teresa is inspired by Sacred Scripture. Yet the *Soliloquies* reflect, above all, the spectrum of religious sentiments that spring forth from the soul of Teresa and inspire her prayer. Perhaps the prayerful motive most present and impelling is the sentiment of God's absence. It is present from the first lines (similar in a certain way to the first stanza of John of the Cross's *Spiritual Canticle*) And it is repeated up to the last, reprimanding again her own life "O life at enmity with my good; who has leave to bring you to an end? I bear with you; because God bears with you; I maintain you because you are his; do not be a traitor or ungrateful to me" (S 17.4). That is to say, together with the sentiment of God's absence is the constant and urgent desire for his presence beyond this life, and it has its formulation in a strong theological hope that persists to the last line, or the last cry: "I want to live and die in striving and hoping for eternal life more than for the possessions of

all creatures and all their goods, for these will come to an end. Don't abandon me" and she spontaneously appropriates to herself the last words of the Te Deum: " I hope that in you my hope that I will not be confounded ."

6. In the same theological line, with a different inflection and expression we have the sentiment of love: she is interested more in the love God has for her than her own love. His love is water and fire: "Do not deny me this sweetest water that you promise to those who want it. I want it, Lord, and I beg for it, and I come to you . . . O Lord how many kinds of fire there are in this life . . . some kinds of fire consume the soul, other kinds purify it . . . O living founts from the wounds of my God, how surely those who strive to sustain themselves with this divine liqueur will advance in the midst of the dangers of this life" (S 9.2).

7. Also strong motives for Teresa's prayer are the horror of sin, amazement before the things of God and before the mystery of human life, the blessedness of heaven, fear before the possibility of losing grace, a special sensitivity before death, and the longing for full conformity of one's own will with the will of God. For this reason she ends the last soliloquy with a suppliant cry of Augustinian inspiration: "may I always serve you; and do with me what you will."

84. The Poetry Of St. Teresa

1. From Teresa's poetic production only 31 poems have reached us. Undoubtedly there were many more that she composed. Yet these few reflect a special facet of Teresa's soul, her sensitivity to beauty and her propensity to celebrate it poetically and musically. There are enough musical poems, composed to be sung. She, nevertheless, is not aware of being a poet. "I know a person who though not a poet suddenly composed some deeply-felt verses well expressing her pain . They were not composed by the use of her intellect; rather, in order that she enjoy the glory so delightful a distress gave to her, she complained of it in this way to God" (L 16.4). A clear fusion of the mystical with the lyrical trance. She assures us of this in the same context: "Oh, help me God! What is the soul like when it is in this state! It would want to be all tongues so as to praise the Lord." She doesn't write poems as a literary exercise, but from the pressure of lived experiences. For this reason her poems are always festive and celebrate the interior feast (mystical poems), or the feast of the group: ballads, carols, the Sisters' profession days, liturgical feast days.

2. Poetic autographs. Almost all of them are lost. They disappeared quickly in passing from hand to hand. Neither Fray Luis de León, nor the critical editors of her works, nor the learned students of her poetry knew of any autograph. Only recently in Italian Carmels have they recovered the carol : "today there comes to redeem us" and various fragments of other carols (P 11, 17, 27, 29). They come from a little notebook brought to the Spanish Netherlands by Teresa's nurse Bl. Anne of St. Bartholomew, and for this they were cut into fragments as relics for foreign Carmels. This lack of autographs

causes a serious critical textual problem for Teresa's poetry, which still today is without resolution. Likewise , it caused the diffusion and publication of pseudo-autographs, as we already noted in previous themes. (cf. Varios autographos de S. Teresa . . ., by A. Seela. Madrid 1884)).

3. *Dates*. There are only a few of Teresa's poems that have a secure date. Yet all of them spring up during the period of Teresa's mystical experiences and accompany her task as founder. The first one datable is the one that celebrates the beauty of Christ ("Oh, Beauty exceeding/All other beauties!"), composed around 1560. Still, in 1577 she recalled it by memory and transcribed three stanzas for her brother Lorenzo (Ltrs. 172 & 182). The humorous poem she recalled and transcribed is of a little later date (1562 - ?) "Now that you give us clothing new, Heavenly King." Both are situated in the two extremes of Teresa's inspiration: the first , in her full mystical experience; the other clearly humorous even though it contains a strange prayer for two choruses. All the other poems correspond to the period of her foundations (1567-1582), with an abundant exchange of Christmas carols with Fray John of the Cross in the last two years of this period at the Incarnation (1576-1577). It is during these years that she sent "a little song for Fray John of the Cross. Tell him that I told you I greatly enjoyed it" (Ltr 171).

4. Thematic groups. Following the order established by Padre Silverio in his critical edition (BMC 6. 79 – 119) we distinguish in Teresa's poetry three series of poetic compositions:

a) poems 1-9: of mystical inspiration and content.

b) poems 11-23: festivities with a liturgical theme.

c) poems 24-31: plus no. 10: community festive poems: reception of the habit, professions, incidental community occurrences, times in recreation.

Of various motives are those in the second and third series.

Monothematic are those in the first series.

5. M*ystical poems.* In the three series, the mystical poems are the most successfully named. As much for their literary value as for their autobiographical content. They celebrate together, something that the author has suffered in the past or is suffering in the present in the deepest layers of her soul: they celebrate the decisive "ýes" of her life. From the first verse of the first poem: "Since I die of love,/ living apart from love" (identical beginning with a parallel poem of St. John of the Cross "I no longer live within myself." The same in the poem "Myself surrendered and given." This already indicates the decisive moment of her arrival on the high seas of mystical experiences, referred to by herself in her *Life*: "the Lord showing me deep love, often speaks these words to me: "Now you are mine and I am yours." (L 39.21). The string of poems that follow celebrate the torrential cascade of experiences: the wound of love ("the arrow he drew full of love . . .Other love I want not. . .) she surrenders all her being to the Beloved ("I am Yours and born for You, What do You want of me?", the personal experience of the Dlectus meus mihi (My Beloved is for me) of the *Song of Songs*. To finalize in a quiet place of the Nada te turbe (Let nothing trouble you), which is not a gnomic poem giving orders to the reader, but a revival of gospel mottos that Teresa imparts to herself and that closes with a final motto: "God alone suffices."

6. Of less depth are the other two series of poems that celebrate the life of the group, whether they are carols and feast days of the saints or professions that are celebrated as feasts by the whole house. They are poems that are in contrast with the mystical poems. They sing of Teresa's immersion in daily life with its noisy joys, yet without backing down from the uppermost regions of transcendence. Despite the poor literary value of these poems ("outlandish" Vicente de Lafuente dared to qualify some of them), they have the merit of

having introduced poetry as a normal spirit in the lifestyle of her Carmels. Starting with Teresa there arose followers of a high poetic reach (cf Theme 6). There arose likewise in her Carmels a patchwork quilt of poems, such as the romances and carols in the Carmel of Valladolid or in that of Santa Ana in Madrid. Teresa herself in learning of the "songs of the soul composed by Fray John of the Cross in the prison of Toledo (his Spiritual Canticle) recommends them to her nuns: "she was delighted that they enjoyed them and sang them."

7. From all this, the most important thing is the humble yet sincere gesture of celebrating the events of life with poems initiated by Teresa. It resonated down through the centuries. . . unto St. Therese, Blessed Elizabeth of the Trinity and Edith Stein. Perhaps this fact has given rise to the Teresian legend commented on by Jacques Maritain who attributed to Teresa the saying that "without poetry life would be unbearable." Textually the words of the philosopher were: "St Teresa used to say that even for contemplatives life would be unbearable if poetry did not exist."

85. Response To A Spiritual Challenge

The work is written with humor, but of a spiritual content. The title is late and foreign. The challenge is worked out by the community under the direction of Teresa and Fray John of the Cross. It is written in the mode of a profane game converted to a spiritual one. In bantering it banters, imparting to the supposed reader an exquisite lesson of community dynamics

1. *Origin of the Challenge.* It took place around 1573. The Carmelite friars of Pastrana sent a list of challenges to the community at the Incarnation in Avila, when Teresa was prioress and Fray John of the Cross spiritual director. The challenge consisted of penitential practices and athletic virtues very much in style in the novitiate at Pastrana despite the corrections made by Báñez and Fray John of the Cross. The extravagant practices of Catalina de Cardona (d. 1577) were increasing there. We do not know the list of challenges. Yet by means of the *Response* the two camps take shape before us: Pastrana against the Incarnation. On the side of Pastrana is present probably Jerónimo Gracián still a novice, but other *knights* and the *Daughters of the Blessed Virgin*, presided over by the Grand Master and maintainer of the field. On the side of the Incarnation a series of nuns present themselves voluntarily, almost all of them sick, among whom Teresa stands out and a knight errant, identifiable with Fray John of the Cross. One team against another team as in as in a tournament between knights. Yet in the text the *response* is only that of the team at the Incarnation.

2. The autograph. The autograph has been lost for the most part. Only a fragment is conserved in the Carmel of Guadalajara. The remainder comes from ancient transcriptions, highly fragmentary. Of the responses given by the nuns at the Incarnation, we possess only

a small part. They are sufficient, nonetheless, for our knowledge of the community dynamic fostered by Teresa. In its brevity , it is one of her writings which witnesses to the sane humor of Teresa, and "the sisterly style that we maintain together." Although in a fictional literary garb, at bottom we are dealing with a lesson that is strictly realist. And serious. The text is divided into two parts: first the new approach of the challenge (nos. 1-4); then the series of responses from the Incarnation(nos. 5-28).

3. The plot of the episode. The point of departure, the Carmelite friars in Pastrana in the fervor of Lent (or perhaps in the middle of September after the feast of the Triumph of the Cross) decided to organize a kind of tournament with a spiritual theme. (The tournament was a sport of knights, which divided into two groups or teams that took up arms in the public square. A game well known by Teresa from the books of chivalry she used to read. She in front of her nuns accepts to respond to the challenge in the tone and with the words of the books of chivalry, yet she rejects the list: "having seen the list . . .no one signed and Teresa of Jesus least of all." More than the list Teresa rejects the approach of the tournament. And she transfers it from the artificial field of exorbitant penances to the field of real life: it must be on the condition that the defender (the principal knight of the opposing team) "must take to the field of the world where we are" And it is she who challenges: "come out, come out from that pleasant life [in a comic sense] we say to him and his companions!". And she challenges them in the realistic field of daily life bespangled with maladies and sufferings, as we shall see in what follows.

4. The new approach to the challenge. We do not know the text and tone of the list sent from Pastrana. (We do know that during these dates Gracián wrote the *Art of Fencing for the Knights of Jesus and the Blessed Virgin* which has been lost). Yet certainly he challenged the practice of heroic penance. In such a way the conqueror carried as the

booty the merits of the conquered. It was a rough way of understanding Christian asceticism and the Carmelite life. For this reason Teresa refused to sign the list. In place of the heroic penances, she proposes a plan of varied virtues yet simple, as appear in the responses. Yet as a novel variant in the combat: whoever wins, will not appropriate the booty, but will offer it to the knight who is conquered. It was a special conversion to the spiritual in the tournament. This she will maintain from the first response to the last.

5. She begins with what the infirmarian does, Beatriz Juarez: "Any knight or daughter of the Virgin who prays the Lord each day to keep Beatriz Juarez in his grace and makes the effort never to speak inadvertently and to direct all things to the Lord's glory will be given the merit she has gained in two years while caring for Sisters with very painful illnesses." A curious mesh of motivations, of practical objectives, and of spiritual intercommunion with the leaders of the opposing band.

6. Facing the "valiant and strong knights," Teresa arranges that the most helpless ones in the house, who at times can neither speak nor write enter the contest. One sick nun very seriously ill, the fifth in the series: Madre María de Tamayo will give to anyone of the said knights the recitation each day of an Our Father and a Hail Mary that the Lord give her patience and conformity to his will in the endurance of her illness; she will give each day a third part of this. And her illness is very serious; for more than a year she has been unable to speak." This gives evidence that Teresa herself writes in her name, as in various other cases of competing sick. With clear intention of making the knights aware that this also forms part of normal life of a numerous community like hers.

7. Spiritual support. Apart from the technique of generous interchange, the mystical background of the responses is notable. The most relevant item is the Christological motivation of the life, with

revealing details: "look at the crucifix three times a day in memory of the three hours he hung on the cross" or "consider the poverty in which he was born and died." Or "the humility with which the Lord stood before the judges . . . recall our Lady's sorrows for a time each day." In such a way that the response is not just a corrective to the ascetical focus of those in Pastrana, but a lesson in Carmelite life in the school of the two holy founders. What is important are not the great penances but the fraternity and the Christological motivation.

86. A Spiritual Critique

In the English translation the title is *A Spiritual Critique*. It is a small composition between the mystical and the humorous. It was written by Teresa toward the end of 1576 (a little before *the Interior Castle*) in answer to a number of writings from a heterogeneous group of friends, among whom was St. John of the Cross. A kind of informal gathering. Of all these writings there have reached us only the reply of her brother Lorenzo de Cepeda and the text of Teresa herself. The autograph is conserved by the Carmelite nuns in Guadalajara. (The word Vejamen [strong criticism] employed in the title is not Teresa's ; she does not use the word in any of her writings).

1. The episode of the *Satirical Critique*. It occurred in the climate of intimacy and spiritual fervor that increased between Teresa and her brother Lorenzo, recently returned from America and taught by her in the practice of prayer. In this climate of confidence Teresa communicates to him a motto engraved in her interiorly during her prayer "seek yourself in me." Lorenzo took it seriously and with the approval of the bishop , Don Alvaro de Mendoza , gathered a group of friends that they seek the meaning of this spiritual motto and comment on it. It will be Don Alvaro who then decides that the commentaries be judged – in the manner of literary contests – by a tribunal of spiritual persons that will be made up of nuns from the community of the Carmel of St. Joseph in Avila. It happened then that it was all sent to St. Teresa in Toledo so that she could also send her opinion. (Teresa in those days was most occupied. Between 7 and 8 February she underwent a serious breakdown caused by stress and the doctor prohibited her from writing in her own hand.

2. *The contestants*. They all lived in Avila. We will list them in order.

Fray John of the Cross who is the confessor at the Incarnation.
Julian de Avila, chaplain of the monastery of St. Joseph.
Francisco de Salcedo, the saintly gentleman who is now an ordained priest.
Lorenzo de Cepeda, Teresa's brother recently returned to Avila from America
The Carmeltie nuns of St. Joseph
At a respectful distance the Bishop of Avila

The next episode extended as far as Seville, from where Teresa had recently returned. On 2 March 1577, she sent the dossier of responses to the prioress in Seville and told her: "enclosed are the responses (Ltr.188.11). As is seen the contest had reached a wide diffusion. It is a pity that in this mix up the response of Fray John of the Cross was lost.

3. The office of judge. Teresa begins her ruling: "If obedience had not forced me, I would certainly not have answered nor for certain reasons would I have accepted the role of judge." The allusion to obedience indicates the pressure of the Bishop of Avila, Don Alvaro de Mendoza, that she pronounce on the mysterious topic of the search for oneself in God. With the answer of the contestants in hand, Teresa noticed that the interpreters had really taken the words seriously. She on the other hand chooses humor. "I love all of the contestants . . . But I have no intention of saying anything good about what they have written. " That is to say, Teresa who through many pains found time to read the papers , adopts the vexatious tone of a literary judge. And she concludes her verdict: "all these gentlemen are so divine that they have lost by going beyond what was asked by the question."

4. The strongest judgments fell upon her brother Lorenzo *("*Your excellency should order the contestants to make amends. I myself

will make amends by not being like my brother in his little humility")
and upon Fray John of the Cross, "who presents very good doctrine for
anyone who might want to follow the exercises they make in the Society
of Jesus." And at the end of her judgment: "God deliver me from people
so spiritual that they want to turn everything into perfect contemplation,
no matter what." (Unfortunately we do not possess this text of Fray John
of the Cross which must have been one of his prime works.)

5. *Obviously,* Don Alvaro had Teresa's critique reach all the
accused. Two of them didn't understand the tone, not caustic but
joking, of Teresa's judgment and had their moment of anger: they were
Salcedo and Lorenzo. The first did not accept the fact that she joked
about so lofty a topic and so he let Teresa know: "I was amused by
good Francisco de Salcedo's response . . .The response was long for
someone of Fancisco's temperament" (Ltr. 172.18). To Lorenzo on the
other hand, she had to give an explanation of why she had not answered
in a serious vein," but jokingly (Letr 182.12). The polite Lorenzo had
contributed a carefully studied answer with some delightful verses.

6. *Teresa's response.* In reality the mysterious topic: "seek
yourself in me." flooded Teresa's soul as it did as well Fray John of
the Cross's or Lorenzo's. And she did not delay in giving her response.
She did so in a beautiful poem entitled *"Soul seek yourself in Me,"* that
unfolded in the refrain: "and in yourself seek Me." Then she developed
the twofold theme in six five-line stanzas: the first three lines on seeking
self in God; the last three on the Augustinian motto of seeking God in
oneself. Both themes condensed in the first and the penultimate stanza.

The first theme on the motto of the *Critique*: "seek yourself in
God."

> With such skill, soul,
> Love could portray you in Me
> That a painter well gifted

Could never show
So finely that image.

The penultimate stanza is a poetic anticipation of the Interior Castle.

Soul, since you are my room,
My house and dwelling,
If at any time
Through your distracted ways
 I find the door tightly closed.

Thus the episode of the *Satirical Critique* ended with the only poem in which Teresa puts the word and the verses on the mouth of a transcendent Person. (the theme also had had left its trace in *Spiritual Testimony 14.2).*

87. The Constitutions

1. A little legal codex complementary to the Rule of Carmel governed the life of those Carmels founded by Teresa. It was a living text that grew and developed during Teresa's last twenty years. The first book published and printed by her. In its being published in 1581, Padre Gracián summed up its evolution thus: these constitutions were drawn up in the beginning from the ancient constitutions of the Order and given by Our Most Reverend Padre, the Master F. Joan Baptista de Ravena prior general. Afterward the very Reverend Padre Fernández, apostolic Visitator of this Order . . . added some acts and declared some of the constitutions , and I too added something in visiting with the apostolic commission . . . and finally in this our provincial chapter celebrated in Alcalá, it seemed to the Very R. Padre Fray Juan de las Cuevas, who presided at the chapter, and to the definitors and to me that it was appropriate to join all the acts and constitutions in the order in which they occurred, declaring, adding or removing some things, although few" (Letter to Mother Teresa, pp prelimnary s.n.)

2. We point out this note of Gracián's because above all there is no mention that Teresa is the author (the original redactor) of this legal text . The jurist mentality of the time hindered this attribution. Gracián avoided it in the whole *Dedication* so filled with praise for Teresa. He is sure that these Constitutions , which Fr. General "gave them "(approved, authorized?), were inspired by the previous constitutions for the Spanish Carmelite nuns ("taken from the ancient constitutions"); although these were not redacted by him; for they grew with new contributions by the Visitator and by Gracián himself: and finally were re-elaborated and officially approved by the Chapter of

Alcalá (1581: neither this time by Teresa!)

3. The first redaction ("at the beginning" according to Gracián). The pontifical briefs for the foundation of the Avilan Carmel of St. Joseph authorized Mother Teresa to organize the community making statutes that would rule it "to the prioress and nuns who for a time were in what concerned the good government of the said monastery, *"we give permission and the faculty to make statutes and licit and just ordinances" (Breve of 72. 1562).* She elaborated them during the first three years of the foundation when in 1565 she wrote the story of the foundation, she testified that in the house they observed in addition to the rule of Carmel , " other observances which seemed to us necessary in order to observe the rule with greater perfection" (L 36. 27). This she assured us a little afterward in the *Way of Perfection* 4.1,4. Teresa conceived the *Constitutions* as a simple extension of the *Rule.* She affirmed that almost all is ordered to conform to our Rule (IX, 14); she quoted the rule seven times in the Constitutions. Yet with clear modifications. They were ratified probably by Bishop Alvaro, and in 1567 they were seen as good by Father General, who at the time did not have jurisdiction over the Carmel of St. Joseph, the only monastery of Teresa's existing at this time. Thus at the time they were simple house statutes in evolution.

4. Their content. We do not conserve the autograph of this first codex. It has reached us by belated copies, into which have filtrated allusions to other foundations (cf WP 16). In that first state, there was a most brief text. With the following plan:

rubric 1-2: on the order to be observed in spiritual matters; the Eucharistic liturgy and the choral recitation , the books for spiritual reading.

rubric 3-4: daily work and poverty; the fasts and the household furnishings.

rubric 5: the cloister.

rubric 6-8: on the novices, the humble offices, and the sick.

rubric 9: meals and recreation.

rubric 10: the suffrages for the dead.

rubric 11-12: the offices of the community and the chapter of faults.

She insisted especially on prayer and on spiritual formation; in the fraternal interrelationship of the community, "without class distinctions" with an equal distribution of service ("the Mother prioress should be the first on the list for sweeping so that she might give good example to all" ("never should the prioress or any of the Sisters use the title Doña") putting love before authority (XI 34) without any exclusion for reasons of pure blood; from the postulants is demanded that they know how to read, so as to follow the choral recitation (21). All have to work, as St. Paul commands (24). That in the house there be books for spiritual reading (8); as something absolutely new, two hours of prayer are introduced matched by two hours of recreation, morning and evening: this latter was an exception to the schedule of silence prescribed by the Rule (26 & 28). In place of the heavy penal code of faults and penalties, which she was later obliged to insert in the text, she had prescribed the "chapter of faults " in which according to the rule the faults of the sisters must be corrected with charity" (43).

5. They live and increase. Redacted for the internal use of only the community of St. Joseph's, the *Constitutions* had to be adapted for various reasons when Teresa founded new Carmels:

a) Above all, because the new foundations remained under the jurisdiction of the Carmelite order and its *Constitutions* had to be approved by the Father General.

b) A little after preparing in 1567-68 the foundation in Duruelo, there is the intention to adapt these *Constitutions* to the community of friars (cf. Regesta Rubei, p 58-65).

c) At the suggestion of a demanding jurist, Teresa added the large section " on faults and penalties," which transcribes literally an old text of the Carmeltie constitutions, but which throws out of balance the simplicity of the first text.

d)She adds – we don't know when – an appendix on the presence and weekly reading of the constitutions in the monastery, an appendix that ends with a concluding "Deo gratias,"yet adds a number more on the disciplines prescribed in the ordinal.

e) Toward 1568 the Carmel of La Imagen, in Alcalá accepts for its own regime the Teresian *Constitutions*.

f) There followed a little afterward the ordnances ("the acts," she calls them) of the Visitators, which were not always to her liking (Ltr 376.5).

g) The situation grew worse with the proliferation of manuscript copies for each Carmel, with various readings due to the transcriber or to the prioresses in each house (Ltr 376.). The official establishment of the text was imperative: "I would like to have these Constitutions put into print . . . a strict unmistakable precept should be set down against deleting from or adding anything to the Constitutions (Ltr 376.8).

6. The edition. The longed for establishment of the text was accomplished in the Chapter of Alcalá (1581). For it, Teresa contributed the text of the Constitutions of St. Joseph's . She entrusted the task of revision and restructuring to Gracián giving him a long series of suggestions, plus the letters of the nuns to the chapter, previously approved by her (Ltr. 371.7). The definitive text was approved 13 March 1581 and at the request of Teresa published that same year, with the title "the primitive Rule and Constitutions of the discalced nuns

of the Order of our Lady the Virgin Mary of Mount Carmel." This new text had acquired a juridical formality, yet at the expense of the simplicity and freshness of the original Teresian text. There was placed first the Castilian version of the Rule and it concluded with an appendix on the manner of giving the veil and receiving the vows of the nuns. Unfortunately it had a short-lived validity, only in force a little while.

88. On Making The Visitation

Written by Teresa at the request of Padre Gracián and destined
for him, this work has for its theme the Canonical Visitation of the
Carmels, which was then a juridical act of high responsibility urged
by the Council of Trent (ses. 25.8 and 20). The visitator looked over
the religious life of the community and the conduct of each nun.
Teresa, nevertheless, writes in the strictest intimacy and gives suggestions to the visitator, at that time Padre Jerónimo Gracián.

1. Composition of the writing. It is the year 1576. Teresa has
returned from Andalusia and is confined to the Carmel in Toledo.
Padre Gracián has also come back a little previously from Andalusia
where he exercised his ministry of visitator and even wrote a *Form
and Manner of Proceeding* which he followed in the visitations
(MHCT I, 304-310). The nuncio Ormaneto had conferred on him
authority over Mother Teresa and her nuns. To exercise now the
office of visitator of the Carmels, he asks Teresa to give him some
advice that would allow him to do so in a beneficial way. And she,
despite her interior resistance ("beginning this work has been the
greatest mortification for me, and I have felt a strong repugnance
toward doing so."no. 1), she writes rapidly 43 sheets of paper and
hands them over.

2. The autograph. It is conserved in its integrity in the Library of
the Escorial, in the reserved section. It is a manuscript of 22 leafs in
minor format. The text is divided into paragraphs, each one pointing
to a series of suggestions. The last page is a letter to Gracián: "I beg
your Paternity . . ." He made notes in the margins with little marks to
call attention to certain things, these were at times mutilated by the
paper cutter. He gave the manuscript to Fray Luis de León for the

1588 edition of Teresa's works, but the Augustinian Master decided not to publish it. After his death the manuscript passed along with the *Foundations* – the two unpublished works – into the hands of Dr. Sobrino (Valladolid), who in 1592 gave it over to the Library of the Escorial at the request of Padre Doria in submission to the requirement of King Philip II. Even after it was in the Royal Library, a late hand gave it the title: "The manner of making the visitation of the Convents of women Religious. Written by the Holy Mother Teresa of Jesus, by command of her provincial superior Fray Jerónimo Gracián of the Mother of God." (A title repeated — and canceled – on the final page of the manuscript.}

3. The content. At the level of full confidence, Teresa imparts practical instructions, including details, to Gracián. With her usual realism, she begins with the material: "It seems an inappropriate thing to begin with temporal matters. Yet I think these are most important for the promotion of the spiritual good, although for monasteries founded in poverty this doesn't seem to be so"(no. 2). She praised Gracián's manner of conducting the canonical visitation. Yet in no way did she want these to be converted into something routine, or that the review of the community or personal life give way to indulgent compromises: "First, let it be presupposed as extremely appropriate that the visitator so behave toward the nuns that even though on the one hand he is affable and loving, on the other hand he makes it known that in essential matters he will be strict and by no means lenient." She recommends that he not make acts: it would be something insufferable if each prelate at each visitation should leave mandates." And she adds in the margin: "this is very important." Ultimately she sketches the profile of a perfect visitator.

4. According to Teresa the day of the visitation marks a special parenthesis in the style of sisterhood and recreation" of the Carmels. As if it were the exact hour set aside for a serious examination and

opportune corrections. She abounds in practical suggestions. She writes them in the spirit of collaboration: her "counsels" ought to serve so that Gracián write on his own account a book in which he incorporates and completes with the authority of a visitator. In such a way that the result will be a model treatise: "Now I am going to begin the final part of the foundations and this can be added there; for it will prove very beneficial" (no. 54). Neither Gracián nor Luis de León seconded this editorial project of Teresa's.

5. Edition of the book. It is the most painful episode of all that happened to Teresa's writings. The autograph of On Making the Visitation lay forgotten in the Royal Library during more than thirty years. And it was not accompanied by the fortune of being printed. In the meanwhile, the one for whom it was written, Padre Gracián, had been banished from the Order and had passed two most difficult years in captivity in Tunisian dungeons (1593-1595). On his return he found refuge in Flanders, and was welcomed by the Carmelites of the Ancient Observance. There he published, on his own account, the Teresian Book of Her Foundations, to which he still did not add the text of On Making the Visitation . He supplanted it with a chapter on the foundation of the Carmel in Granada, redacted by Mother Anne of Jesus. Yet his edition of the Foundations (Brussels 1610) received a bad welcome in the environment of the Spanish Carmels. Above all on the part of superiors and their followers , the official historiographers. The only reason at bottom were the praises heaped on Gracián himself, who was now outside the Order.

6. Probably this was the fact that induced one of his greatest adversaries to publish quickly Teresa's manuscript. The general of the Spanish Carmelites , Padre Alonso de Jesús María in a small volume 11 x 7.50 cm. with the title Treatise on the Manner of visiting the discalced nuns of our Lady of Mount Carmel. Composed by the holy Mother Teresa of Jesus its founder . . ."Printed in Madrid by Alonso Martín in

the year 1613" It consisted of 43 pages, preceded by a long dedicatory letter "to the discalced nuns of our Lady of Mount Carmel., Fray Alonso de Jesús María, their General"; in which he said: "I considered it very opportune to have printed this short treatise on the visitation, which I found in the handwriting of our Holy Mother in the Escorial among the originals that were held there by our King, for being her doctrine directed to this end.

Yet in the printing there was no mention whatsoever of Gracián, still living. Rather all possible allusions to him in the teresian text were eliminated, and the last two pages in which Teresa gave her final recommendations on the further elaboration of the writing were suppressed.

We do not know if any exemplar of the edition came into the hands of Gracián, for he died in Brussels the following year (21 September 1614)), some months after Teresa's beatification. It took centuries before the original text came to light in its integrity. In 1883 it was published in facsimile by Herrero Bayona in continuation of the Escorial facsimile edition of The Way of Perfection. (The Valladolid redaction of the Way was printed by Luis N. de Gaviría.)

89 Teresian Correspondence

1. *The Letters* of St. Teresa are the richest documentary for her autobiographical itinerary. They are at the same time a huge historical document for that period. She wrote them all in the last part of her life, between 1560-1582, which coincided with her mystical life. But above all in dependence on her work as founder which got her involved with the most extreme social classes and put her in relationships with a high variety of persons, from the king to muleteers. They contain at the same time copious information about the nascent Carmel, its ups and downs and ideals, its progress and its setbacks. They are not, in general, doctrinal letters, in the manner of those she read from St. Jerome's letters. They are bits of her own life in progress. Seldom do they speak of her mystical graces. Much more do they speak of her physical ailments and of her medicines, bleedings, popular remedies ("syrup of the king of the Persians," or "The waters from the fount of Antequera," or "resin") and of some of her herbalists or doctors on occasion. Few of the letters are on a strictly spiritual theme. She welcomes in them news from America, about the Andalusian Moorish guerillas, about the great epidemics that are laying waste the nation, rarely about the great wars (neither in Tunisia or Lepanto, or Pavia). Taken together there unfolds a multicolored fan of news about Castile and its surroundings (Portugal, France, Italy, Flanders, and Africa), although Teresa never becomes a reporter of the happenings in the national surroundings, European or American.

2. The makeup of a Teresian letter. As is natural, her letters, vary according to the type of person they are addressed to. She is familiar with the puzzle of social dealings – that were soon codified

in the book *Galateo* by her friend Lucas Gracián – and she respects them, although she does criticize them harshly in her *Life* (37.10). She uses indiscriminately for everyone to whom she sends her letters a quality paper, rather wide (31 x 21), with an ample margin on the right and a side space on the left. She almost never uses — as was frequent at the time — bits of paper. Without an envelope, but at most a simple wrapping. In it is at times included "two doubloons" for the payment (Ltr 85.1).

The heading of the letter. She always begins by printing on the upper margin the anagram JHS (Jesus), putting a cross on the upper line of the h. She follows with the greeting, generally a religious greeting desiring blessings on the on the person for whom it is destined. "The grace of the Holy Spirit be with your honor, my daughter." Or more simply: "Jesus be with you, my daughter." Or to Gracián: "May the Holy Spirit be with your paternity, my Father. And she begins the message.

The body of the letter. She begins as a conversation. At times in response to a message received (which she does not usually keep). Themes come bubbling up. A simple gesture. Religious and sorrowful when it is a means of offering condolences. Yet the dialogue is not merely about things or themes. It personalizes as it goes on. For the letter almost always parades before us a stream of friends. More than twenty sometimes.

The closing formula. As the initial greeting, it is always religious and well-wishing in tone with the quality of the one addressed in mind: "Remain with God, and ask him to give me the spirit not to stray in anything from his will. It is Sunday night. Your honor's daughter and servant: Teresa of Jesus "(to Báñez). "May His Majesty make you a saint" (to her sister Juana). At times repeating: "Your honor's unworthy servant who kisses your hands, unworthy Teresa of Jesus." (to Báñez). They are solemn and sincere to the king: "May

His divine Majesty keep you for many years, as many as are needed by Christendom' (Ltr. 52). "May God give you peace and a long life, as I beg him continually and as is needed by Christendom"(Ltr 86). There follows the place, the date, and the signature: always Teresa of Jesus, except in the first two letters: "Doña Teresa de Ahumada." If necessary, she adds a postscript: "Send the turkeys since you have so many"(to her sister Juana). She folds and refolds the folio and wraps it in a packet on which she writes the name and address of the one for whom it is destined

The address. The name of the one for whom it is destined precedes the respective style. At times simple: For Mother Prioress María de San José, Seville (109); or more detailed: For Mother Prioress of St. Joseph's Carmel of Seville, Discalced Carmelite Nuns, San José Street, behind San Francisco" (i26). "For my padre Pedro Sanchez, confessor of the Carmelite nuns," "He is *mi padre. Alba*" (467). More solemn are those destined for the king Don Philip II: "To His Sacred, Catholic, Imperial Royal Majesty, the Lord King" (52). Already toward the end of her life: "For my dear daughter Sister Leonor de la Misericordia" (449). More than once she adds in the postscript the postage due: "Postage one half *real* (455 and 457, from Burgos to Seville).

3. Mail carriers, messengers, the main mail, special delivery. Gracián in his *Scholias* notes: "It happened that for a certain foundation she had to spend a lot of money to send letters by special delivery. I said to her let us find someone who will bring these letters, so that we don't spend so much money. She responded: If for important business matters one uses special delviery, what is more important than establishing one church more where the Blessed Sacrament is adored? Go on , Padre that we do not lose a critical moment, what do twelve or twenty ducats matter? Finally, with the poverty she observed, which was very great, I never saw a man or a woman with

a greater or more liberal spirit."

In the beginning she made use of humble muleteers who waited impatiently at the door of the monastery while she was writing the last letter. Afterward, when her letter writing became intense and risky, she made use of the royal mail. She made special friends with some of these carriers: with Figueredo in Toledo, in Burgos with Francisco de las Cuevas (husband of the famous Luis Sigea), with Casademonte and Roque de Huerta in Madrid, and in Palencia with Diego de Reinoso. The stream of royal mail from Madrid to Rome, or on the dates of departure of the armada from Seville to the Indies. Only in Avila was she unfortunate. Yet her most humble cell was converted into a special agency for mail. She didn't have difficulty in paying for special delivery; going and return. A little nervous because of the chapter of Alcalá, she writes to Gracián: "would you send me a private courier at once, and I will repay you, for it would be a terrible thing if you didn't receive them" [the letters she sent him]. I truly believe this is a temptation because the courier here [Palencia] is a good friend of ours, and he recommended that the bundle be delivered with great care"(377.8).

4. The secret correspondence. For letters for others, she always has great respect. If for urgent reasons she dares to open a letter addressed to her brother Lorenzo, she informs him immediately. Yet she asks him not to open the letters written by her to Francisco, his oldest son. It occurs nonetheless that her letters as founder become suspicious and others try to get hold of them, including even bribing the muleteers and letter carriers. It is then that she has recourse to an ingenius system of codes. She uses it only to write in code the names of persons: She is Angela or Lorencia; she calls the Lord Joseph or "The Glassworker"; Gracián is Eliseo or Paul or Cyril; Seneca is Fray John of the Cross; Patillas [sideburns] is the devil; Mathuselah or Melchisedech is the Nuncio Ormaneto or the provincial Salazar, and so on.

5. Number of letters. In the actual Teresian correspondence we possess about 500 letters, more than 260 originals among the integral texts and small pieces. But the great majority of letters have been lost due to various causes: people to whom they were addressed who didn't save them. After her death, there was the phenomena of relics (cf Theme 58). Finally, having an influence in this loss was the delay of the first edition, in the middle of the seventeenth century (Zaragosa 1658). At the present time the autograph letters of Teresa are scattered throughout Europe and America.

90. Teresian Correspondence: Diagram

Teresa wrote from the great cities of Castile. Of the nearly half thousand letters that we actually conserve, she wrote more than a hundred from Avila. Also more than a hundred from Toledo. Especially interesting is the block of letters written during the years 1576-77, in the period in which she was writing The Interior Castle (and living in Toledo and Avila). Almost thirty letters were written from Valladolid and just as many from Palencia. Less numerous are those sent form Salamanca (9), Segovia (14), and Soria (10). Interesting is the share sent from Seville, some 25. Moving is the letter she sends from Villacastín to Seville while half way on her journey back from Soria to Avila (Ltr 405). No less interesting are the letters written from Burgos, the last year of her life (27). Still on her journey, she wrote 11 long letters during her final trip from Burgos to Alba de Tormes In the summer of 1582. Almost coinciding with these localities is the sphere of the cities to which the letters are addressed. Worthy of special mention are those addressed to Quito, Lisbon, Evora, Rome, Piacenza, Madrid, or those sent from Castile to the capitol of Andalusia, or from Avila and Toledo, to Alba de Tormes, where her sister Juana lived.

2. The flow of letters intensifies in the measure that her work as founder advanced. Even when the letters we actually possess do not permit us to diagram the statistical curve of the innumerable letters she wrote, we can sketch an approximate assessment of the last seven years (1576-82):

    a. In 1576, 71 letters
    b. In 1577, 53 letters
    c. In 1578, 58 letters

d. In two years 1579-80, 64 letters

e. In 1581, 64 letters

f. In 1582 (January to September), 40 letters

3. There are more than 110 destinations for Teresa's correspondence, individuals or communities. Above all, they are varied, from the king to unnamed aspirants or her nephew and niece, Lorenzo and Teresita. In an arch with so many keystones, it is normal that the levels of intimacy or of simple human relations vary, for they do not only measure the different tone of the text, but also the multicolored mental state of Teresa in her social relations.

4. We can distinguish the different levels of communication in so many other groups of letters.

A first group of letters to family members, with about ten addressees, among which stand out 17 letters to her brother Lorenzo de Cepeda, with whom she begins to deal with money, business, and family affairs (Ltr. 2), and ends by entering into an intense spiritual communication on the themes of prayer and unconditional fraternal service.

The second group is situated at the extreme opposite: letters to persons of high society, civil and religious, interesting for offering us a series of snapshots of Teresa in speaking with the king Don Felipe (4 letters) or with her own bishop Don Alvaro (6 letters) or with the prelate of the Portuguese court (another 6 letters) or with the Grand Inquisitor Quiroga (2 letters) and his secretary, and even a delightful letter to Padre Luis de Granada (Ltr. 82).

Change of record in the third group: intimate letters to Gracián (no less than 114), to the discalced Carmelites (Ambrosio Mariano, Doria, Roca). Gracián is" her Paul" or her "holy of holies." Through this sieve pass one by one hundreds of business affairs, problems, scruples, her projects in the last seven years of her life (1575-82). Of her correspondents, Gracián is number one. He is also the great storehouse of teresian memories. Sometimes he is compared with Fray John of the Cross: "If while having so good a life you become this pessimistic, what would you have done had you had to suffer what Fray John did" (Ltr 261.3).

The fourth group includes the numerous letters written to discalced Carmelite nuns, a whole world apart. In the first and second group there are letters of a feminine tone and feeling, of a woman to women. Yet now they return to being multi-colored and intense, maternal at times, at other times plain and peaceful. There are letters to the Carmels of Seville, Valladolid, Malagón, Avila, and Toledo. But above all there is a case history of intimacy with the prioress of Seville, to whom she tells about incidents in other Carmels, physical ailments, problems of a founder, incidents of Gracián. He consoles her in the saddest moments of her Spanish community, and finally she entrusts to him the safekeeping of the manuscript of her Interior Castle, without omitting strong reprimands in times of disagreement. But the strongest of all, the "terrible letter" addressed to another of her prioresses, Anne of Jesus, founder of the Carmel in Granada under the direction of Fray John of the Cross (Ltr 451).

The fifth group is made up of letters to learned men: theologians, priests or religious. No less than 24 different addressees.. Among them is the correspondence with her preferred theologian, Báñez. Yet, among them figures equally the Roman canonist Diego de Montoya::"for he has given us life" she assures another about him when he got her out of a lot of certain legal jams (Ltr. 295.5).

And finally, the group of collaborator friends, royal employees, a whole band of ladies from the high nobility, Luisa de la Cerda, María de Mendoza,, Inés Nieto , to Juana Dantisco, Gracián's mother, or the admirable Biscayan-Burgalese Catalina deTolosa.

5. Some Specimens . . . to explore. If the teresian correspondence is like a great city and to know it one would have to travel through all of its streets, we can suggest exploring it on the basis of a pattern extreme and select. We propose a half dozen models:

a. the first letter to Lorenzo (Ltr 2) for its thematic and familiar density;

b. the four letters to the king, representative of that theocratic ambient (Ltrs 52,56,208,218);

c. the correspondence with her Father General, Giovanni Baptista Rossi ((Ltrs 83, 102, 271);

d. The letters to the community in Seville, half destroyed by the opposition (Ltrs 283,284,294);

e. The conflict with friends of the Society of Jesus (Ltrs 228,229,342,475);

f. A mistaken letter, the famous "terrible letter" to Anne of Jesus (Ltr. 451).

6. Editions. The first edition of the teresian correspondence took almost a century. It was confided to the venerable Juan de Palafox, who published it in two volumes (Zaragosa 1658), with 41 letters (not all of them authentic) in the first volume and 24 in the second . They were entitled *Letters of the seraphic and mystical doctor Saint Teresa of Jesus.* Each of them was annotated with ample spiritual commentary. The complete edition of the teresian correspondence arrived in the middle of the 19th century through the work of Vicente de la Fuente, who published 403 letters of Teresa's in the second volume of her

works: Madrid, BAE, 1862. In the twentieth century Padre Silverio de Santa Teresa in volumes 7-9 of the BMC (Burgos 1922-1924) published a critical edition, which contained 440 letters with abundant documentation. There followed some years later the precious edition of Frs. Efrèn and Otger Steggink, who gathered together 457 letters. In the recent edition Tomás Alvarez (Burgos, Monte Carmelo, 1979-1997) continued to incorporate the last findings of Teresian autographs and collated 468 letters by Teresa.

X.
Teresa's Spiritual Teaching

Saint Teresa is the first woman proclaimed a Doctor of the Church. With this title the Church recognizes "eminent doctrine" in the field of Christian thought; not only as a writer and teacher in the past but as a thinker of current importance and as a witness to gospel values for people today. Teresa does not have a system of thought ably structured, but yes articulated in an organized way at diverse times, whether in small essays, such as in *Spiritual Testimony 59, or in large treatises such as The Interior Castle. Here we will select some guidelines to her religious thought.*

91. The Teresian Thought

1. A writer of the sixteenth century, Teresa is not a theorist. Yet she is a thinker. Few have thought as insistently as she on the profound meaning of their own life. She was incapable of living it without questioning it so as to understand it. She did so with pen in hand from her first great writing *The Life,* (but already before that in her *Spiritual Testimonies* 1-3), up until the last introspection on her interior life in 1581 (ST 65). One of her most typical gestures is amazement (to be astonished, she says) before the mystery of things, of people, or events. She thinks of these things in a religious key: hers is a religious ideology. Her point of reference as the ultimate criterion of truth is sacred Scripture. Through it she measures what is right and what is wrong, or she discerns between truth and error. Yet at the same time she has an instinctive philosophical sensitivity before the things and happenings of life. ("It would be a great thlng to be able to speak with someone who knows philosophy, for in knowing the properties of things he would be able to explain to me what I enjoy thinking about" she notes in speaking of the properties of water and fire (W 19.3). "I believe that in each little thing created by God there is more than what is understood, even if it is a little ant" (IC 4.2.2). She is aware of the limits of human thinking and the ineffability of the profound mysteries of life, above all of the Christian life. Experiences that do not fit into words. Hence her constant recourse to symbolic mediations, not only in metaphorical language and in her typical recourse to oxymoron , but also in coining expressly symbols having their own literary value. She constantly idealizes historical figures from the bible to charge them with symbolism or to incarnate an idea.

2. Attempts have been made to catalogue the Teresian ideas.

So for example in the *Diccionario de Santa Teresa* (Burgos 2001 and 2002), which in its doctrinal section (670 pages) it has more than five hundred thematic entries, among them more than a hundred words or themes. Almost on an equal plane they have elaborated the *Concordance* of her writings: two volumes with a total of more than 3,000 pages, followed by statistics on the presence of words in the totality of her writings. Which even though they are a material indication of Teresa's vocabulary, they permit us to see certain lines of her thought. An elemental sampling of only two extreme aspects of her religious world – the themes of God and man — produce indicative numbers of the ideological weight of each one:

the words	God (Dios)	4324
	Lord (Señor)	2770
	His Majesty (Su Majestad)	938
	Our Lord (Nuestro Señor)	805
		(in all 8837 references)

the words:	soul-spirit	2349
	body	246
	man-woman	387
	human-bodily	10
		(in all 3084 references)

These are numbers that document the two strongest sectors of Teresa's thought: God and humans. The statistics also indicate the words that testify to Teresa's interest in *thinking*: the action of thinking occurs 1150 times; that of understanding, 2884 times; that of knowing 2672 times. Without granting these material numbers a value other than that of simple indicators, they do bring us closer to what we think are the strong lines of the Teresian thought.

3. Forceful lines of her thought. The central orbit of her thought is the idea of God. Teresa so friendly with the theologians of her time, cannot be said to share their theology. Almost at the beginning of her writings (L 4.10) she offers us a synthesis of what she has often thought about , all condensed in *thinking, amazement,* and *emotion*: "I often marveled to think of the great goodness of God, and my soul delighted in seeing his amazing magnificence and mercy. May he be blessed by all, for I have seen clearly that he does not fail to repay, even in this life, every good desire. As miserable and imperfect as my deeds were, this Lord of mine improved and perfected them and gave them value, and the evils and sins he then hid. His Majesty even permitted that the eyes of those who saw these sins be blinded, and he removed these sins from their memory. He gilds my faults; the Lord makes a virtue shine that he himself places in me — almost forcing me to have it." That is to say, she thought about it a great deal. She was amazed and delighted. "She saw clearly" traces of aspects of the face of her God. Around this image of a goldsmith God, who gilds her human faults, there revolve two other fundamental ideas: the enigma of his "absence- and –presence" : objectively omnipresent, yet with the tremendous mystery of his subjective absence in the orbit of love. And in the second place, the persistent conviction that God enters into relationship with human beings, with human history, with the micro-history of each person: "he finds his delight with humans." It is also certain that God infuses biblical respect and fear, ("love and fear," she will say), yet in the face of God there prevails the traces described in her condensed theology (*Life 4.10*).

4. Around this idea of God and almost fusing with it is the series of thoughts about Christ. Her christological ideas constitute a mental and cordial sphere that is most personal. Before all, the historical Christ of the Gospels reconsidered and meditated upon step by step, deeds and words, the unfathomable mystery of his Passion: Teresa confesses that she "always pondered for a little while this episode" (L 9.4). In

him she was especially interested in his humanity (We shall see this in Theme 98). And then Christ present here and now in the history of each person. "Do you think he is silent? . . .He speaks well to the heart when we beseech him from the heart"(W 24.5).

5. After these fundamental ideas, the ecclesial theme is subsidiary, as are her ethical thought and mystical ideas. In the ethical key, Teresa, shared the ideas of her contemporaries (from Luther to Trent) that man is naturally corrupted by sin; that he needs conversion and grace; that only in these lies salvation. Ideas that extend to the plane of community life and the state of society. Finally the cycle of the mystical is already situated on another plane of ideas. It is for Teresa the world of mystery, of the experience of transcendence. (We will also see this in a theme apart.)

92. Asceticism and Virtues

Although in the Teresian vocabulary the terms asceticism or ascetic do not appear, Teresa does sketch well this period of initiation into the spiritual life. She distinguishes it from the mystical phases, but without confining it to the period of beginnings: the human study and cultivation of the virtues are a task for the whole of life, both ascetical and mystical. She dedicates to it chapters 11-13 of her *Life;* and in the *Interior Castle, Dwelling Places I-III* and almost all the teaching of the *Way of Perfection.* Here we will select only some aspects.

1. The Barrier of Sin. Sin conditions the spiritual life of the person from its base. " We are naturally so lowly, of a nature so weak and miserable" she repeats. There is in our human nature a sediment of inordinate, antihuman forces. Criticizing the image of a contemporary writer who compared man to a "toad that aims at flying," Teresa adds her own commentary "although flying is more natural to it [the soul] than to the toad, it is so bogged down in the mud that through its own fault it lost this ability" (L 22.13). In the symbolism of the dwelling places, sin is the castle in ruins (IC II). From the mystery of evil or of sin, she has a markedly christological concept, with a profound sense of horror."Oh, oh, oh what a serious thing sin is, for it was enough to kill God with so many sorrows" (Sol 10.1). And again: "Oh mortals, return, return to yourselves . . . Understand for love of God that you with all your strength are about to kill the one who to give you life lost his own" (Sol 12.4).

2. A first step in the face of sin is conversion. Conversion is a radical option against the dynamism of disorder present in us because of sin. Teresa lived this decision with special intensity (chaps 8-9 of her *Life).* According to her, conversion is not only an ethical fact but

415

a christological orientation. As much in her autobiographical account as in her teaching in the *Way of Perfection* she describes conversion as a "determined determination" of the will, which affects the whole person "come what may, happen what may, whatever work is involved . . . or if the whole world collapses" (WP 21.2), yet with awareness of the precariousness of human effort unless it is open to the grace of God. Thus she describes it graphically in her own personal case ("I was struggling with a shadow of death" L 8.12).

3. The indispensable struggle. Teresa develops on her own count the biblical concept: "the life of man on earth is a warfare" (Job 7.1). In the teaching of the *Way of Perfection* she proposes it to readers in the military image of the "standard-bearer " who has to raise high the banner, " or of the king who chooses a group of select soldiers. For her nuns she condenses it into "we shall be fighting for him even though we are very cloistered" (WP 3.5). In the *Interior Castle* the struggle is a phase of the process. She dedicates the second dwelling places to the spiritual struggle, "like the soldiers of Gideon." With the arms of mortification and penance. Yet she warns again that this battle against the inordinate forces within oneself will go on through one's entire life. And that our greatest enemy, according to her, is the spirit of evil.

4. The practice of the virtues. To struggle is to do good by practicing the virtues. Teresa never enumerates them, nor does she copy the "tree of moral and theological virtues" proposed by the theologians. Nor does she define them as "operative habits." She conceives of them as living undertakings in the face of God. The first counsel given to beginners in her *Life (12.2)* is, surprisingly, to grow accustomed to being inflamed with love of Christ and his sacred humanity: "They can in this state [of beginners] make many acts to awaken love and many resolutions to render God much service." An approach that remains in the *Interior Castle*: the door of entry into the Castle is prayer, to initiate the personal relationship with God. In the initiating teaching of

the *Way of Perfection* she proposes three virtues that she then develops extensively and which serve at the same time for initial formation of the person and for the shaping of the religious group. This trilogy of virtues begins equally through love: "I shall enlarge on only three things . . . The first of these is love for one another; the second is detachment from all created things; the third is true humility, which even though I speak of it last, is the main practice and embraces all the others"(WP 4.4). Nevertheless, the exposition that follows maintains the primacy of love. (We will see this in the following theme.) The other two virtues are really fundamental in Teresa's teaching. Detachment is at the same time an attitude of interior poverty and an acquiring of freedom of spirit, indispensable for the maturity of the person. Humility is the Socratic teresian calling: knowledge and acceptance of self. In no way does it imply the renunciation of self-esteem. On the contrary, humility is to walk in truth, to accept the truth of our values and anti-values, and the truth of the values of others. To accept the truth before God and before others. A search for authenticity without substitutions. The full development of the virtue of humility will permit us, at the end of the *Interior Castle,* the assimilation to the Servant of Yahweh: to be, like him, the slave of everyone (IC 7.4.8). As a complement to the initial trilogy, at the end of the *Way of Perfection* she will propose to the beginner the binomial "love and fear." With the chapter heading: "Tells how by striving always to walk in the love and fear of God we will proceed safely among so many temptations" (WP 40). The beginner will understand easily what walking in love means. But more difficult will be the second "to walk in fear of God." And nonetheless for Teresa it is an intrinsic component of our singular friendship with him in which are founded intimacy and respect, without watering down the one into the other (the horror and fascination of St. Augustine). In the growing dynamic of this friendship, there increases as well the awareness of who is with Whom, who he is and the truth about oneself.

5. Also at the end of the *Way of Perfection* there arises the fundamental proposal of certain indispensable human virtues. Among them appears surprisingly affability: "So, Sisters, strive as much as you can, without offense to God, to be affable and understanding. . . this is very important for religious ; the holier they are the more sociable they are with their Sisters. . . . with a light underlining "this is very important for religious" (WP 41.7). With frequency she will insist on something that hardly seems to be virtue: gentleness in everything: "His yoke is easy and it is very helpful not to drag the soul along, as they say, but to lead it gently . . .(L 11.16). An insistent theme.

6. The virtues prepare and make prayer possible. In the Teresian asceticism, the virtues are the door of entry into the Castle so as to initiate prayer. To the beginner she proposes simply the common theme prayer: *vocal prayer, mental prayer, contemplation.* To educate oneself to recite the *Our Father* sharing the sentiments of Jesus in his invocation of the Father. To meditate above all on the life or the mysteries of Jesus, his Passion, his words. Yet prayer does not consist "in thinking much but in loving much." The bridge of passage to contemplative prayer is recollection. She dedicates to it the central chapters of the *Way of Perfection* (26-29). And more than recollection, liturgical prayer, on which she concentrates Eucharistic piety (WP 33-35).

7. At the height of the virtues is the theological trilogy: faith, hope, and love. They pertain to the essence of the Christian life. They are important as the foundation of the ascetical life. Yet they reach their highest tension in the heart of the mystical life. Although faith and hope are highly important, we will explore only the highest power of love.

93. Love for One Another

Love for one another is the first of the three instructions that Teresa proposes to readers of the *Way of Perfection*. She expounds it so as to form community, as a first step in the pedagogy on prayer and as the supreme milestone in the mysticism of love.

1. When in 1566 she writes these pages, Teresa is already a master on the subject of love. She has passed through the two great stages that had conferred on her an affective maturity. She had overcome the rough spots of the critical years that followed her time in the convent infirmary, with painful tribute to the excess of her scattered affectivity. And successively had lived through decisive happenings. She recounts them herself in her *Life*: On the occasion of her entrance into the mystical experience, the first rapture cures her of all affective dispersion; the interior voice assured her that from then on she would no longer converse with men but with angels. With its liberating effect: "I have never again been able to tie myself to any friendship or to find consolation or bear particular love for any other persons than those I understand love God "(L 24.6). The numerous friendships that will follow in the future will no longer be scattered, they will have their unifying center in the love of God, her mystical spouse. In Teresa there increased in her soul an overwhelming love without her knowing how it came about or who put it there "I saw that I was dying with desire to see God, and I didn't know where to seek this life except in death. "Some great impulses of love came upon me" and these culminated in "the grace of the dart" that was plunged deep within her (L 29. 8..13)).

Both experiences are reflected in the lesson on love she now imparts to her nuns in the *Way of Perfection*. She proposed to them first her teaching on fraternal love (chaps. 4-7). And then she will lead them deeper into the mysticism of the love of Christ the Bridegroom. (chaps 26-35).

2. Here all must be loved. This is the first instruction. For Teresa the small community that she brought together in St. Joseph's is above all, a community of love: "here all must be friends, all must be loved, all must be held dear, all must be helped . . ." (WP 4.7). Carmel is a school of Christ. Not even relatives must interfere in this convergence of love. In the appearance of the *Constitutions* that Teresa elaborates for the group, she prescribes that the prioress care for them all with "a mother's love" And that she "she strive to be loved so as to be obeyed." The same instructions she gives to the director of the postulants and novices: "treat them with piety and love."

3. For the sisters, she expounds her doctrine on "pure love." Probably the theologians preached to Teresa and her nuns the classic theory of the two loves: of concupiscence and benevolence. Self-interested and egocentric, the first. Altruistic and disinterested the second. But she prefers a simpler exposition: she speaks to them of sensitive love and spiritual love. She distinguishes these by the quality of their objects. The sensitive love is sentimental, it centers its gaze on mediocre, fallen values of mere appearance. It is an ephemeral love, exposed to the ups and downs of life. While the pure spiritual love, loves the person for stable values , capable of being the foundation of eternal love, not exposed to the surgings of daily happenings." It is a love that dignifies the persons who possess it.: "the persons the Lord brings to this state are generous souls, majestic souls. They are not content with loving something as wretched as these bodies, however beautiful they may be, however attractive. Yes it pleases them to see such bodies, and they praise the Creator; but no, they do not stop there. I mean stop in such a way that they love these things. It would seem to them that they were loving something of no substance, loving a shadow. They would feel chagrin and they wouldn't have the courage,

without great shame, to tell God they love him" (WP 6.4).

4. Teresa knows, nonetheless, that the community consists of apprentices in fraternal love. What interests her above all is that there not be in the group a lack of love. While the apprentice candidates are trained in the community life and at times falter in this high ideal of pure spiritual love, what interests her is that the love does not undergo a breakdown. So she ends her first redaction in proposing this ideal of pure love: "Even though your love may not be as perfect as that just mentioned, provided that it go out to all in general, I would rather you love one another with tenderness and delight than that there be a moment of discord" (WP 7. note 5).

5. The mysticism of love. Teresa is convinced that if it does not arise from the root of love of God, we will not reach the perfect love of neighbor (IC 5.3.9). For this reason in the *Way of Perfection* her pedagogy on love is elevated to the mystical plane. She attempts to educate or infect them with the love of Christ, inculcating in the young readers the bridal sense of their own profession. Without this, the life of prayer is difficult. Teresa places a special insistence on directing the gaze of love to Christ. She insists in the instruction: "who can keep you from turning your eyes to this Lord, even if you do so just for a moment if you can't do more? You can look at very ugly things; won't you be able to look at the most beautiful thing imaginable? Is it too much to ask you to turn your eyes from these exterior things in order to look at him sometimes? . . . behold, he is not waiting for anything else, as he says to the bride, than that we look at him" (WP 26.3)

6. Although Teresa intervened with this allusion to the bride in the *Song of Songs*, she does not allegorize. With all realism she refers to the married woman. "They say that for a woman to be a good wife toward her husband she must be sad when he is sad, and joyful when he is joyful, even though she may not be so. . . . the Lord without deception, truly acts in such a way with us. He is the one who submits

, and he wants you to be the lady with authority to rule; he submits to your will" (WP 26.4). And she continues directing the gaze of love to Christ in moments of joy or sadness or of suffering. Later in the *Interior Castle* she will develop fully this bridal image, always in a bivalent sense. In the seventh dwelling places she will touch the ceiling of bridal mystical love. In them she will repeat for the last time the instruction of the *Way of Perfection*: "Fix your eyes on the Crucified and everything will become small for you." (IC 7.4.8)

7. The lesson of *The Way of Perfection* with the binomial love and fear, recalling for readers that the friend and bridegroom is the Lord of transcendence and that in life by striving to walk in fear and love of God we will be proceeding securely. And she concludes with a kind of hymn similar to the Pauline hymn of love: "Those who truly love God, love every good, desire every good, favor every good, praise every good. They always join, favor, and defend good people. They have no love for anything but truth, and whatever is worthy of love. Do you think it is possible for a person who really loves God to love vanities? No, indeed, she cannot; nor can she love riches, or worldly things or delights, or honors, or strife, or envy. All of this is so because she seeks only to please the Beloved" (WP 40.3).

94. Teacher of Prayer

St. Teresa in her state as a Carmelite is a contemplative nun. Faithful to her profession, she speaks and writes about prayer even when dealing with foolish matters and themes. Her teaching is so dense and extended that it is difficult to fit it into one theme. In the present theme we will explain what is most elemental about the theme, her distinctive concept of prayer, which according to her is the life of prayer; and what her teaching is about prayer, without touching her doctrine on contemplation and mystical prayer.

1. Notion. Teresa has an original and simple idea about prayer. To pray, according to her is to enter into relationship with God. She is convinced previously that God is always open to a relationship with humans. For this reason she defines or describes it indirectly, as something obvious: "nothing else than an intimate sharing between friends; it means taking time frequently to be alone with him who we know loves us"(L 8.5). Fundamental in this definition is the central item: prayer is the fact of sharing with God. Stressing the sharing and being alone with him who we know loves us, she indicates an immediacy in the relationship. And the final item "with him who we know loves us" is the theological presupposition that God is love and precedes us in love; we know it! Still she adds the aside "frequently" because she knows that friendship requires frequency. Teresa will repeat, further on, the famous Aristotelian motto: "friendship is lost through a lack of communication."

The teresian expressions, to share or relate with God (*trato, tratar*) are realistic, taken from the common language. A contemporary of Teresa's defines it in this way:"to deal with is to negotiate buying and selling merchandise. To deal with in another sense is to know and converse with someone" (Covarrubias). To deal with God is not a metaphor, but real. "Christ is the true friend, with so good a friend one can endure all things. The Lord helps us, strengthens us, and never fails; he is a true friend" (L 22.6). In Christ Jesus there increases in Teresa this image of God-friend: "His Majesty is testing to see who it is who loves him. . . he loves whoever loves him; how good a beloved! How good a friend!" (L 22.17). In such a way, that for her prayer is a re-circulating of love between two. To enter into conversation with him is to begin a spiral of friendship that will involve the life of the one praying. And a dynamic of friendship will go on developing. With an unforeseen development. Teresa insists that despite appearances God on his part is not silent: "He speaks well to the heart when we beseech him from the heart" (WP 24.5).

Probably, more than one Dominican theologian had explained to Teresa that the theological virtue of charity consists according to St. Thomas in the "friendship of man with God" (*amicitia quaedam hominis ad Deum)* and that the friendship tends to make the friends equal, to level "their conditions" or their manner of being. In friendship a freedom with words or in communicating increases. Teresa had acquired a rare capacity for exclamation: "Oh, what a good friend you make, my Lord! How you proceed by favoring and enduring, You will wait for the others to adapt to your nature, and in the meanwhile you put up with theirs" (L 8.6).

From within the friendship, everything becomes evocative: "fields, water, flowers . . . In these things I found a remembrance of the Creator" (L 9.5). A book, the gospels. A picture . . . to carry about in your heart, she suggests, but on the condition that "you look at it." "since you speak with other persons, why must words fail you more when you speak with God. Don't believe they will; at least I will not believe they will if you acquire the habit Otherwise the failure to communicate with a person causes both estrangement and a failure to know how to speak with him. For it seems then that we don't know him . . . even if he may be a relative; family ties and friendship are lost through a lack of communication (WP 26.9). Even things can bring you to your friend.

2. The life of prayer. Like all friendship, prayer is also a form of life. It is not reduced to an occasional practice. One is not a friend at times. Prayer impresses form on the life of the believer before and after the praying moment. It demands before some virtues that guide it. In the *Way of Perfection,* for the beginner in prayer. Teresa demands above all a pledge of three fundamental virtues: love for one another; detachment from things; humility in regard to oneself: "so as to love God/ with freedom/ and in truth." She then demands a solid attitude before life in progress: the determined determination to persevere in prayer "come what may, happen what may . . . even if they die on the road . . . or if the whole world collapses" (WP 21.2).

Prayer in itself is life. It develops normally in a series of degrees . . . like a garden well watered, or like an interior castle with seven dwelling places. Or like a greater friendship which takes precedence over all other friendships and conditions them. For this reason Teresa insists that prayer has a scale of increase that in its later mystical degrees depends on the other friend who is God and that in any case prayer is not an introverted and solipsist force, but an impelling dynamism. It is operative. It doesn't isolate the soul from the life around it. It always aims for the good of its brothers and sisters: "works are what the Lord wants! He desires that if you see a Sister who is sick to whom you can bring some relief, you have compassion on her" (IC 5.3.11). Prayer is a friend of friends. "The five of us who at present love one another in Christ." Or the episode about the first reader of the *Life* about whom she speaks descriptively: he was a distinguished man but distracted. Teresa prays for him: "I went to the place where I usually prayed alone and being deeply recollected, began to talk to the Lord in a foolish way, which I often do without knowing what I'm saying. It is love that is then speaking . . . I said: 'Lord you must not deny me this favor; see how this individual is fit to be our friend'" (L 34.8). Prayer, according to Teresa is a proselytizing friendship.

3. The teaching on prayer. To form the beginner in prayer, Teresa wrote *The Way of Perfection*, in reality a book of "Advice and counsels." Neither in it nor in her other writings does she propose a method of prayer. She speaks of the three current forms of prayer: *vocal, mental, and contemplative.* The absolute manual for all prayer, above all vocal, is according to her the Our Father, which puts us in conversation with the Father and makes us share the sentiments of Jesus in his praying relationship with the Father and with us. Teresa appropriates these sentiments and radiates them. More than commenting on the prayer, she prays it with her readers. She knows that in reciting it, it is possible to be raised to perfect contemplation.

Yet mental prayer is indispensable, for it interiorizes the recital. For the beginner, she teaches her own manner of recollection: before all dominate the scattered senses calling them inward so as to direct our interior energies to God. And in the second place, concentrate the attention on Christ in his humanity, on a word of his, or in a scene from his Passion.

And finally, on the contemplative plane, Teresa unfurls her mystagogic resources: she herself prays before her readers so as to stir up in them a special empathy, and entice them to God. Her technique consists in teaching to pray by praying. She prays in a living way before the reader. In fact, the moment will arrive in the praying dialogue when the word of the Friend will prevail. It will be the all-consuming mystical prayer, which culminates in the union of the two, the supreme goal of prayer.

95. Life and Mystical Experience

1. Mysticism or mystical theology are learned words that Teresa does not usually use, but we find them only in her treatise on the degrees of prayer (L 10.1; 11.5; 12.5; 18.2). On the other hand she repeats innumerable times the term "experience." In the *Life* she refers to her profound religious experience: "I shall say nothing about things of which I don't have much experience" (L 18.8). In the *Interior Castle* she codifies it systematically. It is what we call "mystical experience." Three items interest us about it: a/ what we understand by mystical experience; b/ in what Teresa's lived experience consists; c/ why and for what reason does she give witness to it with so much insistence.

2. Notions. In Teresa's concrete case, one must distinguish between mystical life and mystical experience. Every Christian life is mystical insofar as it is integrated intrinsically through many mysteries of grace: we believe in them and we live them, but we do not experience them. Something similar occurs in our natural life — the most profound vital processes – the flow of blood, the cellular metabolism, the processes in the brain – we live them but we do not experience them. Only by the power of a special grace granted by God to some – to Teresa concretely – do the experiences of the mysteries begin, for example, our incorporation into Christ, the Eucharistic presence, the Trinitarian life in the soul. These experiences can be sporadic (let us recall the modern cases of Morente or of Frossard) or they can well be stable and continuous. This second is the case with Teresa. She lived them continuously in the last quarter of her life. We are not dealing with ecstasies and visions (which she experienced occasionally), but of living these last 25 years open and sensitive to the presence of God, as if the barrier that for us separates the transcendent from what surrounds us had fallen or had become transparent to her,

with alternating degrees of more or less intensity. Yet Teresa herself will be able to write the adverbs "always" and "never." It seemed to me that Jesus Christ was always present at my side" (L 27.2), "Never, not even in its first stirrings, does the will turn form its desire that God's will be done in it" (ST 65.9). The first assertion alludes to Teresa at the age of 40 years; the second was written in the penultimate year of her life. Teresa had lived the fact of a long mystical experience.

3. The fact of her mystical experience. We can outline if by a development into three periods: a/ her entry into the presence of God; b/ a most intense experience of the Humanity of Christ; c/ the Trinitarian experience in the soul.

a) The entrance of Teresa into the experience of God was sudden and absolutely unexpected. It consisted in a simple and radical change in her relationship with God. From representing him (God or Christ), she passes to a feeling of being established in his presence. The first is active; the second, without any act or personal effort. She refers to this novelty with all simplicity "It used to happen that when I represented Christ within me in order to place myself in his presence, or even while reading that a feeling of the presenc e of God would come upon me unexpectedly so that I could in no way doubt that he was in me or I totally immersed in him" (L 10.1).

A little before she had noted that these experiences were a simple beginning and that they lasted only a very short while. This occurred in 1554, when she was 39 years old. When years later she attempts to arrange in a series the mystical phenomena that happened to her, she will recall again that this was her first experience: "Another prayer I recall which comes before the first kind I mentioned, is a presence of God that is not a vision of any kind. But it seems that when and each time (at least when there is no dryness) one wants to pray to God, even though it be vocal prayer, one finds him." (ST 59.25). And this experience of finding oneself "immersed" (external) in and "impregnated" (interior) by the presence of God grew mysteriously until she asked a learned theologian (L 18.15; IC 5.1.1; ST 49), who gave her reasons for this and clarified the matter for her.

b) But very soon there came upon her in an uncontainable way, the Christological experience of the risen Jesus: "It seemed to me that Christ was at my side . . . I felt very clearly that he was always present beside me and that he was the witness of everything I did (L 27.2). And she repeats it: "the vision of Christ left upon me an impression of his most extraordinary beauty, and the impression remains today [She writes this in 1565 at a distance of 8 or 9 years], one time is sufficient to make this imprint. How much deeper it becomes as the Lord grants this favor more often!" (L 37.4; cf. the Eucharistic experiences of L 38.23 & 39.22).

c) Yet still her experience of the transcendent mystery will culminate in a spacious experience of the Trinity and the fulfillment of the words of Jesus that promise the Trintarian indwelling. In this, Teresa has the experience of her own soul. She perceives it "as a sponge that absorbs and is saturated with water, so I thought, was my soul which was overflowing with that divinity and in a certain way rejoicing within itself and possessing the three Persons (ST 14; ST 40). Still at the end of her life she will continue to give testimony to this mysterious opening of her life to the divine. "This presence of the three Persons is so impossible to doubt that it seems one experiences what St. John says . . .This presence is almost continual (ST 65.9).

4. In synthesis: Teresa's experience is progressive, continual, and undulating; it enlarged her living space; it changed her attitude before ethical and anti-ethical values, without interfering in her perception of material reality; for her" money continues to be money and the pots and pans continue to be pots and pans; If she is cook, her capacity to fry exquisitely a pair of eggs continues; she rides an uncontrollable mule; is capable of restraining it without losing the equilibrium of her composure; she writes a letter, and recounts with realism the crossing

of the Guadalquivir . . . she does not lose her balance or the restraints of her pen in economic altercations, for example, with Pedro de la Banda or the Archibishop of Burgos. The same experience of the Trinity does not upset the trays of the trivial and daily life. In speaking with God, she speaks as naturally as she does with the muleteer.

5. There are in Teresa's psychology multiple nuances originating from the mystical experience. Perhaps the most important are: above all, the enrichment of ideas. Then the enjoyment of them. Simultaneously and contrasting with this, the pain. A whole torrent of emotion (Teresa is always amazed again). And, finally, the alternating between *security* and *insecurity.* These nuances would have to be analyzed one by one. Teresa has recourse insistently on the oxymoron: the delightful martyrdom, the delightful torment, delightful death, the most delightful wound . . .; she says to God: "how delicately and smoothly and delightfully you treat them" (L 25.17). Physically, she has fragile health. The mystical experiences strengthen her. They are what final y cancel the fear of death, "which I always feared greatly" (L 38.5). On the contrary she now hopes against the striking of the clock (L 40.20).

6. *The why* . . . a/ Teresa's mystical experience was so strong that it obliged her to think and think about it with the purpose of discerning and defining it. She found it necessary to submit it to the discernment of responsible experts. She writes about them for herself and for them, the theologians. b/ Personally, she is convinced of the intensity and singularity of these experiences of hers: "I believe there are few who have arrived at the experience of so many things" (L40.8). She writes of them expressly "so as to attract souls to so high a blessing" (L 18.8): this is the mystagogical objective of all her writings. And c/ in the end she does so for her prophetic mission, to testify to God's work in her: as a mystical writer Teresa is the great witness of God. She continues being God's spokesperson even for readers today. In a certain way, an unimpeachable witness.

96. Mystical Phenomena

We call mystical phenomena certain extraordinary (and accessory) manifestations of the mystical experience. In general, they are attractive episodes. They are accessible for their being unusual to the non-mystic spectator who contemplates them from outside. The mystic, on the other hand, suffers them or bears them as a consequence of his adaptation or resistance to the breaking forth of the supernatural life and experience. In the history of spirituality there stand out as supreme reference points the Old Testament prophets, St. Paul with his rapture, or St. John with his apocalyptic visions.

1. In St. Teresa the mystical phenomena acquire a special relevance for various reasons: a/ for the number and variety with which they happened to her; b/ for the climate of fear and opposition on the part of theologians that marked the setting; c/ for having testified herself with every detail, in lieu of the resistance that opposed them: "The disturbance reached the point that, in reflecting upon it, it seemed to me I was more willing to be buried alive than to have these favors made known publicly" (L 31.12); d/ for her care in describing them, ordaining and contextualizing them in her ethical life; e/ for her later influence in art, liturgy, theology, and in the sciences of the psyche. In the present theme we limit ourselves to enumerating them (the first part), reserving the second part to the exposition of only one of them, "the grace of the dart or arrow" or transpiercing of the heart.

2. The influx of mystical phenomena. Teresa refers to them repeatedly in her autobiographical writings. Generally she dedicates to them more space than she does to the mystical experience properly speaking, because this latter is more resistant to verbal exposition. A synthesis of her thought could be found in the title of chapter 20 of the

Life. "Discusses the difference between union and rapture. Explains the nature of rapture and tells something about the good possessed by the soul that the Lord in his kindness brings to this prayer of rapture. Tells of its effects. There is much to marvel over" (cf. also no. 1). Yet the more systematic a enumeration she gives in two later writings, in the years 1576 and 1577: *Spiritual Testimony* 59 and the sixth dwelling places of *The Interior Castle*.

Spiritual Testimony 59	Sixth Dwelling Places
no. 4 quiet and interior peace	c. 2 arrow that wounds
no. 5 sleep of the faculties	c. 3 locutions
no. 6 union of all the faculties	c. 4 rapture or ecstasy
no. 7 rapture and suspension	c. 5 flight of the spirit
no. 8 transport	c. 6 jubilation
no. 9/10 difference between rapture and transport	c. 7 suffering for sins
no. 11/12 flight of the spirit	c. 8/9 intellectual visions, imaginative visions
no 13/15 impulse	c 10 suspension
no. 17/ wound . . . an arrow thrust into the heart	c 11 impulse, fiery arrow
no. 21/22 locutions	

The spiritual testimony 59 concludes: "I have never asked His Majesty to give me knowledge of anything" (ST 59. 24). Neither of the two enumerations is complete. In other passages of her works Teresa leaves evidence of *apparitions, prophecies, levitation* . . . and an episode of *bilocation*. She values them for their ethical effects. Yet she never confuses them with the substance of the Christian life or of mystical experience: "Well do I understand that sanctity does not lie in these favors," she categorically writes in the *Foundations* (F 4.8).

3. *A singular mystical phenomena, "the grace of the arrow."* Among Teresa's mystical favors the grace of the arrow merits special attention for two reasons: a/ for the precision and repetition with which she describes it, and b/ for the impact that it has produced in students, theologians, and psychologists, especially among those resistant to its supernatural origin. Let us specify:

a) Teresa describes this phenomena at least three times in *Life* 29.13-14; in *Spiritual Testimony* 59. 17; IC 6.2.4; there are other numerous allusions in her poems and letters. (It is indispensable to read the first two passages).

b) This grace lasted or was repeated according to her, for various years, probably at the beginning of 1560 (cf. IC 5.11.1 and 29.14) when Teresa had reached age 45.

c) As she herself admits, it was not a bodily phenomenon ("The pain is not bodily but spiritual, although the body doesn't fail to share some of it, and even a great deal" L 29.13), yet in describing it , in the "depths" or in the "heart" she localizes it (metaphorically in both cases): "this pain is not in the sensory part, nor is the sore a physical one, but the pain lies in the interior depths of the soul without resemblance to bodily pain". . . (ST 59.17).

d) She staged it through the mediation of an angel located outside herself; she herself contextualizes it within an affective process . . ."increasing the love of God in me to such a degree that I didn't know where it came from (for it was very supernatural L 29.8); and she categorized it as a wound of love . . . of supernatural origin.

e) She never alludes, not even indirectly, to possible traces of this grace in her physical heart pains.

4. Interpretations and appraisals. The first to appraise the mystical episode after Teresa is Fray John of the Cross, for he interprets it theologically as a charismatic grace given to Teresa in her function as founder. Then after his interpretation follow the versions of the

artists and sculpters, especially among these latter the work in marble done by Bernini. Later they confer on her liturgical honors. And, finally, with the advent of the psychological sciences come naturalist interpretations. Let us mark three of these: / *pathological:* Doctor R. Novera Santos is sure that we are dealing with a pleasing heart attack; b/*psychoanalytic:* among whom are disciples of Freud, H. Leuba is sure that we are dealing simply with en erotic phenomena and that when Teresa speaks of the "depths", one should read "womb, that's all!", although Teresa says that it happens in "the interior of the soul"; c/ still in our days, a century later, the hypothesis is formulated of a feminine episode of orgasm (M. Izquierdo), obviously localized in the genital organs, despite the fact that Teresa never alludes to them and that she expressly excludes them in familiar confidences.

They amount to three interpretations lacking an objective foundation: they are contrary to the autobiographical data supplied by Teresa herself. The supernatural interpretation given coherently by Teresa still stands. as also does the theological appraisal of St. John of the Cross who knows personally and directly what was experienced by Teresa, a good psychologist and, above all, great mystical analyst: "It will happen that while the soul is inflamed with the love of God, . . . it will feel that a seraph is assailing it by means of an arrow or dart that is all afire with love . . . as though it were a sharp point in the substance of the spirit, in the heart of the pierced soul." Graces like this are "granted to those whose virtue and spirit were to be diffused among their children" (F 2. 9, 12). An anonymous allusion to the Teresian episode.

97. Her Sense of the Church

1. Born in Spain in the sixteenth century and in the bosom of a Christian family, it is natural that Teresa would live her faith and customs with a clear sense of the church. Baptized in the parish church of San Juan, she entered from the time she was a small child into the structure of what she would name the holy Roman Catholic Church. From the time she was a child she practiced the commandments of the church (any of the primers from her childhood, for example the primer for teaching how to read . . . of 1526, teaches twice in lines that can be sung "four commandments of holy Mother Church"). At 22 years of age, her profession as a Carmelite nun incorporated her into a Religious state approved by the central authority. And in the following years, now as a founder, she will know first hand the lights and shadows of the hierarchical organization, its frictions and tensions with the civil society. She herself will become the object of interferences from Rome through the meanness of the Papal Nuncio Filippo (Felipe) Sega. She will become aware that her own condition as a woman causes others to question her activity in the life of the Church.

Yet in the process of her personal religious piety, Teresa had two special occasions that obliged her to take a position and refine her sense of the church. The first had to do with the tragic happenings that undermined Christianity in her century. And next her own mystical experience which had to restrain the demands of the church institution, a charism facing the institution.

2. Teresa in the presence of the breakup of Church unity. It is probable that in the monastery of the Incarnation and in the surrounding Castile all that was happening in Europe beyond the Pyrenees took time to enter the people's awareness. Nevertheless, news coming

from the Council of Trent and above all the coming to the Spanish throne of Philip II widened and aggravated the defensiveness before the ultramontane happenings with the promulgation of the Index of Forbidden Books, with severe control of exits to foreign lands, as well as vigilance and repression toward indigenous movements. There reached Teresa in the Incarnation, in 1559, the raid on books that were sequestered on account of the *Index,* and in this same year, or a little after, the alarming news of the things going on in Europe either through the Jesuits residing in Italy and corresponding with their friends, the Jesuits in Avila, or directly through alarmist circulars that the court in Madrid sent to the monasteries — and among them the Incarnation — urgently seeking prayers and processions for the wars going on in France and for the unity of Christians. The royal circulars from 1560 and 1563 have come down to us. In this last one the king writes: "You will know the state in which the things of our Christian religion find themselves and those who have been careless in so many provinces . . . and especially in France which is so close to these kingdoms, and since we hope in our Lord that by means of the holy Council that is gathered in Trent things will have a good outcome . . . we give strong orders that you provide that in all the monasteries of both men and women of your order special care be taken to offer prayers and petitions begging God our Lord with all efficacy for the unity of this religion, for obedience to the Holy See and Roman Church . . . that those who have wandered from it in any way will return to true knowledge . . . and will provide what is suitable for the universal good of Christianity . . . and that in these monasteries they have processions as they did at other times, especially in the past year of 60." Also this other circular of 1560 had arrived at the monasteries in Avila and certainly that of the Incarnation. They sounded the alarm making people aware of the breakup of unity among Christians and the consequent breakup of unity within the church. Teresa was far from being indifferent From her point of view, she condenses the situation with a few strokes of her pen: the harm being done in France, the loss of so many souls, the church on the ground, so many priests lost, churches being destroyed, Christ himself being implicated in the evils of the church.

" From her small point of view she perceives the magnitude of the cataclysm: "the world is all in flames," she exclaims. And she reacts in the first pages of the *Way of Perfection* with a double gesture: to live the Christian life in depth: "I resolved to do the little that was in my power; that is , to follow the evangelical counsels as perfectly as I could." And to assign an objective of ecclesial service to the contemplative life of the little group forming her nascent Carmel: "And all my longing was and still is that since he has so many enemies and so few friends that these few friends be good ones . . . Since we would all be occupied in prayer for those that are defenders of the Church and for preachers and for learned men who protect her from attack we could help as much as possible . . ." (WP 1.2). That is to say: Teresa feels in a living way the catastrophe the Church is suffering. And she reacts with the force of a contemplative nun who intuits Christ implicated in the mystery.

3. No less important for Teresa is the contrast between her own mystical experience and the experience of those representing the church. She has lived in depth the stale problem of the confrontation of charism and institution. Teresa, as other mystics, was accused of directly opposing the institution. As if the mystical experience freed one from the church structures and transcended the frontiers of all religious society.

It is certain that Teresa lived her experience within the Spanish religious climate, mined with multiple episodes of the *alumbrados* that sounded an alert, almost in arms, against the official church. To this was due the fact that Teresa herself, from her first mystical experiences became apprehensive of all that happened to her and submitted her experiences to the opinions of incompetent theologians who were not only fearful of them but imposed their negative criteria and opinion arising out of a bad spirit. They deprived her of Communion for long periods of time and they obliged her to reject the visions with obscene gestures – to show the fig — a gesture doubly repugnant to a feminine spirit like Teresa's "Enough things to drive me insane," she comments. What interests us in this whole dramatic situation is the attitude in depth of Teresa herself. To what point did they serve to refine, or annihilate, her sense of the church, despite the huge abuse.

Well then, the line of conduct constantly adopted by her is the persistent seeking of discernment of her mystical experiences by competent judges. And this was founded on a clear church posture: " I hold it to be most certain that the devil will not deceive . . . a soul that does not trust itself in anything and that is fortified in the faith and understands that it would die a thousand deaths for one item of the faith. And with this love of the faith. . . which is a strong living faith, it always strives to proceed in conformity with what the church holds, asking this one and that , as one who has already made a firm assent to these truths. All the revelations it could imagine – even if it were to see the heavens open – wouldn't move it one bit from what the Church holds" (L 25.12). Two times there emerges in the text the typical Teresian formula — what the Church holds – which will reappear in the front of her books: "I submit to what our Mother the Holy Roman Church holds" (the initial declaration in the *Way of Perfection* , and likewise in the *Interior Castle* and the *Foundations*). With the same spirit of submission she will repeat in concluding the *Interior Castle* "I submit everything to what the holy Roman Catholic Church holds" (Epil 4). That is to say, Teresa is conscious that her mystical fact happens within the church organism, and far from exempting herself from this structures or from its official teaching office, she subjects herself expressly to it; that is to say, she submits to it her experiences as well as her message. Teresa is a mystic of the church.

98. Jesus And His Sacred Humanity

Teresa is not a theologian by profession. In her writings there is no treatise, not even a sketch, on christology. Yet in her life as in her work we have a case of panchristianity comparable to that of St. Paul or St. Francis of Assisi.

1. Perhaps in no other aspect of her spiritual life did Teresa have the fortune of a formation so rich and complete. As we already noted, in her childhood she had the luck of reading the primer pages of the *Flos Sanctorum,* the Castilian version of Gerson's Monatésseron, which offered her the text of the Passion according to the four Gospels, illustrated with a series of vignettes capable of having a strong impact on the sensitivity of the child Teresa. Later, as an adult, she likewise had the fortune of being formed by reading the best and most copious *Life of Christ* by the Carthusian, following step by step the history of Jesus and the biblical texts of both Testaments alluding to him. Each chapter was crowned by an emotive and absorbing prayer. Teresa will follow, moreover, in her religious life the daily course of the liturgy with frequent reading of the Gospels.

2. In the process of her spiritual life there occurred two moments of christological experience. There preceded a period of popular piety. Teresa cultivated a devotion to certain passages from the Passion, such as the prayer in the garden, or she imitates the gestures of the women in the gospels, like the Samaritan woman or the Magdalene, she relives imaginatively the entry of Jesus into Jerusalem on Palm Sunday, she unites with the Blessed Virgin in her transfixion at the foot of the cross. Still at the end of her life, on the occasion of the foundation in Burgos, she pauses before entering the city to venerate an image of the Holy Christ. Her christological piety of popular

inspiration endured and coexisted with the most lofty experiences of her mystical life. Nonetheless, this second period is much stronger, all brilliant with experiences of a christological mark. During more than 25 years, Teresa lived a long time of strict personal relationship with Jesus Christ, her model, her Bridegroom and Lord. It is impossible to give the history of Teresa without fixing the outstanding milestones of this christological experience.

3. The mystery of Jesus. For a contemplative like her, Jesus is an unfathomable mystery. He is the thicket of the mystery of God made human. He is the book where she saw the truths. He exceeds her pen in any of her exclamations: "Oh, our Emperor, supreme Goodness, Wisdom itself, without beginning, without end, without any limit to your works; they are infinite and incomprehensible, a fathomless sea of marvels, with a beauty containing all beauty, strength itself! . . ."(WP 22.6)). It is not easy to follow Teresa in her breakdown of the mystery of Jesus. We can only highlight the more relevant facets.

a) Above all, for her Jesus is the *servant of Yahweh:* she is amazed by the mystery of his lowering of himself. He "had no house but the stable in Bethlehem where he was born and the cross where he died" (WP 2.9). At the end of the *Interior Castle* she will recall his condition of slave (IC 7.4.8): "there is no slave who would willingly say he is a slave, and yet it seems that Jesus is honored to be one." (WP 33.4). Her hair stands on end with only the thought of the humiliation of His Majesty in the Eucharist (L 38. 19). In one of her soliloquies she is amazed at the depth of the Trinitarian mystery and has the boldness to address the Eternal Father and ask him how it is possible that he consented to it: "But you Eternal Father, how is it that you consented?" And again, "O eternal Lord! Why do you accept such a petition? Why do you consent to it? Don't look at his love for us . . . for he allows himself to be crushed to pieces each day" (WP 33. 3-4).

b) Servant yet Majesty. The sovereignty of Jesus is something that was not able to be diluted in his abasement, nor in the mystery of the intimacy of his communion with Teresa: "O my Lord! O my King! Who now would know how to represent your majesty! It's impossible not to see that you in yourself are a great Emperor, for to behold your majesty is startling and the more one beholds along with this majesty, Lord, your humility and the love you show . . ." (L 37.6). In one of her autobiographical confidences in the *Way of Perfection* she tells her readers of "the "special delight" she feels at the recitation of the words "your kingdom shall have no end"(WP 22.1).

c) He is the absolute beauty. Teresa's christological experience is marked by this aesthetic factor. She doesn't tire of proclaiming his beauty (L 28. 1-3). Only in seeing him "left upon me an impression of his most extraordinary beauty, and the impression remains today" (L 37.4). She dedicates one of her poems to singing of it: "Oh Beauty exceeding/ all other beauties."

d) He is the Master. Teresa not only tastes each word pronounced by him in the Gospel, but in her mystical experience relives this discipleship. "There is no knowledge or any kind of gift that I think could amount to anything when placed alongside of what it is to hear just one word spoken from that divine mouth" (L 37.4). Teresa had written in her breviary the words of the Master: "Learn of me for I am meek and humble!" They served as a permanent reminder each time she opened the book for prayer that Jesus is the absolute model.

e) Yet above all, he is the Bridegroom. She identified him with the Bridegroom of the *Song of Songs*. He is the *Christ of love*. And she was enamored of him as the biblical bride who dares to repeat: "Kiss me with the kisses of your mouth." "O my Lord and my God, and what words are these that a worm speaks them to its Creator! . . .But who will dare, my King, utter these words without your permission? The thought is frightening" (M 1.10). Yet at the same time Teresa dares to write a poem of loving power: "If the love You have for me,/ Is like the love I have for You . . ." Precisely for this reason, in the *Interior Castle* she presents the height of the Christian life as a bridal fact! The summit of the Christian life is the supreme love on the part of both lovers, Christ and the soul.

    4. The problem of the Humanity of Christ. Dramatically lived by Teresa, it served to put to the test her gospel realism. Through *the Humanity of Jesus* she understands his gospel history, his Passion, his works and words, divine and human joined, yet historically realized in his human condition, including his body, first capable of suffering and then risen. It happened that there reached her the old spiritualist current, of neo-platonic origin, according to which high contemplation, that is, the perfect life of the Christian, became so spiritual, even to the point of excluding or passing beyond everything corporeal, so that only the spirit remained: to the exclusion as a result of the humanity of Jesus. Teresa after a brief period of wavering in which, badly counseled, she ceded to this doctrine, but then reacted against it with all her energy. "I cannot endure it," she exclaims. She couldn't bear that there be even a moment in the spiritual life in which one intends to avoid the humanity of Jesus. This time she reasons her thesis like a theologian by profession and arrives at the certain conclusion that all our good comes to us through the humanity of Christ. She dares to propose it as an irrevocable postulate to the theologian reader of the *Life* (22.18), and years later she repeats it with energy in the *Interior Castle* (IC 6.7.15). This is undoubtedly is the strongest position taken theologically by Teresa.

99. The Mystery of the Trinitarian Indwelling

1. It is the mystery of the Holy Trinity in Teresa's soul and life, experience and doctrine. The supreme experience of her history of salvation. The presence of the Trinity in the soul in grace is the normal consequence of Jesus' promise in the Gospel of John (Jn 14.23). What is singular in Teresa's case is the mystical experience of this presence. She gives testimony to it in stunning terms at the beginning of the *Interior Castle*. In a passage that collided, like no other of her writings, with the theology of her time and even after her death Teresa brought tenaciously her writing before the Inquisition. In this present theme we will be interested in both things: in Teresa's Trinitarian experience, and in the fortune of this witnessing passage of her work.

2. Within the process of her mystical life, Teresa had in her last years a progressive experience of the Trinitarian mystery. It happened to her that her initial experience of the presence of God – an experience that penetrated her and transcended her (L 10.1) — introduced her into the divine mystery and culminated, first in ineffable experiences of the Trinity and finally established her in the experience of her own soul as a temple, indwelt by the three divine Persons. Halfway through this process Teresa had lived in a prolonged and most vivid manner the presence of the mystery of Christ and his glorious humanity. In such a way that the experience of the indwelling came to her as a surprise. As though it had not been preceded either by her reading or by the contributions of her theologian friends, for we know that they spoke to her or preached about the Trinitarian mystery. She testifies to this experience ingenuously in one of her autobiographical reports, given approximately in the year 1571: "I have experience of this presence of the three Persons, which I mentioned at the beginning [she had referred

443

to it a little before in this same year ST 13]. Since I was accustomed to experience only the presence of Jesus, it always seemed to me there was some obstacle to my seeing three Persons, although I understood there was only one God" (ST 14). She continues her report: "It seemed to me there came the thought of how a sponge absorbs water and is saturated with water; so, I thought, was my soul which was overflowing with that divinity and in a certain way rejoicing within itself and possessing the three Persons." This was on the eve of her entry into the seventh dwelling places and from this moment on the experiences of the presence of the Trinity in her soul was repeated and intensified. The sensation of her soul was like that of a sponge absorbed in God (ST 40). She bore the divine Persons "printed in her soul" (ST 42). "These are grandeurs which make Teresa again desire to be free from this body that hinders their enjoyment" (ST 42).

3. Yet the more categorical testimony Teresa writes on the threshold of the seventh dwelling places (IC 7.1.5-7), being again in Avila, close to Fray John of the Cross and perhaps under his spiritual direction. It is a passage with a twofold value: autobiographical and doctrinal. Fortunately we possess it even today in its autograph form just as it came from her pen, although perhaps mutilated in the second part of the report, as we shall see. We transcribe the strongest part of Teresa's account: "Now then , when His Majesty is pleased to grant the soul this divine marriage that was mentioned, he first brings it into his own dwelling place. He desires that the favor be different from what it was at other times when he gave the soul raptures . . . making it blind and deaf, as was St. Paul in his conversion . . ."

"In this seventh dwelling place the unions comes about in a different way: our good God desires to remove the scales from the soul's eyes and let it see and understand, although in a strange way, something of the favor he grants it. When the soul is brought into that dwelling place, the Most Blessed Trinity, all three Persons, through an intellectual vision, is revealed to it through a certain representation of the truth. First there comes an enkindling in the spirit in the manner of a cloud of magnificent splendor, and these Persons are distinct and through an admirable knowledge the soul understands as a most profound truth that all three Persons are one substance and one power and one knowledge and one God alone. It knows in such a way that what we hold by faith, it understands , we can say, through sight — although the sight is not with the bodily eyes but with the eyes of the soul, because we are not dealing with an imaginative vision. Here all three Persons communicate themselves to it, speak to it, and explain those words of the Lord in the Gospel: that he and the Father and the Holy Spirit will come to dwell with the soul that loves him and keeps his commandments."

"Oh, God help me! How different is hearing and believing these words from understanding their truth in this way! Each day this soul becomes more amazed, for these Persons never seem to leave it any more, but it clearly beholds, in the way that was mentioned, that they are within it. In the extreme interior, in some place very deep within itself, the nature of which it doesn't know how to explain, because of a lack of learning, it perceives this divine company."

4. In the impossibility of commenting on this passage with a simple commentary, we will focus only the impact that it produced in the first theologian readers. From the hands of Teresa the manuscript passed into those of Gracián. He himself tells of the scrutiny to which he submitted the book in the presence of Teresa and the Dominican theologian Diego de Yanguas. From the improvised tribunal of censors we only know the corrections that Gracián introduced into Teresa's autograph, lowering the tone of Teresa's affirmations, sprinkling the Trinitarian passage with things crossed out and emendations that mitigate the force of Teresa's testimony. Years later Teresa's first biographer, Francisco de Ribera erased them implacably. Yet probably

due to the corrections of Gracián Teresa tore out the page in her manuscript that contained the final paragraphs of the chapter and wrote it integrally again. We don't know with what kind of retractions. In any case, it is evident that Gracián's theology did not fit Teresa's. Rapidly he hastened to transcribe the entire book in neat calligraphy, perhaps with his edition in mind including all the corrections introduced into the autograph on Teresa's experience of the indwelling.

5. Gracián never managed to publish his text. Fray Luis de León, after Teresa's death, did it and refused to incorporate into the text the emendations of Gracián, yet he did soften the account of the indwelling. So strong did Teresa's passage seem to him that he added a long marginal note (two pages, 234-235), the only one in the whole book. The note of the editor began in this way: "although man in this life, losing the use of the senses and elevated by God, may see his essence in passing, as probably it is said of St. Paul and Moses and some others, Teresa does not speak of this kind of vision here." The note by Fray Luis did not serve for the safe conduct of Teresa's text, which was hardly published when the sleuths of the Inquisition caught the sight of it. The boldest of them denounced the author and her editor: "El Padre Maestro León – alias vir doctus – did not understand or didn't want to understand that which is clear in this writing [by Teresa] . . . I mean that he is ignorant of the terms of this sect . . . which is evidently heretical stupidity and from a hellish sect and dreams that the devil dreamed, which the Master desired to reduce to Catholic doctrine [in his marginal note}. And in this it is clearly seen that he didn't know anything about this doctrine nor of their mysteries." So the famous Alonso de la Fuente in the spring of 1591 denounced to the Inquistion Teresa and Fray Luis. Fray Luis died some months after (23 August 1591).

6. Teresa did not retract. On the contrary she continued living her Trinitarian experience serenely. She returns to give testimony in her last autobiographical writing. She wrote in 1581: "the presence of the

three Persons is so impossible to doubt that it seems one experiences what St. John says that they will come to make their abode in the soul. God does this not only by grace but also by his presence, because he wants to give the experience of his presence . . . This presence is almost continual" (SR 65 9). Teresa's Trinitarian experience is important for fixing the ultimate goal of her mystical life and for testifying to it with an exceptional text within Christian spirituality.

100. Doctor of the Church

1. Saint Teresa is the first woman to be officially declared a Doctor of the Church. This title, more than any other adjective that qualifies her, such as, seraphic, mystical or angelic doctor, accompanied her ever since Fray Luis de León published for the first time her works and assured us that "there is no doubt that the Holy Spirit spoke through her and governed the pen in her hand," up until Paul VI decided to declare her officially a Doctor of the Universal Church. In the present theme we are interested especially in two items: the historical trajectory of her doctorate and the assessment of the official teaching office of the Pontiff.

2 Historical Landmarks. The doctoral prehistory of Teresa is dense and complicated. Let us sum it up. Teresa's doctorate is in its own way a good indicator of the feminist and antifeminist currents within the church. It was a matter of recognizing the existence of a universal teaching charism, untied to the hierarchical ladder. That is to say:

a) The first publication of her complete works, endorsed by the decision of Fray Luis – man of letters, theologian, and biblical scholar – served as a launch pad , even if the wise Augustinian warns readers that "not belonging to women to teach but to be taught, as St. Paul writes, one at once sees that this is a new marvel," the case of Teresa. An exception to the rule. Nevertheless, already before the publication of the first writing of Teresa's – the *Constitutions* — Jerónimo Graciăn recognized expressly that also to women — and to Teresa , in concrete – the charism of wisdom is given.

b) In the following centuries – 17th and 18th – her teaching office is both supported and rejected by future Doctors within the church,

St. Francis de Sales and St. Alphonse Maria Liguori. On the strictly theological level the *Salmanticenses* pronounced in her favor: "Our blessed mother Teresa has however the matriarchal aureole of teacher whose singular doctrine . . . she received as emanating from heaven and the church approves." (1657).

c) In the 19th century a number of studies were already published to demonstrate the validity of the Teresian doctorate, even though she was not officially declared a doctor by the supreme authority of the church. Let us point out two extreme positions: on one side Enrique do Ossó not only wrote in his review a whole treatise in favor of Teresa's doctorate but also spread hundreds of statues of Teresa with the doctoral gown and biretta and arranged that the most famous architect of the century, Gaudi, should raise in Barcelona the greatest architectural monument symbolizing her doctorate. Whereas the other extreme, the Bolandists (J. Vandemoere), deny her categorically the title doctor of the church ("St. Teresa cannot be placed among the doctors of the universal church: the title of chapter 81, p.360) precisely because she is a woman (that title cannot agree with being a woman), finding support in the authority of St. Thomas (II-II, 177.2).

d) Already in the XX century the possible declaration of Teresa as a Doctor of the church was put to Pius XI motivated by the doctorate of St. John of the Cross, and the Pontiff preferred not to act alleging for the umpteenth time the anti-feminist motive: "obstat sexus" (her sex stands in the way) (1922).

e) This is precisely the problem the Vatican Council II dealt with in general terms declaring the non discrimination of charisms within the church (*Lumen Gentium 12),* with which, and with the numerous expressions of promotion of women, the way remained open to the longed for proclamation of Teresa as a Doctor of the church.

3. The proclamation. In the expression without preamble, on the 15 October 1967, in a discourse directed to The World Congress on

the Laity in the Vatican Basilica, Pope Paul VI announced in Spanish: "We propose to recognize one day for Teresa as also for St. Catherine of Siena the title Doctor of the church." He was dealing with an exceptional fact not only because Teresa would become the first woman declared a Doctor of the church, but also because the declaration was an absolutely personal initiative of the pope. Immediately, through pure formality, a large *Positio*, was elaborated, in which the doctorate of Teresa was looked at historically and justified, and the suspected and stale anti-feminist objections were cleared up. The solemn declaration took place in the Vatican Basilica on 27 September 1970 with the bull *Multiformis Sapientia* in the following words:

"With sure knowledge and after mature deliberation in the plenitude of the apostolic power we declare St. Teresa of Jesus, the virgin from Avila, a Doctor of the Universal church."

4. Asessment of the teresian teaching office. The pontifical bull *Multiformis Sapientia* recalled first of all the Pauline doctrine on the free granting of charisms to "anyone" ("dividing his gifts as he wills"), a doctrine endorsed by the recent Vatican Council II (*Lumen Gentium 12*) so as to confirm then that God endowed the person of Teresa abundantly with the gift of the word so that in "saying and writing" she exercised it in the midst of the church (that to her might be referred these words: in 'the midst of the church she opened her mouth'"). It recalled then that her wisdom welcomed uninterruptedly for centuries by the faithful, by Holy Doctors (and it mentions by name St. Francis de Sales, St. Alphonsus Ligouri, St. Anthony M. Claret, St. Charles of Sezze, St. Vincent Pallotti . . ."and other saints") and a whole series of Supreme Pontiffs adducing one by one their respective praises of Teresa. It recalled likewise that before proceeding to the solemn declaration of her as the first woman doctor of the church there had to be clarified the troublesome feminist problem "whether the title and cult of Doctor of the church can be granted besides men to women."

5. And finally Teresa was declared a Doctor not only for her service to spiritual theology, but more especially for her teaching on prayer and for her singular testimony on Christ and on God. Two points insistently underlined by the pope in his homiletic allocutions on this occasion were:

a) that Teresa be recognized simply for the service she rendered to the church for centuries;

b) and that her word about God is a testimony especially valid for men and women in the world of today.

The Institute of Carmelite Studies promotes research and publication in the field of Carmelite spirituality. Its members are Discalced Carmelites, part of a Roman Catholic community-friars, nuns, and laity-who are heirs to the teaching and way of life of Teresa of Jesus and John of the Cross, men and women dedicated to contemplation and to ministry in the Church and the world. Information concerning their way of life is available through the local diocesan vocation Offices or from the vocation Directors' Offices:

1233 So. 45th Street, W. Milwaukee, WI 53214

P.O. Box 3420, San Jose, CA 95156-3420

5151 Marylake Drive, Little Rock, AR 722206